Genders and Sexualities in History

Series Editors: **John H. Arnold, Joanna Bourke**

Palgrave Macmillan's series, Genders and Sexualities in History, accepts new approaches to historical research in the fields of genders and sexualities. The series provides a home for world-class scholarship that concentrates upon the interconnected themes of genders, sexualities, religions/religiosity, civil society, class formations, politics and war.

Historical studies of gender and sexuality have often been treated as disconnected fields, while in recent years historical analyses in these two areas have synthesised, creating new departures in historiography. By linking genders and sexualities with questions of religion, civil society, politics and the contexts of war and conflict, this series will reflect recent developments in scholarship, moving away from the previously dominant and narrow histories of science, scientific thought and legal processes. The result brings together scholarship from contemporary, modern, early modern, medieval, classical and non-Western history to provide a diachronic forum for scholarship that incorporates new approaches to genders and sexualities in history.

Queer Domesticities: Homosexuality and Home Life in Twentieth-Century London is a groundbreaking study of queer men at home. This fascinating and highly original book explores how queer men described and experienced their homes and home life in London in the twentieth century. Hitherto, histories of homosexuality have examined queer identities through the stresses of the public space – such as the law courts and the street – or in recognisably queer spaces in the public sphere, like protest marches, bars and cruising areas. Matt Cook instead takes 'queer indoors' and analyses queer home and family life. This book engages queer at home with histories of family, gender and home that have all but ignored the home and family life of queer men. This remarkable book problematises ideologies of home that dominated in England, and contextualises broader narratives in the period that regarded queer men's home and family life either as 'pretend', or non-existent. In common with all volumes in the Genders and Sexualities in History series, *Queer Domesticities: Homosexuality and Home Life in Twentieth-Century London* presents a multifaceted and meticulously researched scholarly study, and is a sophisticated contribution to our understanding of the past.

Titles include:

John H. Arnold and Sean Brady (*editors*)
WHAT IS MASCULINITY?
Historical Dynamics from Antiquity to the Contemporary World

Heike Bauer and Matthew Cook (*editors*)
QUEER 1950S

Cordelia Beattie and Kirsten A Fenton (*editors*)
INTERSECTIONS OF GENDER, RELIGION AND ETHNICITY IN THE MIDDLE AGES

Chiara Beccalossi
FEMALE SEXUAL INVERSION
Same-Sex Desires in Italian and British Sexology, c. 1870–1920

Raphaëlle Branche and Fabrice Virgili (*editors*)
RAPE IN WARTIME

Matt Cook
QUEER DOMESTICITIES
Homosexuality and Home Life in Twentieth-Century London

Peter Cryle and Alison Moore
FRIGIDITY
An Intellectual History

Lucy Delap, Sue Morgan
MEN, MASCULINITIES AND RELIGIOUS CHANGE IN TWENTIETH CENTURY BRITAIN

Jennifer V. Evans
LIFE AMONG THE RUINS
Cityscape and Sexuality in Cold War Berlin

Kate Fisher and Sarah Toulalan (*editors*)
BODIES, SEX AND DESIRE FROM THE RENAISSANCE TO THE PRESENT

Christopher E. Forth and Elinor Accampo (*editors*)

CONFRONTING MODERNITY IN FIN-DE-SIÈCLE FRANCE
Bodies, Minds and Gender

Rebecca Fraser
GENDER, RACE AND FAMILY IN NINETEENTH CENTURY AMERICA
From Northern Woman to Plantation Mistress

Dagmar Herzog (*editor*)
BRUTALITY AND DESIRE
War and Sexuality in Europe's Twentieth Century

Robert Hogg
MEN AND MANLINESS ON THE FRONTIER:
QUEENSLAND AND BRITISH COLUMBIA IN THE MID-NINETEENTH CENTURY

Julia Laite
COMMON PROSTITUTES AND ORDINARY CITIZENS
Commercial Sex in London, 1885–1960

Andrea Mansker
SEX, HONOR AND CITIZENSHIP IN EARLY THIRD REPUBLIC FRANCE

Jessica Meyer
MEN OF WAR
Masculinity and the First World War in Britain

Meredith Nash
MAKING 'POSTMODERN' MOTHERS
Pregnant Embodiment, Baby Bumps and Body Image

Jennifer D. Thibodeaux (*editor*)
NEGOTIATING CLERICAL IDENTITIES
Priests, Monks and Masculinity in the Middle Ages

Kristin Fjelde Tjelle
MISSIONARY MASCULINITY, 1870–1930
The Norwegian Missionaries in South-East Africa

Hester Vaizey
SURVIVING HITLER'S WAR
Family Life in Germany, 1939–48

Clayton J. Whisnant
MALE HOMOSEXUALITY IN WEST GERMANY
Between Persecution and Freedom, 1945–69

Tim Reinke-Williams
WOMEN, WORK AND SOCIABILITY IN EARLY MODERN LONDON

Forthcoming titles:

Melissa Hollander
SEX IN TWO CITIES
The Negotiation of Sexual Relationships in Early Modern England and Scotland

---

Genders and Sexualities in History Series
Series Standing Order 978–0–230–55185–5 Hardback 978–0–230–55186–2 Paperback
(*outside North America only*)

You can receive future titles in this series as they are published by placing a standing order. Please contact your bookseller or, in case of difficulty, write to us at the address below with your name and address, the title of the series and the ISBN quoted above.

Customer Services Department, Macmillan Distribution Ltd, Houndmills, Basingstoke, Hampshire RG21 6XS, England

Also by Matt Cook:

London and the Culture of Homosexuality, 1885–1914

A Gay History of Britain (*ed.*)

Queer 1950s: rethinking sexuality in the postwar years (*ed. with Heike Bauer*)

Queer Cities, Queer Cultures: Europe since 1945 (*ed. with Jennifer Evans*)

Queer Domesticities

Homosexuality and Home Life in Twentieth-Century London

Matt Cook
Senior Lecturer in History and Gender Studies, Birkbeck College, University of London, UK

palgrave
macmillan

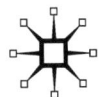

© Matt Cook 2014
Softcover reprint of the hardcover 1st edition 2014 978-0-230-22139-0

All rights reserved. No reproduction, copy or transmission of this publication may be made without written permission.

No portion of this publication may be reproduced, copied or transmitted save with written permission or in accordance with the provisions of the Copyright, Designs and Patents Act 1988, or under the terms of any licence permitting limited copying issued by the Copyright Licensing Agency, Saffron House, 6–10 Kirby Street, London EC1N 8TS.

Any person who does any unauthorized act in relation to this publication may be liable to criminal prosecution and civil claims for damages.

The author has asserted his right to be identified as the author of this work in accordance with the Copyright, Designs and Patents Act 1988.

First published 2014 by
PALGRAVE MACMILLAN

Palgrave Macmillan in the UK is an imprint of Macmillan Publishers Limited, registered in England, company number 785998, of Houndmills, Basingstoke, Hampshire RG21 6XS.

Palgrave Macmillan in the US is a division of St Martin's Press LLC, 175 Fifth Avenue, New York, NY 10010.

Palgrave Macmillan is the global academic imprint of the above companies and has companies and representatives throughout the world.

Palgrave® and Macmillan® are registered trademarks in the United States, the United Kingdom, Europe and other countries.

ISBN 978-1-349-30690-9   ISBN 978-1-137-31607-3 (eBook)
DOI 10.1057/9781137316073

A catalogue record for this book is available from the British Library.

A catalog record for this book is available from the Library of Congress.

Typeset by MPS Limited, Chennai, India.

Transferred to Digital Printing in 2014

*For
Jaya and Chetan
With love*

Contents

List of Illustrations	x
Acknowledgements	xii
Introduction	1
Part I Beautiful Homes	**21**
Introduction	21
1 Domestic Passions: Unpacking the Homes of Charles Shannon and Charles Ricketts	29
2 Queer Interiors: C.R. Ashbee to Oliver Ford	55
Epilogue	78
Part II Queer Families	**87**
Introduction	87
3 George Ives, Queer Lives and the Family	95
4 Joe Ackerley's 'Family Values'	112
Epilogue	131
Part III Outsiders Inside: Finding Room in the City	**143**
Introduction	143
5 Remembering Bedsitterland: Rex Batten, Carl Marshall and Alan Louis	153
6 Homes Fit for Homos: Joe Orton's Queer Domestic	174
Part IV Taking Sexual Politics Home	**191**
Introduction	191
7 'Gay Times': The Brixton Squatters	199
8 Derek Jarman's Domestic Politics	226
Notes	250
Bibliography	298
Index	317

List of Illustrations

1 Speaking about the Brixton squatters at the Sundown School of Queer Home Economics, June 2012   2
© Fritz Haeg

2 Charles Ricketts in the flat in Kennington Park Road he shared with Charles Shannon, c.1889, complete with prints of classical statuary   32
© The Fitzwilliam Museum, Cambridge

3 Shannon and Ricketts' drawing room at Landsdowne House, with display cases and 'penny lampshades', c.1910   39
© The Fitzwilliam Museum, Cambridge

4 Shannon and Ricketts posing in the studio at Landsdowne House, c.1910   47
© The Fitzwilliam Museum, Cambridge

5 The tiled fireplace designed by Charles Ashbee for the hall at the Magpie and Stump – as illustrated in *The Studio*, May 1895
Kings College Library, Cambridge. CRA/23, p. 13   58

6 The fireplace mural by Roger Fry for the drawing room at the Magpie and Stump – as illustrated in *The Studio*, May 1895   60
Kings College Library, Cambridge. CRA/23, p.13

7 Charles Ashbee with granddaughter, Olivia, 1940   62
Kings College Library, Cambridge. CRA/22/1

8 Ronald Fleming at home, as featured in *The Queen* magazine in Oct.1958. Fleming was a proponent of the interwar 'amusing style' in which art and furnishings of different styles and periods were 'pleasurably' juxtaposed to create 'a personal setting'   66
Courtesy of Harper's Bazaar (UK) and V&A Images/Victoria and Albert Museum

9	Oliver Ford at Bewley Court with part of his collection in the background, c.1980 Oliver Ford Will Trust and V&A Images/Victoria and Albert Museum	71
10	Neil Bartlett performing, c.2000 © Dom Agius	81
11	Adrian Goycoolea (aged 11) with his Great Uncle Denis (Quentin Crisp) in 1989 © Frances Ramsay	88
12	George Ives in old Age, c.1945 University of Texas at Austin	95
13	Roger and Joe Ackerley © The estate of J.R.Ackerley	116
14	Carl Marshall in 2005 © Andy and Carol McEwan	164
15	Joe Orton in the bedsit he shared with Kenneth Halliwell, c.1964 © Mirrorpix	185
16	Tony Smith (r) and Alistair Kerr (l) in one of the Railton Road squats © Ian Townson	204
17	A communal meal – with (l to r) John Lloyd, Alistair Kerr and Julian Hows © Ian Townson	206
18	Ajamu, 2012 © Jane Standing	218
19	Derek Jarman and HB (Keith Collins) at Phoenix House © The Estate of Derek Jarman. Courtesy of Keith Collins	235
20	Derek Jarman and HB © The Estate of Derek Jarman	246

Acknowledgements

In this book I repeatedly touch on the significance for the individuals I describe of overlapping networks of family, friends, colleagues, and associates. I've shown how important these networks were in the way those individuals thought about and sustained themselves, their sense of home, their various and multifaceted relationships, and their social, political, and professional lives. These acknowledgements are a further – and conclusive – case study. I find it hard to imagine where and what I would be, let alone what shape this book would be in, if it were not for those who have offered support – practical, financial, emotional – along the way.

Friends, colleagues, and scholars I have never even met have read and commented incisively on the book in part or whole and at various stages. Sally Alexander, Heike Bauer, Deborah Cohen, Anna Davin, Ilsa Colsell, Rosie Cox, Jennifer Evans, Carly Guest, Katherine Holden, Richard Hornsey, Matt Houlbrook, Dominic Janes, Morris Kaplan, Brian Lewis, Sharon Marcus, Daniel Monk, Andrew Gorman Murray, Alison Oram, John Potvin, Victoria Powell, Christopher Reed, Sasha Roseneil, Lynne Segal, Ben Tooke, Chris Waters, and Jeffrey Weeks: I'm hugely grateful to them all. Neil Bartlett, Rex Batten, Keith Collins, Peter McGraith, Angus Shields, Bill Thornicroft, Ian Townsen, and Ajamu X not only allowed me to hear their stories but fedback on what I went on to write about them. Tony Wilburn kindly commented on the sections I wrote using the testimony of his late friend Carl Marshall. I am also hugely grateful to the many others who let me interview them for the book. I haven't used all the testimonies I gathered, but each one contributed to my thinking directly and indirectly.

I owe thanks to the archivists who have made research for this book so enjoyable and especially Stefan Dickers, Sue Donnelly, Jan Pimblett, and Pat Fox. Keith Collins, Diane Courtney, Peter Montieth, Peter Parker, Ian Townsen, Tony Wilburn, and Ajamu X were very helpful in my search for images. Guidance and support from Emily Russell, Clare Mence and Geetha Williams at Palgrave Macmillan and from series editors John Arnold, Joanna Bourke and Sean Brady has been invaluable.

Birkbeck has been a wonderfully collegial place to work on this book. The Faculty of Lifelong Learning, where I started out, put money behind research trips and transcription costs. The intellectual community I've found in the Department of History, Classics and Archaeology, Birkbeck Institute of Gender and Sexuality, and the Raphael Samuel History Centre has meanwhile helped to shape my thinking and argument, as have my doctoral and masters students. I have learnt an immense amount from audiences and participants at talks and workshops I've given along the way – to older men's gay groups Opening Doors, GALHA (the Gay and Lesbian Humanist Association), South London Gays, and more besides. They have reminded me why the stories I tell here matter.

Some of the chapters that follow are based on pieces that have appeared elsewhere, and I am grateful for the permission granted to rework and republish here. Chapter 1 is based on 'Domestic Passions: Unpacking the Homes of Charles Shannon and Charles Ricketts', *Journal of British Studies* 51, no. 3 (2012); Chapter 3 on 'Families of Choice? George Ives, Queer Lives and the Family', *Gender and History*, 20 (Spring 2010); Chapter 5 on 'Love in a Cold Climate: Rex Batten and the Evidence of Experience', in *Queer 1950s*, ed. Matt Cook and Heike Bauer (Basingstoke: Palgrave Macmillan, 2012); Chapter 6 on 'Homes Fit for Homos: Joe Orton and the Domesticated Queer', in *What Is Masculinity? Historical Perspectives and Arguments*, ed. Sean Brady and John Arnold (Basingstoke: Palgrave Macmillan, 2011); Chapter 7 on '"Gay Times": Identity, Locality, Memory and the Brixton Squats in 1970s London', *Journal of Twentieth Century British History* 24, no. 1 (2013): 84–109.

The Harry Ransom Humanities Research Centre at the University of Texas at Austin funded a one-month fellowship to consult their collections. The Arts and Humanities Research Council awarded me a nine-month fellowship in 2012 in which I drew the threads of the book together. Research leave granted by Birkbeck has also been invaluable.

Madeline Joinson, Olivier Lacheze Beer, and Andy Saich and Laurent Lachal gave me literal space to write at key moments, and my circle of friends and family have been interested, supportive, and diversionary by turn. I'm lucky to have them. Ben Tooke has shown me new dimensions to home and family and has lifted my heart.

The book is dedicated to my children, Jaya and Chetan Rathbone. They light up my life.

Introduction

In June 2012 a geodesic dome tent was pitched on the rooftop terrace of the Hayward Gallery on London's South Bank. This was the 'Sundown Schoolhouse of Queer Home Economics' where, for a month, you could learn and hone domestic skills – from cleaning and cooking to flower arranging and knitting. There were workshops on rug making, on '*avant*-gardening', and on queer family trees, as well as discussions, performances and talks. It was, said school founder and Californian architect Fritz Haeg, a 'rogue' component of the Hayward's 'Wide Open School' programme which took place inside the gallery itself.[1] Just next door a few months later, the Royal Festival Hall hosted 'Alternative Fairytales, Alternative Families' – a day of performance and events celebrating 'the rise of the alternative family' and the estimated '10,000 same-sex parent families' nationwide.[2]

By this time civil partnerships had been available to gay couples in the UK for eight years (since 2004); adoption for ten (since 2002). Gay marriage was on the government's agenda and only a year away from passing into law (2013). The hit American sitcom *Modern Family* (from 2009), with its two gay dads, was only the latest twenty-first century show to screen in the UK featuring domesticated or domestically stylish gay men. Aiden in *Queer as Folk* (1999), Will in *Will and Grace* (1998–2006), and Justin Ryan and Colin McAllister in home make-over shows from *Trading Up* (2003) to *60 Minute Make Over* (2009) only the most memorable. The gay columnist in *The Guardian* was no longer a 'PWA' (Person with AIDS), as Oscar Moore had been in the mid 1990s,[3] but soap star and father of two Charlie Condou. His weekly piece, 'The Three of Us' (2011–2012), described his experience of co-parenting with his male partner and a female friend. Scholars in the social sciences and humanities were meanwhile asking what all this might mean in terms of assimilation, difference

1

2 *Queer Domesticities*

Figure 1 Speaking about the Brixton squatters at the Sundown School of Queer Home Economics, June 2012
© Fritz Haeg.

and an apparently dwindling radicalism.[4] Gay households had never been so visible or subject to so much scrutiny.[5]

There is, unsurprisingly, a history to all this. Though contemporary representations and debate about queer homes and 'families of choice' tend to be anchored in the present and very recent past, the relationship between homosexuality, home and family was provoking fear, comment and debate long before Aiden appeared on our screens with a baby and loft-style apartment. 'Even the most scandalous gay lives had a domestic component', writes literary critic Sharon Marcus of the late-Victorian period. Though a male-female couple was then and since seen to be a defining feature of home, it was not only their space and idea. Home was also used by queer men in ordinary and extraordinary ways – as well as by others in characterising them.[6]

The invert's apparently intrinsic stylish flair was described by late nineteenth century sexologists and has been repeated frequently since.

This flair has been used to signal a certain queer cultural superiority but also misogynistically to belittle men who were engaged in 'women's' work and who were apparently all style and no substance.[7] If in these ways queer men were sissy home boys, a law society memo nevertheless declared in the 1950s that 'male persons living together do not constitute domestic life'.[8] Without a wife, without children to support, what could domestic life be for such men? There was, the playwright John Osborne asserted in 1986, a 'solemn fakery to sodomite domesticity'.[9] Section 28 of the Local Government Act declared two years later that such homosexual households could only be 'pretend'. However tasteful the places they lived, however adept at domestic work in their own homes, in hotels, and in the employ of the wealthy, however wrapped up in childcare and other forms of care-giving, queer men have had a deeply equivocal relationship to home and family. They could not quite be fully admitted to a place and an ideology which went to the heart of ideas of home, Englishness and good citizenship.[10] With their undomesticated passions they were often instead conceived as a threat to these things.

This book is about the ways a number of queer men from the late nineteenth century to the present made, experienced and described their homes in London. It is about how they did those things in relation firstly to these broader ideas about the relationship of homosexuality to home and family which circulated in the newspaper press, sexology, sociology, and the arts, and in government legislation and local council edicts. And secondly in relation to the immediate pressing contexts of the areas, streets, houses, flats and rooms where they lived through choice or force of circumstance or a combination of the two. In so doing, the book shows additional ways in which queer men orientated their sense of themselves – behind closed doors and apart from the more public bars, clubs, toilets, cruising grounds, courtrooms, and protest and pride marches that have more often drawn our attention. It takes queer histories more determinedly indoors, and touches and troubles existing histories of home and family which almost entirely neglect queer lives.[11]

The artist couple Charles Shannon (1863–1937) and Charles Ricketts (1866–1931) fashioned their beautiful homes, established their collection of art and antiques, and held 'at homes' for their queer circle in London's bohemias in the late nineteenth and early twentieth century. The romantic socialist and architect Charles Ashbee (1863–1942) and interior designer to the Queen Mother, Oliver Ford (1925–1992), underscored ideas of a queer acumen in domestic design, and also signalled how such style might be politicised in opposing ways. Writer and director Neil Bartlett (b.1958) describes the significance of home, collecting, and a camp eclecticism to his sense of being queer in the late twentieth and early twenty-first centuries. I discuss each of these men in the first part of the book: 'Beautiful Homes'. The second, 'Queer Families', looks at queer homes as a scene of family life, taking in the early campaigner for homosexual law reform, George Ives (1867–1950), who established his 'alternative family' in Swiss Cottage in the early twentieth century with a former 'comrade', his wife and daughters, and some younger working class men. The writer and editor J.R.Ackerley (1896–1967) sought some distance from his birth family in pursuing his queer life, but his writing about his father, his domestic set up with aunt and sister, and his relationship not only with his lovers but their families, shows how entwined queer and family lives could be. Designer Peter McGraith (b.1964) suggests something similar but in a very different social and cultural context as he describes the ways he brought his own childhood, family and the politics he developed in the 1980s and early 1990s into the family home he and his partner have created with their two children in central north London.

In the third part, 'Outsiders Inside', I look more squarely at the difference money – or rather the lack of it – made to queer home making in London. For this I use oral history interviews with sometime DJ and office worker Alan Louis (1932–2011) and drama student turned teacher Rex Batten (b.1928) alongside a hand written memoir by photographer Carl Marshall (1938–2010) and the much better known diaries and plays of Joe Orton (1933–1967). The focus in part three is on the 1950s and 1960s, transitional decades in cultures of home and queer life. Part four, 'Taking Politics Home' looks at the more overt politicisation of queer home life in the years that followed. I explore this through a group of squatters in Brixton, south London in the 1970s and the domestic life of black queer photographer and activist, Ajamu X (b.1964), who has lived in the same area since the late 1980s. Finally I turn to film-maker, writer, artist and gardener, Derek Jarman (1942 – 1994), and his homes in London and Dungeness on the Kent coast formed in the contexts of 1960s and 1970s counter culture and then of AIDS and HIV.

These diverse men don't come together neatly in an exposition of what a queer home or family was or is like. Yet the book shows how claiming a queer identity – as homosexual, inverted, or indeed queer – did and does make a difference to domestic life because of the legal, social and cultural positioning of those identities. As different as Shannon and Ricketts were from the Brixton squatters, Jarman from Ford, or Ives from Ackerley, there was a self-consciousness in the way each of them engaged with an idea and place which was and still is most often conjured in terms of heterosexual lives and lifestyles – and which each of them experienced in that way in childhood. There was a self-consciousness too in entering into an identity which was portrayed in relation to home and family in very particular and contradictory ways. As we have seen, queer men have been characterized both as domestically adept and as homeless 'exiles from kin'.[12]

Local lives, multiple differences

Foregrounding the stories of particular men as I do here allows us to see the genesis of ideas and assumptions which inform our present. But the biographical focus also gives us a complex sense of particular moments, places and people in the past which might not fit or fit entirely comfortably into more sweeping accounts of social and cultural change. A turn to individual, local, and here also home lives, shows that people in the past were unpredictable in the ways they related to ideas about the self and sexuality circulating at any particular time, and so to those discourses – of medicine, the law, and the media most especially – which have been shown to wield such power in these respects.[13] Taking my lead from localized case studies suggests a past which was 'more contingent and less monolithic' than is often assumed.[14] Most of these case studies claimed to be, variously, queer, homosexual, or gay. Through this act of self-definition they plugged into networks of other men and ideas about distinguishing characteristics, propensities and cultures – and not least home cultures. And yet what soon becomes clear is the multiple dimensions of their identities and identifications, and also the complicated ways in which their understandings of their desires were entwined with the particular material, economic, cultural and social circumstances of their lives.[15] For this reason I haven't been able to locate a binding and singular experience or model of queer domesticity. Whilst I have traced trenchant stereotypes, found that they were and are in common circulation, and found too that they were significant for the way many queer men have thought and think about themselves, I have also found that they usually don't apply and certainly don't apply in any straightforward way.[16] I argue that the way these various men made home was as much about the street or area where they lived, about their proximity to or distance from friends and family, about the money they had and the jobs they did, about their understandings of identity, about their relationship status, health, age and much more besides. It was about their queerness in as much as it affected (and was affected by) each these things, but that queerness in itself was not necessarily the decisive factor in the way they organised and made their homes and felt themselves to be 'at home' in London.

Exploring these men on their own terms, in their own contexts, and acknowledging their idiosyncrasies and preoccupations, partially displaces the gay/straight binary distinction that has so compelled us since the 1970s especially. The lines between queer and normal and gay and straight in the way homes and families were formed and experienced have always been rather blurred. Queer men have often been judged against an idea of heterosexual normality. But the ways such (supposedly) 'normal' people have lived has been very variable indeed. Moreover, the queer men I examine here have found a sense of 'composure' in their domestic similarities to 'normal' men and women as surely as in their differences from them.[17] That said, it is also true that the men I discuss were each unevenly invested in a sense of difference which they saw accompanying their desires for and relationships with other men. They did in various ways repeatedly pitch themselves against what they saw as domestic and familial convention and their own formative home and family lives. The investment in a sense of difference arises in the specific context of a country and culture which placed a rather exclusive conception of home and family front and centre, which criminalised sex between men and more broadly frowned upon and was fearful of it, and which yet had a capital city that was (and was seen to be) equivocally accommodating of men who were 'that way'.[18] My case studies allow me to explore such pressures and possibilities and to locate the impress of a particular national and urban context. It becomes clear that home was a crucial site for their experience and for understanding themselves and their sense of connection with others. Home was a way for them to stand out and to be different. It was also a way for them to fit in.

It is men I focus on here because however different the men I discuss were from each other, there was something particular about the relationship between men, masculinity and the home, and something particular too in presumptions about queer men's relationship to the home as opposed to that of queer women. Sexologists and writers of 'new woman' fiction at the end of the nineteenth century certainly suggested a disjunction of the female invert from home and family life. This was couched differently for them than for the men, though, because of the particular familial and domestic roles women were supposed to fulfil. The male and female homosexual appeared to present different kinds of threat to the home and family, and were different kinds of outsider.[19] They encountered different challenges too: some of the privileges that came with masculinity – the scope for greater independence and earning potential, for example – meant queer men were often more able to make their own way domestically. Those stabs at domestic independence and difference were, meanwhile, sometimes viewed with more suspicion than those of women because there was in general a greater awareness of male homosexual transgression. Throughout the book I moreover demonstrate a repudiation of what was considered feminine even as (and in part because) my case studies strayed into supposedly feminine territory in their investments in home.

Slippery terms

'Queer' in the 'flash dictionary' at the end of George Cruikshank's 1849 work *Sinks of London* is said to mean 'doubtful, good for nothing and bad'. Amongst the 28 variants listed below are 'queer gill' ('a suspicious fellow'), 'queer pattir' ('foreign talk'), 'queer lully' ('a deformed child'), 'queer hen' ('a bad woman'), and (intriguingly for me) 'queer ken' ('a gentleman's house without furniture').[20] These varied yet loosely connected associations of oddity, badness, malformation or foreignness resonate through the proliferating and then narrowing meanings of queer in the years that followed. In the last part of the nineteenth century and the first half of the twentieth these touched eccentricity, Bohemianism, and exoticism. Thereafter they signalled homosexual difference more distinctly. All of the men I discuss were familiar with the word. Ricketts used it to describe some flowers in 1919;[21] in the early thirties George Orwell used it in relation to the homeless and their outsider status.[22] Though from 1922 the *Oxford English Dictionary* records queer being used to mean 'homosexual', that meaning was not to the fore until after World War II. It was then that Ives' cleaner affectionately described the old man as 'queer'.[23] Ackerley said the same of his former landlord.[24] The playwright Joe Orton meanwhile felt he and his lover Kenneth Halliwell received a prison sentence for their vandalism of library books 'because we are queers'.[25] Queer, we will see, was often used to describe people but also the way they did things, what they had around them, or how they looked at the world. It did not exactly mean 'homosexual' or 'invert' as sexologists and reformers earnestly used those terms from the 1880s. It might allude to a particular type of homosexual – though what type depended on the context in which it was used. Queer bashers in the 1950s and after did not mean the same as film-maker Derek Jarman did when he used queer in the 1990s to signal his radicalised politics and identity.[26] 'Queer' was by then also being used by sexuality and gender theorists to suggest fluidity in sexual and other identity categories.[27]

When I use queer in this book and in its title I am trying to hold on to these various meanings and associations, and especially to the sense of oddity or eccentricity, and the imprecise way it signals sexual difference but not necessarily in the way we think about such difference now. It is useful in this way because it does not quite mean 'opposite to' in the way 'homosexual' can seem to 'heterosexual' or 'gay' to 'straight', and so allows me to describe a situation that all the men I discuss found themselves in – not utterly at odds with a set of presumed norms but not quite in accord either. Queer in this sense can help to highlight the messiness of everyday lives which rarely fit with homogenising and transhistorical assumptions about homosexuality or indeed heterosexuality.

If 'queer' is slippery, then so too are the other terms in the book's title. None of them has a static or stable meaning. What 'home' has meant culturally, how men and women have been seen to fit into it, what domestic chores have been necessary to keep it up, what modern conveniences have eased that burden and also reshaped leisure time spent there, what homes have looked like and what homes have been available within the city – all these things have shifted across the period I'm describing and in ways that have affected the lives of the men I discuss. It is, crucially, both a material place and an 'extremely coercive' idea, ideal and ideology.[28] The material nature of home and the ideals attendant to it changed with time and also carried with them different expectations depending on many other variables and contexts – most obviously of socio-economic position.[29] Home was important to upper middle class George Ives and to retired teacher Rex Batten, for example, but they experienced and expected different things from it because of the money and class outlook they respectively brought to bear and because of the different periods in which they lived. Similarly, though both men, like most others, saw home functioning in relation to 'family',[30] the nature of the families they remember, created and imagined were also very different. Family life and the heterosexuality assumed to be aligned with it has a changing history too and expectations about parenting, relationships, sibling dynamics, duty and responsibility, and secrets and privacy shifted in the period from Ives' birth in 1867 to Batten's older age now.[31] These shifts have variously shaped, accommodated and pushed away queer fathers, sons and brothers. If 'family' is usually conceived as singular, Ives and Batten and most of the men I describe felt themselves simultaneously to be part of more than one family (of kin, of friends, and of co-residents, for example), and these various families touched each other and home in different ways – in occasional or more frequent visits, in everyday lives, in memory, and in aspirations for the future.

'Domesticity' embraced both home and family, and perhaps more specifically the things that were done to service and to protect them. If men were meant to work to sustain homes, it was often women who did the less visible domestic tasks that kept them and the people that lived there going. Many had domestic roles in other people's houses, in hotels and in restaurants without having much of a home to speak of themselves. There was and is hard and thankless graft associated with the domestic but in more idealized terms domesticity was that elusive quality that made 'house' a 'home'. It suggested clearly defined gender roles, and emotional, relationship and sexual lives enclosed within four walls. Domesticity was, by the period covered in this book, also emblematic and expressive of an individual's interiority and sense of self.[32]

Underpinning these interrelated and not clearly separable concepts of home, family and domesticity was the idea of the 'private' sphere, cast in perpetual contrast to the 'public'. These were again differently valued concepts and physical spaces and were attached to expectations of men and women's place and behaviour. The opposition between them – which has potency partly because it is so often described and repeated – is yet rather equivocal. If my case studies all moved between public and private spaces and if they felt different in each of them, there were also cross-overs in behaviours and expectations. They often acted in private with the public in mind – even if what they had and did there was never observed by anyone else. On the other hand, many public places served some of the supposed functions of home for them – in terms, for example, of retreat, relaxation, and intimacy. The porous boundaries between public and private and between public and private lives caused much concern across this period and brought attempts to shore up the divide. The 'private' realm of home was idealized and separated out through politics and action in the 'public' world of national and local government, town planning, architecture, commerce, and advertising. That same private space was conversely often marshalled to the 'public' service of broader ideas of Englishness, patriotism, gender roles and much more. Though (in historian Judy Giles' words) 'the private sphere has frequently been understood as a refuge from the modern, a repository of traditional values, a haven from the excitements and dangers of living in the modern world', many aspects of modern life were yet 'lived, expressed and imagined' in direct relation to it.[33]

Emerging ideas about the centrality of the childhood home and family in shaping adult sexuality, about a separation of adult homes from those of childhood, about the importance of and right to private life, and about home as a space of self creation and individuality have been crucial to modern experiences and ideas of queer identity and identification. Yet because there has been a strong current in representations of queer men which suggests they don't quite fit into home and family life, there has often been unease with these places, relationships and concepts for them. Tensions between feelings of belonging and alienation on the home front thread through this book, and brace the experiences of the men I discuss.[34] Home was also 'saturated with emotion'.[35] It was a place infused with desires – for love, sex, intimacy, relationships, for pleasure, for security and comfort. Such desires were often strongly felt because they were unfulfilled, and yet might also be a powerful driving force in seeking changes to home and the domestic set up. They came in and out of focus at different times, with different people, in different homes. They were rarely consistent across the course of the men's lifetime; they rarely quite made logical sense. Desires are difficult enough to track in ourselves let alone in others and especially in others long gone. Yet the century covered by this book saw a growing understanding of their potency – largely because of the burgeoning cultural influence of psychoanalysis. I do not try to trace the origins of desires in my case studies or to retrospectively psychoanalyse them. But I do suggest the impetus they gave these men to live in particular ways, with particular things or people around them, and with particular aspirations, hopes and fears.[36] Such strands of subjectivity come into sharper focus when we view queer lives in the context of home.[37]

Period and place

The first of my case studies – Shannon and Ricketts, Ives, and Ashbee – reached adulthood in the 1880s. They had grown up in the 1860s and 1870s and a period when many middle class domestic ideals, the lines between public and private, and some of the gendered dimensions of home and roles within it had become entrenched. This came with the rise of the professions and shifts in the urban economy, and was underscored in a new and burgeoning literature of household management, in the actual shape and design of housing in London's rapidly growing suburbs, in the stock and display of the city's new department stores, and in fiction, social commentary, and sexological and psychological literature.[38] This was when, for example, middle class women came to be seen as the prime domestic consumers and shapers of the look and feel of home and when some middle class men felt distant from these roles.[39] These divisions and ideas were not necessarily new,[40] but by that time Shannon and Ricketts, Ives and Ashbee were making their way in the world they had gained a cultural foothold and had coalesced into a broadly conceived set of middle class 'norms' ('norms' that some would soon kick against, as we will see).

Not coincidentally, by the second half of the nineteenth century more men (though certainly not most) had access to middle class and lower middle class occupations and incomes in the city and were able to live somewhat more independently in adulthood.[41] Partly as a result a modern homosexual or inverted 'type' of person came into view, and was described and represented in sexological, literary, journalistic, and philosophical writing which began to inform the way these first of my case studies understood themselves.[42] The invert or homosexual was supposedly discernible partly in the way he dressed and conducted himself in public; partly in the way he arranged his domestic life.[43] There was nevertheless by no means a uniform and coherent understanding of what men having sex and relationships with other men amounted to. Indeed even those involved in such acts and unions might understand them in quite different ways from their partners. That would be the case for much of the century that followed – even as writing about distinctive queer identities proliferated.

The later nineteenth century is my starting point because this was when some now familiar norms and figures were coming into clearer view. However, the book shows how home and homosexuality did much shape-shifting and also much shape-shifting in relation to each other across the century that followed. I'll suggest some of the reasons for this as I go along, but one key factor was the changing nature of London – the place where all my case studies lived for the bulk of their adult lives. The city – home to very roughly a fifth of the population of England and Wales throughout the period – was in constant flux. During this period new suburbs were built; middle class areas became boarding house districts and then were gentrified back again; councils built and then demolished tower blocks; the blitz in the middle of the century did its devastating work. Housing in the capital often marked an aspiration to a wider English fantasy of home – it famously grew out in suburbs of semi-detached houses or terraces with gardens more dramatically than it grew up in apartment blocks.[44] Each of those houses and gardens garnered a sense of the English home and of homeliness associated with independence, safety, retreat, rest, family life, privacy, stability, warmth, comfort, separation of the self from others, and of the individual from the society. That many of these houses were then subdivided into bedsits (one room apartments) and flats is just one indicator of the difficulty most Londoners had in ever living up to the 'impossible' fantasy of what home and family 'should be'.[45] This was a gap between aspiration and reality that ironically sometimes allowed for queer 'outsiders' to feel more at home in the city.[46] At other times, and given thin partition walls and nosy landlords and landladies, it meant they were under even closer surveillance and at even greater risk there.

I have drawn my case studies from London because I wanted to find out more about how the specificities of one place pressed on the lives of particular men, and how they in turn etched out space for themselves there. In this way the book extends my earlier work on the relationship of London and homosexuality between 1885 and 1914 in terms of both the spaces considered and the period covered.[47] In *London and the Culture of Homosexuality, 1885–1914* (2003) I suggested some of the ways in which London came to be seen as the obvious home for queer men.[48] What I have done here is to look at how queer men did indeed make home there in the very particular local circumstances of Chelsea, Islington, Brixton, Notting Hill and other parts of the capital, and across the long twentieth century.

Choices, sources and stories

In the chapters that follow I give some account of the shifts in meanings and uses of these various terms, places, identities and identifications and also of the ways they intersected. More particularly, though, I show how they mattered in the lives of the men I discuss. Because everyone had a home life of sorts, even if only aspirationally,[49] potential case studies were legion. I could have talked about any number of other men and none of them – nor those I have chosen – can be said to typical. I chose some public figures who made home to a greater or lesser extent in the public eye – Shannon and Ricketts, Ashbee, Ackerley, Orton, and Jarman. I chose others – like Ives, Batten, Marshall, the Brixton squatters, and Ajamu – who though less well-known also sought to tell the stories of their family and domestic lives. They are all (to use historian Carlo Ginzberg) 'anomalous, not [...] analogous'.[50] And this is part of the point. Juxtaposing even the few biographies I gather here suggests a heterogeneity in everyday home life which undercuts pat assumptions, stereotypes and generalisations – even though such assumptions, stereotypes and generalisations informed some of the ways queer men (and my case studies not least) behaved, thought about, and described themselves and their identities.

The book pivots on the stories these men told. It looks at how home was wrapped into a sense of who they were, and how it often had a central if equivocal place in their accounts of their queer lives. These accounts come in various forms – and with more and less anticipated audiences – in diaries, memoirs and autobiographies, in interviews, in art, novels, plays, and films, and (more obliquely but no less surely) in the arrangement of actual homes. The latter attention to the fabric and contents of homes is important. Historians Mary Chamberlain and Paul Thompson observe that

> what we wear or eat, what we discard, how we decorate our homes, the consumer choices we make, or do not make, or would wish to make, give off signs, particular aspects of our personality, with all its complexities of dreams and aspirations, as well as status and position, wealth and class.[51]

The capacity for the men I discuss to consume domestically had much to do with the literal space available to them and the resources they had. The limits to what could be bought for the home are as important to my account as what the men were able to get and put on display. In a similar way, in the oral and written accounts I discuss I pay attention to the parameters of what felt sayable. I look at the silences as well as what was communicated directly, and think about how these things changed across the century – and why. The early chapters which focus chiefly on the pre-World War II period and on written sources feel quite different from the later ones which are structured more around oral testimony and sometimes franker revelation, for example. This is not to say that those later accounts are any truer or more real. It is rather to suggest that the nature of stories about sex, relationships, home and family altered with understandings and expectations of intimacy, with changing modes of communication and revelation (not least the internet), and with a shifting sense of what was significant and conceivable. This again often had a lot to do with gender and with class. If Ives never talked about washing the dishes in his diary it is not only because he may never have done such a thing but also because he could not conceive of it being of any importance to him, to those around him, or to the future reader of his diaries he keenly anticipated. Batten in remembering the 1950s, meanwhile, suggests the significance of such domestic tasks in giving support and assurance in his relationship then.

The men I've chosen who had a relatively high public profile can for good or ill be seen as contributors to (or co-producers in) broader ideas about queer home life. These well known men most obviously, but actually all the men I deal with, had some agency in the way they shaped their home lives, in the way they represented them, and in the way they were understood by others.[52] They sometimes sought validation or distinction in this way – perhaps in the absence of adequate representation elsewhere or to ameliorate their supposed queer degradation through an appreciation of and contribution to a 'higher' culture of domestic taste.[53] This sometimes feels radical, sometimes reactionary and elitist. All the testimonies I discuss were shaped nevertheless by a sense of cultural style (countercultural or otherwise), by art and also by genre – that often untaught sense of how stories are constructed and work to communicate ideas and histories.[54] Telling any story, historian Raphael Samuel reminds us, 'demands a selecting, ordering and simplifying, a construction of a coherent narrative whose logic works to draw the life story towards the fable'.[55] Such story telling (to use sociologist Ken Plummer) allows people 'to imagine and reimagine who and what they are, what they want to become'.[56] I have tried to remain attuned to the different modes and registers of story telling in the sources I use. I have also tried to remember that these sources are not raw and unprocessed, they do not provide unmediated access to the 'truth' of the lives they represent – even when they come in the form of Ives' or Marshall's spidery, handwritten diary entries.[57] This is key to my account. The way in which homes and families were woven into personal narratives and the way they structured those narratives is as important as the substance of what is said. When Marshall sat down to write his memoir in the late 1990s, he devoted one notebook to sketching out the overall structure. He did this according to the places he had lived. This was how he prompted his memories of who he was having relationships with, where he was working, what he was doing, and who he was socialising with at any particular time. It was also how he imagined his story being best understood and appreciated by his reader. Such structuring can indicate the centrality or marginality of home and help us to discern how wider narratives and myths of home and family inform and shape the stories these men told about themselves and those they lived alongside.[58]

Though the book is structured by individual lives, I suggest that understanding them involves following their direct and implicit connections to other understanding and expectations of home – to stories that came through families, through groups of friends, through newspapers, novels, films, government policy, through the things they had and that were available to buy for the home, and through the layout and architecture of the homes themselves. It is no coincidence that a number of my case studies engaged in or referred directly to fairy and children's stories: Oscar Wilde wrote them;[59] Charles Ricketts illustrated them; Joe Ackerley's novel *We Think The World of You* was, he said, 'a fairy story for adults'.[60] Derek Jarman remembered the 1954 homosexual scandal involving Lord Montague and journalist Peter Wildeblood being about 'evil men in the castle', and describes his own home on the Kent coast in the great storm of 1989 being like the farmhouse in Kansas in *The Wizard of Oz*.[61] Each of these men had a use for, and a claim on such mythologies of home and family. They redirect them to speak of a felt difference but in the process also suggest a need to belong in a culture where such narratives had a central place. Negotiating them was a way of developing 'a personal mythology, a self justification', which was in turn part of finding a place in the world.[62]

The distinctive ways individuals use these and other stories – about home and family, and about homosexuality in relation to these things – is not an 'impediment to generalisation'.[63] It is instead a way of indicating diverse experience which yet touches shared reference points and cultures. The result is that there is a shuttling back and forth in the various testimonies. The men orientated and measured their home and family in their present through stories and experiences from their past, through broader expectations of what home and family 'should be' and through the myths and archetypes that circulated about them. There are also repeated comparisons of experiences of home before and after domestic and family ruptures which came when relationships formed and broke apart, with maturity, independence, the acquisition of money or the sudden lack of it, or with coming out. This before and after effect embeds the past in the present and shores up and helps indicate the distinctiveness of the current circumstances in which the individual found himself. Home and family were thus not only here and now for these men, but were concepts, places and relationships which gathered in the past and gestured to a hoped for future – with aspirations for a room of their own, for a garden, for particular possessions, for a legacy, for children. Through the resulting tapestry of past, present and future, of hopes and memories, of personal, family and wider stories and myths we see the interplay of the cultural stories we tell (and which are told about us) and the individual lives we lead.[64]

Structure

My case studies are discussed within four thematic parts, composed of two chapters each. These relate to different circulating ideas about queer home life: about the idea of distinctive domestic style and aesthetics (Part I: 'Beautiful Homes'); about a purported separation of queer men from family (Part II: 'Queer Families'); about queer men in bedsitterland (Part III: 'Outsiders Inside'); and about the ways home became an especially politicized realm for some gay men (Part IV: 'Taking Politics Home'). I bring these themes to the fore in turn and in relation to the different case studies, but they also weave through the whole book. There is thus overall a layering of lives and concerns which give a sense of some shared issues at stake for these men as well as some telling dissonances. These have to do with different and shifting conceptions of queerness, with the interface of other identifications, and also with social and cultural change over time which I track in the chapters and sectional introductions. The case studies help me to highlight the equivocal and uneven effects of such change.[65]

Each of the four parts includes closing reflections on men describing their lives now or in the very recent past. I do this not to make pat connections between past and present but as a way of thinking about how personal and broader histories are remembered, evoked and used directly or indirectly now. For Parts I and II the centre of gravity is the pre-World War II period and I have separated these more contemporary reflections into extended epilogues. This is because they consider different people and contexts from those discussed in the substantive chapters. The inclusion of these epilogues mean that the first two parts of the book reach right across the twentieth century and chart changing conceptions of queerness through the prisms of domestic aesthetics and then of families. Part III on queer outsiders in bedsitterland and Part IV on gay and queer politics and the home are more tightly defined by period – the 1950s and 1960s and the post-1970s respectively. They look at what a close focus on home in those particular historical contexts might tell us about queer lives then and since. Because these parts focus on the more recent past, the final reach to the present is through the men also discussed in the substantive chapters.

The book is partly a series of experiments in getting at past sexual subjectivities and the home in different ways, across different lengths of times, using different scales of analysis, and through different sources. The first two parts are more extended in their chronological reach than the last two, leading to different kinds of analysis of change over time or the specificities of particular decades. The individual case study chapters similarly differ in their scope. Sometimes I look at the sweep of a whole life as with Ives; with Marshall, Batten and Louis I focus on early adulthood. Throughout I make a case for the importance of locality, but it is in the chapter on the Brixton squatters and on Ajamu X that I look in most detail at a particular area to see how it affected the way individual homes were made there. My chapter on Orton, on the other hand, focuses more on the interior of his bedsit than on the wider Islington area. There I look at what the detail of such smaller spaces might reveal.

For that chapter, Orton's plays and diaries are key sources. With Ricketts it is his things and what we can garner of his attitudes towards them that are central to my analysis. Jarman's published life writing compelled me for the book's final chapter, whilst oral testimony is at the core of my investigation of the 1950s. Ackerley and Batten both fictionalised their life stories, shaping memories and experiences of home and family in yet other ways. As I go along I discuss the provenance and reach of these different sources, remembering throughout, as I've said, that no testimony provides us with a base line or absolute truth, but remembering too that writing good history means 'never assuming that one's subjects were incapable of recognising the same "hegemonising forces" subsequently identified by professional intellectuals'.[66] This is especially true when we are talking about people in marginalised social positions who 'must engage' in critical reflection 'to find and redefine [their] identities'.[67] The men I have chosen are analytically astute about their own lives and those around them. Their voices, the stories they tell and the way they tell them are crucial to understanding their particular take on what was queer about their homes and families.

My home

My mother was upset when I came out at 20 in 1990 having just moved to London at the height of the AIDS crisis and press homophobia. My father explained her upset to me by telling me about the ideal as he, they, saw it. They had made that more socially validated transition into marriage at 21 and by the time they were 30 had had five children. I was the baby – born nine years later. My parents' concern when I came out was to do with the dangers they saw in my being gay in London at that time; their sadness was in part that they felt I might not be happy and wouldn't have children. Theirs was a restatement of family hopes and fears, which yet did not impede their emotional and practical support for me over the years that followed. I met my partner of 14 years soon after in 1991 and he was welcomed into the family as a brother, son-in-law and uncle to a growing cluster of nieces and nephews. My parents, meanwhile, and unbeknownst to me, took out an additional life insurance policy on my behalf lest I hit the same trouble other gay men were finding in getting mortgages in the context of AIDS. Nine years later (with no mortgage, but a housing association flat near Soho's gay village), my daughter was born into a co-parenting arrangement with my partner and a lesbian couple; my son arrived two years later. When we had a picnic to celebrate the children's arrival we each said something to assembled friends and family. One of the mums rightly credited pioneer lesbian mothers in the 1970s and 1980s who had blazed a trail for us to follow. I talked about my birth family and the support and inspiration I had garnered from them. Having children together was something that could be read as radical and as part of my wider family story. It was in any case something I yearned to do.

My relationship ended when the children were five and three, but we have continued to parent together. My subsequent partner has taken those existing family arrangements in his stride. If this all seemed rather 'modern' (as a parent at the school gate put it), it was also not so different from the dynamic of his own family in which his parents had divorced, remained on good terms, remarried, and brought other children into the mix as half and step siblings. His family, my own and those of my case studies in this book suggest that there is no queer monopoly on familial and domestic difference; no straight monopoly on conformity.

I completed this book as we bought a house together in London, distilling two flats into one new home. In the process I became acutely aware of my attachment to my possessions. Everything on my walls had been given to me by friends or family – from work by my sister to the two huge photos taken from my balcony at sunrise after a late night with a former boyfriend. I could hardly claim to love my foot high flowery black and pink vase but it was from my mum's house. It was something I picked out after her death perhaps because it seemed kitsch to me, if not to her. In my flat it seemed additionally camp behind a full-size papier mâché flamingo made for my fortieth birthday by my sister-in-law. As I move on now I've hung on to the vase, the pictures, and the flamingo. These things touch overlapping components of my life – where what is camp, queer, homely, and familial are not easily separated out. Such eclectic accumulations of things are important to several of the men I discuss in this book, whilst for others it has been important to leave things behind or impossible to take them forward – because of a lack of money or home, for example. In the chapters to come I show how those choices, possibilities and impossibilities speak of different circumstances and histories.

Amidst the packing boxes we made final plans for our civil partnership. This was paid for by cashing in that insurance policy my parents set up for me 24 years ago. This was a shift from the intended use but is yet still about the intricacies, intimacies, and practicalities of making a queer home and family. How I am using that money signals changes over the course of my adult life in the parameters of debate about gay life and in terms of what is or feels possible. It makes me mindful of how each decade I've looked at in this book saw possibilities in domestic life for queer men close down and open up – and for a whole panoply of reasons. These were sometimes to do directly with social and political responses to homosexuality but were sometimes about other changes – in the housing market, fashion, council and government policy, and in transitions between war and peace, for example.

In entering a civil partnership now I could be doing any number of things: being conformist, taking up a right we should have had long ago, declaring a difference, showing some solidarity with an international struggle, showing off, celebrating my relationship and the love I have found there, gunning for a party with my friends and family, seeking some uplift in the wake of grievous losses for the both of us. In truth I can not pinpoint my motivation. It could be some of all these things – the personal and more broadly political and cultural intertwine in ways that are hard to separate. And if this is personally confusing to me, it has yet helped me to come to terms with my case studies who were radical and reactionary by turn; expansive, inconsistent and determinedly, singularly dogmatic; iconoclastic and wittingly and unwittingly conformist. Recognising our own complexity can perhaps alert us to the different complexities of historical subjects from whom we yet often expect consistency.[68]

My brief biography is of course full of omissions and is an account my co-parents, my children and my 'husband' would tell rather differently and with a different emphasis because of their own life experiences, understandings and perspectives. It is not intended as a smug rehearsal of achievement: my family and home life has felt more accidental, chaotic, and bumpy than that – and is not finished yet. If home and family are ideas, ideals, and material and interpersonal realities, they are also ongoing processes that are never done, settled or 'achieved'. I give a snapshot here rather to indicate where I am coming from, what has drawn me to histories and ideas of home and family, and some of what has taken my investigation in particular directions. How, I found myself asking, might I historicise my investment in home and certain objects and possessions, or the creation of my so-called 'family of choice'?[69] How, moreover, has my own home and family history inflected my own queerness, history writing, teaching, politics and conformity?

As I have written about different men from across the twentieth century, I have found myself positioning myself in relation to them – shuttling between their stories and my own, their pasts and mine, and finding muted echoes, distorted reflections, familiarity and distinct moment of alienation. Some have spoken to me more than others. Readers might find the same. It is, I want to suggest, the play of such stories and histories that does significant work in shaping and bringing into focus our individual and cultural sense of home and family as a place and as an idea – whatever the direction of our desires. What the stories in this book (and my own) show is a certain muddling through. If homes and families were and are often forged in idealism they are rarely lived in those ways.

Part I
Beautiful Homes

> The home-life [of the Uranian] has a different colour from that of most homes which women control, but it is, none the less, a home-life.
>
> Edward Perry Warren (1860–1928).[1]

Introduction

On 11 February 1873, 32-year-old artist Simeon Solomon was arrested for indecent exposure and 'attempting to commit sodomy' with 60-year-old stableman George Roberts in Stratford Place Mews just off London's Oxford Street. Roberts received an 18-month prison sentence; Solomon six weeks in the Clerkenwell House of correction and a hefty (for the time) hundred pound fine. We do not know what became of Roberts, but for Solomon the prosecution presaged a rapid descent.[2] Many members of the artist's circle deserted him – most spectacularly his close friend, the poet Algernon Swinburne, with whom he had reputedly 'cavorted naked' in Dante Gabriel Rossetti's studio in Cheyne Walk, Chelsea.[3] After a couple of months with more supportive friends in Devon (supportive, that is, until his drinking became too much for them), Solomon was largely homeless, a state that seemed to befit his status as a sexual outcast and Jew (Swinburne dismissively referred to him in this period as 'the wandering Jew').[4] He briefly entered a mental hospital in 1880 at the behest of his family, and then fended for himself on the streets as a pavement artist in Brompton, west London, and as a match and shoelace seller in the more poverty-stricken neighbourhoods around Mile End Road and Whitechapel to the east. Some family and remaining friends offered piecemeal help, though after entering St Giles Workhouse, just north of Covent Garden, in 1884 he wrote to a cousin that he was happy where he was and refused alternative accommodation. 'Thank you', he wrote drily, 'but I like it here, it's so central.'[5] Solomon spent a further 22 years based largely at St Giles until his death in 1906. When Robert Ross, Oscar Wilde's close friend, sought him out in 1893, he found him 'extremely cheerful. [...] Unlike most spoilt wastrels with the artistic temperament he seemed to have no grievances, and had no bitter stories or complaints about former friends, no scandalous tales about contemporaries who had remained reputable; no indignant feelings towards those who had assisted him'.[6] Solomon continued to paint and draw, drank at a local pub when he could afford it, and – looking like a tramp – hung out at the National Gallery and gave impromptu tours.[7]

Solomon's story is certainly a sad one in many ways. It suggests the terrible losses that could accrue to a queer life exposed. Solomon's apparent contentedness with his later lot, however, also indicates some advantages to a life beyond the constraints of middle-class and even Bohemian homes and society. He chose to 'join London's teeming vagrants rather than submit himself to further discipline'.[8] This was perhaps more plausible for a man who still had the resources of some family and friends to draw on occasionally (he had his first heart attack in 1906 *en route* to a cousin who gave him clothes and pocket money) and who had seen some revival of his reputation in the 1890s. But for other homeless men too there might be comradeship, intimacy, and sometimes sex in London's public spaces, shelters, workhouses and lodgings. For some it was an alternative culture of sorts which, though riven with multiple difficulties, might also offer occasional pleasures and support denied elsewhere.[9]

This introduction to Part I looks at the flip side to the lives presented in the two substantive chapters that follow. It considers the association of homosexuality with homelessness and overcrowding in the late nineteenth and first half of the twentieth century. In the last two parts of this book I take up the stories of some of those making their way in London with little or no money in the second half of the twentieth century, in part by using oral history testimony. For this earlier period it is more difficult. While there is a paper trail giving us access to the homes of artists and collectors Charles Shannon and Charles Ricketts, architect C.R. Ashbee, and interior designer Oliver Ford, the lives of the homeless and those in makeshift accommodation were most often not documented. *En masse* these men were a source of concern to those fearing moral and physical degeneration at the heart of Empire.[10] Their individual biographies were seen to be unimportant, though, not least because they stood outside the home and family and the associated respectability and active citizenship these things were seen to signal. The men I discuss in the main chapters meanwhile showed that they had a place within cultures of home. They contributed to – and were exemplars of – a stereotype which ran in parallel to that of the homeless homosexual: these were men who seemed to have an inimitable sense of how to make homes that looked and felt good. They did this in opposition to the (supposedly) less sophisticated taste of some of their 'normal' middle- and especially lower-middle-class contemporaries, and to the homeless or those living in cramped, overcrowded accommodation. Queer men in these circumstances were visible daily to my case studies. Although the latter most often ignored them, they sometimes took them as lovers (as Wilde famously did) or helped in piecemeal or more sustained ways (in the Guild of Handicraft that Ashbee founded, for example). These 'other' men and the circumstances in which they lived were not utterly separate from Wilde, Shannon, Ricketts, Ashbee and Ford. They were not only counterpoints but also interlocutors for those who had the money to make their homes beautiful.

Out on the streets

Homelessness endured across the period (and of course beyond), and predictably worsened in times of economic depression – in the 1880s and 1930s especially.[11] Any accommodation homeless men could find – in workhouses, casual wards (providing one or two nights' accommodation for vagrants), or lodging houses – was temporary, and usually for just a night at a time. There was little chance for them to establish the kind of rootedness that Solomon seems to have found at St Giles and which men with more money could afford. This lack of a domestic base was associated with a lack of moral compass: sexual dissipation, overcrowding and the lack of a permanent place in which to live were casually and frequently connected in writing from the period.[12] Social reformers pushed for new housing partly on the basis of the apparently morally improving effects of a properly constructed, clean and neatly furnished home.[13]

Homelessness and homosexuality were sometimes interchangeably envisaged as the cause and effect of each other. Solomon's homelessness resulted from the sex he had with another man; for others, sex with other men arose out of the places they took refuge – under the bridges, on the Embankment, in Hyde Park and in countless other parts of the city. Reports of such activity, coming through court cases especially, suggested that this was an undomesticated passion and the city was a dangerous place where men were apparently more likely to stray and to become – as *The Daily Telegraph* had it in 1895 – the enemies of 'the natural affections, the domestic joys, the sanctity and sweetness of the home'.[14] Richer men cruising and having sex in these various places had a home, hotel or chambers to retreat to; bases which could offer more safety and privacy than poorer men could enjoy. The poor ended up in court more often as a result and their apparent sexual dissipation was thus exposed more frequently.[15]

The Lambeth Workhouse was judged a 'breeding ground' for unnatural passions in 1866. The workhouse, wrote journalist James Greenwood, had been 'transformed into a chapel of ease to the Cities of the Plain for the hideous enjoyment of those who are already bad, and the utter corruption of those who are obliged to hear what they cannot prevent'.[16] Pioneer sexologist Havelock Ellis' *Sexual Inversion* (1897) later drew attention to 'Homosexuality Amongst Tramps' in an appendix he commissioned from American Josiah Flint. Flint wrote that 'every hobo in the United States knows what "unnatural intercourse" means [...] talking about it freely, and, according to my findings, every tenth man practises it, and defends his conduct. Boys are the victim of this passion'.[17] He described a kind of queer reproduction via the seduction of boys between the ages of 10 and 15 by tramps who 'excite [their] imagination with stories and caresses', and so encourage them to enter an alternative world and set of relationships which stood in for family and were cemented by sex.[18] Though apparently less entrenched in England, Flint had nevertheless met there 'a number of male tramps who had no hesitation in declaring their preference for their own sex, particularly for boys'. Whether this 'liking' was something picked up on the road or was what led them away from home and family in the first place, Flint was 'unable to say'. 'That it is, however, a genuine liking, in altogether too many instances' he did not 'the least doubt'.[19] The presumption was underlined legislatively in 1898 when the Vagrancy Law Amendment Act included measures against male importuning in public.[20]

In 1932 George Orwell suggested that there were no 'essential' differences between beggars and ordinary 'working' men, and the homosexuality that was practised was situational, the result of a separation from women. He nevertheless cemented the association directly and indirectly in his comments and rhetoric. 'It is queer', wrote Orwell, 'that a tribe of men should be wandering up and down England like so many wandering Jews.' Tramps were, he said, 'a queer product'.[21] Though 'queerness' was not yet broadly understood as a synonym for homosexuality, it certainly indicated eccentricity and a difference from the norm.[22] Because this was also a chapter dealing with the supposed homosexuality of tramps, Orwell's use of the term suggests sexual strangeness too. The homeless, the homosexual, and also the Jew were in this way loosely linked in Orwell's account – and in ways that echoed Swinburne from half a century earlier.

This conflation endured, and still in 1967 the campaigner for homosexual law reform, Anthony Grey, felt the need to counter it. 'Sex deviancy is no respecter of persons', he wrote. 'It isn't only the homeless, the wanderer or the drop-out who discover themselves to be homosexual or bisexual in a heterosexual world.' Grey was nevertheless alert to the particular problems faced by homeless homosexuals: in a period when such 'types' were more widely recognised and discussed, the homeless hostels prepared to take avowed homosexuals were, he wrote, 'few and far between'.[23] And yet, such places had been and still were important to those who had sex with other men.[24] Some became notorious in the interwar period for the traffic in casual sexual encounters – albeit curtailed by the danger of interruption and exposure.[25] George Orwell described the 'nancy boys' in a boarding house on the Strand and wondered if the 'old Etonian' staying there was in fact in search of them.[26] It was partly in such texts and representations that homosexuality was conjured as alien to those elusive 'norms' of home and family life and incompatible with all they represented: respectability, restraint, containment, and 'true' (middle-class) Englishness.[27]

Overcrowding

Many men could not afford any form of permanent or semi-permanent housing; many more could only get the most basic of places to live. Overcrowding was common. A third of London's population in the 1930s lived more than three to a room – and even this was an improvement on the situation as it stood 30 years earlier.[28] The vast majority of queer working-class men in London lived in close proximity to others in the first half of the twentieth century and for most of the second – in boarding or lodging houses, with families, or cheek-by-jowl in cheap rented accommodation and bedsits (the homosexual was one of the 'types' to be found in bedsitter land according to a 1967 study).[29] Secrecy and privacy were well-nigh impossible in these kinds of home.[30]

Local councils covering London did begin to develop a stock of social housing in the first half of the twentieth century and especially in the interwar period.[31] Such housing was, though, generally designed and designated for families.[32] Just 277 of the 68,629 London County Council dwellings in 1935 were one-room tenements.[33] Even though married couples were a bare majority in the interwar years, housing policy and design underscored the pre-eminence of that particular marital and familial ideal – one that was also touted in the growing number of magazines focussing on home in the 1920s and 1930s.[34] The distance between such depictions and what was practically available and pragmatically possible was huge, however, and if the English domestic ideal of one house per couple or family was rare enough nationally, it was exceptional in London.[35]

Houses shared with others invariably brought restrictions. The companionship and emotional and practical support of family and co-residents should not be underestimated, but these other people could also be inhibiting.[36] Police only rarely searched private property in cases of homosexual crime, but there were almost invariably others who made caution and discretion necessary. Three landladies and one fellow tenant were called to testify against Wilde's co-defendant, Charles Taylor.[37] Many working-class men who had sex and relationships with other men were, moreover, also married and had homes with their wives, children, and often with lodgers and members of their extended families.[38] These homes were shaped – for good or ill – by these other affections and imperatives and also fundamentally by household income. Homosexual sex often took place beyond the home or else clandestinely within it.

Self- and individual expression – those hallmarks of the middle-class home – were clearly limited in such contexts. Decorating cost money and London County Council homes were, for example, decorated from a prescribed palette of yellow ochre or pale green (unless the tenant could afford to pay for an alternative).[39] Private landlords and landladies were unlikely to be receptive to requests for a lick of paint. Postcards or pictures might be as far as it was possible to go in terms of individualising a room, though these might still be important in alluding to a sense of difference – for the 'young prostitute' in Edward Carpenter's epic prose poem *Towards Democracy* who 'arrang[ed] the photographs of fashionable beauties' in his room.[40] For many poorer or working-class men, how they acted, what they wore and where they went was more important than the décor and arrangement of the places they lived.[41]

The same was often also the case for men who were working in the service sector – in hotels or the private houses of the wealthy. There seems to have been a preponderance of queer men in these roles in the first half of the twentieth century.[42] Many servants 'lived in'. The 1901 census showed, for example, that 176 live-in servants (78 male;

98 female) were employed to service the 132 households at the 'modern' Queen Anne's Mansions in fashionable St James.[43] For some queer servants, 'living in' provided an opportunity to find sex, relationships, some camaraderie, and a means of living away from possibly restrictive family homes. Living on site, though, often also meant compromised privacy and a double insecurity: both job and home could be lost if they were found out. Though in domestic roles, these men paradoxically often did not have a home of their own – or at least not the kind that was being idealised more broadly.

It was those with money who could do something materially different. As we will see in the two chapters and epilogue that follow, the relative safety and comforts of the middle-class home, the descriptions of inverts and homosexuals emerging through sexology, and the self-conscious way in which some homosexual men related to art and culture, made a domestic flourish a tacit marker of queer difference in the first half of the twentieth century and a trenchant stereotype in the second. This was the case even though it was far from the majority experience or impulse, and even though ideas of the homeless and rootless homosexual endured alongside.

1
Domestic Passions: Unpacking the Homes of Charles Shannon and Charles Ricketts

In 1924, *Country Life* magazine featured a home made in the Keep of Chilham Castle in Kent. Such unusual landmark properties were standard fare in this and similar publications from the late nineteenth century onwards.[1] They detailed domestic histories and interiors that seemed to perfectly frame and reflect the character and distinction of the inhabitants – in this case, the artist couple Charles Shannon (1863–1937) and Charles Ricketts (1866–1931). The author of the piece, historian of domestic architecture Christopher Hussey, waxed lyrical about the 'two painters [who] now imitate the way of Montaigne and dwell in a tower: two painters whose long and productive friendship is scarcely less "perfect, inviolate and entire" than that of Michel de Montaigne and Étienne de la Boétie'.[2] The pair had preserved and 'beautified' 'one of the most ancient habitations in Britain', and in these surroundings, were to be 'left in their tower overlooking the fat meadows of the Stour, among the peacock bowers and ilex [holly tree] shade of their field, at peace to raise castles of canvas and weave tapestries in paint'.[3]

Shannon and Ricketts were given Chilham Keep for life in November 1918 as what Ricketts described as 'bakshish'.[4] They had advised their friend and patron, Australian collector Edmund Davis, on the purchase of paintings that, once re-sold, had raised enough money for him to buy the whole Chilham Castle estate. Though they retained a London base (at Lansdowne House in Kensington and then from 1923 at Townshend House near Regent's Park), Shannon and Ricketts used the Keep as their country retreat after the horrors and what they saw as the philistinism of the war years. They took on the transformation of their new home with great relish. 'Old windows and old fireplaces are being found', wrote Ricketts to a friend. 'For the moment we are securing or making furniture for the place. Shannon has designed a cretonne [a kind of fabric] and I may do another to suit the octagonal room downstairs, which needs huge stalactite-like falls of curtains, and possibly curtains on the walls.'[5] To another friend he promised 'gradually [to] coax the skin back to the place; already we have sent down Japanese irises, Chinese peonies, hollyhocks, and queer dear flowers to the big house gardens'.[6]

Chilham Keep was a place of creativity and craftsmanship for the couple. They aligned themselves in this with a particularly English and especially late-Victorian and Edwardian middle- and upper-middle-class domestic culture,[7] and a new impulse from the 1870s and 1880s for the home to reflect 'the character of its inhabitants'.[8] Historian Judith Neiswander convincingly connects this to tenets of Victorian liberalism espoused most famously by John Stuart Mill. Mill defended private freedom of expression in ways which 'exactly parallel[ed] the concerns expressed in the [burgeoning] literature on interior decoration. Its writers condemned the mindless conformity to correct appearances that stifled creativity and personal expression in the home'.[9] 'Different persons', wrote Mill, 'require different conditions for their spiritual development, and can no more exist healthily in the same room, than all the variety of plants can in the same physical environment.'[10] Though there were also strong conventions about what the middle-class home should look like, such tenets suggested the scope to express difference and 'personality' there.[11] Middle-class men and women were increasingly expected to put something of themselves into their domestic surroundings – for themselves and also for visitors, who would then bear witness to the knowledge, culture, and taste of their host and hostess.[12] Such domestic eclecticism, individuality and artistry were facilitated by London's status as the centre of Empire. There was an astonishing array of goods brought from across the globe into the vast docks to the east and often sold alongside home-produced goods in the new department stores which were opening their doors in the West End from the 1860s. Such shops widened the scope to buy things for the home and so to make the kind of individualised mark that had previously been afforded only by the very wealthy.

With this understanding of home, Shannon and Ricketts could speak of themselves in part through the things they accumulated and the way they arranged them. In this they conformed to prevailing aspirations for the middle-class home but also found a way to suggest a certain queerness. This was partly because the home and interior decoration were increasingly feminised and women were seen as the primary 'beautifiers'.[13] Shannon and Ricketts were not being quite the men some of their domestically distant male peers appeared to be.[14] In addition, specific homes and items within them could be read for clues to queer character. Hussey was, for example, alert to Chiham Keep's association with Edward II and the final (unnamed but notorious) 'crisis' of his reign (the king was purportedly murdered by the anal insertion of a hot poker). This was, it seemed, an appropriate domestic heritage for the new residents. By imagining them in a 'peacock bower', meanwhile, Hussey nodded to late nineteenth-century Wildean aestheticism which was tainted after the playwright's trial for gross indecency. The connection to Montaigne referred the reader back to an especially intense example of male friendship and love.[15] Having established Shannon and Ricketts in their ancient setting and rendered them respectable in that way, he also subtly signalled their queerness. The couple, I argue in this chapter, did something similar for themselves in the way they decorated, furnished, and lived at the Keep and in the London homes they shared from 1886 in Kennington, Chelsea, Richmond, Kensington and Regent's Park.

Home and the muddle of identification

Shannon and Ricketts first met at the City and Guilds Technical Art School in Kennington Park Road, south London, in 1882. Shannon had been studying there for a year when Ricketts arrived, aged 16, to start an apprenticeship to a wood engraver. Ricketts had recently lost his father (a naval lieutenant turned painter) and, two years previously, his (probably illegitimate and aristocratic, certainly penniless) French mother. Ricketts had spent much of his childhood in France and Italy, though for periods the family lived in south east London near the Crystal Palace (which the young Ricketts loved for its concerts and exhibitions) and then in South Kensington (the capital's new museum quarter). Shannon, meanwhile, had had a more settled, less peripatetic upbringing as a vicar's son. Brought up in the Lincolnshire countryside, he attended a boarding school for the sons of the clergy in Leatherhead, Surrey, before going on to study in Kennington.[16] The training Shannon and Ricketts received there was resonant with the intersecting aesthetic, applied and practical aspirations of the Arts and Crafts movement, which sought to counter mass production through a re-engagement with individualised design and craftsmanship.[17] That influence endured for them, and we see it in the way Ricketts talks about refurbishing Chilham Keep some 30 years later.

This domestic relationship began in democratising times. Shannon and Ricketts moved in together in 1888, just four years after the Third Reform Act had given all male householders who had continuous residence at one address (and also £10 lodgers) the vote. Men who could be trusted to vote were those who had a secure sense of home.[18] The measure enfranchised around eight million more men nationally – leaving around 40 per cent of all adult men, including those discussed in the introduction to Part I and of course all women, without a vote. It fell far short of earlier Chartist demands articulated famously at a mass rally on Kennington Common in 1848 – just a stone's throw from Shannon and Ricketts' new address (and by now transformed into Kennington Park). The local Lambeth workhouse in Princes Street was the one James Greenwood had exposed for (homo)sexual dissipation in 1866, and though Shannon and Ricketts' road was middle class, Charles Booth's poverty maps drawn up between 1886 and 1903 show a real mixing of income levels and classes in the streets behind.[19]

Once they had a little more money (partly through Ricketts' work as an illustrator) they moved on to artistic Chelsea. From this point on, the couple repeatedly chose artistic districts and residences, enfolding art into

Figure 2 Charles Ricketts in the flat in Kennington Park Road he shared with Charles Shannon, c.1889, complete with prints of classical statuary

© The Fitzwilliam Museum, Cambridge.

their domestic and daily lives, setting themselves apart as Bohemian,[20] and framing themselves in these ways to others.[21] They had two successive homes in Chelsea. They first took over aesthetic artist James McNeil Whistler's house in the Vale in 1888 and then from 1894 lived in nearby Beaufort Street – closer to the river and to their friend Oscar Wilde. Though there were streets in the area (nearby Flood Street and Flood Walk, for example) which Booth marked in dark blue and black to indicate 'chronic want' and 'the lowest class' (no area of central London – even Mayfair – was without them),[22] Chelsea also had a substantial middle class and a reputation as a literary and artistic home-based bohemia.

From what novelist E.M. Forster described in *Howards End* (1910) as 'long-haired Chelsea',[23] the pair moved for three years to Spring Terrace, Richmond, before returning to central west London in 1902 and a 'palatial studio-flat' in Lansdowne House, Kensington – one of a cluster of new and specially designed artists' homes within easy reach of the Victoria and Albert Museum.[24] Ultimately – in 1923 –Townshend House, Regent's Park, became their London base. This was a less frenetic but also artistic district, and their home had previously been occupied by that great of the Victorian art world Sir Lawrence Alma-Tadema (1836–1912).

Over the years the couple's income 'rarely exceeded a thousand pounds per year, and [was] seldom half this'.[25] This was a good sum but was uneven and sometimes felt precarious to them. At first they relied on sharing their homes with other artists to cover costs, and they would sometimes scrimp on basics to purchase arts, collectibles, and ('exotic', 'queer dear') plants and flowers. As their reputations grew (both became fellows of the Royal Academy; Ricketts was offered but turned down the directorship of the National Gallery in 1914), their income became more stable and their homes grander. They were by now able to afford live-in domestic help. Overall, this meant that in more than 40 years together – and between the housemates and the servants – the pair never lived alone. Home for them and for others of their class and status was not the private secluded realm that many couples of the post-World War II generation found it or hoped it would be.

Neither Shannon nor Ricketts described himself as homosexual, Uranian or inverted, nor did they allude to the sex they might have had together.[26] Ricketts playfully refused to answer the questions of classicist John Addington Symonds on the subject, though in relaying the anecdote down the years he indicated an ease and a certain mischievousness about it.[27] Instead, Shannon and Ricketts' bond and relationship was articulated by the men themselves and by their circle of friends in terms of their co-residence, their emotional, practical and aesthetic investment in their homes, their vast collection of art and antiques, and the artistic and design work that was closely identified with the places where they lived (their Vale Press, for example, was named after their first Chelsea home).[28] Shannon and Ricketts sustained their coupledom and also protected it from criticism in part through what literary critic Sharon Marcus has described as 'their intensely domestic existence' and also their open, visible and highly cultured rendition of home.[29]

I look in what follows at Shannon and Ricketts' aestheticism and collecting, then at some queer domestic markers and sensibilities, and finally at their everyday domestic and home-orientated social lives. This is not as straightforward a structure as it might at first seem. The interplay of art, collecting, presumed queer sensitivities, friendship, intimacy, and the 'everyday' is one of the most striking and, I will suggest, telling things about their households. Because of the available source material, the chapter is skewed in its focus. Ricketts was the more prolific of the two men in his diary and letter writing, and attracted more attention from commentators and critics in his lifetime and subsequently. This coverage and his own life-writing has perhaps bolstered perceptions that he was the queerer of the two men,[30] raising questions about how we think about intimate domestic relationships between couples whose desires and sexualities do not ostensibly match. Shannon had affairs with women and contemplated marriage on more than one occasion, giving Rickett's biographer J.G.P. Delaney cause to suggest that he was basically heterosexual. He makes sense of Shannon's (apparent) 'sacrifice' of the 'ordinary joys that his life with Ricketts denied him' through their joint and home-based passion for art and collecting.[31] This does indeed help in understanding some of what energised and underpinned Shannon and Ricketts' relationship, but Delaney's fixing of Shannon and Ricketts' sexuality (as heterosexual and homosexual respectively) does scant justice to the intensity of their bond, or to how they and others perceived it. Even if this couple did not have a sexual relationship (which is possible), that should not detract from the strength of their connection and intimacy. Neither should their bond with each other diminish the significance of their other multiple and differently organised and appreciated friendships and relationships.[32] While we have tended to look to homosexual sex, homosociality and homosexual couples in our analyses of queer lives in the past, it is worth remembering that Shannon and Ricketts and their friends and acquaintances – Oscar Wilde, John Addington Symonds and Robbie Ross amongst them – had connections and affections that cut across gender, sexuality, age and class divisions in conventional and also less conventional ways. These connections and affections do not necessarily mean these men were any less queer but might instead be part of that queerness, as we discern, for example, the particular value placed on friendship over or in addition to family. Part of this relates to a Hellenic tradition in which all these men were well-versed, but it is also a feature of all the case studies I consider in this book. Friendship has been key in contexts where men felt their outsider status or wanted self-consciously to explore emotional and sometimes sexual bonds in more expansive ways than through conventional coupledom.[33]

It is not necessary to prove that someone like Shannon had sex with other men in order to view him rather queerly. He, Ricketts and their circle were accommodating of different kinds of desires and relationships, and they marked out their own difference and expectations in multiple and not only sexualised or eroticised ways – most notably via art, collecting and literature. This is worth observing too in relation to the artist Roger Fry, who crops up repeatedly in Part I of this book. He was married to Helen Coombe and seems to have been attracted to women sexually, yet he was also part of Shannon and Ricketts' early circle, which largely comprised avowedly inverted or homosexual men. Fry also became a close comrade of Charles Ashbee and of Duncan Grant. He was rather queer in this network of association and in the way he validated intense emotional (if not sexual) relationships with other men.

Shannon and Ricketts' queerness can be thought about in similar ways. We need to consider the multiple threads of identification and belonging within groups and between individuals that might signal homosexuality or represent a homosexual milieu but not precisely or exclusively or in ways that deterministically lock down the sexual identities of men like Shannon and Ricketts.[34] This is especially the case in a period when rigid binary sexual identity categories had not yet crystallised. The prism of home, I suggest, allows us to comprehend their subjectivity, relationships and circle in rather different and more complex ways than if we were to look at them only via court cases, sexology and the newspaper press.[35] The pair used home to give a sense of distinction and difference and simultaneously to show that they fitted in. These twin currents of conformity and non-conformity are key to understanding Shannon and Ricketts and their passion for theatricality, aesthetics, collecting and each other.

The house beautiful

Ricketts declared himself (it is tempting to say 'came out as') an aesthete and atheist at 15, and art and the pursuit of beauty became his own and the couple's preoccupation.[36] They prioritised these things in their domestic expenditure, judged and analysed the world and the people around them on these terms, and were in some ways guardians of the aesthetic 'house beautiful'.[37] The term was used first by Oxford don Walter Pater as 'a general metaphor for a space of art and pleasure'.[38] Oscar Wilde deployed it more specifically (though with similar import) in relation to home decoration for his 'House Beautiful' lecture delivered during his American tour of 1882. He placed the onus on beauty for its own sake rather than on the moral, ethical or sentimental value of pictures, ornaments and furnishing. Wilde had by this time already shown his aesthetic domestic flair. The apartment he shared with the painter Frank Miles at 13 Salisbury Street, just off the Strand, in 1879–1880, had a white panelled sitting room decorated with blue china and lilies – a style synonymous with aestheticism and famously parodied in the pages of *Punch* and by Gilbert and Sullivan in their operetta *Patience* (1881).[39] From 1885, at Tite Street, Chelsea, Wilde and his new wife Constance created an aesthetic showpiece.[40] The couple 'threw their mahogany into the streets' and broke with domestic convention in their enthusiasm for 'bizarre tapestries, furnishings and ornamentation' that invoked other times and spaces – and especially North Africa and Japan.[41] These rooms became places where the appreciation of beauty in the here and now was key. Prior to Wilde's prosecution in 1895, these interiors spoke of a 'modern', advanced artistic couple who did not want to replicate embedded values and a fusty traditionalism associated with other contemporary Victorian interiors.

The domestic compelled Wilde creatively and allowed him to give voice to his concerns and sense of difference.[42] He 'marked his work in every genre with his investment in domesticity' – in his editorship of *The Women's World* from 1887 to 1889, in the lush interiors of *The Picture of Dorian Gray* (1891), in his drawing room comedies and in his fairy tales for children.[43] Home was central to Wilde in the articulation of his subjectivity. In his careful analysis of the decoration and furnishings in Wilde's study, art historian Michael Hatt shows how he produced himself as an expansive, cultured writer, artist and family man – and also as somewhat queer. The latter was signalled not only by overt (homo)eroticism but also by the evocation of particular histories and cultures – of Greece and Morocco especially.[44] This was not, however, about the precise articulation of identity but rather a more diffuse indicator of difference from circulating norms.

The aesthetic decoupling of furnishing from morality and tradition, and the invocation of exotic places meanwhile slipped for some towards decadence. It seemed a small step from the appreciation of beauty for its own sake to the validation of broader sensual pleasure. Oriental and North African ornaments and rugs, for example, were hardly the exclusive preserve of queer men, but they were part of a chain of contemporary association which might evoke such experimentation. This had been suggested to the small elite readership of the homoerotic pornographic novel *Teleny* (1893), to which Wilde is supposed to have contributed and in which the 'soft Persian and Syrian divans' seem continuous with the 'consummate lewdness' enacted upon them.[45] At the trial of Wilde and Charles Taylor in 1895, meanwhile, the court heard that Taylor's rooms 'were furnished sumptuously, and were lighted by different coloured lamps and candles [...] the windows were never opened or cleaned, and the daylight was never admitted'.[46] If other Victorian homes were supposed to represent and to nurture harmonious marriages and gender relations, family lives and upright citizenship, Taylor's interiors seemed to promise something else altogether.

In this context, Ricketts was doing something quite deliberate when he aligned himself with the disgraced playwright via their respective homes in the opening pages of his *Recollections of Oscar Wilde* (1932). He noted Wilde's approval of his house in The Vale: 'What a charming old house you have and what delightful Japanese prints [...] And you have yellow walls, so have I – the colour of joy!' A few days later, Ricketts continued: 'We were invited to hear him read *A Portrait of Mr WH*. His small study was painted buttercup yellow [...] On the walls hung a Monticelli, a Japanese painting of children at play, and a drawing by Simeon Solomon of Eros conversing with some youths.'[47] Aesthetic and queer markers converged: they had gathered to hear Wilde's *A Portrait of Mr WH*, his Platonic and homophile re-interpretation of Shakespeare's sonnets, in a study hung with 'Love Amongst the Schoolboys' – a homoerotic piece by Solomon, who was by this time living in penury at St Giles workhouse.

Ricketts noted the beautiful things in Wilde's Tite Street home. Ricketts and Shannon accumulated many more. At Kennington Park Road, and with limited funds, they covered the walls with prints of art and classical statuary (see figure 2). At the Vale there were the Japanese prints Wilde liked.[48] Then, with more money, they began to accumulate art and antiques in a collection initiated with purchases from the sale of artist Lord Frederick Leighton's effects in 1896. The couple's collection was ultimately valued for probate at £36,203 – very roughly £1.75 million today.[49]

Always alongside their art and collection in these various homes were gorgeous displays of flowers. Floristry was increasingly seen as a domestic and feminine pursuit,[50] and in its more exotic and florid dimensions had a queer tinge.[51] It was a particular passion for Ricketts. In a thank you letter to a friend in 1902 he described a floral gift in extravagant prose:

> Shannon joins me in grateful acknowledgment of your superb gift of flowers. It looks as if you had ordered all the flowers to be picked, just as an Eastern Potentate orders the execution of all his wives. The Blue salvia is still alive and perpetuated in one of Shannon's canvasses. It is a most noble and haughty flower, at once half a nettle and half an exotic; it looked precious and blue blooded when brought next to some quite haughty foreigners I had brought back from Regents Street, these last being profoundly undemocratic flowers with tyrannical scents.[52]

Again we get the links to the 'exotic' East and language which resonates with late nineteenth century decadent and homophile or homoerotic literature and with the lush interiors of J.-K. Huysmans' *À Rebours* (1884), Wilde's *Picture of Dorian Gray* (1891), and *Teleny*. Ricketts' rhetorical flourish in relation to the gift of a bouquet was small fry by comparison to these other writings, but here and in his writing more generally there is a connection to this recent literary history. In this way he suggested a distance from the nation of philistines who had (in his view) prosecuted his friend Wilde in a 'social vendetta' born of 'a deep hatred of the artist in the British mentality'.[53] His own (partially French) heritage and upbringing allowed him to imagine himself as an outsider to this, and suggested too an associated politics: he indicated in his description of the flowers the value he placed on the exotic and exceptional, the 'elite', the 'blue blooded' and the 'undemocratic'. These social and cultural values and hierarchies were eroticised, brought home, and encapsulated in this bouquet and in the extraordinary collection the couple accumulated.[54] The omnipresent flowers in their homes and their antiquities and *objets d'art* were clear signals of the couple's cultural distinction and oblique signs of their queerness.

Austerity and eclectic collecting

Despite these various connections to earlier and concurrent artistic, literary and decorative movements, Delaney suggests that 'it was not an aesthetic house that they made for themselves': 'No fashion ever imposed on [Ricketts], he never accepted or rejected artists, movements or period wholesale.'[55] If there was a suspect tinge of louche *fin de siècle* decadence in their domestic display and certainly in the way they described it, and also something palatial and luxurious in their last two homes especially, there was also a compensating seriousness, eclecticism and austerity, which commentators observed carefully.[56] Cecil Lewis, co-founder of the BBC, described a series of rooms at Townshend House that served subtly to legitimise the couple in these ways. They kept, he wrote, a 'small museum' there:

> Egyptian antiquities, Greek vases and figurines lived in glass cases. Below were drawers full of antique beads and Chinese hair ornaments [...]; there were Adam sofas and chairs, Italian side-tables, a marble torso, a bas-relief, a picture of Don Juan by Ricketts, a portrait of [the actress] Mrs Pat[rick Campbell] by Shannon [...] But this room was never lived in. Days would pass when it was not visited. It was open only when they received, when friends who cared to see, and would understand its rarity, were shown round. Yet it was not, like a museum, cold and detached. It was a set piece, true; but it was none the less a room. Arranged in perfect taste.[57]

Like the aristocratic private-house collections of the eighteenth and early nineteenth centuries, the room signalled exquisite taste and culture and

Figure 3 Shannon and Ricketts' drawing room at Landsdowne House, with display cases and 'penny lampshades', c.1910
© The Fitzwilliam Museum, Cambridge.

also substantial knowledge, restraint, refinement and a sense of a mission to save and preserve.[58] This was a room to view rather than a room to be lived in. There was a broader general trend for collecting at this time but not with the kind of specialist knowledge and seriousness displayed by Shannon and Ricketts.[59] They carefully photographed the artefacts and bequeathed these along with much of the collection itself to the Fitzwilliam Museum in Cambridge. All this aligned Shannon and Ricketts with an established masculine and highly respected pursuit,[60] and the collection and photographs of it marked a difference from the feminised 'amateur world of taste and domesticity' of the period.[61] This was not superficial and frivolous home-making, nor was it louche or decadent. This was domestic fashioning of a different order.

If this small 'museum' was not used domestically, the dining room at Townshend House certainly was. It was, Lewis wrote, 'a bridge from [this] work to entertainment' and was 'the most perfect' he had ever seen:

> Ricketts had that unique quality of taste which enabled him to distinguish an object of merit, whatever its period or use. You would not think that Old Master drawing would be at home with a Chinese bird cage; you would not think that red and green marble topped tables could live in amity; you would fancy that Empire chairs might swear at Morris chintzes, French knives could never harmonise with Georgian silver, and a modern blue glass bowl could never stand at the feet of a Grecian statuette; the whole certainly could not be lit hard with clear bulbs hanging from six penny porcelain shades. Yet [...] each object, being in itself perfect, added its lustre to the whole, so that the room, which was, besides, winter and summer, filled with flowers, glowed with a radiant and compelling beauty.[62]

The aesthetic, decadent echoes were there again, and the arrangement was (Lewis repeats and repeats) not one 'you' would think of. It was full of unexpected conjunctions which nevertheless worked together (like Shannon and Ricketts themselves). The room and its contents were luminous ('lustr[ous]', 'lit', and 'radiant') and marked out the couple (and Ricketts especially) as exceptional. The society painter Jacques-Émile Blanche had felt a similar 'air of culture and refinement in the surprising and eclectic choice of drawings' in the hall of their earlier home at Lansdowne House.[63] There was certainly a nod in both houses to an earlier and late-Victorian fashion for domestic eclecticism, but Shannon and Ricketts' persistence with it into the 1920s, when they were well into late middle age, set them apart. They shaped Townshend House at a time when an interest in interiors and aesthetics had been even more determinedly feminised and when the individualism prized by the late Victorians and Edwardians had given way for some to a modernist suspicion of such idiosyncrasy.[64]

Importantly, though, these domestic arrangements were not about the 'indulgence of luxury' – as the bare bulbs and the 'six penny lampshades' suggest. 'The rooms where they habitually spent their days', wrote Lewis, 'would be almost poverty-stricken puritan in their simplicity.'[65] Ricketts observed that Wilde had 'smiled at the austerity of my habits';[66] the painter Edmund Dulac caricatured the pair as monks in one painting. Their homes were, in part, about hard work and productivity, suggesting a laudable and respectable 'protestant austerity [… and an] uncompromising work ethic'.[67] Ricketts' studio was 'Spartan', furnished with easy chairs 'almost devoid of padding' and a sofa 'as uncomfortable as a waiting room seat at a railway station'.[68] Blanche pinpointed this in his description of the couple's simple bedroom at Lansdowne House with its 'twin bedsteads of spotless white [and] two washstands' – similar, in fact, to the portrayal of Lord Leighton's cell-like bedroom in his Holland Park mansion.[69] Blanche, like Lewis, seized on such domestic asceticism as tacit evidence of respectability. They intimated in this way that there was nothing going on behind the scenes and that Shannon and Ricketts' passions were not indulged in the bedroom but front of house and associated with art, culture and collecting. The art historian John Potvin argues something similar in relation to Edward Perry Warren's 'Spartan simplicity of interior and furnishings' at his house in Lewes, Sussex, which provided 'an alternative queer domesticity' to that represented in the trials of Wilde and Alfred Taylor. Such furnishings, he observes, could 'stave off any pejorative connotations […] associated with both the domestic realm and queer bachelorhood'.[70] Blanche, Lewis, Hussey, and Ricketts himself were thus perhaps both signalling and redressing the couple's queerness in the careful note they took of simplicity and propriety in their commentaries.

'Domesticity', as Marcus succinctly puts it, 'celebrated privacy that could be put on display.' The emergent homosexual type, meanwhile, 'coalesced around secrecy'.[71] Shannon and Ricketts in part sidestepped an association with the latter by conforming sufficiently to the former.[72] Their homes were spaces of work, of retreat, but also of display. There might be in relation to all this, art historian Jason Edwards writes in his work on Lord Leighton, a playful interweaving of secrecy and revelation that was 'pleasurabl[e]' rather than 'defensive' because there was nothing specific to be exposed, no particular identity to be revealed.[73] Rather than a 'sublimation' of homosexuality through collecting, there was in such passionate display instead a celebratory expression of distinctiveness.[74]

Collecting was not of course a queer pursuit *per se*. Indeed, it connected Shannon and Ricketts to a longstanding male elite tradition of connoisseurship as well as to the imperial project. But it also had a whiff of non-conformist masculinity to it and a loosely associated queer pulse. The art historian Barrett Kalter locates something similar in the eighteenth-century antiquarianism of Thomas Gray, Horace Walpole and William Beckford.[75] Others have observed the bachelor status and/or queer desires of many late nineteenth- and early twentieth-century antique collectors who saw themselves as 'married to their collections' and with 'a passion to preserve'.[76] In a riff on legal and newspaper rhetoric about gross indecency between men, Shannon and Ricketts' friend Sydney Cockerell (director of the Fitzwilliam Museum between 1908 and 1937) quipped to Ricketts that the price he paid for one object had been 'unnatural and indecent'.[77]

Shannon and Ricketts spoke of themselves through the things they crafted and collected.[78] In the portrait of the actress Mrs Patrick Campbell hanging in their 'small museum', they linked into the London theatre scene (and a queer campiness settling around it),[79] while the Hellenic sculpture and art in the collection affiliated them to a cultured homophile milieu. Ricketts described himself as a 'confirmed Greco–Roman', and, like some of his similarly classed queer contemporaries, orientated himself towards these ancient civilisations.[80] Wilde famously evoked the ancient Greeks in his courtroom defence and in elements of his Chelsea home, while Charles Kains Jackson celebrated them in the tellingly titled *Artist and Journal of Home Culture*, which he edited between 1888 and 1894.[81] Edward Perry Warren became a famed collector of Hellenic artefacts and created his home, in Sussex, in ascetic classical terms as an 'all male "monastery"' where 'the outside world shrank to a memory' (and which Ricketts visited twice).[82] These men – who either knew or knew of each other in what was a relatively small network – differentiated, elevated and separated themselves from others by drawing Hellenism in one way or another into their homes.

Shannon and Ricketts' home-based collection thus gave them a place within a masculine tradition and within metropolitan Bohemian and artistic cultures that linked also to national and imperial investment in certain histories and civilisations.[83] It secured and established them in this way. And yet it also queered them. Theirs was not an open collection. It was housebound, which meant they could be proprietorial – amassing it and arranging it to their lights, controlling who could view it, and using it in particular ways to speak somewhat theatrically for them. In his analysis of the artist duo Jasper Johns (b.1930) and Robert Rauschenberg (1925–2008), historian Jonathan Katz describes the way in which 'as a couple they were able to reap the benefits of a shared subjectivity without having to identify or affiliate with a larger gay or lesbian community'.[84] Without collapsing two very different places, eras and individuals, Katz's analysis is suggestive. Shannon and Ricketts were part of a milieu familiar from subsequent analyses of the queer 1890s, but the pair did not link into this grouping specifically in terms of sexual difference. Instead, it was their investment in aestheticism, in collecting and art, and in exclusive and exquisite homes that connected them to these others and was a mode and means of speaking of themselves. This was perhaps true too for other readers of the *Artist and Journal of Home Culture* under Kains Jackson's editorship.[85] The conjunction of art and the domestic sphere in the title of the journal alone had by this time become queerly evocative for Shannon and Ricketts and their circle. It is telling that the second part of the title was dropped after the Wilde trials – it was perhaps too feminising; too queer.[86]

Domestic sensitivities

Ricketts sought visitors who appreciated culture and beauty and could understand the rarity of their possessions. These visitors were men (chiefly) who had a sensitivity to art and its arrangement and display and who were responsive to exceptional spaces.[87] Classicist John Addington Symonds wrote that 'places exercise a commanding influence in the development of certain natures', and himself gave vivid details of his childhood homes and the effect they had on him – linking material objects and art to his 'inverted' sensibility. He wrote that art 'stimulated while it etherialised my inborn craving after persons of my own sex'.[88] Havelock Ellis (whom Shannon and Ricketts knew slightly) and fellow sexologist Richard von Krafft-Ebing both observed such heightened artistic and environmental sensibilities in the invert or homosexual. Max Nordau made a similar connection in *Degeneration* (1895).[89] For Symonds, Wilde, and Shannon and Ricketts the aesthetic sense – which they exercised keenly in their homes – in part legitimated their desires and gave them 'form' and 'ideality' (as Symonds put it).[90] Ricketts, with his 'unique quality of taste', keyed especially into these broader emerging assumptions about the sensitivities of the elite, cultured invert. He did not make that connection directly, however, and instead used it to signal a more diffuse, queerer sense of distinction. Ricketts recounted the environmentally transformative effect of listening to Richard Wagner (already by this time a queer icon)[91] at the home of a female friend in Plumstead, Essex: 'Magic lakes, subterranean seas, rushing waterfalls, twilight forests, and starlit peaks of ice, where strange flowers blossom under the snow, became visible to me in this humble seven roomed house.'[92] Spaces, for Ricketts, could be wildly recreated through art, music and beauty, and the home, already more broadly conceived as a retreat and sanctuary, gained additional significance as a place that could produce these distinguishing and individuating effects in the face of a 'philistine' society and culture.[93] Ricketts' arrangements of art, objects and flowers, and his decorative flourishes (those 'huge stalactite-like falls of curtains' at Chilham Castle Keep, for example) were thus far from incidental. They were a way for him, for them, to give shape to their felt difference, to idealise and legitimise it.

The theatricality in this was apposite. Ricketts was passionate about the theatre and opera, and the Ballets Russes especially (all early twentieth-century queer markers). He gained a reputation as an innovative and striking set and costume designer.[94] He often strove in this work for continuity between the two. For Laurence Binyon's *Attila* at His Majesty's Theatre in 1907, for example, set and costume for one scene were both almost entirely blood red, in a merger of actor and setting, individual and environment that suggested an ineffable connection between them. It was possible, Ricketts suggested in this, to read place and person from each other in an aesthetic interplay of colour, surface, appearance and character. The domestic environment could similarly reflect and frame the inhabitant and even modulate mood, feeling and persona – ideas rehearsed earlier by Wilde in 'The Decay of Lying' (1889).[95]

Ricketts measured his affinity with others partly on the basis of their homes. The aunt and niece couple Katherine Bradley and Edith Cooper (who together wrote poems about their erotic love for each other under the name 'Michael Field') were described by Ricketts through their cottage in Reigate, Kent:

> Its interior showed the modifications brought by my two friends on a typical, comfortable English home as it then was, Morris curtains and wallpapers, on the walls photos of Italian pictures. The place spoke of a love of books, art, travel and flowers. I noticed on one of the tables

one of those early paper covered editions in which Nietzsche first appeared; otherwise the general atmosphere was that crystallised by Walter Pater, a survival of the less flamboyant phase of the Aesthetic movement.[96]

Bradley and Cooper were conjured as aesthetic, artistic, cultured and different through their home, and simultaneously Ricketts showed himself to have the requisite sensitivity and critical acumen to read the signs ('*I* noticed', Ricketts wrote; others perhaps might not). This reading of the self and others from the domestic relates to a broader and burgeoning sense of the home as an aspect of interiority and part of the expression of individuality. But this was especially significant for those with these heightened artistic, nervous or theatrical sensitivities, supposedly possessed by degenerate, grossly indecent, inverted or homosexual men.

If, from Krafft-Ebing or Nordau's perspectives, these sensitivities were pathological and socially destructive, for Ricketts they distinguished him from 'suburban minds' and from the mundane, philistine 'normal' home. When Ricketts visited Wilde in prison, his distress found voice through a description of the dour décor of the 'small putty coloured waiting room, decorated with a chocolate dado and an ebonised clock'.[97] His disdain for such 'suburban' interiors was edged or even underpinned by misogyny and dismay at the effect women could have on the domestic life of men. In 1900, Ricketts recorded in his diary a schema for a possible novel that had come to him in a dream. It featured a man trapped in a marriage with 'one of those common, coarsish, lower middle class types that develop with age a half masculine appearance':

> I realised in this common case of a loveless home [the husband's] days would grow more and more grey and cold [...] the wife grows hard and dull, engrossed in the badly managed circumstances of her home. The happiest moments of his life will be in his solitary walks to and from work [...] The wife's vanity never leaves her. She is of the type which howls and fumbles over a piano she is unable to play when nobody is in the house but the servant who laughs in the kitchen.[98]

This man is thwarted in home-making by his wife, and what results is quite different from the artistic and cultural productivity of Ricketts' own domestic relationship with Shannon. The home in Ricketts' imagined novel lacks the cultured, masculine input and receives instead the clumsy attentions of this 'coarse' 'type'. 'As soon as a woman is concerned in a man's life', Bradley and Cooper reported Ricketts saying, 'it becomes unintelligent and trivial from the senseless marriage festivities onwards.' 'Marriage ought to be forbidden by law', Ricketts apparently told them.[99] To his friend, the artist and poet Thomas Sturge Moore, Ricketts promised to 'make for your wedding the pendant of pendants which will tear all lace and scratch babies' – imagining a piece of jewellery that would rip at the domestic fabric.[100] Like George Ives and Edward Perry Warren, his near contemporaries, Ricketts saw men together achieving something politically, artistically and domestically that was not possible with a woman. Warren wrote that the Uranian 'despises the pretty, the unnecessary, the superficial, the artificial, the accessories of decoration and manners, which [woman] is apt to import. But he goes further than most men, because the instinct for the beauty of the masculine drives him on'.[101]

In contemporary commentary, the emergent figures of the invert and homosexual were commonly depicted as anti-domestic and an enemy to the home and all it represented.[102] Shannon and Ricketts refused to stand outside, however, rejecting not home, but what they saw as a mundane lower-middle-class English version of it. When Ricketts painted an imagined portrait of Mr WH for Wilde's story, and Shannon provided the frame, the playwright exclaimed gleefully, 'Our English homes will totter to their base when [the story] appears.'[103] In this, the couple colluded with Wilde in the desecration of this wider English domestic and also imagined and produced alternatives in the way they shaped their own homes and validated the unusual or eccentric domestic intimacies of others in and beyond their circle – of Wilde, of 'Michael Field', of the devoted artist couple Glyn Philpot and Vivian Forbes.

Everyday lives, everyday intimacies

Shannon and Ricketts' domestic aestheticism and collection were integral to the couple's home and everyday life together. Their correspondence with each other was alive with new purchases and accounts of antiques and works of art, and through these things they articulated both their mutual affection and their troubles. When the painter Jacques-Emile Blanche heard that Shannon and Ricketts had lived together for twenty years and that their collection was in common, he told the latter: 'But this is an ideal existence that you lead – everything for art.'[104] They were, Blanche later wrote, 'two inseparables [...] who

Figure 4 Shannon and Ricketts posing in the studio at Landsdowne House, c.1910
© The Fitzwilliam Museum, Cambridge.

had amassed a princely legacy' – bracketing again the couple's intimacy with their treasures and gesturing to what this promised for the future.[105] When Shannon contemplated marriage to one of his female models, meanwhile, Ricketts focussed on their collection and spoke metonymically of the impossibility of dividing it. Shannon did not leave; the collection (or perhaps rather the relationship with Ricketts) won out.[106] Edith Cooper wrote that Ricketts had again been 'frightened' at the prospect of Shannon marrying in 1905: 'What would become of the collection?' he had asked her.[107] Whatever Shannon's desires (and in pondering marriage he was not necessarily indicating that he was 'really' heterosexual), the collection and their homes together provided an impetus for their relationship, a joint passion that allowed them to endure even though both also had intense emotional and sexual relationships with other women (chiefly for Shannon) and men (for Ricketts).[108] There was something similar, Potvin suggests, in the connection between Edward Perry Warren and his secretary and companion John Marshall: 'Collecting and subjectivity', he writes, 'quickly became mutually sustaining aspects of their joint venture and reciprocal feelings.'[109]

If Shannon and Ricketts' relationship was couched in and sustained by collecting, art and culture, however, it was also the product of muddling through in the everyday with each other. In letters and diaries we see snippets of conversation, annoyance and teasing, and touches of concern and intimacy between the two men. 'Remember my instructions about Calais', wrote Shannon to Ricketts in 1900, 'and mind you arm yourself with port. It makes one much younger towards the end of the journey.'[110] Ricketts wrote romantically from Florence: 'Dear Old Chap [...] At each meal time they plonk down a plate of strawberries which make me think of you – no, this is not quite accurate. I really think of the strawberries. Only when they are done, "I think of thee."'[111] Ricketts mentions in passing 'the shouts of laughter' together as they read from the paper, and of 'making [Shannon] drunk'.[112] When Shannon buys pet Japanese mice, they together hope their 'very intimate conversation [...] may have been unnatural vice', lest they be overrun by 'mouselets'.[113] Both men talk in the plural: 'Captain Brinkley's sale. One of the greatest hauls of our lives', wrote Shannon in his diary in 1898; Ricketts added a note – an intimate act in itself – that 'both our banking accounts vanished in this sale'.[114] There were the decisions they made as a couple about the division of domestic tasks, pooled income, the support of one by the other (the early arrangement was for Ricketts to work so that Shannon could paint), how to sustain their expenditure on collecting, and where and when to move (Shannon was generally keen, Ricketts less so: moves tended to upset and depress him in ways resonant with those presumptions about queer hypersensitivity, or what Freud described in a 1911 letter to Jung as 'homosexual touchiness').[115]

There was in Shannon and Ricketts' homes a ready interplay of friendship, socialisation, art and collectibles. The latter were sometimes described as intimates: Shannon and Ricketts introduced Michael Field to 'Fatty', 'Swallow' and 'Bullfinch', three Staffordshire jugs; to 'Jennie', an old chair; and to 'Dr Ibsen', a jack-in-a-box (in a telling reference to the Norwegian playwright whose contemporaneous plays lifted the lid on the idealised middle-class home and family).[116] Conversely, visitors and co-residents were sometimes objectified, becoming part of the collection. Two new servants in 1923 were 'useless, ugly' but their replacements, Mr and Mrs Nicholls, were 'two new treasures'.[117] Earlier, Ricketts described a visitor as 'a beautiful, untidy looking chap who would make a good model for Christ, only his nose is too small and weak'.[118]

The collection itself energised and provided a context for enduring friendships and thus carried a cargo of affection.[119] This energy ebbed when it was transferred from the final house the couple shared to the Fitzwilliam Museum after Ricketts' death. Lewis described entering the

'Shannon and Ricketts Room' as akin to 'going to a cemetery, gazing at a mummy in a crystal coffin':

> The presence that once informed it all, the daily life which flowered among these things, the flow of conversation, of laughter, the sense of being in the intimate company of great art collected by a zealot, himself a genius, all that is gone, gone. [...] It is cold when we come out into the street again and I am tired.[120]

As Lewis suggested, Shannon and Ricketts' homes were the core of their social life. Though the couple were reclusive at first (something the Vale – 'a shady, time forgotten lane' – seemed to facilitate), as their work became better known 'the legend of [...] the two young artists completely devoted to art and to each other' attracted more attention – and a growing numbers of visitors.[121] The Vale became 'one of the most socially important and vibrant homes in Chelsea'.[122]

Shannon and Ricketts' 'at homes' were personally sustaining and artistically productive. Ricketts especially could sometimes feel out of place or uncomfortable elsewhere. After the Wilde trials, he observed that 'anything unusual, an Inverness coat, for instance, or longish hair, would elicit from the street Arabs the cry "hello Oscar"'.[123] They socialised at home more exclusively and with less propriety than they would have been able to in other places, though there was a felt need for some self-censorship there too: Ricketts destroyed private letters and sections of his journal following Wilde's prosecution.[124] Such home-based socialising was important for many queer Londoners across the first half of the twentieth century – with small gatherings and bigger parties providing a greater margin of safety than the streets or more public venues.[125] Shannon and Ricketts were often as 'merry as boys' in company at home: 'There was a great deal of teasing and pantomime between them.'[126] The poet John Gray described being transported by his visits to the Vale: 'How many times did I walk home to the Temple in the small hours dreaming sunnily all the way from the palace of enchantment which the [...] Vale really was.'[127] Wilde observed to a guest he took there: 'This is the one place in London where you will never be bored, and where you will not be asked to explain things. Nothing should be explained.'[128] If Shannon and Ricketts' 'at homes' were a version of the Victorian tradition of artists opening their studio-houses so that their work (and impeccable domestic taste) could be viewed in *situ*,[129] theirs were less publicised, more intimate, more Bohemian – and altogether queerer. This showed in the roster of visitors. Wilde, was, of course, a guest, but also John Gray, Robbie Ross, Charles Kains Jackson, on at least one occasion John Addington Symonds, Roger Fry, Forbes and Philpot, and Vaslav Nijinsky and Sergei Diaghilev of the Ballets Russes.[130] Aside from fostering artistic collaboration,[131] the gatherings allowed Ricketts especially to meet, befriend and guide a new generation of artists and writers – Lewis, Philpot, Forbes, Fry, and Gordon Bottomley amongst them. There was a fantasy of (queer) reproduction in Ricketts' anticipation that these men would carry on his artistic lights in the face of what he saw as the travesty of modernism. If Fry was a disappointment in this respect, Forbes and Philpot would, he hoped, become 'the Shannon and Ricketts of the near future'.[132] He was delighted when they took over their home and studio at Lansdowne House in 1923. Lewis was 'adopted' by Ricketts when he was in his early twenties and was given various treasures and a small property in Italy. Lewis was in awe of him; he seemed to fulfil a paternal or an avuncular role. Riffing on the reproductive theme, he wrote that Ricketts had 'midwived my earliest efforts'.[133] As with Warren and his acolytes in Lewes, there was something of the Hellenic pedagogical bond in these relationships in a context and period where cross-generational relationships were sometimes idealised rather than denigrated.[134]

Shannon and Ricketts' friendship network was not only male, however, and it included a number a married couples (including George Bernard and Charlotte Shaw, Thomas and Marie Sturge Moore, and Edmund and Mary Davis, their own patrons), single women like Ricketts' friend in Plumstead, and of course the queer female couple 'Michael Field'. These friendships were again domestically focussed, and Shannon and Ricketts were seen by these others as arbiters of domestic and artistic taste. Michael Field asked Shannon and Ricketts to help them to find and furnish a 'home for our marriage'.[135] This is precisely what they did in a high cultural and Edwardian version of a home makeover. Ricketts, as we have seen, took careful note of the couple's Reigate home when he first met them, and thereafter the domestic was a constant pulse in their correspondence in terms of décor and collectibles, and also in their day-to-day domestic lives as couples. Ricketts sent camp notes to them. In a postscript to one letter, he quipped that 'Shannon would send his love but is just now thoughtless from having shampooed his head'.[136] The potency of this friendship with Michael Field and with others was especially evident when Wilde died in 1900. 'I am too upset to write about it', observed Ricketts; 'I feel wretched, tearful, stupid [...] Moore had hardly finished giving us the news when a loud ringing was heard and Michael Field arrived, sobbing loudly in the hall'.[137]

The nature of these bonds was marked in part by the artistically oriented pet names they gave each other. 'Shannon and I were called "the painters"; sometimes I was called "the lizard" or "the basilisk"', noted Ricketts – omitting to mention two more suggestive nicknames, 'fairyman' and 'fay'.[138] Such nicknaming was part of a trend in their milieu – Rickets and Shannon did it too, as did Wilde and Ives. It suggested a heightened and artistic connection which was distinct from but parallel to the familial. 'I think', wrote Ricketts, 'the private nicknames given [by Michael Field] to their friends carried with them a separate and legendary view of their lives and characters'.[139] Relatives, meanwhile, were to Ricketts like 'cinders, ashes, dust',[140] and the deep connections that developed between Shannon and Ricketts and their friends, protégés and co-residents created an alternative way of conducting relationships that we can also identify in the homes established by Ives and Warren.[141] These structures of intimacy and the ways in which they were established and sustained is yet another tentative but significant queer marker – one that became more visible, overt and politicised in the later twentieth century.[142] Shannon and Ricketts' use of home as a base for 'shared tastes and emotional bonds' was certainly in line with broader conceptions of the domestic,[143] but the nature of those home-based bonds was also rather different. Their homes were in this way not orientated towards the procreative family but rather to a cultural legacy and the nurturing of collectors and artists who were usually male and often queer. The flow of men and women, queer and 'normal', in and out of Shannon and Ricketts' homes meanwhile suggests degrees of queer knowledge and localised acceptance that underscore the frequent heterosociality of many queer lives.[144] Ricketts noted with a certain satisfaction that his friend in Plumstead, Essex (whose love of Wagner had transported him) was 'a declared atheist [...], had distrust for her sex and a liking for exaggerated character in men, and, for that matter, men without character'.[145] He was, in this, measuring their connection to each other, but also observing and confirming something about himself. He was one such man.

* * *

When Shannon suffered a fall in 1929, Ricketts shifted his gaze from aesthetics to the practicalities of nursing or finding nursing care for Shannon. This involved the sale of parts of the collection that had been so central to their bond and life together. Their domestic and work lives changed, as Ricketts revealed movingly in his letters from this period:

> [Shannon] recognises me, responds to simple stimuli, food, shaving, washing etc., but he lives in an incomprehensible world of his own [...] I think I told you he is in my studio, he has only two nurses (men) now instead of three. [...] Latterly I have lunched out and left the house for three hours at a time. I shall strive to return to normal occupations, but the strain on everyone has been constant, the cost amazing, and the result nothing except perplexity and anxiety [...] A month ago we had freezing fogs, burst pipes, no baths, water through ceilings. In fact, there has been an epidemic of small bothers, which, I suppose, have helped to keep me alive.[146]

The rhythm of daily life – shaving, feeding and 'epidemics of small bothers' – took on a new, even sustaining, significance for Ricketts in these changed circumstances. Shannon, meanwhile, in Ricketts words, 'developed a subconscious resistance to doctoring; he refuses point blank to be punctured anymore and argues over everything'.[147] With nurses and doctors resident and visiting, there were now different sorts of intrusion into their home; intrusions which were less desired and artistic. When Lewis came to stay, Ricketts was 'cheered': 'I feel less in the hands of paid persons', he said.[148] Soon after, 25-year-old Henning Nyberg moved in as Ricketts' secretary, companion and possibly also sexual partner.[149] Nyberg brought a gramophone with him to Townshend House, and the pair went out to the theatre and cinema at least three times a week. Ricketts was nostalgic ('I now view old Vale work with a sort of affection, and the past seems flooded with sunlight')[150] but also resigned: 'I realize that, viewed as a whole, this trial is small compared to the forty years of perfect companionship I have enjoyed.'[151] In these later years, Townshend House – or as Ricketts now had it 'The Townshend House Hospital' – in London was no less queer,[152] but there were new dimensions and relationship dynamics. This is a reminder that the way the self is experienced, the way lives are lived – queer or otherwise – change markedly over the course of a life, due to the pragmatics of money and health, and the tensions between such contingencies and what is idealised and sought. When Ricketts died of heart failure on 7 October 1931, the house he and Shannon had shaped together was sold to pay for a new home for Shannon in Kew, west London, and for his care there by two nurses and the loyal 'treasures' Mr and Mrs Nicholls. Shannon lived on there without his companion for a further six years until his own death on 18 March 1937.

Returning to Chilham

Shannon and Ricketts clinched the deal on Chilham Castle Keep days after the armistice of 1918. It was a literal and symbolic retreat for them, addressing a sense that Ricketts now had of belonging to a different age. He was horrified by the lack of care for the nation's treasures during the war – a sign to him of a growing disregard for art and beauty, and of the loss of a body of cultured men who could 'properly' appreciate it. 'We are all suffering from Democracy', he wrote. 'I read every morning whatever news there is from Italy, re: Musolini [sic] and his incomparable *fascisti*. Are they the counter revolution? Are they the sign of a world returning to order, duty, sense of real values, a return to constriction and to veneration for firm things?'[153] With the end of the war, there was a sense more broadly of deep loss and a desire to reconnect to the past and tradition.[154] This was the era of suburban 'Tudorbethan' development and the growth of gardening as a hobby.[155] There was a new conservatism that is perhaps reflected in Shannon and Ricketts' narrowing perspective.[156] Their hoped-for 'return' to earlier and supposedly less compromised cultural forms and structures speaks to the way they constituted their homes and shared them with others. They had looked to a cultured queer elite with an appreciation of beauty, set apart and above the rest. At the Keep, the talk was of restoring, of securing something otherwise endangered. This was coupled with a nostalgia and yearning for friendships now over. 'How it would have excited Oscar, the Michaels and Robbie Ross', Ricketts wrote.[157]

Ricketts and Shannon associated themselves with forms of art and culture that were being challenged, modernised, and re-inflected by some of their queer contemporaries. Yet while the pair increasingly looked to the past, there was nevertheless a forward impulse for them too. They were outlived by their protégés and of course by their collection (installed at the Fitzwilliam Museum, and in the 1950s under the care of Carl Winter, who gave evidence to the Wolfenden Committee as an avowed homosexual under the pseudonym 'Mr White'). There were, in addition, muted echoes of Shannon and Ricketts' particular investment in the home to be heard down the queer generations in the 'pretended family' of Ives in the interwar years;[158] in the outlandish snobbery of collector and Mass

Observation survey diarist 'B. Charles' in the 1940s;[159] in the classical and Renaissance prints plastered on the walls of playwright Joe Orton and Kenneth Halliwell's Islington bedsit in the 1960s (see figure 15);[160] in the way that home and domestic eccentricity figured in artists Gilbert and George's self-conscious performance of their coupledom;[161] in film-maker Derek Jarman's creation of an extraordinary garden at Dungeness in Kent at the height of the AIDS crisis in Britain; and in novelist and playwright Neil Bartlett's accumulation of a *'bricolage'* of objects and photographs that he saw fortifying a sense of gay identity in the absence of stronger validation from elsewhere.[162] These various men are very different from Shannon and Ricketts and from each other, but in the threads of connection there are elements of a particular queer investment in the home and a related re-imagining of intimate ties there.

2
Queer Interiors: C.R. Ashbee to Oliver Ford

Shannon and Ricketts' contemporary, near neighbour and sometime collaborator, Charles Ashbee (1863–1942) was making his way at the start of the period covered by this book. Interior designer Oliver Ford (1925–1992) died towards the end, just two years before Derek Jarman, my final case study. Ashbee was motivated in his architectural and design work by his romantic socialism and the homosocial comradeship he associated with it. Ford, interior designer to 'HM the Queen Mother' (as he always respectfully called her in his diary) had an eye to tradition which endeared him to the establishment and allowed him to endure even after his prosecution for 'indecency' with two guardsmen in 1968. These men are connected by their strong ethic of friendship, their professional prominence, and their serious missionary zeal which was aligned with ideas of social or personal and royal service. They each underscored the developing association between queerness and a flair for interior styling, but I argue here that this association could mean very different things personally and politically. The chapter is in three distinct parts – looking at the pre-World War I, the interwar, and then the post World War II periods. I look first at Ashbee and in particular his interior work in the late 1890s. Using the interwar 'amusing' style and the words and work of designer Ronald Fleming (1896–1968), I then survey the growing queer resonance of modern, stylish, individualised interiors and a shift in awareness about queer lives in the period between Ashbee and Ford's respective professional practice. Finally I turn to Ford, Fleming's younger colleague and friend, and the ways he negotiated that association in the post-war years in part through his quiet conservatism and investment in English tradition and culture.

Arts, crafts and C.R. Ashbee

Ashbee had a privileged though not particularly happy upbringing in Bloomsbury before the area gained its literary and artistic cachet.[1] His father, the businessman Henry Spencer Ashbee, is now remembered as the compiler of bibliographies of erotic literature under the scatological pseudonym Pisanus Fraxi. His mother, Elizabeth, who had suffragist sympathies, ultimately left the family home in 1893 to live alongside her son in Chelsea. Perhaps already disillusioned with the much-touted respectable middle class family, at Cambridge University between 1883 and 1886 Ashbee's politics moved towards romantic socialism and, in design terms, towards Arts and Crafts. In these movements he marked a difference from his domestic and familial past and found space (both literal and metaphorical) to conceptualise his relationships and desires. His thinking was shaped in part by William Morris and John Ruskin, more personally and pressingly by Edward Carpenter. His time at Toynbee Hall, a university settlement in the East End of London, in the late 1880s meanwhile gave him a keen awareness of some of the realities of poverty, its causes and what he saw as some of its cures. Cross-class contact and affections were, he believed, 'one of the motors to social reconstruction'.[2] These bonds could be energised by desire and a particular empathy which Carpenter attributed to the 'intermediate sex'.[3] Such 'intermediate types' were, Carpenter felt, especially fitted to social and settlement work, and might find through it some temporary respite from bourgeois domestic culture.[4] Toynbee Hall was a community beyond the family matrix which suggested the potential for different social, work and domestic arrangements. It was from here that Ashbee, aged just 24, set up the Guild of Handicraft to tutor and employ working class men in traditional and domestic craftsmanship. The Guild moved in 1902 to Chipping Campden in rural Gloucestershire, where Charles and his wife Janet Forbes (whom he married in 1898) tried to realise a bucolic alternative crafts community.[5] The comradeship Ashbee sought in both settings was underpinned by affection between men. 'More obviously homogenic' men in the guild were, Ashbee felt, 'more responsive to the friendship and support of other men, a link in the ever growing chain of comradeship'. These were the men 'in whom he put his highest hope'.[6]

Carpenter's influence is absolutely tangible in this. He had himself moved away from his suffocating upper middle class family in Brighton and from associated expectations and what he saw as artifice. He sought out 'the simple life' in Millthorpe in Yorkshire. His stripped back cottage consisted of just a living space and kitchen, with bedrooms above. This spoke to Carpenter and to many of his visitors of his socialism and ideals of authenticity and honesty – not least in love, relationships and desire. Carpenter lived openly at Millthorpe with his lover George Merrill and with guests who stayed for a night or much longer periods. It was this home and open lifestyle that was part of the attraction for Ashbee. He wrote that:

> The feeling of home and of peace and satisfaction that you feel at once in the atmosphere of his cottage, the absence of 'things' and of their attendant fuss and care make an evening with him a scarlet letter in the calendar. The housework is divided among him, a young Sheffield artisan, George Merrill, and a Polish Anarchist (whom Ed. C. [sic] has rescued from a scissor factory and who is dying of consumption under his roof) [...] Everything is managed without a hitch and in perfect quiet and order, because it is begun from the right end of the dual of keynotes of simplicity and temperance.[7]

Ashbee's idealised rendition of Carpenter's home life was a counterpoint to Victorian convention and expectation, and to the kind of home he experienced as a child.[8] Carpenter modelled for Ashbee a different kind of living space which might accommodate relational, sexual and emotional frankness, sexual difference, and an open ethic of care.

This played out in Ashbee's vision and practice not only in the Guild of Handicraft but also in the homes he designed and built for himself and his sister and mother on and adjoining the site of the Old Magpie and Stump pub in Cheyne Walk in Chelsea – just round the corner from Wilde. It was indeed in the midst of Wilde's trials in May 1895 that the homophile art magazine *The Studio* congratulated Ashbee on his achievement there in an extended illustrated piece. In implicit contrast to the lush interiors exposed in court, *The Studio* lauded the sense of space and simplicity and the lack of artifice Ashbee had achieved. The electric lights were not disguised as candles or gaslights, bucking what the journal identified as a contemporary 'endeavour to hide some hideous but essential item'. Like Shannon and Ricketts, Ashbee instead allowed 'the item in question to serve its purpose thoroughly with no added ornamentation whatever'.[9] More broadly Ashbee's designs were shorn of Victorian cornices and mouldings in favour of 'honest' simple lines. His furniture was an 'austere or earthy version of existing furniture types' – a conscious reaction against more ornate and elaborate contemporary styling.[10] The idea of unadorned simplicity running through Ashbee's design resonates with Carpenter's domestic, sexual and social ethos. It also links obliquely to *The Studio's* tacit justification of homoerotic desires through the art and photography it published in the early to mid-1890s.[11] This often

58 *Queer Domesticities*

featured young naked men in natural, simple, neo-Hellenic settings, suggesting desires and desirability untainted by urban sophistication.[12]

Readers of the piece on Ashbee's house might have picked up on some further queer indicators – especially as they were likely to have been reading about the Wilde trial in newspapers alongside. *The Studio* observed the personal expression, individualism and perfect taste of Ashbee's design, and obliquely alluded to aestheticism and to the Wildean 'house beautiful': '[The house] expresses [...] its owner's idea of a beautiful house to suit his personal requirement, and because it satisfies him fully, because

Figure 5 The tiled fireplace designed by Charles Ashbee for the hall at the Magpie and Stump – as illustrated in *The Studio*, May 1895
Kings College Library, Cambridge. CRA/23, p. 13.

his taste is good and his knowledge of practical needs ample, it becomes admirable in itself'. The piece goes on to describe a certain decadence in a fireplace composed of metallic tiles with their 'spots of gorgeous crimsons, purples and greens, inserted apparently by chance among the plain copper squares, giv[ing] a jewelled effect to the whole'.[13] In this way the *Studio* gestures to some of the markers of Bohemian and queer difference I identified in relation to Shannon, Ricketts and Wilde.[14]

The Studio presumes that the readers would be most interested in the 'artistic aspects' of the house at 37 Cheyne Walk. For Ashbee himself there was an important additional dimension which further queered the pitch. At odds with some of the tenets of aestheticism and the broader drive to unique expression in the home, William Morris and John Ruskin inspired Ashbee to resist the exclusive focus on the beauty of domestic objects. These men were not only engaged in the desires of the consumer, but with the experiences of the producer – the worker or craftsman.[15] There was in this an aspiration to democracy of design, production and consumption, and a transparency in those processes. Alan Crawford, Ashbee's biographer, writes that devotees of the Arts and Crafts movement – Ashbee primary among them – 'saw things with a double vision'. 'The object [was] never quite distinct from the maker – and when they started talking about art they could easily end up talking about society'.[16] These things were connected in ways that suggested a chain of responsibility between consumer, designer and craftsman, and between the home, social awareness and justice.[17] Art historian Michael Hatt observes how the copper tiles around the fireplace were initialled by Ashbee as designer and guildsman Arthur Cameron as their creator, drawing the two men together in an artistic pact.[18] This link was eroticised for Ashbee. His sturdy unpretentious designs evoked the craftsmen who had worked on them.[19] They provided an anchoring (masculine) backstory to the (feminised) superficiality associated with interior decoration. Shannon and Ricketts found such an anchor beyond the object in the origin and history of the items in their collections. For Ashbee it was the links to these craftsman that particularly compelled him.

For all their simplicity, Ashbee's interiors incorporated some exquisite art and craftsmanship – insistently not reproductions or mass-produced design. The handles of the entrance doors to the Magpie and Stump house were, for example, formed of naked boys fashioned in bronze.[20] Though naked forms were relatively common artistic design motifs, they also spoke directly of Ashbee's desires and incorporated (homo)eroticism into the domestic fabric.[21] Roger Fry painted a mural around one chimney breast – including a glimpse at a pleasure garden, a reference perhaps

Figure 6 The fireplace mural by Roger Fry for the drawing room at the Magpie and Stump – as illustrated in *The Studio*, May 1895

Kings College Library, Cambridge. CRA/23, p.13.

to the nearby Cremorne Pleasure Gardens which had closed in 1877. *The Studio* was again impressed: 'the painting by Mr Fry is cleverly planned in the same key of colour [as the Peacock blue wallpaper], so that it grows out of the walls as part of them, and does not at first sight detach itself as a painting is apt to do'.[22] There was another pastoral mural by Ashbee's sister around the dining room showing aesthetic peacocks, deer, trees and rabbits. A guardsman friend of Ashbee later added in some nude boys – part of what Hatt describes as a sometimes 'embarrassingly literal' integration of homosexual desire into this interior amidst more 'subtle connections' (like the jointly signed tiles).[23] Murals were an important part of contemporary design – including in William Morris' Red House and James McNeil Whistler's famous Peacock Room – and they became a hallmark of later Bloomsbury group homes, painted often by Fry, Vanessa Bell, and Duncan Grant. Unbounded by frames and hanging conventions, the mural might signal an expansiveness and resistance to containment, reflecting, perhaps, the kind of relational and sexual freedoms espoused and to a degree lived out by these artists and writers.[24]

None of this is to say that Ashbee self-consciously sought out a queer style or to establish one when he worked on these designs. Rather he keyed into contemporary currents in the arts, culture and politics which could express a felt difference and a distance from the kind of home he had experienced in his childhood. He wanted something different because of that past and because he did not feel he could squeeze himself into a conventional home and family in adulthood. Before they married, Ashbee had written to Janet that the one guiding principle of his life had been 'comradeship […] – an intensely close and all absorbing personal attachment, "love" if you prefer the word – for my men and boyfriends'. His proposal to Janet was for a 'comrade wife', and she accepted.[25] The accommodation of their other loves in the relationship was not easy. Janet told Charles that she cried when she learnt that he had fallen for guardsman Chris Robson in 1913 after they had met at Charing Cross and walked back to their respective (and differently queer) Chelsea homes – in Cheyne Walk and the Chelsea Barracks.[26] 'I confess I had a few tears this morning over your description of your lover', she wrote, 'but I never can repay your understanding and generosity of five years ago save "in kind" […] so bless you both'.[27] Charles had struggled with Janet's earlier relationship but also supported her in it. They were markedly open with each other about these other affections, and in an act of deep intimacy kept a joint journal.[28] Janet was actively engaged both with the Guild of Handicraft and in contemporary sexuality debate. Charles was an associate of George Ives and possibly a member of the secretive Order of the Chaeronea which Ives formed in the early 1890s to press for legal change in relation to homosexuality. Janet became one of Ives' close friends – sharing letters whose 'frankness would certainly have made any lesser woman quail'.[29]

The Ashbees, like Shannon and Ricketts, Carpenter, members of the Bloomsbury set, and Ives, placed a particular value on friendship. Such men and women in these queerer circles articulated the potency and political and social importance of friendship bonds more self-consciously and directly than most. For many of them – and in a reflection of developing expectations that marriages should be companionate – friendship

Figure 7 Charles Ashbee with granddaughter, Olivia, 1940
Kings College Library, Cambridge. CRA/22/1.

was also seen to be a key component of a successful marriage.[30] Contrary to convention and expectation, though, sex and additional emotional support and love might be found beyond marriage – as it was for the Ashbees and for those in and around the Bloomsbury set. The monogamous union was not necessarily at the centre of their domestic lives, and while this could be said to be the case for other contemporary couples too, in these circles it was more explicitly avowed and validated.

It was the sense of embarking on something different that led the Ashbees to leave London – first to Chipping Campden in Gloucestershire with the Guild in 1902 (letting their Chelsea house to James McNeil Whistler who had earlier preceded Shannon and Ricketts at the Vale) and then, after the virtual collapse of the Guild enterprise, to Kent in 1906. It was there that they settled and brought up the four daughters they had in rapid succession in the 1910s. Kent – alongside neighbouring East Sussex – had in the interwar period a reputation for Bohemian and queer Londoners seeking rural retreats (aided partly by a growing car culture). Aside from Shannon, Ricketts and the Ashbees, Noel Coward, Radclyffe Hall, the Bells and the Woolfs, Vita Sackville West and Harold Nicholson, and (more briefly) J.R. Ackerley had footholds in these counties.

Homes in Chelsea or Bloomsbury, country retreats in Kent or West Sussex, simplicity and 'honesty' in design, an engagement with murals or Arts and Crafts can hardly be described as necessarily queer. Yet they could be part of a mix for those wealthier men and women who wanted to mark themselves out domestically and who sought out places to live near others who might be in sympathy with them, be that in Chelsea or the counties south of the capital. That the homes of the Ashbees – like the Bloomsbury artists, Carpenter, and earlier Wilde and Shannon and Ricketts – were relatively open to others suggests that these were not self-enclosed or self-indulgent private realms. Instead, as Hatt argues, these experiments in domestic difference were part of a self-conscious and tacitly politicised attempt to re-consider the parameters of relationships, friendship and social interaction.[31] These people had the resources – emotional and monetary – to do this, and had less to lose than others who lacked the money to sustain more than one home or for whom a loss of respectability could be socially and financially crippling.[32] It is important to remember that the vast majority of people did not depart from general expectations and 'norms' of sex and relationships in the first half of the twentieth century.[33] The visibility of those who did and the way they shaped thinking about (homo)sexual, relational and domestic non-conformity has nevertheless been significant. Ashbee, Carpenter and members of the Bloomsbury group suggested that home could be a space to express sexual difference and to articulate and live out an associated politics.

Amusing ourselves

As Ashbee was working with the Guild and at Cheyne Walk, interior decorating was emerging as a new profession. Houses of the wealthy had been furnished and designed before the late nineteenth century of course, but this had tended to be overseen by craftsmen.[34] By the late nineteenth century, however, and with the much stronger association of women with home making, interior design became a professional arena in which wealthier women especially could apply 'their feminine accomplishments to the world of work'.[35] Agnes and Rhoda Garrett, Mary Eliza Haweis, Jane Ellen Panton, and American Elsie de Wolfe were pioneers in the field. They published popular works on home decoration from the 1870s onwards, underscoring and elaborating the idea that the pursuit of good domestic taste was something women were especially good at.[36] The suffragist sympathies of several of these women also suggested a not incidental radical politics.[37] Decorating homes, setting up related businesses, publishing, living out apparently unconventional domestic lives (Agnes lived with sister Rhoda in a close domestic and professional partnership; Elsie de Wolfe had a long relationship with another woman) signalled independent mindedness (and means). These women suggested, alongside Ashbee and Carpenter, that the organisation and decoration of the home could indeed be political.[38] If they were politicised and gained independence through their work, however, their designs for others were person-centred and stripped of an ostensible politics. There was an emphasis on the creation of comfortable, pleasurable individual interiors which were at one with the client and which referred more to fashion than suffrage or socialism. In creating this look and feel, the Garretts, Haweis, Panton and de Wolfe traded on putatively feminine qualities – of fashionability, good taste, and intuitiveness.[39] These qualities seemed to match those of the inverts described around the same time in works of sexology,[40] and some queer men followed these women into interior design, finding a professional and cultural space for themselves there (and rather as others were finding space in the theatre and the arts more broadly).[41] Queer men could accrue some cultural value and perhaps also a sense of self-worth in such work even through the skills required suggested effeminacy and a compromised masculinity. When 'bachelor' interior designer Ronald Fleming died, the *Times* obituary commented on his apparent ability to 'introduce [...] the owner's personality rather than his own into the rooms he created so that they came to believe the good taste displayed was theirs, and hardly realised they had been tactfully guided down the right path'.[42] Such 'tact' and subtlety were by now feminised qualities – and qualities often associated with queer men living on the edge of the law and acceptability. The bachelor label applied to Fleming here and in earlier pieces meanwhile obliquely signalled a certain queerness[43] – an association that had begun to develop from the later nineteenth century and became stronger after the second world war when marriage rates increased and singleness became more exceptional.[44] In coverage of Fleming and post war designers like Oliver Ford, Carl Toms and Alan Tagg the pairing of 'bachelor' and 'interior designer' was neatly suggestive.

Fleming rose to prominence as an interior designer in the 1920s. He had served in the Cold Stream Guards before training in interior design at the New York School in Paris. By the 1930s he had an extensive and elite clientele. He organised an exhibition on 'Modern Designs for Mural Decoration' in 1932 (opened by queer writer and socialite Osbert Sitwell, and including work by Bloomsbury-ites Fry and Grant), and was by this time also giving public lectures on his ethos and technique. In his 'Talk on Decoration' (1931), for example, Fleming described the 'the amusing style', insisting it still had a 'definite place' in 'decoration'. 'It implies', he said, 'something that tickles the fancy – that strikes an original and unexpected note – something that shows a certain courage – so if you can say your room is "amusing" you needn't be ashamed of it'.[45] This style, akin to what was later labelled 'art deco', was marked by eclecticism and the inventive, pleasurable juxtaposition of furniture and art from different periods. The Sitwell brothers – Osbert and Sacheverell – famously brought together baroque, Victorian and modern pieces (including some by Roger Fry) in their home in Chelsea in the early 1920s, for example.[46] Osbert, who met his lifelong male partner in the mid decade, described a 'modern' sensibility being one in which tired convention might be shaken up – in which, for example, 'Victorian objects [were] displayed for qualities other than those of the Victorians themselves'.[47] When *Vogue* featured the brothers' interiors in 1924, there was, art historian Christopher Reed shows, a celebration of this playfulness. The article accompanying the images of the Sitwell's dining and living rooms noted that in their interior vision 'nothing will be in a room for any reason save that it amused the owner the day he put it there. It is his character, not his possessions, that give the room quality. Hence if his character be sufficiently amusing his room will also be loveable'.[48] There is in this the clear potential to showcase identity and a link back to *The Studio's* appreciation of Ashbee's character via his interiors (though without the politicised reach that Ashbee so valued). Home in these circles was increasingly a place to be yourself rather than to demonstrate conformity or respectability. Each of these factors in middle and upper class home-making had been in play before, but the balance shifted in the interwar period. For those who could afford it, individualism, comfort, pleasure and ease in the home were now to the fore in an economy which was moving from being producer to consumer led.[49]

The 'amusing' emphasis on surface, performance, pleasure and eclecticism was, meanwhile, rather camp – a matter of style which yet suggested (to use John Babuscio) that 'life itself is role and theater, appearance and personification'.[50] Wit and unexpected conjunctions could speak of a distance from projected norms and expectations as surely as Ashbee's unified design aesthetic or a unique handcrafted piece of furniture.[51] More obliquely, the amusing style suggested that there was no natural or obvious way to be. Even convention was a kind of performance and the home was shown to be a stage for striking a pose or for representing the kind of individual psychic complexity psychoanalysis and surrealism were revealing to *avant garde* and Bohemian circles in the 1920s and 1930s.

In his lectures Fleming underscored the importance of such individual expression in the home – a place which was to him 'as much of ourselves as the clothes we wear'.[52] He stressed 'personal imagination'

Figure 8 Ronald Fleming at home, as featured in *The Queen* magazine in Oct.1958. Fleming was a proponent of the interwar 'amusing style' in which art and furnishings of different styles and periods were 'pleasurably' juxtaposed to create 'a personal setting'
Courtesy of Harper's Bazaar (UK) and V&A Images/Victoria and Albert Museum.

in interior styling as 'a tonic' to the inhabitant and their friends, and pitched his styling against impersonal and depersonalizing modernism.[53] Like those early female interior designers, Fleming was an enthusiast for the lightness of eighteenth century design, yet cautioned:

> respect Queen Anne certainly, but not being married to her is there any logical reason to go on living with her exclusively? Is it snobbery and affectation, or laziness and lack of imagination? Can't we be ourselves in 1932? If we know what we are – and some of us think we know – but the architects are afraid of us it seems [*sic*].[54]

Fleming's rhetoric throughout is telling. The interior for him was about knowing and being oneself, about being original and unexpected, and about not being 'ashamed' of the self-disclosure these things might imply. He imagines Queen Anne style in terms of a marriage or rather (preferably) an open association which might accommodate other loves and desires. Fleming describes 'courageous interiors' which dared to be different in their fusion of tastes. His language is redolent of the qualities needed by many queer men who 'knew' themselves and yet who were unacknowledged or marginalized socially. In his swipe at 'the architects', meanwhile, Fleming was pitching in to what has been dubbed 'the curtain wars' between architects engaged in (masculinized) hard surfaces and the substance of buildings on the one hand and, on the other, interior designers who looked to (feminised and queered) soft furnishings and to the presentation of rooms.[55] Fleming was perhaps alluding particularly to the designs and design theory of Le Corbusier and Adolf Loos which sought to iron out individualism and idiosyncrasy in favour of clean lines and utilitarianism.[56] Theirs was an attempt to democratise architecture and also represented a particular and particularly stark aesthetic without that personal pleasurable twist.

Modernism in this latter incarnation left little room for the kind of stylistic self-expression valued by queerer contemporaries – by some in the Bloomsbury set, by the Sitwells, or indeed by Fleming. There were yet some common values between these different attempts to forge something new in the interwar period. There was a shared emphasis on space, air and light and on a trimming back of fussy lines in modernist and Fleming's more personalized and 'amusing' interior design. In his 1932 lecture Fleming advocated 'simplicity in style'. 'We can stimulate you to a realization of the present and its possibilities', he said. 'You need not feel arty and crafty but practical and efficient – as in your car or aeroplane – and at the same time satisfy your artistic inclinations'.[57] There could be, he suggested, a neat fusion of stripped back modernism and the individualized style (and again for those with money: note the unthinking presumption of car – if not plane – ownership). The modern world with its putatively democratic and liberal values could thus be brought together with the expression of individual inclinations, eclectic pleasures, and domestic difference. No surprise that the retrospectively named 'art deco' style of the 1920s and 1930s – which braces both design pulses – came to be seen by some as a particular queer look in its 1970s revival.[58]

More broadly, modernist domestic design and architecture could accommodate difference as well as erasing it. The Isokon flats in

Hampstead (1934) downplayed the scope for individual self-expression for sure, but in catering for fold-away lives in the design of the individual flats and the incorporation of a restaurant in the block they were also geared towards single men and women or childless couples. The architects Wells Coates validated different ways of living, different kinds of relationships, and the single state. They suggested that homes could be designed specifically for such lives. In a similar vein Molly and Jack Pritchard's 1933 design for actors Charles Laughton and Elsa Lanchester in Gordon Square in Bloomsbury created a flat that was 'open, liveable and free from the oppressive weight of the past' (the latter perhaps key).[59] The couple, associated with both Bloomsbury and Hollywood, led busy transatlantic lives, had no children, and a marriage which accommodated Charles's affairs with other men.[60] Their flat – complete with the latest mod cons – facilitated and reflected their 'modern' departure from the norm and their deliberate recalibration of what marriage might be. While the London County Council and suburban developers were building housing for couples with children, some self consciously modern architects were thus catering specifically to demand for different kinds of living space in apartment blocks across central west London. These soon had a reputation for their cosmopolitan, single, and in some places queer residents.[61] Fleming had an apartment in one such block in Spencer Place in fashionable St James (see figure 8).

The queer associations of modern flats and of stylish, amusing interiors were becoming clearer by the 1930s. They were showcased, for example, on the West End stage in Mordant Sharpe's *A Green Bay Tree* (1933). The play centred on middle-aged aesthete Dulcimer's tussle for the affections of his adopted son, Julian, who has been drawn away by his fiancée and the reappearance of his biological father. Critics were quick to spot the 'repulsive' and 'abnormal' implications and – as the *Weekend Review* had it – 'the Anglo-Hellenic' 'domesticity' of the protagonist's 'way of life'.[62] Sharpe established this at the outset with directions for the set – the interior of Dulcimer's Mayfair home:

> The atmosphere of the room is one of luxury and fastidiousness. The owner is an artist in the sense that everything in the room has been chosen for its intrinsic value and given its absolutely right position in the general scheme of decoration. He never puts up anything because of its associations, nor leaves anything about because the room is well used. To the outsider the room is artificial, but it

excites curiosity about its owner. To him, it is a constant source of pleasure: it reflects his personality, his sensitiveness, and a delicate appreciation of beauty [...] Mr Dulcimer enters. He is a man of about 45, immaculately turned out [...] He speaks exquisitely [...] he has an alert vibrating personality. A man who could fascinate, repel, alarm.[63]

Dulcimer's interior is certainly amusing and pleasurable to him and keys into that wider design pulse endorsed by Fleming and the Sitwells. It also harks back to a Wildean aesthetic of art and beauty for their own sake. If the late nineteenth century aesthetes were much parodied, however, they nevertheless had a philosophical seriousness in their concern with seeing the world differently and in countering a restrictive morality. Dulcimer's style, Sharpe suggested, was more narrowly about himself and his own pretentions. When Leo (the significantly masculine abbreviation for Leonora, Julian's fiancée) asks if he had ever considered design as a profession, Dulcimer, taking up his embroidery, replies: 'I couldn't endure planning rooms for other people. My taste would have to be theirs'.[64] Dulcimer is domesticated in his keen eye for style, but is also depicted as anti-domestic in his selfish conduct there. When he hosts a dinner party for Julian and Leo he sets the room up as a restaurant as a 'joke'. He sits alone at a table separated from his guests. The dinner party was an established domestic ritual but Dulcimer renders it anti-social, a (cruel) joke rather than a convivial domestic meeting. This is not courageous, liberating self-expression but an indictment of queer narcissism.

Dulcimer's fashionable flat is directly contrasted with that of Mr Owen, Julian's biological father. Act two is set in Owen's sitting room in Camden Town:

A small neat, simply furnished room. [...] It is comfortable and contains good solid furniture, but the wallpaper is crude and the pictures and ornaments are chosen without taste. MR OWEN is proud of it. JULIAN detests it. [...] It is suggested that there might be photographs of MR OWEN's family, and perhaps one of JULIAN as a child, on the mantlepiece and elsewhere.[65]

Mr Owen's lack of taste but 'good solid furniture' shows he is 'normal'. The interior speaks of an investment in family, in a connection to the past, and in the comforts of home rather than the pretensions of pleasure and fashion. He lacks that somewhat queered skill of discerning good from bad taste.[66] The home is in Camden rather than in wealthy, fashionable Mayfair, and suggests a firm base for him to re-engage with his son following his journey from alcoholism to religious faith. It shows domestic pragmatism and redemption and links to wider and supposedly shared (family) values coalescing across classes in this period.[67] If the 'amusing style' had been *avant garde* and Bohemian in the 1920s, by the 1930s it seemed queer, dissipated and decadent in the context of economic depression and a growing re-emphasis on home as epitomized by the proliferating suburban semi.[68] This was perhaps why Fleming was on the defensive in his lectures in this decade.

After World War II suspicion of stylish modern interiors seems to have spread. Reaction to home exhibitions in London in 1946 and 1952 examined by cultural historian Richard Hornsey shows how sensitive observers of all classes could be to such designs. A contemporary-styled living room was judged by members of the public to be 'out to impress'. It was 'not sincere' and must belong to 'a rather immoral type of person'. Another felt the same room was 'flippant' and didn't provide 'the right background for children'.[69] A brightly decorated bedsit, meanwhile, was unmasculine: 'the colour scheme is completely wrong for a man to wake up and see'.[70] Morality and gender had of course long been inscribed in the decoration of the home. These post-war responses nevertheless betray growing and more generalised knowledge and concern about gender and sexual non-conformity, and the ways in which these things might become evident in interior design. Such signs were being used in reformist film and literature as a way of differentiating the acceptable from the unacceptable queer. In Mary Renault's *The Charioteer* (1953), for example, the flamboyant and self consciously modern interiors of the discreditable queer (Bunny) are contrasted with the restraint of the model, respectable and subdued homosexual (Ralph). Rodney Garland's *The Heart in Exile* (1953), characterises and legitimises psychologist Dr Anthony Page's dead lover, Julian, through his domestic interior which 'gave a masculine impression in negative good taste, extremely English and genteel'.[71] Barrister Melville Farr in the landmark Basil Dearden film *Victim* (1961) displays a similarly 'traditional' and uncontroversial taste in the home he shares with his wife on the Chelsea Embankment – near to where Oscar and Constance Wilde and the Ashbees had lived just over half a century earlier. Two sympathetic film portrayals of Wilde were released in 1960 (*Oscar Wilde* and *The Trials of Oscar Wilde*), and *Victim* can be read as a resonant retelling of how the Wilde saga might have turned out differently if only the playwright could, like Farr, have kept his house in order and his desires in check.

Oliver Ford

The interior designer Oliver Ford (1925–1992) rose to prominence in these post World War II years and this restrained design became his hallmark. With a studio in Soho for a period, Ford was ostensibly at the heart of London's nominally democratising youth and counter cultures.[72] In his life, his work, and his aesthetic he yet alluded to that more conservative, nascently respectable queerness which was at odds with that of Joe Orton and Derek Jarman who were making their homes as younger queer men in this same period and who I come to in later

Figure 9 Oliver Ford at Bewley Court with part of his collection in the background, c.1980

Oliver Ford Will Trust and V&A Images/Victoria and Albert Museum.

chapters.[73] His passion for collecting, and (literal) investment in English country homes and gardens came as a tacit repudiation of the unapologetic queerness of these others. Such caution allowed Ford to make a cultural mark and to feel a sense of belonging in a changing but still censorious social and legal climate.

Ford served in the Royal Air Force during the war. As for Fleming before him and many queer men of their respective generations, the forces, active service and barrack life was a feature of his early adulthood. After the war, Ford's father wanted him to follow him into the leather retail business he had built up in the west country but he supported his son's decision to train instead in design and the decorative arts in Bournemouth. 'It's rather nice', Ford told the *Times*, 'to have had parents who didn't reproach me for not going into the family business and wanted me to be happy in what I was doing'.[74] This was not only good luck but part of developing cultural tendency to value personal happiness and self-realisation over family duty – and indeed for the family to encourage such personal fulfilment in its (especially younger) members. Ford became director in charge of decoration and display at Harvey Nicholls and then moved to the French decorators Jansen where he began to accumulate a royal client base including the Duke and Duchess of Windsor (the former King Edward VII and his wife Wallis Simpson). He formed his own company in Nassau in the Bahamas in 1959, returning to London in 1962 as a partner in Lenygon and Morant – another firm of decorators. He worked on the redesign of the Dorchester Hotel in the 1970s and became decorator to the Queen Mother in 1974 (how is not clear, though his elite contacts and clients must have helped). Though he worked early on in theatre design and on marquee and party decoration, his avowed preference was for such private clients.

Ford's archive at the Victoria and Albert Museum includes appointment diaries, press cuttings, photos and some personal correspondence – giving more of a sense of his professional than his private life. There are glimpses of his friendship network – an affectionately signed photo 'after 30 years, Oliver, love Kenneth [Williams]';[75] a note to 'a dear, generous old friend' from poet John Betjeman (who shared Ford's 'passion to preserve' most famously in his campaign to save St Pancras Station);[76] lunch dates with Ronald Fleming (whom we have already met) and links to other bachelor interior designers – including Carl Toms (who worked on Princess Margaret's homes) and Alan Tagg.[77] Tory politician John Profumo and Lord Lucan were in his address book, and there are photos of the Duke of Windsor and the Queen Mother visiting his country homes.[78] He attended a dinner for Mrs Thatcher at the

Garrick Club in 1978 alongside some other notable gay men – Kenneth Williams again and actor Sir John Gielgud.[79] Also in the collection are a couple of more intimate letters. One is from a friend asking for help with accommodation and who signs off despairingly: 'Oh for peace and quiet. I wish to hell I wasn't gay'. Letters from his mother send 'love' to 'Osbert' and money for his Christmas present. It is unclear, but the frequency with which this man appears in the diaries suggests that it was a particularly close relationship.[80]

Some of these names may of course have been clients rather than friends. The archive is nevertheless suggestive of a life lived amidst a rich, privileged and partially queer set, and as part (unsurprisingly) of a network of interior designers – of his own and the previous generation. His own addresses underscore this. He had a London apartment in South Audley Street in Mayfair and three country homes: from 1966 at Sparksholt Manor in the Vale of the White Horse in Berkshire ('among the best examples of a Queen Anne manor House'),[81] from 1967 at the now grade I listed fourteenth century Bewley Court at Laycock in Wiltshire, and soon after at Courtenay Lodge in Sutton Courtenay, Oxfordshire (and which appeared in *Ideal Home* in June 1972). The Mayfair apartment linked him to that tradition of modern moneyed bachelor living, while his country homes, his exquisite gardens, his peacocks, and his antiques allowed him to style himself as an English country gent, firmly embedded in an associated conservative if also another tacitly queer tradition.[82] Ford's homes featured on his annual Christmas cards and were testament to taste, distinction, and his professional status. They showed that he had earned good money and that he was invested in English history and tradition. His Royal connections further valorised his standing – as did the profiles in various newspapers and his appearance on Desert Island Discs on BBC Radio 4 in 1977. The luxury item he said he would take to his island was an orchid – an echo of the *fin de siècle* decadence and of Shannon and Ricketts's taste in floristry.

Ford's work and the way he shaped his own homes resonated with some of the presumptions about queer style, tendencies and aptitudes from earlier in the century. Like Fleming before him, he fused eighteenth century with modern styling. Also like Fleming, he preferred his private clients over commercial ones – enjoying those empathetic intimate personal relationships that were seen to be 'typically' queer by some. 'I am a father confessor, a universal aunt, a protector and a buffer', he told the *International Herald Tribune* in 1981.[83] Literary critic Katherine Snyder observes that the interior designer's 'intimacy with his female patrons coupled with his first hand understanding of the crucial role interiors play in human self fashioning – permits him to be trusted, to become, in a sense "just one of the girls"'.[84] A *Times* portrait of Ford commented on his sharp wit, his 'cheerful' admission to 'living on his nerves' (he 'savagely grind[s] out one of his innumerable cigarettes' during the interview) and his perfectionism.[85] He 'preferred to call [him]self an interior architect, not an interior decorator', he was quoted as saying in *The Evening News and Star*, aligning himself to a more respected and 'masculine' profession.[86] The *International Herald Tribune* was having none of it, though, dubbing him more effetely a 'cushion of elegance'.[87]

Ford's particular queerness may have fitted with an ongoing tradition of tacit knowledge and discreet acceptance. It yet also caused him considerable angst and heartache. His homosexuality was hinted at in these various characterisations, and underscored by his much mentioned bachelor status, his work and home life, and maybe even by his holidays in Tangiers (which Orton notoriously visited at around the same time). It was clinched for a wider public, though, in a scandal that hit the headlines on his arrest on gross indecency charges in September 1967 and his trial the following May. Ford's appointment diary logs legal conferences for 21 February and 3 May of that year, and for Monday 6 May he crossed out all appointments and wrote 'ON TRIAL'.[88] In his desk diary for the same date is written in red capitals 'NO APPTs AFTER AND INCLUDING TODAY UNTIL FURTHER NOTICE'.[89] There is no other mention of what happened in his archive or amongst the press clippings in the scrapbook he kept, but this date was that of his trial at the Old Bailey alongside two soldiers for procuring men for acts of gross indecency. The strike through in his diary suggests his anticipation of a custodial sentence though he was ultimately instead fined £700. His two 'accomplices' – troopers Barry Brook and Jeffrey Sheffield – were given a two-year conditional discharge. The wide coverage – in newspapers ranging from the *Liverpool Echo* to the *Daily Express* – described how Ford had met these men in Tattersalls pub near the Knightsbridge Barracks and had invited them to his country homes. Between February and September 1967 they had procured other guardsmen for Ford, and acts of gross indecency had been committed with them in private at Bewley Court and Courtenay Lodge. There was, the court had heard, no corruption; the acts committed were consensual.

The case prompted an investigation at Knightsbridge Barracks. This found that a third of the troopers in the guards – between 30 and 40 men – had been involved in 'such practices'; Brook had 'heard through general talk [at the barracks] that if you needed to earn a few bob you went to Tattersalls to meet "queers"'.[90] Most, the *Blackpool Evening*

Gazette noted, 'were not homosexual' but did it for the money.[91] The judge felt that a more 'contemptible way for any young man to earn his money is hard to imagine'[92] – though the revelations can hardly have been news to him: guardsmen rent had been a recurrent feature of trials for male-male sex in London across the century and before.[93] When Ford was arrested in October, he had said he 'didn't intend to tell any lies about this matter'. It emerged in court that he had been consulting a doctor to try to deal with his 'bisexual feeling' and had been given drugs for this, and also for depression and asthma which, the doctor testified, 'may have increased his libido'.[94] He was 'ashamed and distressed' by what he had done, and 'honestly believed he was not offending against the law'.[95] Throughout the newspaper coverage the link was made to interior design. The *Blackpool Evening Gazette* proclaimed 'Interior Designer Fined £700/Invited Guardsmen to Country Homes';[96] the *Liverpool Echo* noted he was a 'single man' and a decorator 'of a very high category'.[97] The *Daily Express* mentioned the royal link and alluded to his work at the Royal Lodge, Windsor; he had, it noted, 'many titled' clients.[98]

The case underscored a number of already circulating presumptions about homosexuality. It replayed ideas about a class dynamic of middle and upper class queers having sex with 'normal' working-class men, and stressed the difference between their country and barrack homes respectively. It suggested something of the queer culture of rent that operated in the latter. If the barracks and boarding houses were not designed with a queer flourish, they were still rather queer residences in terms of the sexual cultures they seemed to foster. The coverage stressed too the cross-over between such spaces and the more carefully decorated, self-consciously cultured homes of men like Ford. The risks associated with male-male sex were especially high in cases like this where there was a trail leading through different sites and involving cross-class and monetary exchange. That Ford and his two 'procurers' could still be prosecuted pointed to the limits of the 1967 Sexual Offences Act which only legalised sex between two men in private.

Finally, the case tells us something about Ford. Though it may have been overstated in court in the hope of some clemency, he seems to have struggled with his desires and suffered depression quite possibly because of them. This perhaps gives us some sense of the importance of the affirmation Ford found elsewhere – professionally, socially and from family and friends. This endured. A letter from his mother after the trial was reassuring. 'How lucky we are to have two such good children', she wrote. 'We all have [faith in you] and thank god you spoke the truth right along my dearest'.[99] Whether she is referring to the court case directly is unclear, but what is apparent is the accommodation of his friendships and affections by his parents and also by his wider circle of friends and clients. The royal warrant from the Queen Mother was awarded after the trial – in 1976 – and the multiple invitations to events at Buckingham Palace and Clarence House (the official residence of the Queen Mother) did not suddenly dry up; they continued into the 1980s. Though the classic portrait of the post-war period was of the lonely sad homosexual, many queer men did not 'stand apart'.[100] Ford was integrated within and cushioned by a wider heterosocial network and by his professional and aesthetic acumen. Ford's obituary in the *Independent* made no mention of his sexuality and focussed on his professional expertise, taste and interior design philosophy. 'His rooms were noted for being elegant but understated, very much in eighteenth century country house taste'.[101] *The Independent*'s portrayal is of a self-effacing man in the way he sought to 'enhance' the personality of the owner in his designs, rather than to 'impose his own' (and like Fleming in this respect).[102] This was perhaps the kind of homosexual who could be culturally acceptable and even valuable: conformist, understated, and willing to deploy apparently inimitable interior design skills in the service of others.

* * *

Both Ashbee and Ford had guardsmen lovers; both were perhaps turned on by class and occupational difference. But whilst Ashbee romantically imagined seeds of social transformation in such contact, Ford valued the *status quo*. His designs spoke of commitment to tradition and the security it might provide. With an eye to his legacy perhaps but also reflecting a clear generosity of spirit, Ford's will established The Oliver Ford Foundation partially for the 'advancement of knowledge of the history and techniques of interior decoration'.[103] The gesture was in a similar spirit to Shannon and Ricketts's bequest to the Fitzwilliam Museum. They each sought to encourage an appreciation of culture and taste in future generations. Ashbee in another vein linked his architecture and design to a sense of social change and responsibility. He fostered a more radical vision in his work, drawing in rather than effacing the craftsmen he employed and suggesting the scope for different social formations and relationships in the way he reworked domestic spaces. Fleming and the Sitwells in their advocacy of the 'amusing style' conjured interwar something more camp and more centred on the domestic consumer and his 'personality'. These different pulses in design relate to different queer identifications associated with radicalism, conservatism, an apolitical playfulness, and (as conjured by Mordant Sharpe in his play) pretention and selfishness. Together they clearly did not amount to a coherent queer design aesthetic. There was no singular idea of what queerness might be in the first half of the twentieth century, how it might appear in the home, or how it might be configured in the way you lived there. Just in this chapter we have encountered men living alone, with wives, with other men, in stylish Mayfair apartments, in barracks, in a university settlement, in a rural community, in country homes, and between country and city. Charles Ashbee, Charles Shannon, and Roger Fry each had intense emotional relationships with men but were also involved romantically and sexually with women. Their respective aesthetic investments in the home were not markers of a singular direction of desire and emotional attachment but on the contrary reflected its variability and multiplicity. For them and others I have discussed – Ricketts, Wilde, the Sitwells, Fleming and Ford – it could yet also suggest individuality, difference, and a loose queer network. Tracking these lives and those associated with them suggests the significance for some of an aesthetic ethos and of an artistic or design training like that undertaken by Shannon, Ricketts, and Ford, and offered by Ashbee to men in his guild. If there was a social and cultural conformity in their investment in the look, feel and design of the home and what it contained, these men also distinguished themselves by being leaders and taste shapers in these respects. Given the kind of relationship to home men were supposed to have, there was something queer in this enterprise, engagement and expertise. By the time Ford was working in the post World War II period, this queer association had become culturally entrenched.

Epilogue

In 2004 Darren Brady, founder of gay lettings agency Outlet, told the *Independent* newspaper that gay men 'are more imaginative and more aesthetically minded with our homes – we also tend to be cleaner. Just look at gay men's obsession with grooming, which applies to our homes as well as our bodies'.[1] Brady signals a particularity in gay men here whilst also reflecting a broader cultural 'fetishisation of the home, its possessions and its decoration'.[2] The rise in individualism and disposable income had by this time contributed to an extension of what was already an intensely home-focussed culture.[3] Many more people had their own homes or their own space within a shared home,[4] and they 'gained the space, comfort and stimulation indoors that they had previously encountered only by going out'.[5] This had knock-on effects for the conduct of sex lives and relationships – and in ways which accelerated 'the privatisation of gay life'.[6] The increase in personal space meant something too for the way homes were styled and organised – more often now according to one person's preferences. Gay men gained a particular profile in this respect and gave further visibility to the tendency and identification I explored in the preceding chapters.[7] In 1982 *The Economist* noted the greater disposable income of gay couples and cited a *Gay News* survey which had found that gays were more likely to buy household consumer goods than the average.[8] Mortgage companies were also by this time lending to gay couples on the same basis as straight couples – a situation which soon changed in the face of the AIDS epidemic when sexual identity and an HIV test were often determinants in gaining life insurance and associated mortgages.[9] As house prices increased, being ahead in terms of income and mortgage capacity could make buying in London more of an option, especially as there was apparently a greater readiness among gay men to buy in down-at-heel areas and where the standard of local schools was usually not at issue.[10] A 1982 *Sunday Times* piece on Islington's gentrification identified gay men as key. 'It was really the queers that opened Islington', said one resident. 'They were very much into interior décor and had the imagination and physical strength to do the work'.[11] Such gentrification was aligned with striking out rather than fitting in. Early gentrifiers, London historian Jerry White notes, 'rejected consumerism and the mass market of suburb or luxury flat or New Town house. Their energies went into revising, with individual flair, the beauty of neglected old buildings'.[12] This included a developing London trend for the kind of loft style living that had housed countercultural and artistic New York in the 1970s (most famously Robert Mapplethorpe and Andy Warhol)[13] and which subsequently became big business both sides of the Atlantic.[14] Gay men seemed to be part of a 'creative class' key to 'urban regeneration'.[15]

If some gay men were observed doing their own refurbishing and gentrifying in the later twentieth century – at least in the metropolis – others were moving into new and already modernised apartments in central London areas like Hoxton and Shoreditch. These were the successors of 'modern' apartment blocks built from the late nineteenth century around South Kensington, St James and Mayfair, and providing different kinds of living space to the concurrent family-oriented terraces and semis.[16] If in the 1950s queer residents from these blocks had been exposed in scandalous court cases,[17] by the 1990s gay men were being actively courted as buyers. In 1997 *The Sunday Times* was proclaiming 'a gay house boom' with 'scores of housing developments specially adapted for homosexual residents' including Bow Quarter in east London, Auckland Heights in Crystal Palace and the Ziggurat building in Clerkenwell. This latter development saw 'gay men and couples queuing up at 4 am on the day the first apartments were released'.[18] One estate agent reported that gays 'love good quality architecture' and 'are very particular': 'they do not want lots of bedrooms because they do not have children. Loft conversions and spacious apartments are ideal for our buyers. They like them even more if there are other gays around because they feel safer'.[19] Gay men seemed to be at the forefront of new and fashionable residential cultures in the city.[20] By this time – and following the introduction of anti-retroviral drugs for people with AIDS – mortgage lenders had again changed their policies on lending to gay men because they were apparently less likely to default.[21] Gay friendly letting and estate agents like Outlet (in Soho) and Housemartins (in Surrey Quays) meanwhile dealt directly with what they saw as the particular needs and requirements of gay men buying and letting in the capital.[22]

If one strand of commentary in this period was representing gay men as in need of social housing,[23] others pushed the image of wealthy, metropolitan and usually white gay men demonstrating an inimitable and particular taste in homes and home styling. The continuities between gay men, their homes, their bodies and their desires in Darren Brady's comment cited at the start of this epilogue carries with it a risible sneer at straight men. His presumptions were and are nevertheless trenchant, and have been repeatedly underscored on television in the later 1990s and 2000s. In *Trading Up* (2003), *Colin and Justin's Home Show* (2008), and *60 Minute Make Over* (2010), for example, Justin Ryan and Colin McAllister showed their own queer design savvy and worked to transform the homes of supposedly less stylish straights in ways which elevated ('we know better than you'), trivialised ('we care about how things look and not much else'), and further feminised and domesticated gay men (as well as queering home a little too).[24] Partially through such TV, gay men became typecast as 'aesthetic service providers'.[25] Their new prominence in this respect rendered them more acceptable to some as they became domestic consumers *par excellence*.[26] By the late twentieth century the association was so culturally embedded that it was Colin and Justin's gayness as much as anything else that qualified them to advise on interiors. For Ford and the preceding generation it was a self-consciously acquired and presented cultured taste which equipped them – and which in turn tacitly suggested they were queer.

Representations of domestically stylish gay men tend to screen out housemates (male and/or female), those gay men who continue to live with family, those who have children, those in economic hardship and who might not have the resources to style, redecorate or ornament their homes, and also those without homes.[27] If popular imagery has represented gay men in swanky central London apartments and renovated Islington terraces, this is far from the reality for most queer men – just as the homes of Fleming and Ford in the 1950s were far from typical of that decade.[28] This section has shown nevertheless that collecting, design, and a distinctive aesthetic sense coalesced for some men as a way of articulating their queerness. This fed broader conceptions of what it meant to be queer, homosexual or gay. It is this multifaceted history that writer and director Neil Bartlett self-consciously keys into in the way he describes himself and his home in Brighton.

Neil Bartlett and the queer 'comfort of things'

Bartlett's novels,[29] plays and performance deal with almost exactly the time span covered by this part of the book, from a piece on Simeon Solomon ('A Vision of Love Revealed in Sleep' [1987]) to a puppetry work exploring the domestic lives of a contemporary aging couple facing illness and imminent death (*Or You Could Kiss Me* [2010]). In each work Bartlett conjures home as a place which can signal and anchor a sense of queer selfhood and difference – and this is evident too in his own domestic life. 'I've always been a very material person, I've always loved things', Bartlett said in interview.[30] This is something he associates with a strand of queer culture but also with his childhood and upbringing. He was born in 1958 and brought up in Chichester in West Sussex, about 25 miles to the west of Brighton where Bartlett and his partner now live (though they spend a lot of time in London, their former home, too: 'we've never turned our backs on it', he says). 'My

Figure 10 Neil Bartlett performing, c.2000
© Dom Agius.

mother was a commercial artist, and my grandfather was a commercial artist so I grew up looking at beautiful things'. This appreciation first gained a queer impress partly through an early, older lover and the house he was invited to visit in London as a 16-year-old. Home, he then realised, could be accommodating of queer life, and could shape, frame and give meaning to it:

> He has one or two proper paintings, lovely paintings from antique shops which he told me all about, and he has a kitchen, and he used to give dinner parties for other gay men [...] It was both incredibly familiar – you know, this is a proper house with a kitchen and a bathroom and a bedroom and stuff. [...] Yet it was also completely [...] unlike what I had experienced before.

The mixed tenses in Bartlett's description suggests the enduring significance of this particular queer home. It had something 'uncanny' (or to use Bartlett 'unlike') about it as the familiar was a made a little strange or queer.[31] That feeling suggested to Bartlett as a gay teenager that there was space and possibility for him. The affair and this home taught him that 'if someone else can do it I can do it too'. 'When I was young I sometimes think one of the primary reasons I was so promiscuous was that fantastic thing of getting to see the inside of other people's houses, because I never imagined it was going to happen to me [...] I had the straight narrative in my head'.

Bartlett shapes his queer fictional creations in part through their different homes and the things in them, and he has done the same for himself with his partner. This has made his 'ordinary house, for a duplicate family, like those stretching out up the hill' more than a little queer. What might have been a child's bedroom is their dressing-up room; the living room, says Bartlett, is enough to 'turn anyone gay'. After visiting their home, a friend's teenage daughter described the pair as wizards – domestic alchemists conjuring home in ways which spoke of the texture of their queer lives. 'The family home is a machine for producing children. That's the motor of that architecture, and for most gay lives that's not the case, and indeed for most gay lives there's almost an active refusal of that style, and that architecture and that sense of domesticity'. Instead, he explains:

> An important part of our life together has been the treasures that we've accumulated over the years [...]. It was going 'we want somewhere where we can create something beautiful [...] and create a

garden', and so we didn't want to be two bachelors sharing, we didn't want to go: 'actually we don't care about the kitchen because we'll be in the restaurant every night'. We actually really wanted somewhere we could make a home. So that was a very conscious choice to explore values which weren't the values or the lives [...] that we were leading when we met.

Bartlett is careful not to reify home as 'the true destination' and does not believe 'for an instant [that] everyone should settle down and get married, and have a nice house with a garden'. He nevertheless sees other spaces functioning differently. If gay bars have been described as places where 'queers readily feel at home',[32] Bartlett found something else in them:

I went out six or seven nights a week, and it was a great source of pleasure, and you met fantastic people, but the actual bar thing, you always go back to where you started, is my feeling. [...] The room itself doesn't move you to a different place. [...] The way in which those bars really changed my life is that that was where I met men who I went home with, and engaged to a greater or lesser degree with their lives. You get an incredible glimpse of someone's life.

This, he says was 'an education'.

The couple have accumulated art and things associated with several of the men and movements discussed in this section – Solomon, Philpot, Wilde, the Arts and Crafts movement, members of the Bloomsbury set. There is a self-conscious attention to queer genealogy in this: this is the couple's cultural inheritance. It is also, Bartlett says, a 'tradition of drag' 'of radical second-hand taste [...] the re-discoveries of stuff from the past which nobody else wanted, which gay men in particular have discovered and loved, and cherished'. 'I think it's very easily identifiable why [queer men] were collectors, because we had to cherish what we had, and where we didn't have anything we had to make up things to cherish. [So...] what I'm interested in is that kind of décor which creates something out of scraps'. Bartlett in this way assembles a noticeable queer life through items from the past and by investing 'trash' with value.

In *Who Was That Man?* (1988) Bartlett showed how Oscar Wilde and other late nineteenth century queer men forged cultural space for themselves by piecing together in new resonant formations existing places, objects and styles. This is what Bartlett describes as 'bricolage'[33] – a process in which prevailing ideas and ideologies were not so much opposed as reworked and repositioned so that queer men like Wilde could (often with an air of camp) make sense of themselves for themselves and for others in a culture which had become newly if unevenly preoccupied with them. We have seen this process at work in the lives and home-making of the Sitwells and Flemming, and we'll see it again in Joe Orton and Kenneth Halliwell's bedsit in the 1960s and in the way Derek Jarman made his home and garden at Dungeness.[34] Gathering things together for the house is of course common enough but it has been an especially self-conscious process for men like Bartlett and these others who had and have a sense of being culturally at odds.[35]

This kind of eclecticism is not to Bartlett about authenticity but about individuality. We have seen in this part of the book how some designers accumulated items and references to the past and then twisted them with the modern. This mix of old and new is 'not at all incompatible, I mean […] it's a very gay thing to go to a house which is full of lovely old stuff, but the music will be absolutely the latest thing'. 'This impulse to modernity is there' and suggests the scope to evade censorious or stifling histories and traditions. Histories which might more comfortably couch queer difference are meanwhile retained as we saw with Wilde, Shannon and Ricketts. In this way a sense of queer culture and things invested with queer meaning are passed down from friend to friend. A photograph once owned by Wilde, for example, now belongs to Bartlett, having passed from Wilde to his friend Robbie Ross to artist Duncan Grant to activist and writer Simon Watney and then on to Bartlett. The tiny erotic image of a young man is now imbued with its journey and with each of these successive owners.

This idea of queer inheritance and of bricolage is one form of queer home-making for Bartlett – and one he distinguishes from others. 'I can't bear all that Queen Anne furniture, and all that nonsense: it's very conservative and it's very Kensington antique market taste', he says. 'It's not about beauty or meaning, or rather the meaning of it is money. It's saying: '"have you noticed how much my sideboard cost?"' And I go in and go: "yeah but where are the bits? Where's the thing that's got the texture? That's got the past that you've picked up and gone, look at that, that expresses me."' To Bartlett this style 'feels very un-queer', though he also articulates a sense of its value to other gay men because 'it is about reassuring yourself and the public that they were well-bred, long-pedigreed, and [have] good taste'. Ironically, to Bartlett, this stab at cultural authenticity is the fraud. The camp, drag and amusement of interiors is for him where 'real' queerness is to be found. Capturing this, he says, is part of entering and being part of queer culture. 'Why do lots of working-class boys gets fascinated by football?', he asks. 'Well they grow up in households where that's the culture. Well I entered a culture where lots of the men that I was meeting, had houses decorated with variations – radical variations – on this theme'. And this has been important, Bartlett argues, because it materialises and gives value to desires and relationships which for a long period were derided or ignored, 'considered trash'. 'It's chipped, and it was found in a gutter, but it's mounted and lit as if it was the real thing. In other words it's invested with value'. There is scope to redeem trash for the home, to remake, reframe, reproduce it, and in the process suggest the person who does those things is worth something too. This isn't the precious elite sensibility we have seen amongst some of the men discussed in this section. It yet hits a similar note in terms of finding distinction through homes and things in them in the context of broader social and cultural disdain.

That might be one reason why queer men have become identified with domestic aesthetics and home styling. Another, Bartlett says, might be that '[queers are] hard-wired as psychological freaks and we love glittery old tat'.

Part II
Queer Families

Introduction

In 2009 a documentary film – *Uncle Denis* – was screened for an event at the South Bank Centre to mark the 100th birthday of writer, raconteur, film critic and notorious homosexual Quentin Crisp. His great nephew Adrian Goycoolea had edited interviews with home movie footage to show a different side of Crisp to the one he himself presented in his published writing and interviews.[1] Crisp is shown by Goycoolea embedded in family life – at weddings and other family events. The film was an opportunity for him to explore the 'troubled position' that his great uncle held within the family.

> I began by looking through my old family photographs and home movies. I then contacted my extended family and asked them to rummage through their personal memories of Quentin with me. I discovered that like any gay man Quentin had a complicated relationship with notions of the nuclear family. He felt excluded from it yet at the same time, given who he is, Quentin has always held a privileged place in our family narrative. This tension played out in various ways throughout his life and this film is my attempt to reconcile his position within our family structure together with his wider significance in society.[2]

The youngest of four children, Denis Pratt was brought up in suburban Sutton to the south of London. After school he moved to central London – studying journalism and then art and taking a new name for 'my new self'.[3] It was an opportunity to start again at one remove from his family – and that 'stately homo', the lone, brave 'naked civil servant'

Figure 11 Adrian Goycoolea (aged 11) with his Great Uncle Denis (Quentin Crisp) in 1989
© Frances Ramsay.

is the image that stuck. 'He had a style', observed his niece, 'that he was all alone in the world; the family spoilt that image'.[4] Yet he is there in the family albums, and was the 'closest thing to a grandfather' Goycoolea had.[5] It was for his generation in particular that this accommodation occurred. Crisp's mother and siblings had been upset by the way they and their home life were depicted in Crisp's autobiography *The Naked Civil Servant* (1968) and the film adaptation staring John Hurt that followed in 1975. His nieces, nephews and great nieces and great nephews meanwhile 'enjoyed him', signalling shifting attitudes and also a permissiveness that can come with more distant bonds and more attenuated affections. Crisp himself felt they were interested in him because of his notoriety; this was perhaps the only way he could account for it. Goycoolea, on the other hand, writes that: 'at least for my and my sister's part I can say that this is most definitely not true. We enjoyed him, not his notoriety'.[6] *Uncle Denis* nuances Crisp's self-presentation and also broader representations which suggest a divorce of queer lives from family lives.

Goycoolea's account of his great uncle and in this section my explorations of George Ives, Joe Ackerley, and, in the epilogue, of gay adopter Peter McGraith, are not attempts simplistically to re-forge a link between queer men and their relatives as if sexuality and an awareness of it did not matter. Instead I look at the attachment to and disavowal of family for these men, and at the way families, family homes, the language of family, and familial ways of thinking and relating weave through their testimony and experience. They had to be self-conscious about how they interacted with their families emotionally and in practical everyday terms. This was because of what was culturally expected of family relationships, because of the (shifting) social positioning of queer men, and because of the distance that was presumed to lie between such men and their families. The omission of family from the history of homosexuality matters, historian Deborah Cohen argues, because 'whether your family cast you off or not (or something in between) could make a great deal of difference in the life of an individual'.[7] The potency of family relationships is tangible in the way the men I examine organized their own households, in the way they experienced and conceptualised their connections with other people, and in the way they thought about their pasts and futures. Analysing this interaction suggests that family was malleable enough, conceptually and practically, to accommodate – sometimes uneasily, sometimes more comfortably – the queer difference of uncles, fathers, brothers, sons, and nephews. The analysis also suggests a muddling through in those relationships and in the everyday which is less about an ideal of what families should or should not be like, and more to do with the immediacy of the people involved and with the desire for intimacy, for reassurance, and for some form of progeny or legacy.

The main part of this section is concerned with Ives and Ackerley, and so contextually with the ideas of family, family homes and of homosexuality during the century from 1867 (the year of Ives' birth) to 1967 (the year of Ackerley's death). The epilogue shows how debate about the relationship of gay men to family escalated from the 1970s and often pivoted on the question of parenthood – reconnecting with some late nineteenth-century commentary which I'll say more about in this introduction. The possibility of parenthood has been part of a significant recent reorientation of the way gay men have been seen to interact with and to be part of families (and even though queer men had of course been parents before). Through my brief final case study of McGraith, however, I'll suggest at least some continuity with Ives and Ackerley's earlier experience in terms of the self-conscious negotiation of family practically and conceptually – and also a parallel (and related) eagerness to preserve a distinctive lifestyle and sense of queer difference.

'Exiles from Kin'?

As the notion of a distinctive inverted character was postulated in the late nineteenth century, so the seeds of a more decisive divorce of homosexual from heterosexual, and homosexual from family were sown.[8] Sexology and psychoanalysis both suggested that the invert or homosexual was the product of family – through inheritance or deviations in Sigmund Freud's Oedipal triangle. In adulthood, though, the invert would ideally shun fatherhood and with it the conventions of respectable family life. It was not possible, wrote sexologist Havelock Ellis in 1897, 'to view with satisfaction the prospects of inverts begetting or bearing children':

> Often, no doubt, the children turn out fairly well, but for the most part they bear witness that they belong to a neurotic and failing stock. Sometimes, indeed, the tendency to sexual inversion in eccentric and neurotic families seems merely to be Nature's merciful method of winding up a concern which, from her point of view, has ceased to be profitable.[9]

Other turn-of-the-century sexologists – Richard von Krafft-Ebing, August Forel, Charles Féré and Iwan Bloch – agreed. Bloch claimed that 'among homosexuals the impulse towards the preservation of the species is almost entirely wanting – not more than 3 per cent have the wish to possess children'.[10] Forel even argued that homosexuals should be allowed to embark on same-sex marriage as a means of staving off the possibility of reproductive sex.[11] In this way the homosexual would die out and become a curiosity of the past[12] – 'unprofitable' (in Ellis' telling phrase; note too Bloch's notion of 'possess[ing]' children) in a capitalist economic system which Frederick Engels had recently shown was dependent on a particular form of family and particular gendered roles within it.[13] Ironically, this very system and the expansion in the number of wage earners had enabled more men to live away from their families and in part facilitated the emergence of an autonomous (middle-class) homosexual identity. If the homosexual as a type was unprofitable in that culture in eugenic terms he was also arguably a product of it.[14]

In a different vein but at around the same time as the sexologists, Edward Carpenter, Oscar Wilde, Charles Shannon and Charles Ricketts gestured to a different mode of reproduction and an artistic, philosophical and spiritual queer genealogy extending from Plato and David and Jonathan, through Michelangelo and Shakespeare, to these men themselves and then on into the future.[15] Bloch was again dismissive:

> The greatest spiritual values we owe to heterosexuals, not to homosexuals. Moreover, reproduction first renders possible the preservation and permanence of new spiritual values. [...] Spiritual values exist only in respect of the future, that they only attain their true significance in [...] the succession of the generations, and that they are, therefore, eternally dependent upon heterosexual love as the intermediary by which this continuity is produced.

Homosexuals were 'permanently limited to their own ego' and were 'in their innermost nature dysteleological and anti-evolutionistic'.[16] Those values touted by queer artists, writers and thinkers were secondary to the evolutionary process as Bloch envisaged it. Without a 'proper' investment in family they could apparently not contribute culturally either.

Such men were seen by some actively to threaten English society and culture. In 1909 M.D. O'Brien attacked Carpenter for the threat he posed to 'private property, private homes, and private families' through his politics and his advocacy of 'homogenic love'. The 'socialist and anti-private property principle of unexclusiveness', he wrote, 'strikes inevitably at the monogamic union, without which the separate private family, composed of children who have [...] the same father and mother, cannot in the very nature exist'.[17] O'Brien signalled the anarchic potential of a queerer social organisation. He saw it in paranoid fashion radically disrupting the capitalist system and fracturing a culture and society which put home and family at the centre in terms of national and imperial well-being. Carpenter was a threat because he had set up home outside this system with a male partner with whom there was no legal contract and no children. Lacking this legitimising framework, it could not be a 'real' home – a version in a different key of the *faux* domesticity, fake marriages and mock birthing rituals that took place in the Molly Houses of eighteenth and early nineteenth century London (and of which readers of Iwan Bloch's *Sexual Life of England: Past and Present* were reminded in 1908).[18]

While we can pinpoint concern about the relationship of the homosexual to family in the first half of the twentieth century, however, this debate was not far reaching. Sexology was initially of minority interest in Britain, Ellis's *Sexual Inversion* was banned,[19] and O'Brien's critique of Carpenter appeared in a privately printed pamphlet. Homosexuality was not commonly pitched against family at this time because it was not yet broadly used to denote a clearly separate and distinct category which existed in opposition to a larger and reproductive heterosexual grouping. Though various 'types' might have been recognisable on London's streets, and certain men – Ives and Ackerley amongst them – used the sexological labels for themselves, many men who had sex with other men did not comprehend their desires in these terms or see them as incompatible with home, marriage and children (something we will see with various of Ives and Ackerley's lovers). Sexology and psychoanalysis were nevertheless important because they did have some currency for the men I discuss, they also coded the relationship between homosexuality and family and sewed important seeds in this respect – seeds which took root after the Second World War when hetero/homo, gay/straight understandings of sexuality gained more general currency and family was imagined being more radically dissociated from homosexuality.[20] Though heterosexual reproductive family life was certainly idealised before the 1950s, it was not so homogenous (in terms of the number of children, for example) nor so commonly defined against an unfamilial and undomesticated queer menace as it was during and after that decade.[21]

Lived experiences of family were moreover as mutable as those of sexuality and sexual identity. While the eighteenth and nineteenth centuries saw the rise of the middle-class domestic family unit headed by the male breadwinner and with the conjugal couple at its core, the boundaries of such families were porous and extended outwards.[22] In *John Halifax, Gentleman* (1857) – Dinah Craik's popular novel modelling and espousing domestic, familial and middle-class propriety – the conjugal couple Ursula and John watch over their growing family with a third live-in adult: the eponymous hero's besotted lifelong invalid friend Phineas. Such an arrangement was clearly conceptually compatible with developing ideals of the middle-class home and family for Craik, and is emblematic of 'a more broadly based topography of kinship' in the past than we tend to assume.[23] This was not least because families were so variable in size and composition compared to the period from roughly the 1930s when most married couples began to limit themselves to just two children,[24] and when more and more parents were surviving into old age. In the earlier context when most people died before they were 60,[25] children were commonly bought up by one parent, by other family members, or in informal adoption arrangements (adoption was not formalised by the state until 1926).[26] This earlier expansive conception of family could potentially accommodate men like Phineas in avuncular, care-giving roles.[27] His single state was then and for the first half of the twentieth century moreover a very common if not quite majority experience – though the denomination often feels inappropriate given the intense friendships, attachments and ongoing relationships many nominally single people had.[28] Family was thus an uncertain and changeable entity which yet in its idealised and lived forms couched the way people (single or married) were seen and also saw themselves. This was true for everyone. For those with queer desires and identities there was, we will see, additional and self-conscious work to do in negotiating family and family relationships.

3
George Ives, Queer Lives and the Family

Figure 12 George Ives in old Age, c.1945
University of Texas at Austin.

In 1917 George Ives (1867–1950), the well-heeled early campaigner for homosexual law reform, gave a roll call in his diary of his 'family' home, a large suburban villa in Adelaide Road, Swiss Cottage. Using pet names for his co-residents, he wrote: 'Kit has been with me some

35 years. His wife over 20. Pug 9 or 10. [...] and the 2 Kit girls all their lives'. 'Kit' (James Goddard) had been a servant at the Ives' family seat in Hampshire and then moved with George to London. When he married he bought his wife Sylvie into the household too; 'the 2 Kit girls' were their daughters. 'Pug' (Harold Bloodworth) was a working-class former footballer who eventually outlived Ives and inherited the house jointly with a later addition – 'Elephant', an apparently lovable but nevertheless difficult alcoholic called Stanley Suanders. A few other working class men lived with this group for longer and shorter periods over the years. Together they formed what Ives called 'my little circle in the world'.[1]

Ives' affectionate roll call came as he was grieving for his half-brother, Victor, who had died in the war. 'I loved Victor', he wrote, 'and had no secrets from him'.[2] Cecil, his other half-brother, died in 1923; he was, for Ives, 'just the child I should like'.[3] Victor and Cecil came from Ives' father's marriage to Amy Pullen in 1880, when George was 13. His own mother never publicly acknowledged her illegitimate son, and he was brought up by his paternal grandmother, the Hon. Emma Ives, at the family home at Bentworth Hall in Hampshire, and the Villa Ives in Nice. He referred to her throughout his extensive diary as 'mother'. Elsewhere in that diary he talked of his own urge to father a child, and wrote too of his feelings of 'brotherhood' for fellow members of the Order of the Chaeronea, the group working in the interests of 'homosexual' men which he formed in the early 1890s.

Ives mentioned 'family' in one form or another on virtually every page of his diary, and I show in this chapter that in his birth family, his desire to become a father, his household, and the Order of the Chaeronea he was more or less self-consciously negotiating different ideas and experiences of family. Through this negotiation he found ways of shaping and asserting his masculinity and his sexual identity; a framework for his campaigning work; and a means of finding intimacy and companionship. Though family was the cause of considerable angst for Ives, it was something he valued not in spite of his homosexuality but at least partly because of it. It was fundamental to the ways in which he understood and articulated who he was and how he related to others. 'Family' to him meant enduring, non-negotiable attachments with relations, friends, and co-residents – attachments which were perhaps especially precious because of his feeling of being on the edge of respectability; he was, after all, single, illegitimate and homosexual.

The diary which gives us such detailed access to Ives' world begins in 1886 and ends in 1950. It runs to 122 volumes and about three million words.[4] It became part of Ives' rehearsal of himself for himself and the future reader he envisaged.[5] It is an essential source in thinking biographically about him. It is also suggestive, though, of some of the complex ways in which he and others accommodated and resisted entrenched and changing understandings and experiences of family.

Family life

Ives was cared for initially by a nurse in Croydon, south of London, before moving into Bentworth Hall and his grandmother's care at around the age of five. He writes poignantly of how Emma Ives 'loved me more than anyone else ever has'.[6] Ives met his birth mother twice; once as a child, and then again in 1933 after years of trying to trace her and a period when they exchanged their work with each other. She was aloof and mysterious in correspondence – on account possibly of dementia and perhaps also an anxiety lest her youthful indiscretion be exposed.[7] Ives knew his father much better. There was nevertheless a distance between them which, though he regretted it, he also seems to have accepted on its own terms – probably because this kind of undemonstrative fathering was not untypical.[8] He was close to his half siblings and also formed a bond with his father's second wife Millicent, puzzling with her over how to respond to his mother's strange letters, for example. Millicent thought him 'mad' at first, and 'a dangerous influence' but Ives wrote that 'he won her over to be an affectionate friend'.[9]

Ives did not live for any extended period with any of these people apart from his grandmother, but what becomes clear in the diary is the way he worked hard to forge relationships with them – and relationships that endured. The circumstances of his birth meant none of them was obvious or automatic. They each required definition and redefinition – his grandmother becoming his mother, for example; his much younger half-brother imagined as a son. In working out this family, Ives combined a sense of biological connection with a careful negotiation of the individual relationships themselves. His loyalty related to his pride in the Ives family name (including its own scandalous past), to his deep affection for the particular individuals, and also to the feeling of belonging he gained from these connections. His illegitimacy, his birth position (as the much older brother) and his homosexuality nevertheless modulated the ways in which he interacted with and valued this family. His physical separation from the conjugal unit formed by Colonel and the first Mrs Ives gave him a sense of alienation but also a certain latitude in defining the terms of his family relationships – more, for example, than his half siblings had. For them these relationships were more of a given – automatic because of their direct presence in the family home and also because their desires were (apparently) 'normal'. Such individuals 'did not need to do too much identity work' because they were in contexts 'in which heterosexuality [was] taken for granted' and their (literal) legitimacy was a given.[10] What this fostered for Ives was a sense of separateness and independence which he cherished partly because he considered his mission to be one of challenging sexual taboos and jaded norms. Standing at one remove from his family – however emotionally close he was to them – permitted an analytical distance and a lifestyle which was often at odds with conventions of domestic and family life.

Making home

This distance was underscored when, as a 23-year-old Cambridge graduate, Ives took bachelor chambers at 56 St James Street, off Piccadilly, in 1891. He continued to live at his grandmother's at Regent's Park, but he said in his diary that it was in these chambers that 'I can be left entirely to myself'.[11] The area was 'the inner sanctum of the masculine city',[12] and – with its gentlemen's clubs, bachelor chambers, gentleman's tailors and Turkish bath – was an enclave of elite homosocial privilege offering additional emotional and social resources to those which might be found at home.[13] Ives relocated two years later to Albany on Piccadilly itelf. This address – rather than his grandmother's – became his permanent residence so he could 'get a glimpse now and then of the beauty still in life'.[14] Established in 1803 Albany was one of the best known blocks of bachelor chambers in the West End – with a distinguished lineage of residents including the poet Lord Byron, and Prime Ministers William Gladstone and Henry, Lord Palmerston. The journal *Leisure Hour* noted that the 'bachelor of the Albany was a recognised variety of the man about town',[15] and Ives' friend Oscar Wilde subtly marked out the chambers a little queerly in his writing. Lord Henry Wootton drops in to see a bachelor uncle there in *The Picture of Dorian Gray* (1891), and Ernest is given an Albany address in the original four-act version of the *Importance of Being Earnest* (1894). Miss Prism announces that Ernest is 'as bad as any young man who had chambers in the Albany, or indeed in the vicinity of Piccadilly can possibly be'.[16]

The Albany sets (as the chambers are called) were part of a recognisable bachelor tradition and were spacious, self-contained, and with room for a live-in servant – in Ives' case James Goddard/Kit (though he seems also to have shared Ives' bed). 'By custom', wrote the Chair of the Board of Trustees in 2003, 'residents are not gregarious, so there's no identifiable community in Albany'. Residents and visitors should 'refrain from drawing public attention to Albany'; photographs are not allowed without permission.[17] These contemporary regulations resonate with the culture of the chambers as Ives described them. Though he took a set there to gain some independence and freedom, he was also affected by the onus on preserving certain standards. He refused to allow a third man to join him and Lord Alfred Douglas, Wilde's intimate friend, for sex, for example, because 'it wouldn't do at the Albany'.[18] This sense of restraint, though, was coupled with a quiet culture of tolerance. There had by Ives' time been Bohemian residents from the arts and theatre, and in his wake some well-known queer men including Harold Nicholson, Terrence Rattigan and Terrence Stamp. Ives set up his Order of the Chaeronea here, and nine years after his death in 1959 playwright J.B. Priestley and his wife, the archaeologist Jacquetta Hawkes, established the Albany Trust as the support and counselling wing of the Homosexual Law Reform Society. They named it after the chambers where they lived.

Albany captured and still captures certain ideas of English upper middle-class domesticity, but adapted to suit discreet, childless (children under 13 were and are not permitted as residents), and especially wealthy bachelor residents. One of my interviewees, 'Ben',[19] moved to Albany in the 1950s with a 'rather camp' servant from the Oxford and Cambridge Club, who left when Ben's wife moved in. When she became pregnant in the early 1960s the couple set up a family home outside London, but retained the set at Albany. These two homes have fulfilled different functions in Ben's life, in a model of queer living which endured across the century for some few relatively privileged men. Albany represented for him a strand of life that was not primarily familial. For Ives it was similar. Albany was not his family home; that he established from 1897 in the Regent's Park home of his now deceased grandmother, and then from 1905 at Adelaide Road.

Adelaide Road was developed in the second half of the nineteenth century with semi-detached homes and in an area that was becoming a comfortable Bohemia following the construction of artists' studios in nearby Steele's Road in the 1860s. Charles Shannon and Charles Ricketts, Arthur Rackham, Stanley Spencer, Duncan Grant, folk revivalist Cecil Sharp, amongst other artists and musicians, all lived nearby. It was, wrote one commentator in 1913, 'a city of refuge for those who fled Philistinism [and the] intolerable respectability of more conventional London'.[20] If a West End bachelor chamber had served Ives in his twenties, the greater amount of space and sense of seclusion in this Bohemian inner suburb permitted a different sort of domestic life from his thirties onward. Kit and his wife Sylvie kept house for Ives in a relatively familiar – though rapidly diminishing – tradition of live-in domestic service. Also in the house were Pug and Elephant and other intimate male friends of Ives who became housemates for often extended periods before moving on – often to marry, or in the case of Freddie Smith to move in with Robbie Ross who was a good friend of both Ives and Wilde. These housemates appear to have moved with relative ease between these positions, something Ives seems to have both expected and, with some sadness, accepted. Ives saw them all as his 'family' – a family connected by co-residence rather than by blood ties.[21] James and Sylvie Goddard remained with Ives until their deaths; their daughters until the early 1940s. They could no longer put up with the Elephant's alcoholism, and left to open a shop using money Ives had settled on their father. Ives effectively chose Elephant over them – even though, as a teetotaller, his drinking was a source of considerable angst for him too.[22] The sisters nevertheless continued to visit Adelaide Road regularly and when one of them, Therese, went in 1944 she was described by Ives as 'the youngest of my adopted family – and she is 47!'.[23]

While Carpenter and the Ashbees were framing their actual or idealised living arrangements in their politics, Ives did not describe his in these terms. He preferred the by-now familiar language of domestic sentiment which had developed across the nineteenth century. The Registrar General had announced in his introduction to the Census of 1851 that the Englishman's home 'throws a sharp, well-defined circle round his family and hearth – the shrine of his sorrows, joys and meditations'.[24] At Adelaide Road, Ives actively engaged with this role of paterfamilias and embraced the sentimentalised centrality of this figure. He referred to his housemates affectionately but patronisingly with infantilising nicknames (Cubby, Pug, Kit, Elephant – Therese was Chooki) and also frequently as his 'children'. He was their 'old bird',[25] and they teased him (to his face) for being 'a stingy old b'.[26] 'My children all laugh at me', he complained, 'but they have not the responsibility of running a house with six or eight people in it; all to be milked for'.[27]

Ives was founder of – and provider for – this home and family, and yet also saw himself as its attentive mother figure, fretting over his 'children's' welfare, late nights, arguments, lack of consideration and happiness. 'Have my boys been a success to themselves I wonder?', he mused in 1921; 'they have never done much but they are much liked and they are really lovable souls'.[28] When two of them got work for a while away from London he wished 'his sons might find work near home'.[29] While a late night for Pug left Ives feeling 'pretty sure he had arranged to stay with a girl', he observed that 'a wise parent does not ask too many questions' (even though usually 'we have no secrets between us').[30] Ives was always happiest when 'the whole family' were present at home.[31]

Ives keenly observed any attachment between his household and his family of origin. Each perhaps became more substantial and real to him if they were affirmed by the other – suggesting a mutual affection not reliant on Ives himself. Thus when Ives' half-brother Cecil died he watched the reaction of his co-residents closely: 'Pug's face', he said, 'clouded over with visible melancholy […] this is a great loss to the family'.[32] He had nicknames for his siblings similar to those for his housemates – Victor, for example, was 'Sheep' – and there is a sense that together they formed his brood: he had, he said at one point, 'so many children'.[33] His sense of responsibility towards them was elaborated further in his affection and concern for their respective families.[34] He frequently visited Pug's family during the Great War to share news, for example, and also called on Kit's mother near the Bentworth estate where Ives had been brought up. He carefully wove and maintained an affective web between these different people, crossing and re-crossing class and conventional family boundaries as he did so.

Though Ives' relationships with the other men at Adelaide Road possibly started sexually, they seem quickly to have become platonic – even though he continued to sleep with them from time to time. When Pug and another long term resident Cubby (Charles Gee) were both away he wrote in his diary: 'I feel sad. I love those two, deeply, tenderly […] Love's quite different from passion […] to sleep side by side with one's comrade is beyond all worlds beautiful. Not exciting, but oh such a protection and sympathy, of healing to the heart's many wounds'.[35] When Cubby failed to return home to join him in bed on another evening Ives could not sleep.[36] The men thus shifted from (possible) lovers to sons and, in bed, to comrades. Ives seems to have been unsurprised when his sons/comrades married (as indeed Cubby and Kit did). He did not think about his acknowledged love for them in terms of sex and coupledom. He rather negotiated and experienced that intimacy by taking on a role that he – and possibly also other members of the household – considered to be maternal. He was, remember, their 'old bird' and 'mother hen'. Historian Michael Roper has observed the language of care and mothering between men on the front in the Great War. He shows how it was used as a way of describing and understanding intimacies which might otherwise be unpalatable or suspect.[37] Such language between men in the domestic setting could serve a similar function and alerts us to slightly less rigid gender divisions at this time than have often been assumed. These were rarely as clear-cut as contemporary literature, journalism and other writings suggested.[38] As Ives was 'mothering' his 'family' in Adelaide Road, for example, Toynbee Hall in the East End of London (where Charles Ashbee – Ives' friend – had earlier set up his Guild of Handicraft)[39] was running classes in household and caring skills specifically aimed at working-class men.[40] From 1919 the father-craft movement began to encourage men to be more actively involved in caring for their children.[41] Meanwhile, by looking after his own 'children', Ives took on a similar role to the one his widowed grandmother had had in his own childhood. This was the case even though he also maintained elements of the paterfamilias who 'establishes a home, [] protects it, [] provides for it, [] controls it, and [] trains its young aspirants to manhood'.[42] The Goddards (Kit and Sylvie) were the conjugal heterosexual couple in the Adelaide Road household who might theoretically have displaced Ives in these maternal/paternal roles. Ives' class and money prevented this, however, and these factors stood before sex and coupledom in the household hierarchy.

The Adelaide Road set-up was not created out of immediately comprehensible family ties and as a result the various relationships could have been understood in a number of ways. We have no real sense of how the rest of the household conceived of what Ives saw as his family, and the bonds were possibly conceptualised more loosely by these others. Though Ives saw the various men as his sons, for example, we do not know if they saw each other as brothers and sisters. Therese and Adele clearly had little time for Elephant (Stanley), and though their parents were very attached to Ives, it is unclear whether they understood themselves to be more staff than family, or more family than staff. However blurred the servant/master dynamic at Albany, at Regent's Park and then at Adelaide Road – and Ives did not refer to the Goddards as servants – this dynamic was surely present.[43] It was far easier for an employer to make these inclusive gestures than it was for those who had neither the cash nor the class standing. Moreover, if the Goddards became visible in such gestures, their work and broader significance to the household were largely invisible. As with the nanny and nurse who had cared for Ives in his childhood but rarely get a mention, Sylvie Goddard's work also went largely without comment.[44] This was perhaps because an account of her domestic labour might upset the family story Ives was telling, or more probably because Ives did not fully register what she was doing in servicing the household. For Sylvie herself we can conjecture that she made sense of her life via her domestic role and what historian Judy Giles identifies as circulating concepts 'of privacy, motherhood, homemaking and "service" '.[45]

From the outside it is likely that Sylvie's presence and that of her daughters allowed the Adelaide Road house to appear relatively conformist, embodying a particular organisation of gendered and class service. When Ives' friend Edward Carpenter set up home with George Merrill in 1898 at Millthorpe, his radical friends, advocates of free love and the rest, were appalled at the absence of a 'women's touch': 'they drew sad pictures of the walls of my cottage hanging with cobwebs, and of the master unfed while his assistant amused himself elsewhere'.[46] With Ives, it was only after Sylvie died and her daughters had left that we can find comments about the eccentricity – and the queerness – of the Ives household. With no live-in women 'to do', Ives employed a cleaner. Ives, she said, 'was very nice, very quiet, always sticking things into his black and gold books [his scrapbooks]. He was "queer", and lived with two men [...] I think he kept them both'. Asked about his eccentricity she observed that 'he had a passion for melons. He kept them everywhere. The whole house used to stink of melons'.[47] Here was a homosexual and two 'kept' men languishing in a house of rotting fruit. The respectable household of the interwar years had turned decidedly queer postwar.

There was less romantic socialist idealism and more pragmatism and conformity in the ways in which Ives constituted his 'adopted family'. He wanted domestic intimacy and secured it through his independent means and deep-seated loyalty to the people with whom he lived. Shortly after Pug returned from the trenches, he wrote (with a certain lack of self awareness) that 'nothing is more contemptible in a diary than to chronicle one's dealings with the great [...] and to leave out all ones intimacies with people who constituted one's life'.[48] These were ties 'beyond blood' but he worked as hard to sustain them as he did with his biological kin.[49] In this he was 'doing' family self-consciously and in ways which allowed him to be open about his desires and sexual behaviour. Although his diaries are marked by an obsessive secrecy (in his use of code, for example),[50] Ives seems to have been relatively candid about his life and loves to his friends and broadly conceived family, who, in turn, were tacitly or explicitly accepting. For Ives, homosexuality was acknowledged in personal networks of association that crisscrossed class boundaries.[51] Ives' investment in family in various forms, his mode and code of conduct, and the domestic set-up which was often not so distant from the supposed 'norm', perhaps made it easier for others to sideline or overlook his sexuality and indeed criminality.

Making babies

Though the sexologists I discussed in the introduction to this section suggested a clear line be drawn between the invert and parenthood, for Ives the conjunction of fatherhood and a self-consciously claimed homosexual identity was certainly imaginable. He knew and/or was strongly influenced by a number of men who saw themselves as inverts or homosexuals and yet who also married, had children, and took that parental role seriously – John Addington Symonds, Oscar Wilde and Charles Ashbee amongst them.[52] These men wove these parts of their lives together with varying degrees of candour, and Ives – often quick to judge – made no adverse comment about their arrangements. He was close, for example, to Janet Ashbee, who knew about her husband Charles' male lovers, yet did not see this as an impediment to starting a family with him.[53] John Addington Symonds maintained a strong relationship with his wife and daughters, and also had their understanding in his relationships with men. He combined his homophile passions with a strong sense of familial responsibility. He set up home not only with his wife in England but in Venice with his lover Angelo Fusato, Fusato's wife and their two children. Symonds had encouraged Fusato to marry and so to do his 'duty' by the children. The couple's housekeeping role for Symonds meanwhile gave them a home and income in a set-up which provided Symonds with a second domestic base.[54] Oscar Wilde, most notoriously of all, was married, had two children and also 'feasted with panthers' in London's West End in a more widely comprehended pattern of upper middle-class male sexual philandering involving his family home on the one hand and bachelor chambers and hotel rooms on the other.

After his prosecution, Wilde never saw his children again. Once his sex life had been revealed he was seen to be an unsuitable influence. He had also desecrated the sacred space of the family home by taking his lovers there.[55] It is clear, nevertheless, that he, like Symonds and Ashbee, had formed close bonds with his children and had taken his paternal role seriously by contemporary standards. Fatherhood and queer desires were not, at this point, seen to be incompatible by the men themselves or by their intimates despite the current of commentary which suggested just that. Though Symonds, Ashbee and Wilde struggled in different ways with their queer desires and identities, these were not necessarily so difficult to accommodate within the domestic sphere – partly, of course, because of the privileges that came with being moneyed, male, higher class, and/or self-consciously 'Bohemian'.

Though Ives recognised a mutability in desire (and indeed had affairs with women himself), he also saw himself clearly as a homosexual and viewed this as marking him out as different from other men. He did not, though, see his life as necessarily childless. Neither did he see 'normal' men as necessarily the fittest parents. On a train from Redhill to London in 1942 Ives encountered a sailor: 'a coarse animal with a wife and four children', who opened the carriage door and pissed out of it. Ives wrote, 'I could not help thinking, that while this low, common creature has had children, Edward Carpenter [had had] none'.[56] Earlier, when he noted that ' "young" Somerset was engaged to be married', he added that he 'affords one more instance of homosexuals leaving flourishing families'.[57] ('Young Somerset's' father was Lord Henry Somerset who lost custody of his children and fled the country in 1878 after a scandalous divorce case in which his wife testified to his preference for 'sodomitical practices').[58] Ives – influenced strongly by eugenic thinking, but refusing to accept the idea of the degenerate taint of the invert – clearly saw more danger in the reproduction of a 'coarse' working-class 'creature' than the middle-class or aristocratic homosexual. He was moreover influenced by burgeoning debate about contraception and the scope for 'normal' couples to choose whether and when to have children.[59] These were choices he felt he might be able to make too – despite being single and avowedly homosexual.

Ives' desire for a child was related to his urge to continue the family name and to 'pass on' something of himself to the next generation. 'The joy of passing on my personality', he wrote in 1935, 'of course one would love it'.[60] This was not only idle conjecture in older age. In 1920 he described how he had often considered having children and had talked the matter over with 'a certain girl'. This was Matilda (Tilly) Hayes with whom Ives had a long running affair/friendship from the 1910s to the 1940s.[61] Ives wrote that

> she attracted me physically (not the romantic love; no girl can win that from me) [...] she said she wanted a baby but only under married conditions. I said that with marriage as it is now [...] I would get married on no condition or in any possible circumstances. So there was nothing doing.[62]

Later he described his concern that he may have conceived a child accidentally and we get a clearer sense of why he thought it would have been a bad idea – not so much because of his homosexuality, but because of the state of the world in general, his own financial situation, and his refusal to enter into a domestic relationship with a mother and child. 'I might have had a child by x' (presumably Tilly), he wrote in 1936, 'which we have always guarded strictly against – but then I could simply not have retained my home and have done my duty towards the kid and its mother'.[63] It nevertheless played on his mind as something he half wanted to do as part of his investment in the future. 'Oh the vanity of wishing to breed. I cannot afford to attempt it. It would be absolute ruin and bourgeois in present and probable circumstances', he wrote.[64]

Though Ives ultimately decided against it, he did at least consider – and seriously consider – having a child without marrying. Aside from this potential arrangement with Tilly, he was interested in news from Australia in 1945 of a 'woman who advocates that childless spinsters should be allowed to have children by insemination'. 'The method', he wrote, 'opens up new possibilities, one of which is that children may be produced – as with fish – without personal involvement on the part of the parents'.[65] Though Ives followed a line against marriage rehearsed in radical late-nineteenth and early twentieth-century journals like *The Freewoman* and *The Adult*, and in debate in the British Society for the Study of Sex Psychology with which he was closely involved,[66] this did not preclude parenthood for him. Having children without being married was something Ives could certainly imagine in the context of these radical debates and in a deliberate version of his own conception outside wedlock.

Ives, then, did not measure his fitness for fatherhood in the light of his desires. He rather considered it in terms of his ability to financially sustain a parenting arrangement without marrying – which for him would have involved providing for two households. In the way he described potentially being a parent, meanwhile, we hear ideas which resonate with those of his own father. He imagined being removed emotionally and physically during the child's early years while doing the 'honourable thing' financially. In this he keyed into a tendency to rather distant fathering in the late Victorian and Edwardian middle class.[67] His thoughts also reflected the renewed significance accorded to mothers during this period which had the effect of marginalising men in parenting.[68] In this respect it is perhaps not surprising that Ives did not seem to register that there was much less at stake for him than for Tilly in having an illegitimate child in the 1920s. It was the state of his finances and – given his interest in eugenics – the quality of his sperm that worried him more than the practicalities of hands-on parenting. Having a child would affirm Ives' class and masculine status as well as his commitment to the Ives family line. What is notable in all his pontificating, though, is that the sexuality question which so obsessed late twentieth-century commentary on fit parenting was markedly absent.

Brothers-in-arms

Vertical structures of sentiment and intimacy were woven through Ives' household, family of origin, and desire for a child. More horizontal notions of brotherhood and comradeship were important too – in the way he described sharing a bed with his male housemates, for example, and especially in the way he conceptualised the Order of the Chaeronea and his relationships with his fellow middle and upper-class champions of the 'cause'. In this he followed an established radical tradition of fraternity identifiable in French revolutionary rhetoric, in the British labour movement, in elite circles at Oxford and Cambridge Universities, and in the romantic socialism of Walt Whitman and Edward Carpenter.[69] Though Ives was at the centre of the Order in terms of its foundation around 1893, he also specifically structured it non-hierarchically. Any two existing members could invite a third, theoretically creating a level playing field of brothers rather than establishing a hierarchy with presidents, vice presidents, committees and subcommittees. This latter approach was used by others organising around sexual radicalism, from the British Society for the Study of Sex Psychology (of which Ives was treasurer and Carpenter life president) to the later (post-Second World War) Homosexual Law Reform Society and Campaign for Homosexual Equality. The ritual for joining the Order meanwhile emphasised mutual responsibility, duty, loyalty and endurance.[70] Such rhetoric was familiar from other models of political organising, but by ritualising the order along almost Masonic lines, Ives inculcated a sense of unconditionally and permanence which brushed closely against notions of family. It helped to suggest less a voluntary allegiance and more a pre-existing bond of sexuality, a homosexual 'family', which Ives saw the ritual acknowledging rather than creating. This was to him an elite family with a heroic lineage, stretching back to the Theban Bands, whose battle at Chaeronea in 338 BCE Ives commemorated in the name he selected (a reference point for Derek Jarman too).[71] It was a family with historical depth and one which commanded his allegiance as surely as his relatives and household did.

When he was debating having a child in the 1920s he observed a clash not just with his own domestic set-up but with his broader goals and politics: 'I have my mission to think of', he wrote somewhat grandly; 'one must not grudge the burden of one's embassy. [...] Have I not my own people?'[72] Ives envisaged a form of family bond apart from the biological and the domestic, one cemented specifically by sexual difference. He nevertheless conceived of the Order in ways which struck a chord with the expectation that a family be committed to its history and honour.[73] Though the Order's ritual stressed the importance of individual self-expression, the bond between the men was meant to be inviolable. Ives was scathing in his diary of those who did not take that commitment seriously.[74]

There was a distinction between Ives' egalitarian ideals in his homophile politics and the hierarchies observable in his domestic life. Though he once or twice wished his housemates would live more according to the credo of the 'cause', the differences in class, gender, wealth and age perhaps made this kind of horizontal fraternity difficult for him in the domestic setting. It was much easier with peers who, like him, had passed through Oxbridge and shared similar Hellenic and sexological reference points in conceptualising their sexual identity. This was the only context in which Ives self-consciously connected rhetorics of family with those of homosexuality and the homosexual 'cause' – possibly because it was only in this elite context that he could conceive of an exclusive and shared identity like the one conferred by a family name. However egalitarian in its internal structures, the Order signals Ives' inability to think through friendship and democracy 'beyond' (to use philosopher Jacques Derrida) 'the homo-fraternal and phallocentric scheme'.[75] 'The fratriarchy', Derrida observes, 'may include sisters and cousins but including may also mean neutralising. Including might dictate forgetting'.[76] The Order may have had some women members (Radclyffe Hall and Una, Lady Troubridge seem to have been considered) and Ives did have an interest in the court cases relating to A.T. Fitzroy and Hall's 'lesbian' novels of 1918 and 1928 respectively.[77] He also kept up a close and open friendship with Janet Ashbee and with Tilly Hayes.[78] Women, though, were not ostensibly part of his political fight and, as in his home life, were marginalised – possibly included, but largely forgotten. Ives' politics were not expansive or imaginative enough to make such connections between issues and spheres even though his intimate, personal and family relationships often crossed class and gender lines. Perhaps Ives' investment in the rhetoric and sentiment of home and family curtailed his radical potential, preventing him from thinking beyond the ideologies and structures that had become so symbolically and practically central to English moral and sexual governance.[79] There was no way of thinking that was completely outside of family. Family (variously and multiply conceived) nevertheless enabled Ives to conceptualise and shape a homosexual politics (however constrained) and also a network of personal support at home, among his kin, and in relation to a wider circle of friends.

* * *

Ives made his will in October 1939, as war threatened untold destruction. He produced an extraordinarily detailed and complex document running to eight closely typed pages.[80] Over the decade that followed he added ten codicils – revoking and reinstating bequests and adjusting executors. Wills can reveal much about the way queer men comprehended and underwrote networks of affection beyond kin. The people in those networks are drawn into a legal document in the place of and in addition to family – sometimes 'as if' they were family, and sometimes showing how relationships with kin and with queer friends and household members differed. The care Ives took over his will suggests the value he placed in the various bonds and commitments I have described in this chapter. Novelist E.M. Forster's will, writes legal scholar Daniel Monk 'attests to a desire to record an alternative history, genealogy and temporality. At the same time it can be read as highly traditional'.[81] The same can be said of Ives – he, like Forster, meshed difference with conformity in both his lifetime and in his legacies.

Ives' commitment to his family line and name, and his affection for his half-sisters is, firstly, clear: aside from some money, they received 'any pictures, portraits, miniatures, books, or seals which relate strictly to the Ives family'.[82] With a level of detail that is, legally speaking, unnecessary, he made his relationship to each family member mentioned clear, and also the lines of succession should any of them predecease him. He meanwhile sought to look after his household practically. Therese and Adele Goddard – his 'adopted daughters' – each receive £400; their mother, Sylvie, £60. This bequest was reapportioned after Sylvie's death, and the gifts to the girls were revoked, rebalanced (in favour of Therese – perhaps his favourite of the two, perhaps the most in need), and eventually largely reinstated in codicils. The two men he was living with – Harold Bloodworth and Stanley Saunders (Pug and Elephant) – were left the Adelaide Road house and contents; Tilly Hayes was next in line to inherit after them. If conventionally there might be a single spouse, Ives recognised the three-way affections between himself and the men he lived with. Bloodworth, who had lived with Ives at this point for around 30 years, was also appointed one of his executors. In these ways he acknowledged and differentiated his relationships. His kin and the family he was part of at Adelaide Road were each covered in the will, but in different ways. Pug, meanwhile, was ultimately trusted more than Elephant.

Ives distributed clocks from different rooms ('the leather covered travelling clock which usually stands in the upper sitting room', 'the gilt bronze clock', 'the tortoiseshell clock which usually stands in the dining room of my house') to friends beyond the home. Therese received 'my oak sideboard with two cupboards which stands in the dining room and a Vase with a china bird on its lid which stands on a glass cabinet in the drawing room of my house'. Such bequests give us a clearer glimpse at Ives' interior than the diaries do. Whilst Ives' family of origin received heirlooms, these others got keepsakes, those things which might 'conjure up feelings and reminiscences that keep that person alive'.[83] If we can't know the dimensions of those meanings for Ives and the recipients, we can note the importance of material things in the way relationships were remembered and also perhaps how bequests might touch desire. Perhaps nostalgically for Ives, certainly tantalisingly for us, he remembered with a £10 legacy a certain Charles French 'who at one time worked at the Spread Eagle Hotel, Midhurst Sussex and who lately was at 1 Greek Street, London W1' (in the heart of Soho – in these war years relished by Quentin Crisp and others for the ease of queer encounter). Probably working-class, employed in the service sector (which we've already seen had a reputation for attracting queer men), French was perhaps a former lover, though was also one of the men Ives went on to call 'Ducks' (short for 'lame ducks' – men he helped out intermittently but thought hopeless cases).[84] The bequest was later revoked in a codicil. Perhaps French had fallen out of touch, out of favour, out of memory, or was simply a casualty of a general move Ives made to streamline the will. By the time of his death it was squarely focussed on his kin, close friends, and household, with an additional nod to his causes and comrades-in-arms. He left the poet and fellow member of the Order of the Chaeronea, Laurence Housman, a ring bearing the numbers 338 (the date of the last battle of the Theban Bands). The Howard League for Penal Reform, the British Society for the Study of Sex Psychology (later the British Sexological Society), and the Sex Education Society received books and/or money.

In this will we find the residue of Ives' multiple affections, desires and commitments, and a reach into the future. It is an expansive and nuanced final familial reckoning.[85] The will of writer and editor Joe Ackerley could not be more different. It runs to just one line, a line in which he remembers the author Francis King, his literary executor, with a gift of £100, and his sister, Nancy, 'who lives with me', with the 'remainder of my property'.[86] Therein lies a complex tale, however – one which suggests some of the ways in which experiences, ideas and ideals of family might have intersected with homosexual self-fashioning in the inter and post-war years.

4
Joe Ackerley's 'Family Values'

Joe Ackerley was part of the next generation to George Ives. Born in 1896, the year after Wilde's prosecution, Ackerley died just seven weeks before the Sexual Offences Act of 1967 partially decriminalised sex between men in England and Wales. By the time he was doing most of his writing – in the post-World War II period – the idea that you were either heterosexual/homosexual had more cultural purchase and sexological and psychoanalytical explanations were in wider circulation.[1] As a result there is a different self-consciousness in Ackerley's work than we saw with Ives' and he interrogates sexual difference in relation to his family much more directly. There are yet some echoes of Ives' experience. Both were Cambridge graduates and were inspired by the ancient Greeks and by Edward Carpenter; both had a passion for working-class men. They each lived in central north London – Ackerley for a while in Little Venice, another literary queer enclave in the interwar period and about half an hour's walk from Ives in Adelaide Road. The men were linked too by a deep but complex investment in families and family-like relationships. While Ives committed his thoughts on the 'private' realm of the family to the at least notionally private space of his diary, however, Ackerley wrote directly for publication – 'deprivatize[ing] the modern gay man's sexual anguish' in his astonishing frankness about his desires and sex life, and his relationships with his parents, siblings, dog and lovers. He writes what literary critic Susan McHugh describes as a 'family focussed history of queer England'.[2]

Ackerley's father, Roger, was a working-class guardsman who went on to make a substantial living as a banana importer. Joe was the second of three children (Peter was a year older; Nancy three years younger) from his father's relationship with Netta Aylward, a woman whose 'family tree [was] a network of illegitimacy and sexual irregularity'.[3] Roger and Netta married in 1919 after the loss of their eldest son in the Great War. Joe survived the war and returned to England after a spell as a detainee in a hotel in Switzerland – an experience which inspired his play, *Prisoner of War* (1925). Like Ives, Joe fretted over money and often felt short of it, but he had a privileged upbringing and education, an allowance during his twenties, and a job – as Literary Editor of the *Listener* – which meant he was relatively comfortably off throughout his life. He excelled professionally and the list of reviewers he recruited to the magazine reads like a literary 'Who's Who' – Virginia Woolf and his close friend E.M. Forster amongst them. He left behind some extraordinary work of his own: an account of his five months in India as Private Secretary to the Maharajah of Chhatarpur – rendered by Ackerley as Chhokrapur [or 'City of Boys'] for *Hindoo Holiday: An Indian Journal* (1932); his celebration of his relationship with his dog Queenie, *My Dog Tulip* (1956), which novelist Christopher Isherwood described as 'one of the greatest masterpieces of animal literature';[4] and a novel based on his relationship with his working-class lover Freddie and with Freddie's wife and family (*We Think the World of You* [1960]). Ackerley's autobiographical masterpiece, *My Father and Myself* (1968), was the product of 34 years' labour. It 'marked out', historian Deborah Cohen writes, 'a frank new frontier of confessional literature', though in tune both with obscenity laws and perhaps with the family secrets he grew up with, it only appeared posthumously (as did sections of his journal *My Sister and Myself* [1982]). Of *My Dog Tulip* he wrote to the novelist Francis King (his literary executor) that 'it is autobiographical of course; I have no creative ability'. His work was, he said, 'terribly terribly Freudian'.[5]

Ackerley's preoccupation with family resonates with Ives, but Ackerley also digested and of course presented it differently – more analytically and more publicly. His work underscored, challenged and extended circulating perceptions of queer lives and the way they related to home and family. It appeared largely in the years after World War Two and amidst burgeoning representations of homosexuality in literature, the press, sociology, film and theatre – work which was often produced with a reformist agenda.[6] Though Ackerley supported reform it was not the driver in his writing as it was for others and he does not shy away from revelations which some might have thought did 'the cause' little good. His work preceded the 'coming out' writing of the post 1970s period and Ackerley's story of himself is not structured around that moment which later often marked rupture and separation from family actually or conceptually.[7] Those later narratives were written amidst more overtly politicised debate about family; Ackerley, meanwhile, makes his own family drama public but does not link it to a wider movement or activist pulse. His work in some ways foreshadows the 1970s and 1980s and in others signals differences in the way families might be configured, experienced and understood before and after liberationist politics.[8]

By the time Ackerley named his sexual difference at Cambridge, sexological and psychoanalytical modes of thought and interpretation were in circulation among men of his background and class. 'Are you homo or hetero?', a 'hetero' friend had asked him in 1923, recommending that he read Otto Weininger, Edward Carpenter and Plutarch when he opted for the former of the two terms that were both new to him.[9] The identities were yet clearly there to occupy and Ackerley was not in this sense grappling for the co-ordinates to his sense of self in quite the way Ives and his contemporaries had had to do. There is perhaps in consequence an assurance – albeit deeply pessimistic – in the way he writes about his identity, his desires, his sexual problems, and his lifelong search for an 'ideal friend'.

Ackerley's story extends and re-directs the discussion I began in the last chapter. If Ives encapsulated a thirst for a legacy, a child, a future reader, a sexual and social revolution to come, then Ackerley gathers family into his narrative to account for himself – to recoup a genealogy and to find a model of his own idiosyncrasy. If Ives mainly found comfort in his family and family home, Ackerley was more often attuned to the way his family (and his family's presence in his home) restricted and frustrated him. He speaks of the tension between a desire for (queer) bachelor independence and a duty of familial care. He yet also willingly enters into the family and family lives of some of his lovers and eroticises aspects of his own. In what follows I track Ackerley's 'bachelor' homes and quest for independence from family when he was in his twenties, before showing how the dynamics of his different relationships – with his father, with other family members and visitors to his childhood home, and with his working-class lovers and their families – encroached upon and shaped that everyday queer life. Desire, eroticism, guilt, and resentment weave through each of these relationships in different ways. His queer and family lives were – for good or ill – inextricably entwined.

Bachelor about town

At Cambridge University immediately after the First World War, Ackerley's rooms were hung with homoerotic prints by Charles Ricketts' protégé Glyn Philpot, Henry Scott Tuke, and Jean Hippolyte Flandrin.

In London he took rooms in artistic bohemias: in St John's Wood (walking distance from the now aging Ricketts, Shannon and Ives – though he seems to have known none of them); in Charlotte Street in the mid-1930s ('an artists' colony in those days', he wrote);[10] and then in Maida Vale, known by then for its queer literati whom Virginia Woolf labelled 'the lilies of the valley'.[11] In the summer of 1936 he followed the monied, literary queer trend for weekending in Dover in Kent. The town at this juncture was 'alive with literary homosexuals, becoming a sort of Maida Vale *sur mer*', and taking that mantle from Portsmouth (which Ives had earlier favoured).[12] It was 'the lintel of England's continental doorway', noted Ackerley's friend, serviceman Leo Charlton, giving it an aura of permissiveness.[13] He took rooms in a house because he could not afford one of his own, but when his landladies objected to his visitors he was asked to leave. 'To the average person', wrote Ackerley, 'this sort of thing is disgusting, especially when it obtrudes its creaks-and sheets-end first upon their notice'.[14] Ackerley mentions such risks and upsets a number of times. In his short stint as Private Secretary to the Maharajah of Chhatarpur, Ackerley was frustrated by the comings and goings and constant presence of servants in houses where privacy was seemingly even less valued or expected.

Between St John's Wood and Charlotte Street he lived in Hammersmith Terrace on the river with the Needhams, an 'odd' family group – composed of a sister and two brothers. One of the brothers, Arthur, was 'recognizably "one of us", "that way", "so" or "queer"'.[15] According to Ackerley, Arthur 'enjoyed the vicarious excitement and vicarious pleasure of admitting youthful, friendly [and largely working-class] callers' to visit Ackerley's rooms. These rooms were, according to occasional visitor the actor John Gielgud, were 'spartan'.[16] Gielgud remembered the inevitable 'statue of a Greek youth' (the queer signifier), a large bunch of bananas on the dining table (the familial link – to his father's work), and 'a rather anonymous looking disciple ironing shirts in the kitchen'.[17] Ackerley threw parties on the day of the Oxford and Cambridge boat race to which writers, actors and BBC acquaintances, policemen and guardsmen, his mother, his aunt and neighbours were invited in an eclectic and (for Ackerley) somewhat erotic mix.[18]

For the first 20 years of his adult life Ackerley found places to live in London which were artistic and queer friendly, but in 1941 his Little Venice flat was bombed out – one of around 409,000 homes across London destroyed or seriously damaged in the war.[19] He moved from there to a 'dingy' one bedroom apartment at Star and Garter Mansions, just upstream from Putney Bridge and his interwar Hammersmith

Figure 13 Roger and Joe Ackerley
© The estate of J.R.Ackerley.

home. It boasted a huge roof terrace and was handy for the river's cruisey tow-path ('a dreamland' according to Quentin Crisp).[20] This last home was, we will see, conflicted for Ackerley: he shared it for an extended period with his sister, aunt and dog – not quite the home of an urbane bachelor and more akin to that of the Needhams of Hammersmith which he himself had earlier described as 'odd'. The Star and Garter flat especially saw the conjunction of Ackerley's queer and family lives, but the overlap preoccupied him throughout his adulthood and he sought it out through his examination of his family's past – and especially his father's.

Queer genealogy

Ackerley pursued his own and his father's past as a means of coming to terms with himself and a queerness which often left him feeling discontented. In this extended genealogical project there were muted echoes of sexological case studies and of a wider modern search for clues to personality through inheritance, family and infant experience. 'I have some record of heredity in 32 of my cases', concluded Havelock Ellis in *Sexual Inversion* (published first in 1897, the year after Ackerley's birth). 'Of these not less than ten assert that they have reason to believe that other cases of inversion have occurred in their families, and, while in some it is only a strong suspicion, in others there is no doubt whatever'.[21] In the introductory comments of each case study, there is invariably some reflection on any eccentric heritage. This is grist to Ellis' theorization, of course, and for him heredity took precedence over the infantile influences that Freud plumped for subsequently in his *Three Essays on the Theory of Sexuality* (1905). But aside from this 'science' of causation, the lineage the men each detail suggests an active interest in tracing a queer past – perhaps not only to help Ellis but to give themselves a sense of personal heritage, worth and a reason and way to be.[22] A 26-year-old actor, for example, 'believe[d] that his mother's family, and especially a maternal uncle who had a strong feeling for beauty of form, were more akin to him in this respect' than his father's family.[23] A married 52-year-old 'of independent means' had forefathers 'in the last and earlier centuries' who were 'supposed to be inverted'. Another case – a man '30 years of age, high bred, [and a] refined and sensitive Englishman' – had 'paternal and maternal uncles who were both sexually inverted'.[24] These links suggest the importance for queer men of relations apart from parents who might affirm different ways of being and suggests too the significance to them of knowledge – tacit or explicit – which circulated within families.[25] Classicist John Addington Symonds, Ellis' collaborator, traced his own family's history, character and eccentricities briefly in the case he supplied to Ellis and in more detail in his own 'Memoir'. He found not inverts but strands of temperament which he saw coming together in himself and his queer life. In his narrative of homosexual becoming Symonds fused a neurotic strand in his mother's history and an aesthetic and ethical sense from his father's side.[26] Author and poet Edmund Gosse did the same in more guarded ways in his landmark biography *Father and Son* (1907). There he describes an affinity with his 'reprobate' maternal grandfather and bachelor uncles.[27] If tracing family character and history was and is hardly restricted to homosexuals there was perhaps an additional imperative when difference was keenly felt.

Ackerley was writing significantly later than Symonds, Gosse or Ellis' case studies, and by this time that way of thinking about the self and sexuality had become more culturally embedded; it was an 'obvious' route for Ackerley to take in his self-examination. He was fascinated by ideas of inheritance and especially from his mother's side.[28] In his published writing, though, he placed himself in determined relation to his father, making connections between the entrepreneurial banana king and the queer literary son. Piecing together aspects of his father's relationships and sexual past and relating them to his own life for *My Father and Myself* left, he said, 'the established image of the paterfamilias, the respectable, dull, suburban householder, the good, poor, old dad, [...] in pieces'.[29] Yet Ackerley was unable to prove much conclusively and was haunted by the gaps and silences in his narrative. The literary critic Joseph Bristow finds a 'failure in sexual genealogy' in the book. We simply don't know what Ackerley senior's sexual life involved. But *My Father and Myself* is also richly suggestive of what Bristow describes as the latter's 'obscure desires' and certainly signals Joe Ackerley's felt desire to seek them out.[30] If family therapist John Byng Hall talks of 'the disabling legend' of familial myths and memories for succeeding generations, for Joe Ackerley unearthing them might, he felt, have brought him a sense of belonging.[31]

Ackerley 'divined' that his landlord, Arthur Needham, at six Hammersmith Terrace was 'that way' immediately. What took a while to unfold was the connection between him and his father.[32] Arthur had been a friend of the Count de Gallatin, who in turn had taken a shine to Joe Ackerley's father when he was a young, handsome guardsman. Roger Ackerley had enlisted in the Blues at Albany Street Barracks in 1879 – two years before the pornographic novel *Sins of the Cities of the Plain* flagged it as a source of guardsman renters (a connection Joe himself makes).[33] The Count, meanwhile, had cruised guardsmen at the Napoleon pub in Knightsbridge in the late nineteenth century – just as Joe did later.

It is not clear where Roger Ackerley and the Count met, nor whether they had sex, but they certainly bonded. For the summer of 1885, the Count rented a house in New Brighton, Cheshire, and invited Roger and his friend and future partner in a fruit business, Arthur Stockley, to spend time with him there. Stockley recalled that 'there was no female society of any sort' at the house and that they created 'quite a sensation'. 'The local residents were not used to, were suspicious and perhaps jealous of so strange a household which contained a rich foreign nobleman with rather poppy eyes and two strikingly handsome young men'.[34] Someone even wrote to Stockley's mother to warn her that her son was 'being ruined by an adventurer and his confreres'.[35] After the summer the Count set Ackerley up in business as a pony farmer near his family home in Windsor – in the process securing 'his heart's desire, my father's permanent companionship'.[36] Ackerley soon fell for a wealthy Parisienne visitor to the De Gallatins, however, got engaged and left the farm and the Count to marry her. 'I tell you frankly', the Count's mother wrote to Stockley, 'his heart is broken'. In that letter Mme de Gallatin used the language of family to describe Ackerley's position in the household: 'Roger came to us and took the place of my dear son I lost [...] he was James' brother and James and I treated him as a son and brother and gave him all our affection and devotion'.[37] These were the terms in which Mme de Gallatin could comprehend her son's love for the young working-class former guardsman, but her letter also betrays signs of the Count's lovesickness. He 'has never been able to remain at home since – I see it he cannot – he says everything is so connected with Roger that he suffers too much'.[38]

Roger Ackerley's new bride died early in 1892 leaving him bereft but with an allowance settled on him by his in-laws. It was perhaps for this reason that Roger did not immediately marry Netta (Joe Ackerley's mother) whom – in their son's phrase – he had 'picked up' on a channel crossing.[39] On Roger Ackerley's death from tertiary syphilis in 1929, a letter left from father to son revealed that alongside the household in Richmond in which Ackerley was raised with his brother and sister, was another – a second family of three half-sisters.[40] Roger was 'Uncle Bodger' to these children, who he visited regularly and lavished with gifts – an arrangement that was not altogether uncommon.[41]

In *My Father and Myself* Ackerley tried to trace intimate friends and lovers in his father's life in ways which might somehow couch his own.[42] He got tantalizingly close to a queer family history which was more immediate than 'the tradition of the ancient Greeks [...] and all the famous homosexuals of history' amidst whom he had placed himself at Cambridge.[43] 'What fun it would be', wrote Ackerley, 'if I could add the charge of homosexuality to my father's other sexual vagaries! What irony if it could be proved that he had led in his youth the very kind of life that I was leading!'[44] Bristow shows how Joe Ackerley repeatedly makes connections in his testimony between his own life and that of his father.[45] Joe was like the thwarted Count in his relationship with working-class Freddie; Freddie was meanwhile akin to Roger in choosing a female over a male companion. Both father and son took a keen interest in the lives and families of lower-class men. Joe notes, for example, the way in which his father 'delighted' in his chauffeur, 'gave him handsome tips and presents, such as hands of bananas, sent presents to his family and talked about him so much that we used to ask after him, as though he were a pet dog'.[46] If this passage seems to head towards an assertion of Roger's love for the chauffeur, Joe diverts at the end: this was the kind of affection you might have for a pet not for a lover (though Joe understood both and experienced them in complicatedly intersecting ways, as we will see). Roger Ackerley's actual pet, a dog called Ginger, meanwhile served a similar role to Joe's Queenie, the dog owned first by Freddie and then by Joe. 'I'm taking the dog for a walk' Roger Ackerley would say when he went off to visit his other family, just as Freddie said to his wife when he went to visit Joe.[47] Roger had only a weekend presence in the family home because he kept a flat in Marylebone where, according to Ackerley's Aunt Bunny, 'he led a gay, free, bachelor's life – "all the fun of the fair" as she put it – and to which my mother was never invited'.[48] Like his father, Joe also relished the space he gained for his affairs in the rooms he rented away from his family.

By placing his own sexual adventuring beside what he could find out about his father's, Joe demonstrated how they might have known and understood each other better.[49] This is the book's central theme. Speaking to both his sons, Roger Ackerley had said:

> That in the matter of sex there was nothing he had not done, no experience he had not tasted, no scrape he had not got into and out of, so that if we should ever be in want help or advice we need never be ashamed to come to him and could always count on his understanding and sympathy.

'That this', Ackerley wrote, 'was an excellent and friendly speech I realised when I was older; that I never took advantage of it is the whole point of this book'.[50] Yet when Ackerley did indeed go to his father with a confession, Roger closed down the discussion – albeit in a friendly way. Caught out in a lie, Joe had told him: 'I'm very sorry to have lied to you. I wouldn't have done so if you hadn't once said something about me and my waiter friends. But I don't really mind telling you. I went to meet a sailor friend'. Roger interrupted him: 'It's alright, old boy. I prefer not to know. So long as you enjoyed yourself, that's the main thing. Thus did he close the door in my face'.[51]

After his father's death, Joe saw all this as a 'stupid story'. It was, he felt, 'shamefully stupid that two intelligent people, even though parent and son between whom special difficulties of communication are said to lie, should have gone along together, perfectly friendly, for so many years, without ever reaching the closeness of an intimate conversation, almost totally ignorant of each others' hearts and minds'.[52] Ackerley perhaps overstates that ignorance: he picked up on clues to his father's behaviour and Ackerley senior also clocked the queer themes of his son's play, *Prisoner of War* (1925), and observed his son's penchant for 'waiter friends'.[53] Though the equivocation and distance in his relations with his father were troubling for him,[54] the unspoken truths Joe despairs of were commonplace for many of his contemporaries.[55]

My Father and Myself was an attempt to track a queer heritage and to find a place for the errant son in the family story. But it was also about the struggle for frankness, honesty and intimacy between father and son. This was a common enough tale in this late Victorian and Edwardian middle-class context, and Ackerley senior seems to have been more open than many. As the years passed after Ackerley senior's death in 1929, however, and as the parameters of what it felt possible to say shifted, there seemed to Joe to have been a missed opportunity. What is especially moving in *My Father and Myself* is the sense Joe had that the two men could have been in sympathy with each other, and that in that sympathy and understanding he might have found a firmer grounding for himself in adulthood. The book took 34 years to write and was only published posthumously. Deliberately or not, Joe made his investigation of his relationship with his father and his own queer roots last most of his adult life. In this respect his father did serve as an enduring ballast of sorts.

Hom(e) eroticism

Joe Ackerley's eroticized interest in his father extended to other family members and to men employed in the Ackerley household. His physical description of his brother Peter quickly slips from his 'straight dark brows' and 'narrow palate' to his 'loins' 'buttocks' and 'abnormally long dark cock, longer than my own or any other I had seen'.[56] He also looked back keenly to the first homoerotic signs emerging in childhood – through hazy memories of a bootboy, for example:

> In Apsley House, the first of our Richmond residences, I place him, and he is a game, a childish game, possibly and unwittingly suggested by my weekend and sometimes retributive father himself, for in this game my brother, the bootboy and I take down each others trousers by turn and gently beat the bare bottoms that lie, warmly and willingly, across our laps.[57]

The (nameless) bootboy, the Ackerley home, father, and brother are bound together in this memory – which, the use of the present tense suggests, was still pressing and keenly felt. They figure as part of Joe's account of the genesis of his adult love life and sexuality. 'It began', he writes, 'with a golliwog' (a gift he requested from his father) 'and ended with an Alsatian bitch; in between passed several hundred young men, mostly of the lower orders and often clad in uniforms of one sort or another'.[58]

Embroiling domestic employees and those servicing the household in various ways in the erotics of home was hardly new – post office telegraph boys had, for example, an established place in the queer imaginary.[59] For Ackerley the bootboy was only a beginning. He had an affair with 'a Richmond tradesboy who delivered groceries to [his] parents'[60] and later asked his father to employ a waiter boyfriend as a butler. 'Certainly not!' came the reply, adding that exasperated, 'Joe and his waiter friends!'[61] Ackerley was repeatedly drawn to those who were 'in service' – of the home, of their country; in any case, as he himself says, often in uniform. These encounters were mostly fleeting, sometimes expensive, and often potentially dangerous. They each also spoke of erotics pivoting on class difference.[62]

The tradition of live-in domestic service meant that men of different classes often lived together within equivocal relations of power. Because of the intimate knowledge an employee might have of his employer, there was always the risk of gossip, exposure or blackmail. A London clergyman 'Mr X' was blackmailed for three years in the 1950s by a former valet on account of the queer knowledge he had of him, for example.[63] On the other hand, there was also the scope for relationships of deep trust, of love, and of mutual support – as we saw between George Ives and James Goddard. Some men used domestic employment as a cover. The collector Edward Perry Warren's live-in 'secretary' in Lewes, East Sussex, for example, was actually his lover and life partner. The erotics and affections around workers coming into the home meanwhile endured after World War II. Derek Jarman and cookery writer Nigel Slater both remember their fascination and affection as boys for the housekeeper's son and gardener respectively – men who played with and sometimes took care of them. As adults, Jarman and Slater cast these men as their first loves, opening up for them the experience of affection and care between men.[64] More overtly sexual was the subsequent video, DVD and then internet pornography in which the handyman, gardener, plumber and delivery man were recurrent fantasy figures. There was, in short, an ongoing erotic frisson associated with home derived from the men who delivered to, worked in, repaired, or in other way serviced it. The dynamics of this changed across the century as live-in domestic service declined and car culture and supermarkets made home deliveries less common. There was yet some continuity in the erotics Ackerley felt relating to the divide between those who 'belonged' in the family home and those who came into it as employees or to offer goods and services.

Overbearing women

Those who 'serviced' homes were not always men, of course. Though bachelor living was idealised in popular literature as a blissful domestic alternative to living with 'fussy' females, women were nevertheless present in one way or another in most of the contexts in which middle-class bachelors lived.[65] Ackerley became close to his cleaner, Molly, and through her met her son Freddie with whom he became besotted. He also had an awareness of 'the speculation[s]' and also complaints of his other 'chars'.[66] At the Star and Garter one objected when Queenie (the dog) arrived, complaining that 'first it's niggers, now it's a wolf'.[67] Ackerley's dog was an untrained Alsation; Afro-Caribbean immigrants were, meanwhile, commonly judged predatory and untamed.[68] Neither were suited to the domestic scene according to this woman. Sociologist Judith Stacey describes the 'postmodern gay man' making home without women. This was far from the case for queer men in Ackerley's lifetime (and has often not been the case since).

Aside from the intimacies Ackerley had with the women he employed, his life post-war was dominated by his sister who he felt crushed whatever bachelor independence he had enjoyed in the 1920s and 1930s. Nancy's marriage ended in 1949 and she moved with her young son into her mother's home. Ackerley didn't warm to his nephew, but nevertheless felt a duty of care towards him and his sister. He wrote that he 'was endlessly involved in the troubles that disturbed [that household]':

> Indeed they all now fell upon me, for after all my father was dead, and as the only surviving male in the family, the burden of desperation and appeal was narrowed and focused upon myself; it was upon me only that the wretched task endlessly fell of attempting to protect my mother and keep the peace.[69]

Once his sister went to live in Ackerley's flat in Putney he became especially embittered. He was, he says, 'deeply attached to her' but also saw her as 'a parasite' 'living at the expense of others'.[70] He sought to live out and tell his story via his male lovers and male friends, and reacted against what he saw as the dominance of women – and especially this woman – in his life. He claimed to have had far less sympathy than his father because of the direction of his desires, but was bound in by a sense of duty and (though he rarely admits it) strong affection. Ackerley's literary executor, the writer Francis King, wrote that 'together [Joe and Nancy] were more like a married couple than brother and sister; but like a married couple who have decided that, on balance, they had better stick together, even though everyone else knew that a divorce would be best for them'.[71] 'But there are so many viewpoints' Ackerley himself wrote:

> She was my sister only, my only sister, and her assault upon me was more the assault of a lover, a wife. Was I to give up everything for her, my independence, my life, my own character? As a lover, indeed, I see I failed her. But as a brother, did I do so badly? I never wanted anyone to live with me. I have a right to my independence, have I not? I wanted to live alone, with my dog, visited by my friend, her indeed too if one could have trusted her not to abuse one's hospitality, to have my flat to myself for Freddie's visits or those of an other similar friend I might make. [...] My sister, not my lover or my wife.[72]

There is a sense here of roles slipping and of an incompatibility between his family and queer lives. And yet brother and sister proved indivisible in their relationship of mutual dependence. In a letter to Ackerley, his friend E.M. Forster describes his relationship to his mother in similar terms. Their accounts were mutually reinforcing, riffing on similar complaints and upsets and signalling the importance of their friendship and (more grudgingly) of their respective relationships with live-in relatives. For Forster there was a good deal of comfort to be found from this relationship despite the irritations; Nancy was more troublesome to Ackerley, but he could not turn away either. Such emotional sibling bonds were every bit as powerful and psychically formative as those founded in cross-class erotics or Oedipal rivalries.[73]

In martyred prose Ackerley wrote repeatedly and often misogynistically of the women he lived with and supported – pointing out (what he saw as) the irony that his primary and immediate domestic relationships were with women not men – with Nancy, his aunt Bunny (who also lived with him for a while) and with Queenie the dog. This set up, though, marked a continuation of the scenario of Ackerley's childhood – one which was commonly seen in the postwar period to be the root cause of homosexuality. 'We were brought up and surrounded by women', wrote Ackerley: 'my mother, aunt, grandmother,

her sisters, old Sarah and various nurses, governesses and maids'.[74] I have noted already that the 1950s was the decade when psychoanalytic ideas of normative – and also aberrant – sexual development gained more general currency and to an extent displaced sexological theories of inheritance and the 'third sex'.[75] The structure and functioning of the nuclear family, and in particular the relationship between parent and child, was the subject of ever greater scrutiny as Ackerley was writing.[76] Popular psychologists and sociologists – most famously Talcott Parsons and Robert Bales – suggested that gender role modelling (with a distinction between masculine 'instrumental' and feminine 'expressive' roles) was key to the good functioning and well-being of the family and to the emergence of the healthy and family-orientated heterosexual.[77] Absent fathers and overbearing mothers were seen to be at the root of sexual dissidence in adulthood. The supposed increase in homosexual men in the 1950s was explained by some in the enforced absence of fathers during the war years.[78] In the groundbreaking ITV *Man Alive* documentary 'Consenting Adults: the men' (screened in 1967 – the year of Ackerley's death) interviewees indicated how they had internalized this logic. One observed that he became a homosexual because he grew up 'with a dislike of his father and a tremendous attachment to his mother'.[79] It was a logic of sexuality repeated for some time to come[80] – and was not lost on Ackerley who nevertheless wryly and bitterly observed the paradox of childhood and adult homes shared with women while his lovers visited only fleetingly. This was not the kind of queer home he had envisaged for himself. If these women had caused his queerness, he also saw them inhibiting it.

Lovers and Kin

We have seen already how affections spill over and intersect in Ackerley's writing, in sometimes satisfying, more often frustrating, ways. In his autobiographical novel *We Think the World of You* Frank's (Joe's) relationship with Johnny (Freddie) also takes in Johnny's mother, wife, and his dog. These other bonds are in constant play as Frank/Joe seeks an emotional and physical relationship with his lover. The dog, Evie (Queenie), was once Johnny's and was part of the bond between them. In an expurgated passage from the novel she literally connects Frank and Johnny with her saliva:

> Uttering little quavering cries of doubt and concerns, she sat first upon our mingled clothes, gazing at us with a wild surmise, then upon our mingled bodies, excitedly licking our faces as though

she would solve her perplexing problem either by cementing them together with her saliva or by forcing them apart. She lay with us throughout the afternoon, her fur against our flesh, and we talked most of the time of her.[81]

Queenie, fictionalized here as Evie, is the focus of this sex scene, it is her whimpering and doubts and reactions that are monitored, not those of Johnny (Freddie). The nebulous bond between the two men is rendered clearer, firmer through the dog – although her perplexity also echoes Frank (Joe's) uncertainty about the relationship.[82] Meanwhile, beyond the novel, Joe bound himself to Freddie partly by helping his lover's wife and mother financially. There was an ongoing resentment for him in this, feeling he must accept his lover's other attachments because of his 'normality' but struggling nevertheless with the feeling that he came second. Ackerley considered – perhaps flippantly, perhaps (biographer Peter Parker suggests) more seriously – murdering Freddie's wife as a way of getting his lover to himself.[83] Such triangles of affection were relatively familiar in the years before more exclusivity in sexual identity was expected and especially whilst 'normal' working-class men were apparently relatively at ease with having girlfriends or wives as well as male lovers (though there was clearly a strain for Freddie too as he negotiated the various calls on his time from mother, wife, children, Ackerley and dog). This story of intersecting love and sex and so also of intersecting home and family lives is one repeated in fiction, film and theatre across the inter and immediate postwar years.[84] Oral history testimonies describe how deep bonds (sexual and/or emotional) forged between men in the war or subsequent National Service (which remained in force until 1960, with the last tranche serving in 1963) played out in post-service years as men became godfathers to each other's children, friends of each other's wives, and were incorporated with varying degrees of frankness into new home and family formations.[85] Though there was certainly an increasingly separatist strand in rhetoric about queer men in the immediate postwar period, many queer lives and experiences were still folded into 'normal' homes and 'normal' families.

Ackerley's story shows that queer encounters between classes were not only about brothels and public sex cultures in the capital but also about domestic and family life. Ackerley wrote: 'I found a number of decent boys who attracted me, and of whom I grew fond, as they grew fond of me, who entered my family life as I entered theirs, and who afforded me further rests along the way'.[86] His four-year affair with a sailor in the 1920s ('a simple, normal, inarticulate, working-class boy') began because Ackerley already knew the family. On some of his visits to see him in Portsmouth, Joe also introduced him to his father:

> Now that my father had chosen Southsea for his convalescence (was it because he knew I went there often?), the most convenient arrangement seemed to be to bring them together. This worked well; my father was charming to this inarticulate, monkey-like boy […] he must surely have wondered – if he had not guessed – what his son […] could possibly see in so dumb a companion, yet he accepted him with grace and good humour, invited him two or three times to dine with us in his grand hotel, joked with him and teased him to make him laugh. […] The sailor was helpful and attentive to him too.[87]

Once the affair ended, Joe received an apology via the sailor's brother ('a homosexual, oddly enough')[88] – again flagging the significance of family networks in sustaining, embedding, and here closing down relationships. This was the case with George Ives too: his love and sense of duty for his (possible) lovers turned 'sons' extended to their families. They in turn seemed to accommodate their son's older, differently classed 'friend' rather as Freddie's family did Ackerley.

If Ackerley could be painfully patronizing in his descriptions of his working-class lovers (the sailor not least) he also idealized their home and family lives. In the family home of an early lover from the mid-1920s he described 'such solidarity such sensitive kindness and sensibility',[89] whilst of a visit to Freddie's family home he wrote:

> At Freddie's this evening. Nancy was asked too, but didn't want to go. So I went alone. I had not visited there for some time. Molly was there, and Irene and the three children […] Looking around at the happy family group, peace and calm now restored and established, in which I was an old friend liked and welcomed, I saw in the hackneyed phrase, that we had reached harbour and without loss, with gain indeed, for we all knew the best and worst of each other, and had accepted both.[90]

This tender moment belies the complexity and frustration that dominates his depiction of his involvement with this family but also indicates the appeal of what in more romantic moments he saw as a 'genuine' family and home life – in contrast to what he felt his own to be. In this there are echoes of what the poet Stephen Spender, Ackerley's near contemporary, said of the attraction of his working-class guardsman lover Tony Hyndman: 'I was in love', he said, 'with his background, his soldiering, his working class home'.[91]

Though Ackerley cruised the streets and pubs incessantly, he yearned to have this kind of domestic life with his working-class lovers.[92] 'One wanted them in one's home', he wrote plaintively, seeing in an increasingly home orientated culture validation for relationships that took place there.[93] Before the war and his relationship with Freddie, Ackerley rented an apartment in Portsmouth for himself and Jack, his sailor boyfriend, so that they could more easily spend time together. 'Like any possessive housewife, I catered and cooked while he was at work, impatiently awaiting the moment of his return. One evening Jack said irritably, "What, chicken again!" It is the only speech he ever made that has stuck in my mind'.[94] It is this domestic put-down he remembered, alongside the highly gendered role he saw himself taking. This, though, was complex. Like Ives he was both 'housewife' and provider in this context. There was a fraught sense in which conventional gender roles and divisions of labour could not be deployed straightforwardly as class-inflected ideas of masculinity and masculine independence clashed with broader ideas about what a romantic, sexual and domestic partnership entailed. Ackerley took on the supposedly subservient role of housewife here; elsewhere and in other relationships he felt a martyred sense of being used by working-class lovers who did (he felt) whatever they wanted, visited when it suited them, and said what they liked. This tugged at the middle-class bachelor independence Ackerley coveted and also his sense of intellectual and educational superiority. He described Jack, remember, as an 'inarticulate, monkey-like boy', whilst Roger Ackerley – perhaps because he had himself been similarly patronised as a working-class guardsman – accepted Jack on his own terms. For Jack, on the other hand, there may have been a problematic sense of being 'kept', which, historian Matt Houlbrook suggests, 'could be experienced as effeminizing and emasculating'.[95] 'Middle-class expectations of intimacy, particularly their role as provider or "husband"', could, Houlbrook writes, contradict 'workingmen's understanding of manliness'.[96] There was for both a deep attachment to a sense of masculinity and at least an ambivalence about what was perceived to be feminine. This could come into sharp focus in the context of home.

Such dynamics were not fixed, however, and they played out in different ways at different times. In a touching description of his lovemaking with Jack, for example, Ackerley pays (putatively feminised) attention to cleanliness and potential embarrassment, but Jack 'readily accepts' the female role when they dance together:

> The red Lavender lozenges [for halitosis] had to be handy, a towel also, though hidden from him, to obviate the embarrassment of turning out naked, and to prevent, if possible, stains on the sheets as a speculation for my char. He liked dancing with me to the gramophone, readily accepting the female role, and often when I had ascertained that he too was in a state of erection we would strip and dance naked, so unbearably exciting that I could not long bear the pressure of his body against mine.[97]

We can certainly pull the relationship apart in class-based terms and via Ackerley' ungenerous commentary on the physicality of this and other working-class lovers (their smelly feet, their halitosis). But at such moments there was a tenderness, affection, passion and excitement which seemed to accommodate power dynamics and differing expectations. There is in the way Ackerley experienced and imagined Jack and Freddie, in the way he experienced and idealised their homes and families, and in the way he experienced and criticized his own, a record of the complex ways in which fantasies and realities of home, family, relational and erotic life intersected unevenly for him. He certainly conceptualized a queer life separate from his family, but neither he nor his lovers were able to enact and sustain that division – and nor perhaps did they ultimately want to.

* * *

There was not in this period (or after) a straightforward or uncomplicated intersection or separation of queer and family lives. Wilde's forced separation from his children tragically attests to this and there are multiple other accounts of the tensions and anxieties experienced by queer men in relation to family. What becomes clear, though, is that the experience and/or the rhetoric of family were crucial for Ives, Ackerley and others – not least in finding and conceptualising intimacy, love, commitment and responsibility. For Ives, family provided a link to the past, a sense of personal power, and accorded feelings of self-worth, social connection and endurance. Ives' masculinity, class status and, to an extent, his respectability were preserved not only by distancing himself from the 'silly [effeminate] inverts' he refers to dancing in the streets in Paris,[98] but also by having a family and domestic life. However eccentric in many ways, this family anchored him in convention. Ives thus negotiated the fine lines between conformity and idealism (the 'families we live by') on the one hand, and, on the other, practicality and the everyday (the 'families we live with').[99] Ackerley cared less about how he appeared – as his disarming revelations in his writing suggests. He was also considerably less sentimental about familial attachment and was more clearly embittered because of the pressure and demands they placed on him. He certainly fantasized about a separation of queer and family homes. But in the way he describes his genealogy, his desires, and the actual conduct of his love affairs, family was omnipresent – anchoring not so much his respectability and convention but his sense, for good or ill, of who he was. There was thus no clear inside and outside of family for Ives or Ackerley. Instead it braced and shaped their queer lives.

Epilogue

Peter McGraith was born in 1964 to a working class family in Lanarkshire, Scotland, three years before Ackerley's death and the partial decriminalization of homosexual acts in England and Wales. That legal change was not extended to Scotland until 1981, by which time Peter had come out to his family and was about to move to Glasgow where he worked as a freelance designer, journalist and activist. This period saw a new stridency, visibility, and sense of urgency amongst many gay men, which together with broader social and cultural changes, made for very different intersections of queer and family life than Ives and Ackerley had experienced. I'll return to these broader shifts and contexts in the final part of this book which focuses more squarely on the post-1970s period. Here I look at Peter's experiences of sustaining dual identities of 'gay man' and 'parent' after tracking the battle lines which formed in the 1970s and 1980s over their apparent disjunction: 'It seems', said Professor James Walters in an interview in *Family Coordinator* in 1978, that the term "gay father" is a contradiction'.[1] This apparent mismatch had of course been touted by late nineteenth century sexologists, but it was not the subject of broader debate until these post-liberationist years when gay fathers began to become more visible[2] – initially in relation to formerly married men who had come out and thereafter in relation to surrogacy, adoption and co-parenting arrangements. These 'new' families and the accompanying debate suggested possibilities to gay men like Peter even as they raised ire in others. In this controversy child welfare was not the only issue at stake. It was also and crucially about the broader positioning of gay men as insiders or outsiders to Britain's home and family oriented culture. For Ives and Ackerley queer and family lives intersected and were indeed indivisible and mutually constitutive. The same is true of Peter in the late 20th and early twenty-first century. But by this time there was a more sharply defined, politicized and in some ways polarized quality to the negotiation of family because of the ways in which issues relating to gay life were more clearly in the public realm – in political and (via social and adoption services) institutional discourse, in gay activism and lobbying, and in coverage in the media. Some echoes of Ives and Ackerley experience can thus be heard in Peter's testimony, but as we'll see in the first part of this epilogue there were also new imperatives and perhaps an even greater self-consciousness in play.

Gay dads?

In his review of *The Orton Diaries* in 1986, fellow playwright John Osborne brought together the contemporary furore surrounding the children's book *Jenny Lives with Eric and Martin* (1983) and Orton's murder at the hands of his partner Kenneth Halliwell almost 20 years earlier, to make an apparently obvious point.[3] Orton, he wrote, 'would have relished the solemn fakery of sodomite domesticity embodied in the spectacle of Jenny cuddling brain-soaked teddy between Ken and Joe's own prick-proud, severed body'.[4] Osborne keyed into the by now familiar story of the anti-domestic and anti-familial homosexual (and perhaps himself relished the iconoclasm). How could the 'prick proud' queer make a happy home and happy family?[5] The incongruence was underscored elsewhere. Gay fathers were parodied in the *Spectator* and *Private Eye* in the late 1970s and early 1980s,[6] and were the subject of court rulings and wider controversy. A drawn-out case between 1975 and 1977 began with a County Court ruling that a gay man should relinquish his parental rights and allow his son to be adopted by his ex-wife's new partner on the grounds that 'he had nothing to offer his son at any time in the future'. 'A reasonable man would say "I must protect my boy, even if it means parting from him forever so he can be free from danger" ', the judgement went on.[7] The ruling was overturned in 1976 in the Court of Appeal but the same suspicion ran through that decision.[8] The Appeal Court judge said he would have upheld the original decision if it was being proposed that the child was going to live with his father. In revising the ruling the father had to agree that the boy 'would not be subjected to homosexual influences'.[9] Eight months later the Law Lords reversed the Court of Appeal decision and allowed the adoption to proceed, decisively cutting the biological father out of the picture. Parts of the legal press branded the ruling 'ridiculous' and 'arrogant'.[10] But common sense in the final legal decision had in other quarters been seen to prevail and was rearticulated in the more frequent custody cases during the 1970s and 1980s involving lesbians who had previously been married.[11] 'Only when no other acceptable form of care is available should courts allow children to be brought up in a homosexual household', announced Lord Justice Watkins in his ruling on a case in 1981.[12] 'The best interests of the child' were then as now paramount in legal decisions – a not unreasonable but also culturally changeable index.[13] In the 1970s and 1980s it was the spectre of the pernicious homosexual home that was raised in assessing those interests, and even the sympathetic Professor Walters in his interview with gay dad Bruce Veoller in 1977 worried about the impact 'of so much gay exposure in a household'.[14]

Such households were, though, becoming ever more visible via the newspaper and magazine press. A feature piece in *Woman's World* in 1977, for example, focused on a formerly married man, Bill, who lived with his three children by that marriage, and his boyfriend Ross. The interview took place in the family home in Cambridge in 'a room tastefully decorated with antique furniture, Japanese prints, and oriental vases'. This taste lent Bill a certain respectability (even as it also marked him out as queer), especially as he also retained the masculine roles of breadwinner and dad; Ross was the 'substitute "mum"'. The piece worked the family into conventional roles and relationships in order to make it sympathetic. There had to be a 'mum' it seems, and younger stay-at-home Ross was the obvious candidate.[15]

The focus until this point had been on gay fathers who had been married,[16] but other paths to queer parenting began to gain more coverage in the 1980s. The press 'exposed' local councils which used gays and lesbians as foster parents (facilitated, ironically, by Conservative government reform in 1981 allowing single men to foster). Hackney hit the headlines for the permissive stance it took.[17] Bexley (1985) and Wandsworth (1991) banned such placements.[18] *The Sun* in 1992 reported an 'outcry' at the adoption of a disabled girl by a gay man who worked with handicapped children. 'A child', observed Tory MP Anthony Beaumont Dark in response, 'should be in a family relationship' – something two gay men could clearly not provide unless as fosterers of last resort.[19] A later opinion piece in the *Daily Telegraph* opposed gay and lesbian fostering because a 'homosexual household does not constitute normal surroundings for the upbringing of a child'.[20] As a number of papers reported, there was Tory 'fury' that the 1993 proposal for adoption reform and the ensuing legislation failed to close the 'loophole' which allowed single gay men to adopt.[21]

There was by now a small but growing literature on gay parenting (chiefly coming from the States)[22] and the *Pink Paper* was regularly carrying wanted ads for gay sperm donors and for surrogates. The 1996 film *Hollow Reed* gave a sympathetic portrayal of a gay father in his battle for custody of his son with his estranged wife and her abusive new partner. The film's message was clear (if somewhat didactic), and was echoed in a trio of cases in Scotland in the same year which highlighted different modes of gay parenting and support for each. The national press coverage in May 1996 of a Scottish gay couple who shared the care of their toddler son with his two mothers revealed local support and indifference. The gay dads were said to be good neighbours (a key index of acceptability); the child happy, well dressed and cared for; and social services were not interested in intervening saying it would be an invasion of privacy.[23] A *Scotland on Sunday* feature piece reflected critically on the scandalized press response.[24] Three months later, in July, the Court of Session in Edinburgh approved the adoption of a disabled boy by a male nurse who lived with his male partner. There was, the ruling insisted, nothing to stop a single person adopting, whatever his or her sexual orientation and irrespective of a relationship with a third party.[25] Finally, in August, came more widespread coverage for an Edinburgh gay couple who had a surrogacy arrangement with an American woman. Alongside Conservative and Church of Scotland outrage and concern (as in each of the other cases), the papers cited support for this 'inseparable', 'stable', 'responsible' couple. Though social services were going to check the legal status of the child, they would, they said, only intervene if there was a lack of care.[26] Family lawyer Gill Knight in the *Observer's* coverage of the case noted that gay men 'are in a similar position to lesbian mums in the early 1980s. There are only a handful of custody cases, but a growing number of men are trying to gain access'.[27] Many now saw that being gay and being a parent were not incompatible.

Gay men who had fathered children were by now in a stronger position legally. The 1959 Legitimacy Act had allowed 'putative [that is unmarried] fathers' to apply for access and custody rights. Thirty years later the Children Act (1989) enabled unmarried men to apply for parental responsibility and to be awarded it if the mother agreed.[28] These measures unintentionally opened up the possibility for unmarried gay men to take a legally endorsed role in parenting children they had fathered whether through sexual relationships or artificial insemination arrangements with the mother.[29] The Children Act ironically came just a year after Section 28 of the Local Government Act poured scorn on such 'pretended' families.[30] In 2002 joint and step adoption by gay couples was permitted and it was not anymore so unusual for a gay male household to include children for all or some of the time.[31]

This sense of possibility for gay men in terms of parenting emerged in a period marked by a broader loosening of attitudes. In post-Thatcherite and neo-liberal times there was a re-emphasis on the individual and the idea of self-determination in many areas of life – from the economic and professional to the domestic, relational, and sexual.[32] Bonds and a sense of responsibility to friends and relatives certainly remained,[33] but family forms diversified once more after a narrowing in the inter and post war years.[34] They now commonly included a range of roles and relationships including step-sibling and parents, half-sibling, and closely involved friends.[35] The nuclear-family ideal remained 'embedded in aspiration as well as in reality',[36] but people increasingly felt they had the right and ability to make these active choices about the way they constituted and conducted their home and family lives. The ability to make those choices was and remains highly contingent, but a key area in which the concept of choice was frequently deployed was in relation to reproduction – especially following the introduction of the pill in 1960 and the partial legalization of abortion in 1967.[37] This was allied to the easing of the connection between sex and reproduction and between marriage and parenthood – culturally, in legislation,[38] and because of scientific advances in artificial insemination.[39] Though the associations between these things were still strong and idealized, the opening out of previously tightly bound ideas and protocols cleaved space for gay men to consider and explore the possibilities for having children alone, with male partners and in arrangements with other co-parents. If such parenting alternatives were not celebrated and championed, they were often in the 2000s greeted with a live-and-let-live indifference and pragmatism.[40] This relates to the rise of a generation into professional life and positions of public influence (not least the media) who had grown up in a post-Gay and Women's Liberation context and amidst the debates they generated. The arguments being put forward by Stonewall (from 1989) and other lobbying and campaigning groups had come to be seen by many as more obvious than outlandish – partly because these arguments were often now being framed by ideas of privacy and equality rather than an overtly politicised difference or sexual and social revolution (though Outrage and the Lesbian Avengers continued to battle along these latter lines). While there was certainly stiff resistance to legislation on adoption (2002), to the repeal of Section 28 (2003), and to Civil Partnerships (2004), there was sufficient support for them to pass through parliament and without a huge backlash. The panic around AIDS had by this time receded (especially following the introduction of anti-retroviral therapy in 1996) and gay men – increasingly visible in a range of public contexts, on TV and in the media, in the workplace, and as neighbours, family and friends – seemed less of a threat and more a part of everyday life.

Many families were still often uncomfortable, outraged or ashamed by the sexuality of their sons or brothers, and unsure how to deal with their roles as uncles let alone parents. Many gay men still did not feel able to come out to some people even if they wanted to, and most experienced some form of homophobia. A British Social Attitudes Survey of 2008 showed 32 per cent believed homosexuality was always or mostly wrong and 40 per cent did not think that gay couples 'made suitable parents'.[41] This was clearly no panacea. Moreover, in my survey of newspaper coverage of gay parents since the 1970s, the men profiled were exclusively white, apparently middle class and largely either nurses or in white-collar jobs. The developing framework for thinking about gay parenting and gay families was relatively narrow, with an arguable loss of some of the sense of possibility around home and family that circulated amongst early 1970s radicals.[42]

On whatever terms, though, something had changed. A piece by journalist Rupert Haselden in the *Guardian* in 1991 echoed sexologist Iwan Bloch's pronouncements of almost a century earlier in announcing that gay men were 'the end of the line': 'there is an inbuilt fatalism to being gay. Biologically maladaptive, unable to reproduce, our futures are limited to individual existence and what the individual makes of it. Without the continuity of children we are self-destructive, living for today because we have no tomorrow'.[43] That sense of 'no tomorrow' was devastatingly acute for many gay men in the context of the AIDS crisis, not least because the way it was being described nihilistically in the media and elsewhere. Children are not, of course, the only way of having a sense of the future. But it is nevertheless telling that just a decade later the same paper was featuring regular coverage of gay families. Historian Deborah Cohen writes that 'of all the changes in the watershed decades of the 1960s and 1970s, it was perhaps this widening definition of family that was most unanticipated and has been most durable'.[44]

Queer theorists Donna Penn and Lee Edelman have emphasised what they see as conformism and accession to a neo-liberal 'homonormative agenda' in these shifts. Penn suggests that this was a politics 'that does not contest dominant heteronormative assumptions and institutions but upholds and sustains them while promising the possibility of a demobilized gay constituency and a privatized, depoliticized gay culture anchored in domesticity and consumption'.[45] In his 2004 polemic *No Future*, Edelman argues that the all-pervasive figure of the child in Western culture represents a 'reproductive futurity' from which queers have been systematically excluded.[46] This is an exclusion which, he suggests, they should grasp. Though apparently a capitulation to cultural positioning, such a refusal of the future and a celebratory embrace of the present, of playfulness and also of the death drive could, Edelman argues, be politically radical and particularly queer – a defiant rejection of heteronormativity. I echo some of Edelman's analysis: I showed in the introduction to this part of the book how queer men were often seen to be a dead end and that heterosexual reproduction was much touted as the means to social, cultural and spiritual advance. Penn certainly has a point in her critique of the direction or apparent faltering of a radical politics surrounding queer sexuality, and crucially she underscores links between consumption, sexuality and politics which were highlighted vociferously in the early 1970s and have often been glossed over more recently. Both suggest some of the new conditions for political inclusion and the exclusions those might bring about. Their arguments are important politically but are made in a different vein to mine. They have little purchase on the way the men I'm discussing in this book thought through and lived out their home and family lives. The association of the private, the domestic and the familial with the apolitical is moreover a common and casual connection which ignores the complexity of people's everyday and home lives. These can include multiple and contradictory investments in politics and ways of being which can be radical and reactionary by turn. There has not been a clear divide between family and non-family for men who identified as inverted, homosexual, gay or queer, and the testimonies I've examined suggest an uneven investment, rejection and indifference to prevailing norms, expectations and representations. If civil partnership, gay adoption and now gay marriage might seem to some to be about taking 'a place at the table',[47] to others they represent opportunities to expand the meanings of marriage and to shift debate on (good) parenting.[48] For many the two are inextricably entwined. Difference – and sometimes a radical sense of difference – has often been unevenly twisted with an ordinariness and conformity in behaviours, expectations and desires.

Peter

Peter McGraith gives a potent sense of this complexity. He carries an acute sense of gay difference which relates to metropolitan gay life, to his gay and AIDS activism in the late 1980s and 1990s, to his commitment to a rights agenda, and to his careful thinking about gender role playing within families. What became clear in my interview with him and in his written comments on one of my early drafts was his felt need to preserve that sense of difference as he became a parent and as he experienced shifts in his relationship with his family of origin.[49]

Peter straightaway stressed the significance of his Scottish, working-class upbringing. He described the determination of his grandmother to keep – rather than offer up for adoption – her illegitimate daughter (Peter's mother), and also the independence he was given and expected to take during his childhood. He noted his 'early passions for Latin American ballroom dancing, for drawing, for gardening, fashion' and for 'the ritual of family celebrations' – things his parents and grandparents encouraged him in and which he in retrospect sees prefiguring his gay identification. 'I think some of it was [...] traditional old Irish stuff passed down, but it was also a gay sensibility towards it all'. In Glasgow from the early 1980s life, work and politics were closely connected for him. 'They were and are the same things for me' and the connections were made easy because of 'the small world that was Glasgow'. Such connections took longer to make in London, where he moved to be with his current partner. His life became 'very quiet and domesticated' until they bought and restyled a flat near Regents Park and began entertaining there. His work on that flat was, he says, more about 'self expression than fashion'. It was, he wrote, 'almost an expansion of our desirability as a couple'. Desire, sex and interior design were in this way bound together in the way Peter thought about home. Wrapped up in this was the expressive individuality and sense of difference valued by Shannon and Ricketts, Ashbee, Ford and Bartlett whom we met in Part I. Peter and his partner's 'very central, very sexy bachelor pad' was in this way not just somewhere to live but was part of who he and they were professionally, personally and sexually.

To facilitate their adoption application in 2005 (which was when the 2002 adoption reforms in respect of gay and lesbian parents were being implemented) they moved to a three-bedroom flat in Holloway which they reorganised and restyled. They were keen still to live in central London in addition to having children, and this Peter associated explicitly with holding on to his, their, gay sensibility and lifestyle. 'We weren't giving up being ourselves, and we were never the kind of gay men that wanted to live in [...] some far flung suburb with a caravan and a people mover, [...] – all of the paraphernalia that people like around family life'. Peter and his partner were determined to have a home which spoke to their queerness *and* their new parenthood.

> I think for me having the kids in a place that reflected my ideas about style was important. I mean I did want the kids to feel instantly that their new home was theirs, but that shouldn't be about shoving Sponge Bob Square [Pants … or] Bob the Builder mobiles in your face every corner you turn.

The children, he says, 'weren't made to feel like they were living in some sort of show home […] but the integrity of the actual interior under the surface layer of kiddie stuff was still intact'. What Peter described was building into the fabric of the new family home a sense of continuity from the time before he was a parent. What we might observe too is the continuity with a number of my other case studies in making interiors that were individualized and could speak of sexual difference and of a gendered identity. They refurbished their new home to be 'a stylish pad, and it was very grown up and it was very masculine' – something which meant for Peter 'the material that you use, and the finish that you achieve, the colours and the textures' and an emphasis on 'space' over 'possessions'. It was not 'feminine', he said – a quality it was yet difficult for him to pin down. The sense of masculinity and femininity in relation to style was, is, entrenched and has become so apparently obvious that it is difficult for Peter – and us all – to unpick.[50] Later he wrote that the main material elements of his interior designs 'came from those old heavy industries that were staffed almost exclusively by men and were imbued with masculinity'.[51] In this he harks back to production and producer in the look, feel and associations of the home in ways that are resonant with Charles Ashbee.[52] They tacitly draw in a homoeroticism associated with craftsmen and here heavy manual labour. This look was, Peter says, embedded, robust and child friendly: it could relate both to what he saw as his gay sensibility and the practicalities of having children.

The couple continued with their mealtime rituals after the children arrived in 2007 – 'a continuity that was partly to do with our families and partly to do with a gay sensibility I would say'. Peter highlights here and elsewhere how his new family life was shaped from these two directions. 'I liked the idea of [my partner] knowing my big Scottish family. That sort of laid the way for us [… to] mov[e] forward to adopt because part of what I liked about the idea of having kids was that I could be part of my family in a different way'. They had played a different role as childless, gay, metropolitan uncles who brought 'a little bit of gay London magic' to their nieces and nephews. This position shifted somewhat once they became parents and brought new cousins into the mix. With their own children, meanwhile, they necessarily behaved differently because of the additional responsibilities that were involved. Peter describes quite self-consciously navigating this shifting terrain whilst observing a consistency in his 'gay life and family'. The change for Peter was in their way of being with their families of origin and in an expansion of their friendship circle to include other, especially female, parents.

The sense of difference deriving from his gay family and their 'typical metropolitan sex lives' was something Peter felt they had to play down in the adoption process itself. 'We could really have ruined our chances of adopting by shocking some people whose sensibilities and whose experiences and attitudes to sexual emancipation are quite different from mine.' 'We weren't asked', he said, 'and we didn't offer any frightening information'. 'We were playing the system and felt that we were expected to in a way'. Though Peter felt their open relationship or a majority gay and lesbian support network shouldn't weigh against them, he also felt it would. It is important to him that the adoption and fostering systems understand that 'we aren't necessarily just like heterosexuals' and that these can be 'very positive attributes'. In this, visibility is important. He is, he says, 'against using this buzz word phrase "same sex adoption", "same sex parenting", "same sex" is a loss of visibility and a loss of power politically. [...] It's important to be able to say she is a lesbian, she's not a same-sex anything'.

Peter identifies a distinctiveness too in the way he sees gay men modelling ongoing relationships with former lovers and boyfriends and so 'doing' intimate life, friendship and 'families of choice' somewhat differently from the perceived 'norm' – and in ways which, he suggests, could be positive for children to observe. His experience of gay networks in Glasgow and London have been key to this, as are his gender politics and his commitment to challenging gender role playing at home. 'I don't even like to talk about fathers and mothers too much because a mother is a female parent, a father a male parent. It's not a different job [...] and if you happen to have two parents or more parents then those parents divide the jobs amongst them':

> People kind of have this expectation that if you deviate from the norm of having one mother parent and one father parent that there's something lacking, or that you should be trying to replicate that, or

that there is something special about mothering or fathering that is related to men and women specifically.

In this sense Peter feels he and his partner 'are a bit freer to do what we as individuals feel'. This understanding of parenting roles might allow space for them as two male parents but it is also undercut by broader expectations Peter encounters about fathers being inept and somewhat clueless. He is resistant to such gendered presumptions even as he deploys gendered ideas about style in the way he describes his flat. The respective insignificance and significance of gender as he sees it in these contexts is yet in both cases about marking out a queer difference.

* * *

Peter describes an aesthetics and politics of difference in the way he has constituted home, partnership and family, and strongly refutes the idea of assimilationism. This stridency on the home front arises in part out of the post liberationist, AIDS and Section 28 politics in which he was and is involved and relates as well to the broader changes in family form discussed earlier. It is also, though, about other aspects of his life and experience. These include his personal, sexual and professional history and status, his metropolitan and gay life and lifestyle, his sense of what might constitute a gay sensibility, his class and his Scottishness – which speaks to him of independence, of making it by himself, of a certain authenticity and lack of pretension. This weaving together of multiple scripts, ideas and practical imperatives in the way he conceives of his families – his immediate family and household, his family of origin, his gay family – resonates with the complex processes we saw with Ives and Ackerley earlier in the century. Ives shared Peter's desire for children, and also had to think hard about the decision to have them outside of the heterosexual matrix, for example. However, Ives and Ackerley expected homosexual and heterosexual desire, love and affairs to overlap for themselves (as we saw with Ives) and/or for their lovers in ways which brought family lives together with queer lives in *ad hoc* and pragmatic ways. For Peter and his generation there were still such overlaps but there was by now and in general a more distinct separation of gay from straight. This often made for more self-conscious, rationalized and politicized negotiations of queer and family lives, bringing into focus wider changes in conceptions and experiences of family across the twentieth century.

Part III
Outsiders Inside: Finding Room in the City

Introduction

So far I have looked at the home lives in London of some relatively privileged men and told their stories in relation to domestic aesthetics and families. As I have done that I have touched fleetingly on the lives of other men too – Simeon Solomon, Charles Ashbee's boyfriend Chris Robson, Joe Ackerley's lover Freddie, and Oliver Ford's guardsman renters. These men had fewer resources and had to make a home in London more contingently and under different pressures. In this part of the book I shift focus to look squarely at men who came to the city with little or no money and describe how they made home, experienced family, and shaped their sense of themselves as men and as queer men in more straightened circumstances. More specifically I explore the early adulthood in the 1950s and 1960s of drama student turned teacher Rex Batten (b.1938), office worker Alan Louis (1932–2011), musician and photographer Carl Marshall (1938–2010), and playwright Joe Orton (1933–1967). I thus look at a narrower period than the previous parts of the book in order to discern the impact of the intensifying post-1945 debates about home, family and homosexuality which I have touched on already and which I discuss in more detail in the first part of this introduction.

The focus on this period and on young men who moved to London from elsewhere brings further perspectives on the queer draw of the capital. That move was a pivot in each of the life stories I discuss here: London was the 'home' where they could be themselves. I explore how the four men differentiated between homes within and beyond the city, and so also between the homes of their adulthood and homes of their youth. In different ways, they shuttle in their testimonies between these places and times. They reveal some of the pragmatics of finding and sustaining somewhere to live, the dangers and possibilities associated with bedsit living, and the mobility and contingency of home for poorer queer men especially – something I discuss more broadly in the second part of this introduction. 'Home' or rather 'being at home' did not necessarily mean where these men slept. Bars, other peoples' homes, even churches and cinemas might have been easier places to retreat to and relax in for men who found little privacy in the rooms where they lived.

Home and homosexuality in the 1950s

The 1950s were rhetorically, symbolically and practically 'unprecedentedly home-centred'.[1] The interwar period had seen a growth in suburban housing, in the availability of domestic consumer products, and in magazines flagging the significance and virtues of the English family home.[2] All this chiefly benefited and reached the middle classes, however, and the broadening out of the fantasy (if not the reality) of the ideal home was most marked after the war. A greater proportion of people married then than in the previous half-century. In 1951 three quarters of men between the ages 25 and 34 were married compared to only just over half in 1921.[3] Marriage as an institution and home as a material place and as an ideal represented what could go right for the nation after the crisis and dislocation of war and the disruption wrought by war-time evacuation, mobilisation and rehousing.[4] After the war, home suggested a space of safety. The interior designer Ronald Fleming said in a lecture of 1949: 'more than ever today the Englishman's home is his refuge and comfort from the bitter winds of a cruel world'.[5] If the domestic and associated familial ideal remained way out of reach for most Londoners (not least because of destruction in the blitz), it was still widely touted in novels, films, media, popular psychology, and through the words of politicians, lawyers, medics and more.[6] The new welfare state was based on presumptions about the tight form and functioning of the nuclear-family unit, further ingraining it as the obvious and ideal basis for domestic life.[7] The 'biggest improvement in the material standard of living in Britain since the middle ages', allowed many more to buy for – and indeed to buy – their own homes.[8] The growing availability of private domestic space saw a retreat from the streets as places of socialization, courtship and sex.[9] Home and family were moreover rhetorical tools in attempts to counter 'war-time morality' and to shore up the institution of the family in the face of a rising divorce rate.[10] Not for the first time,[11] but more pervasively and intensely than before, the home became emblematic of – and instrumental in – the project of national renewal and the cultivation of a putatively shared set of values.[12]

These values were illuminated in part through a fresh focus on those who did not fit in. Deviating from the trumpeted models of home and family was 'not merely a matter of personal failing but a very public symptom of bad citizenship and lax patriotism'.[13] Those without a home, those who didn't take care of it, or who took care of it a little too frivolously, boded ill. In these respects the homosexual was conjured with renewed paranoia in the newspaper press especially. While home and family were figured as intrinsic to a civilised, modern and forward-looking culture (and also as protection against its exigencies), the homosexual in this coverage threatened these things.[14] Rex Batten wrote that for his first lover Ashley 'the heady years of his teens [in the interwar years] when anything went [...] had given way to something very different [in the 1950s]. It was called normality, and that was returning with a vengeance [...] His ilk had no place in the new planned economy racing headlong to Utopia'.[15] No wonder that homosexual public sex and socialization were more comprehensively attacked and aggressively policed than ever before.[16] No wonder either that the 1957 Wolfenden Committee recommendations for the partial decriminalisation of homosexual acts – and the legislation that at length followed in 1967 – related only to men who had sex together in private and as a pair. The homosexual was rendered acceptable to the degree he might mimic imagined 'normal', 'respectable', and implicitly middle-class domestic lives.[17]

This imagined intersection of the (respectable) homosexual with (idealized) 'normal' lives was predictably problematic. Apart from anything else those supposedly 'normal' lives were very variable indeed. Although marriage had become 'nearly universal' and families 'more homogenous' (most obviously in terms of their size),[18] many 'normal' men and women in the 1950s felt alienated and crushed by the sense that they didn't measure up either.[19] Historians have given an account of the low levels of home ownership, of the chronic housing shortage, of the shared and cramped conditions many people lived in, of the mundanity of everyday domestic life, and of the extent to which 'divorce rather than death became the great disrupter of marriage'.[20] Though almost a million homes were built nationally between 1945 and 1951, at least that number were needed in the capital alone (and an estimated three to four million in the UK as a whole) to fulfil the government's stated aim of a separate home for each family.[21] If people clearly paid attention to domestic fashion, to home and family, and to what these could signify, relatively few were in a position to do very much about their own living conditions or about who exactly they lived alongside. It was thus in the interstices between a set of cultural fantasies and ideals on the one hand and material realities and pragmatic circumstances on the other that people muddled through in the everyday with varying degrees of resentment, shame, anger, fun, and love. And muddling through amongst them were homosexuals and queer men. Far from 'stand[ing] apart' as one contemporary commentator had it,[22] these men lived alongside other 'normal' men and women who had similar and also rather different troubles and joys. They had to negotiate the practicalities of finding somewhere to live, sustaining a home in the context of illegality, and also navigating consciously and less consciously those potent cultural fantasies of what home and also homosexuality meant.

Michael Schofield's 1960 survey of 127 men (two thirds of whom lived in London), if hardly representative, gives some sense of the diversity in living arrangements for queer men. It suggested continuing involvement in family and the extent to which an independent home was out of reach for most in his group of (largely middle-class) respondents. Seventeen per cent lived in the parental home; 3 per cent with wives; 1 per cent in hostels; 11 per cent in their own property; 29 per cent in rented accommodation with an absent landlord/lady; and 36 per cent in rented premises where the landlord/lady lived. Of that same group 36 per cent lived on their own; 24 per cent lived with their own or their landlord/lady's family; 7 per cent shared with heterosexual men; and 32 per cent shared with other homosexuals (though it is not clear from Schofield's analysis whether these 'other homosexuals' were friends or boyfriends).[23] It was unlikely in this period that a pick-up would be able to take you home; more unlikely still that a man might have the resources to live just with a boyfriend in a jointly owned home. Even for those among that latter minority there was a felt need for particular discretion in this period because of the increased focus on the 'problem of homosexuality',[24] broader knowledge about the existence and supposed threat of the homosexual, and a rising prosecution rate. Such men also remained absent from the official record (unless they were caught out and arrested). While under census definitions a married couple without children constituted a 'family' and the place where they lived a 'family home', there was (unsurprisingly) no such designation for a homosexual couple.[25] Homosexuals seemed to be out in the cold. This was not a new position for queer men as we've seen, but in the 1950s the homosexual was depicted functioning more determinedly outside and in opposition to supposed norms of the home and family. This was the case even though there was frequently a degree of localised acceptance and support as well as some fluidity. 'Normal' men like Freddie (whom we met in the last chapter) also took male lovers, for example. Such men had a fine line to tread if they were still to assert their masculinity and heterosexuality, however. They should be invested in the home, family and what they both represented, be a participant in the growing trend for do-it-yourself as a brand of manly home-making, yet also display a disdain or charming incapacity for day-to-day childcare, housework, and the details of domestic furnishings and décor. My mother was taken aside by a neighbour in the late 1950s on account of allowing my father to hang the nappies out to dry. As homes became ever more tightly bound to ideas of subjectivity and identity for more of the population, and as the 'cult of the domestic' became less elite and more generalized after the war, so growing numbers of people became attuned to signs of conformity and deviance therein. 'People are very aware of homosexuality nowadays', wrote Schofield, 'and any bachelor with a nice flat is suspect'.[26]

The professional, discreet and domestically conventional protagonists in reformist film and fiction of the 1950s and 1960s were often rewarded ultimately with stable companionship.[27] In this work feverish, uncertain and dangerous passions were left outside and the home secured a more or less compromised but safer future. Schofield's sociological case study of a middle-class homosexual couple in their 30s captured something similar:

> Case XVIII. D is a successful businessman who lives with H, the editor of a trade paper. Both are in their early thirties and except in working hours, they are seldom apart. They both earn good salaries and they live in an expensive flat. It is furnished in excellent taste and they are extremely proud of their home and lavish attention on it like young newlyweds. There is a certain amount of physical love between them but the most striking thing about them is their complete emotional harmony and the way they rejoice in each others' company. The editor described the sexual side of their love affair as 'unimportant'. Both of them have masculine physiques and neither of them take, or want to take, the part of the passive partner. They occasionally visit one of the London clubs together, but most evenings they are content to stay at home or entertain friends. Although they are careful to keep their relationship secret from their business associates, they have a number of heterosexual friends.[28]

Here, in the early 1950s and just prior to the escalation of anti-homosexual rhetoric, Schofield sets the scene for normalisation.

He notes the 'attention' H and D 'lavish' on their home (rather as you might on a child), and uses the couple's home-centredness to mark out their equivalence to 'young newlyweds'. Their openness to visitors at home, their good taste, their domestic compatibility, their restrained passions and refusal of the feminised 'passive role', and their professional and class status are all also part of Schofield's attempt to squeeze them into the mould of normal middle-class masculinity. This was perhaps partly self-justification too. Schofield, from a middle class family in Leeds, identified as homosexual himself. In the year this book – *Society and Homosexual* (1952) – came out he met the partner (Anthony Sykrme) with whom he lived for the rest of his life. Schofield's case study couple neatly capture the mode of homosexuality which those beginning to press for reform felt might gain some cultural approval.[29]

Not so the 'effeminate', 'isolationist' homosexuals charted in 1948 by the *Mass Observation Survey*;[30] the criminal, sexually 'twisted' 'aimless young men' described by Gillian Freeman in her fictional exploration of London's 'youth culture' (*The Leather Boys* [1961]);[31] and the homosexual, to return to Schofield, who entered queer culture at 'the queer bar level', and who 'will [...] have to be able to hold his own in a vicious, jealous, back-biting society where no affair is sacred and every effort will be made to hinder his search for happiness'.[32] There were too the press reports of dangerous criminal types preying on such men. A retired army captain 'became terrified at the sound of a ringing telephone bell' and moved address several times after blackmail threats he received in 1955 and 1956.[33] The blackmailer – a Trinidadian immigrant Kelvin Randon – 'always found him' and 'bled' him of nearly £9000. Another case in 1955 – the year which saw the most arrests and prosecutions for homosexual offences – involved a doctor being phoned repeatedly with demands for cash, while a company director in 1957 was door-stepped for money by a former boxer he had earlier picked up in Soho.[34] Each story replayed ideas about the erotics and dangers of working class and now also Afro-Caribbean men. In these reports, as in the film *Victim* (1961) and Garland's novel *The Heart in Exile* (1953), such men crossed over dangerously into or were at least seen to threaten the middle-class home. They highlighted again the apparently porous divide between public and private space for queer men – something which seemed especially troubling in a period when there was such a premium on having a separate and secure home.

If the homosexual was sometimes imagined partially redeeming himself through a conventional middle-class home and family life, at others he was presented as inimical to the domestic sphere and so also to what it represented. The cultural centrality of home in terms of individual and national identity was reaffirmed on both counts, leaving queer men to negotiate for themselves (and more self-consciously than most) quite how they were to relate to it.

Making home in London

The growing literature on homosexuality in the postwar period almost invariably focussed on the capital, feeding existing perceptions of a city which drew in queer men and also formed and shaped them.[35] It was the 'obvious' home for homosexuals who did not fit into 'normal' homes and families. Such families were conversely often imagined outside the centre of the chaotic metropolis – in its suburbs or the provinces. Schofield notes that while half of the capital's population came from elsewhere, three quarters of his homosexual interviewees were provincial exiles. 'Two homosexuals living together in a small village or even a small town would almost certainly be a subject for gossip', he wrote. Yet, he went on: 'two living together are less noticeable among the millions of Londoners'.[36]

There were, he went on, places in the capital where it was especially possible for homosexuals to feel at home. I noted the reputation of Chelsea, Maida Vale, and Little Venice in earlier chapters; in the postwar period we can add Earl's Court and Notting Hill. 'I expect you know there is a huge homosexual kingdom just below the surface of ordinary life, with its own morals and codes of behaviour', one of Schofield's interviewees observed. 'In Notting Hill Gate this kingdom within a kingdom seems to have come to the surface. That's why I live there. [...] When I walk through Notting Hill Gate I feel I'm at a gigantic homosexual party'.[37] The ease this man felt here – which Alan Louis experienced too – relates in part to the area's broader countercultural reputation associated especially with Afro-Caribbean immigration in the 1950s.[38] A sense of home in the city could be as much about an area which felt safe, permissive and accommodating as about a particular flat, room or house.[39]

In Notting Hill as in other areas of inner London like Paddington, Islington, Pimlico and St Pancras, Victorian and Edwardian terraced housing had been divided and subdivided into flats and bedsits as middle-class residents increasingly moved to the new more spacious suburbs roughly from the 1930s onwards. The exodus might appear to alleviate the capital's housing crisis, but housing in central London remained very poor and overcrowded just at the moment when expectations of living standards were rising.[40] Men and women newly arrived in the capital from other parts of the UK or abroad, those who didn't have the resources to live elsewhere, and those working anti social hours who needed to live near their work places crowded into central boarding houses and bedsits.[41] These areas were characterised by a high ratio of non-Londoners to Londoners (somewhere around 50 per cent) and by large numbers of people working in poorly paid jobs in the city's hotels and restaurants.[42]

Multiple occupancy was hardly unique to central London, but it was particularly common there.[43] This type of housing – and bedsits in particular – suggested a rupture from family, a state of moral uncertainty, and proximity to the pleasures and dangers of the city.[44] In 'kitchen sink' literature, drama and film,[45] the mid-sixties' sitcom *Bedsitter Girl*, and in social exploration and 'how to' type guides,[46] bedsits were associated – with singleness, loneliness and solitude and simultaneously with a lack of privacy and constant intrusion. Tenants usually shared bathrooms and toilets and were often only separated from others by thin plasterboard. This could lead to conflict and/or close friendships between apparently very disconnected individuals.[47]

Press reports underscored the dangers associated with bedsitter areas. In 1962 news broke of the murder of two men 'who lived in the twilight world of the homosexual and [...] died in the garrotter's noose'.[48] The *News of the World* salaciously re-imagined the murder scenes in Notting Hill and Pimlico, and the lives of the two victims. Norman Rickard was 38, 'a muscle man with a background of Civil Service respectability. [Alan] Vigar was 23, a slim pretty boy with a weak chest and theatrical ambitions'. They were, the report went on, 'both bachelors; they lived alone; they were both apparently people who minded their own business, and they shunned women. They both entertained men friends in their room'.[49] Vigar's clothes were folded away and 'his room was almost too neat – like Rickard's'. The *News of the World* slotted the men into an urban queer typology: the weak, effeminate ('pretty') theatrical type, and the man with a double life (civil servant by day, kitted out in 'tight blue faded jeans, a cowboy plaid shirt, cowboy buckled boots and an epaulletted leather jacket' by night).[50] What connected them was that tell-tale neatness and their residence in liminal bedsitterland which seemed almost to incite such crime. The newspaper noted that Rickard was murdered in his basement flat 'where the carpet is blood red'.[51] A week later the *Sunday Pictorial* carried a front page story of a man who 'escape[d] the wardrobe killer' (as the murderer was known: the bodies of Rickard and Vigar had been bundled into their respective wardrobes).

Patrick Lambert (pictured anxiously clutching a telephone) had taken a man home before being attacked. The paper doesn't label him homosexual but three paragraphs in some seeds were sown: he was 'a bachelor' who lived 'in a part-furnished bed-sitting room' and 'work[ed] at a local restaurant'.[52]

The men discussed in the coming chapters remember often insecure and *ad hoc* living arrangements in central London in this period. Cheap accommodation was scarce – a situation exacerbated by the removal of rent controls from some 800,000 houses under the Rent Act of 1957.[53] In my interviews several men nevertheless recall finding places fairly easily – through lovers, word of mouth, friends, or adverts in shop windows. Queer black men had difficulty more because of their colour than their desires: 85 per cent of landladies in 1952 said they would not let a room to students who were 'very dark Africans or West Indians'. Alan Louis, we'll see, had to leave one bedsit because his landlady could not tolerate his black boyfriend.[54] He, Rex Batten and Carl Marshall generally found a live-and-let-live attitude amongst tenants and landladies, however, and others found queer men to share with and to rent from.[55]

Overcrowded central London rooming districts stood in sharp contrast to the new suburbs built between the wars and consolidated in postwar developments. One commentator wrote in 1946 that 'the suburban environment determines the style in which – for good or ill – England lives'.[56] Whatever the realities of life in these areas,[57] the suburbs and the specific design of much of their new housing seemed directly to reflect and entrench prevailing ideals about normative and nominally middle-class home and families. They were associated with 'privacy, status, pride in ownership, and a fear of being left behind (literally) by the tide of fashion'.[58] Such developments pushed out the edges of London so that between 1931 and 1961 the area covered by the city doubled in size even as its population fell slightly. Outer London and the eight satellite new towns provided better housing than many working-class inner Londoners had had access to before, and there was 'a huge migration' from 'slum-ridden or blitzed' inner areas of a city that looked 'broken, drab, patched, tired out and essentially Victorian still'.[59] Thus while the population of inner London shrank by over a million between 1931 and 1961 (from 4.4 million to 3.2 million), the population of greater London fell only marginally in the same period (from 8.1 million to 7.99 million). Suburban housing clearly demarcated one family unit from the next and if suburbia was much parodied, it also represented postwar domestic ideals and aspirations in ways that the bedsitters of central London decidedly did not.[60]

The differences between housing in inner and outer London were of course not absolute: suburban houses were not only lived in by families. Single people, house sharers and lodgers often lived in them too, some of them of course queer – Joe Ackerley, for one, lived outside central London in Putney. Families, meanwhile, still lived in central London – not least in the developing though still insufficient stock of council housing. Some bedsits might be sound-proofed and self-contained and with that commodity much sought after by queer men: direct access from the street.[61] Bedsit accommodation could also be stable and enduring: Quentin Crisp lived in his bedsit in Chelsea Square for 40 years before his move to New York in 1981.[62]

There was nevertheless a conceptual divide between inner and suburban London which several of the men discussed in this book replay.[63] Central London bedsitter living did not in fact separate queer men out as contemporary commentators on the 'homosexual problem' suggested, but such (inadequate) homes certainly represented outsider status and existence on the cultural periphery of a society that was looking ahead to better things and to better, more spacious living conditions.[64] The heady mix of queer urban life, immigration, juvenile crime, and youth cultures threatened what a suburban home and companionate marriage seemed to promise.[65] London's bedsitterland did not fit the culturally restorative and modernizing agenda, though I argue in this part of the book that it did cleave some home space for men like Rex, Carl, Alan, and Joe Orton. I discuss Rex, Carl and Alan in Chapter 5 via their memories of this time, showing how postwar experience shaped their lives and conceptions of home in the period since. I look at Orton separately in Chapter 6. This is partly because my discussion of him is more focused on the 1960s, but also because his testimony is not reminiscence but a diary written at the time. In this way Orton gives a different sort of access to the postwar years.

A study from the 1950s found that inner London areas had the highest rates of suicide in the capital and were characterized by social dislocation, loneliness, and anonymity.[66] In what follows I show that these were not the only ways in which these places were experienced. Sex, relationships, friendships, and community were also a part of bedsitter living – and in ways that were personally and socially formative. London more broadly provided a place for my queer case studies to find and to 'be themselves' in terms of sex, desire, and relationships. The city, or rather particular areas within it, in this way served some of the functions of home.

5
Remembering Bedsitterland: Rex Batten, Carl Marshall and Alan Louis

This chapter looks at the ways in which three gay men tell their stories of coming to London penniless in the 1950s and finding 'home' there. Their testimonies suggest ways in which the city and particular areas within it could accommodate and shape queer lives in different ways. They also suggest shared concerns about making home which relate to the social and cultural positioning of homosexual men in the post-war years. Rex Batten (b.1928) gathered his memories of the 1940s and 1950s in a fictionalised memoir, *Rid England of this Plague* (2006). There he describes his rural working-class upbringing and his first love affair with a middle class man called Ashley; his move to London to take up a scholarship at RADA; and his life in a bedsit in Camden, where he and his boyfriend John experienced a frightening brush with the law. I contacted Rex after reading his book and interviewed him at his current home in East Dulwich which he shared with John until his death in 1994. The novel, he told me then, was 90 per cent autobiographical.[1] Alan Louis (1932–2011) got in touch with me after I advertised for project participants with older gay men's groups in London, and I interviewed him in 2010 in the common room of his sheltered accommodation in Hackney. This for him did not feel like home and he reminisced chiefly about his 'camp' life in various houses in Notting Hill in the 1950s. He had moved there from his working-class family in Portsmouth, on England's south coast, and over the years that followed worked in a series of relatively low-paid office jobs as well as DJ-ing. A friend gave me Carl Marshall's hand-written health diary and memoir after his death in 2010. I had met him once before at his flat in Kennington on a social rather than research visit and so whilst Alan and Rex talked to me with my specific project in mind, Carl's testimony was not geared in that way. He was born in 1938 and brought up in

Kent largely by his poverty-stricken grandmother. He moved to London in the late 1950s after deserting from the army where he had served in the band. He worked in a variety of low paid, largely service sector jobs whilst also making music. Latterly he focussed on his photographic work. His memoir traces the development of that work and his social and sexual adventuring (including on the burgeoning leather and SM scenes) until the late 1960s. It is, however, tellingly structured by the places he lived. This is the main way in which he orientated himself in London then and remembered the city and that period when he looked back from the 2000s.

Like Alan and Rex, Carl's account is retrospective, coming – as with the others – some 50 years after the period he describes. He, they, shuttle back and forth, comparing times and places in their differently formulated accounts, and bringing into particular focus the complex dance they had to perform as they lived out their daily relationship, social and sexual lives in the city. This 'evidence of experience' allows us to recoup aspects of queer life in the 1950s and 1960s which would otherwise escape the archive.[2] It is not, though, some base-line truth. It is necessarily partial and modulated by experiences and circumstances since – Rex's more settled home from the 1960s, Alan's disaffection with his later accommodation, and Carl's ill-health from the late 1990s, for example. Their testimonies are laced sometimes with nostalgia and sometimes with relief at having moved on, and are shaped in particular ways by generic conventions of the novel, the memoir, or the structure of interview.[3] These things do not invalidate what is said and they are not things I want to screen out. They indeed tell us something about the ways memories of earlier homes are caught up in complex and unpredictable ways in the later lives of these men. Domesticity is as much about the play of memory and personal history as it is about the circumstances of home life in any particular place and moment. The first part of what follows thus deals with Rex's recollections of rural life and how those memories are wrapped into his account of his subsequent time in London in the 1950s. Alan's and Carl's testimonies then help to give a sense of the dangers and possibilities of the capital in those years – dangers and possibilities which, I suggest finally, are gathered into their later experiences and understandings of home.

Homeward bound: Rex

When Rex was 20 he moved from his family home in Dorset into his lover's house in a nearby village. He lived with Ashley (not his real name) for a year, and then in the same house with his subsequent lover John before moving to London. He and John lived first in a bedsit near Russell Square and then in another in Camden. In 1957 the couple moved into a house in East Dulwich in South East London and lived there together until John's death on Christmas Eve 1994. Rex still lives in the same house, and his novel is dedicated to his new partner, also called John. Rex's account in *Rid England of this Plague* stops at the move to East Dulwich and the greater sense of security that marked the subsequent period for him and for him and John as a couple. He took up that part of his life story more fully in interview. His account in both mediums hinges on and returns again and again to his family home in Dorset. In *Rid England of this Plague* concerned calls and letters to London from Dorset provide the key narrative markers in Rex's account of the fearful months after Ashley's arrest on indecency charges. They were 'a good accommodating family', and while he never 'came out' in a post-liberationist sense and his parents never directly asked, they accepted Rex and also his relationship with John. Another of my interviewees, 'Terry', reported something similar: he 'kept in very close touch with his family' and took his boyfriends 'home' to Kent. His parents 'knew' he was 'homosexual', he said, but 'it wasn't a topic of conversation'.[4] As historian Heather Murray convincingly shows in her examination of familial relations between parents and their gay and lesbian children in the north America in the 1950s, this pattern of support was relatively common and constructive in ways that a later generation schooled in the liberatory rhetoric of openness and visibility tended not to grasp or else saw as repressive.[5] Many men experienced a rupture from family because of their sexuality – and not least because heightened awareness of the 'homosexual problem' attuned parents and family to tell tale signs. Many more seem to have found some sort of accommodation with family in this period, however – as Ackerley and Ives had done before. Family was an important resource for them as for Batten and was meshed into their understandings and experiences of homosexuality.

Family and the family home brace Rex's account of himself and his close ties. They represent for him some of those broadly understood values – of safety, support and retreat especially. As they are figured in the novel they also represent a time before: before London; before his brush with the law; before what he saw as the 1950s drive to normalcy. Rex's sexual awakening when he was living with his parents seems not to have been clouded by guilt or tainted by some dangerous underworld in the city. His parents were unruffled when he moved into

Ashley's cottage. In Rex's fictionalised account that simplicity, naivety even, was indelibly linked to 'this idyllic, quintessentially English setting' and to a pre-fifties moment.[6] It is contrasted with Ashley's more sophisticated, urbane middle-class world and persona, which Rex conjures in his novel through a rendition of his lover's cottage. Looking back Rex identified something 'almost theatrical' about it:

> Ash's cottage, in common with all the other dwellings, had neither running water nor mains drainage, though it did have electricity and could boast a telephone. When they arrived Ash seemed far more interested in showing Tom [the Rex character in the novel] his house than getting him into bed. Tom knew only too well what cottages were really like to live in. He had known nothing else. A rural slum was an apt description [...] Here in Lower Budleigh was another world. Tom was impressed [...] The transformation Ash had worked moved the man into a realm well beyond simple sex. He had created a showpiece [...] the perfect recreation of the archetypal cottage that never existed.[7]

Rex marks the difference in perspective of his younger and older selves here, and conjures too his 'authentic' family home through a contrast with Ashley's mock-up of the rural cottage. The latter is surface, show and pretension, furnishing 'simple sex' with some cultural identity and identification.[8] Ashley's interior transformation was an adjunct to and partial articulation of his homosexuality – and of a particular upper middle-class and self-consciously tasteful homosexuality.[9] While Rex characterises his parents' home primarily through the people who lived there and so the associated emotional bonds (this is the first time we get a direct description of their cottage in the novel), he describes Ashley's home materially and in ways which produce and frame its owner. Ash's cottage, Rex writes, 'had flair and style, as did the man who lived there'.[10]

Ashley had an eye for quality and value. When he divorced it had been the 'better pieces of furniture' he had clung to tenaciously, hiding them in a barn 'to prevent her family getting their hands on them'.[11] Rex's description of Ashley resonates with the self-depiction of Mass Observation diarist B.Charles at around the same time. B.Charles – a collector – relished beautiful things and was proud of the way he had put his home together, comparing himself favourably on that score to his heterosexual neighbours and acquaintances.[12] Hearing of a project to instruct working-class 'lads' in 'cultural matters', B.Charles wrote 'to say that if there is any organisation in Edinburgh interested in giving working-class lads instruction in interior decoration or antique furniture, I shall be pleased to receive visits from lads for chats on old furniture, etc'.[13] B. Charles and Ashley aligned themselves with that loosely queer tradition of culture, good taste and antiques in the home.[14] The upsurge in discussion and debate about home and homosexuality in the postwar period consolidated this association; there was, as we have seen, a heightened sensitivity to domestic signs of queerness.[15]

For Ashley, as for B. Charles, the queer tasteful domestic twist was also associated with elitism and class position. Ashley 'would casually mention country house parties in the days before the second world war', writes Rex.[16] At these parties and in these homes queer men were associated with privileged and higher-class living in an echo of late nineteenth-century queer scandal which often highlighted the involvement of supposedly dissipated aristocrats.[17] At one 'the footmen served dinner nude with their cocks and balls painted gold'.[18] This is what some 1950s newspapers feared might be going on at *louche* queer gatherings in luxurious Mayfair apartments leading to the corruption of working-class men and guardsmen.[19] Ashley's recollections of a decadent queer past structured around class difference yet seemed out of kilter with postwar austerity, a new social democrat pulse, and a reorientation of queer identifications.[20] Ashley's time had passed. He 'could no longer afford to mix with the real landed gentry'; 'the war had blown the smart world of the 1930s into the past'.[21] These privileged, privatised and elite domestic affiliations differentiate Ashley from Tom and Michael (the Rex and John characters in the novel); he was, Rex suggests, something of an anachronism.

Tom and Michael are, meanwhile, shown to be more equal to each other in terms of age, class and money. Their companionate domestic relationship is apparently more in tune with the new era – quite different from the cross-class and cross-generational relationships of Ashley, Ives and Ackerley. This was part, perhaps, of shifting expectations of relationships and a drawing together of ideas about what relationships 'should' be like – whether queer or normal.[22] Michael moved into the cottage with 'no consultation' and ostensibly 'no great plans' – the move to cohabitation itself signalling the desire for a relationship with Tom (he didn't want to 'risk being turned down').[23] Ashley meanwhile went to 'take care of his ailing widower father' and left the two younger men to it.[24] Rex characterises this time as 'a simple domestic period' with little intrusion from the outside world. He emphasizes repeatedly the equality of the partnership in terms of sex and domestic chores especially, and in the novel and in interview the home is pivotal to the way Rex describes the initial and subsequent stages of their relationship. At moments of crisis the domestic stands in for normality and continuity and comes as a mode of reassurance. When they receive news of Ashley's arrest after their move to London:

> They both sat looking at each other not knowing what to do.
> 'There's the washing up to finish'.
> That prosaic domestic task seemed to break the tension.
> 'You always do so well with our meals and I know it isn't easy', Michael said.
> Tom smiled.[25]

Further down the same page the narrator remarks that 'both, in their different ways, had been bought up to conform'.[26] Their shared experiences and understandings of home provide a means of speaking to each other and to family, friends and neighbours about their relationship and intimacy in ways which might not have been easy to articulate directly. For Tom and Michael (as for Rex and John) the domestic space offered a haven in which discretion was not a burden, and the unspoken was not seen as oppressive or repressive. The men were held by the benign inarticulacy of those around them and the ongoing ordinariness of the day-to-day. In the novel, when Tom returns to Dorset in the wake of Ashley's arrest, 'his mother was waiting'. 'She cooked him breakfast. His father was at work. Everything was fine. Vic wagged a welcome [... and] jumped and barked insisting he would take Tom for a walk'.[27] Though they had not been arrested, the association with Ashley made it a real possibility, leaving the fictional and actual couple reeling. In that context Rex talks of turning more to his family because 'support was there without having to ask or explain'.[28] Rex and John did not tell any of their London friends about what had happened to Ashley and the consequent risk to them. The wartime slogan 'careless talk costs lives' perhaps found new meaning and resonance for them and for queer men more broadly in the 1950s. In turn, and precisely because of this pernicious climate and the escalating arrest and prosecution rate, Tom/Rex took care not 'to put [his family] in the line of homophobic abuse'; he 'valued [them] far too highly' for that.[29] Rex speaks here and in interview of a felt need to accommodate and protect his family and this seems relatively easy for him to do partly because of his own domestic circumstances and his validation of home and what it represented; partly also, of course, because his family were at a geographical distance. This domestic and familial pulse beats against wider press characterizations of 'evil men' haunting street corners and public toilets.[30] It echoes 1950s reformist literature and film which stressed domestic accord as a way of legitimizing homosexuality. As we saw earlier, Rodney Garland's *The Heart in Exile* (1953) and Mary Renault's *Charioteer* (1953) were both important in this respect,[31] and we see it too in Andrew Salkey's *Escape to an Autumn Pavement* (1959) which charts the relationship between Jamaican immigrant Johnny and Englishman, Dick. This relationship is articulated and normalized through their co-residence and domesticity. 'We [Johnny and Dick] took a flat in Whitcomb Street, quite near Leicester Square. We shared the rental, which was exorbitant. We cooked for each other, and when that was becoming a bore, we decided to employ a woman who'd cook our evening meal and hover over us on Sundays'.[32] In this way their partnership is set apart from the one Johnny has with Fiona whose 'sexuality' he finds 'depressing'. An agonised Dick ultimately asks Johnny to choose between him and Fiona 'for our sake, for the pleasant memories we've stored up through the months of partnership in the flat and before at Hampstead'.[33] It is their domestic life and the memories associated with it that anchor the relationship for Dick.

Safe in the city: Rex, Alan and Carl

This fictional relationship between Dick and Johnny in *Escape to an Autumn Pavement* and the way it is conducted first in a bedsitter house in Hampstead and then under the eye of their domestic help reflect the local acceptance or toleration some queer men describe in this period. London's status as a city of incomers ('half the population were born elsewhere')[34] made conjunctions of difference common for those who couldn't afford more secluded homes. Though real caution was still needed,[35] the mixed bedsit rental market facilitated or perhaps necessitated a strand of live-and-let-live indifference and sometimes solidarity between people living cheek-by-jowl. Landladies and landlords could also be actively supportive. One of Schofield's subjects described his landlady as 'a sweetie'.

> The boy in the next room was having an affair with another boy, and this boy's ex-boyfriend, if you understand me, came to the door and showed a photograph of Martin to the landlady and asked if he visited this house. The landlady said: 'sure enough he does. They're two very nice boys. They make no secret of what they are and they're no trouble at all. They like their bit of fun the same as everyone else but they keep the place nice and clean so don't you

be interfering with them. They're very respectable and have women up there and all. So be off with you'.[36]

Domestic cleanliness, propriety and respectability were key here and it was in these ways that homosexual men might earn the support of their landlords and landladies. They were more cautious and careful than 'normal' men who perhaps had a greater sense of entitlement.

This resonates with Rex's experience. His first bedsit near Russell Square had a potentially tell-tale double bed (though with only one comfortable side; they took it in turns).[37] People came and went very quickly in this house and the fact they were two men sharing brought no trouble. 'In bedsitter land who would bother to look? [...] who would know or care what happened next door?'[38] The landlady in Camden ejected an intolerant man upstairs and there was a general sense of in-house solidarity here and also in the bedsits of friends.[39] This is a recurrent feature of Alan and Carl's memories of this period, and gave them both a strong sense of belonging and of being 'at home' in London. Alan, for example, had fond memoires of his first London lodgings with a Mrs Valentine – 'a wonderful woman', widowed in the war and caring now for her son and daughter alone. 'She knew I was gay, everyone knew I was gay [...] I was camp and all the rest of it and I was just out and out gay'. He would take lovers back ('I know more about you than you think I do', she told him), and if Alan was out Mrs Valentine would let them wait in his room. Such support shored up his confidence and allowed for self-realisation and assertion. Alan recalled that when his brother and father visited him in a subsequent flat in Notting Hill from Portsmouth and made comments about his queer flat mates and friends he 'got so flippin' angry I called my father into the other room and said "listen [...] you come here as a guest, you know I have other people here as well [...] we are not going to put up with Ian [his brother] and all his friends making jokes." [...] My [father said Ian] doesn't like it and I said "he doesn't pay my rent!" '. They never came again. So I'm afraid we were divorced'.[40] On this home turf Alan felt able to stand his ground – a queer rejection of parents rather than the (more usual or anticipated) opposite.

Alan found his feet in Notting Hill in part through Flora Macdonald – 'the matriarch' of the Notting Hill queer community in the mid-'50s. 'She was quite eccentric, looked like Cat Weasel, hair and all ragged beard and god knows what else, rattled along the road with her bike and she was like the contact for people'. 'She knew everybody and she gave [girls'] names to a lot of them'; Alan was 'Nelly Bagwash'. Flora provided contacts for sex and places to stay, and put Alan up for three months. Flora would go out to cut the hedge at 11 p.m.; 'that was the time they would come out of the shebeens [...] you would get the black guys coming down the road [...] she'd bow in front of them and say "hello sexy"'. When Alan walked past her into the house on one occasion and went to bed, Flora guided one of these men in afterwards. 'The next thing I knew there was this guy stark naked [...] he jumped into bed and that was that! Good night Diane!' Flora and Alan seem to have associated black men with 'the classic stereotype of a natural, spontaneous sexuality'.[41] This was not (in Alan's view) codified and categorized like his own and other white camp men in his network. Though this perceived sexuality was more broadly seen as part of the threat of Afro-Caribbean immigrants,[42] it contributed to their desirability for Alan. It was what had drawn him to London. When Alan had accompanied his mother from Portsmouth to Paddington Station in the early 1950s. 'I went outside I saw all these black guys walking up and down, I thought to myself "hello this is another world". That's what made me come to London. I wanted to get away from Portsmouth, it was very dreary dull; I was beginning to feel the urge I think!' Earlier in the interview Alan related one of only a few childhood memories – of suffering panic attacks when he was in hospital as a nine-year-old and being comforted there. 'The nurse put me next door to someone I swear was a black man because I can hear his voice now. When I had a panic attack I heard this voice talking to me "down, down, down" and calming me down'. There is perhaps a connection in Alan's testimony between this childhood incident, the attraction he felt to the black men he saw at Paddington station, and the home he made in Notting Hill alongside newly arrived Afro-Caribbean immigrants, several of whom he lived with as boyfriends. For Alan, as for Joe Ackerley in the last chapter, there was seemingly an acceptance of partners who had a different understanding of sex and sexuality. Whilst he and Ackerley labelled themselves as exclusively gay and homosexual respectively, their Afro-Caribbean and working-class lovers did not. This was a transitional period in British sexual cultures when it was still just possible to sleep with men and women and have a claim on 'normality' (not least through a repudiation of effeminacy). For those like Alan and Ackerley who embraced a singular sexual identity yet largely desired men who had not, there were repercussions for the way they lived domestically. If there was certainly a deep and often enduring affection between these men and their lovers, in these cases girlfriends, marriage and children took precedence in terms of where those lovers lived and the frequency with which they were able to see their boyfriends. Alan saw his relationships as necessarily temporary. 'They all got married', he said, 'every one of them'. In response to this Alan suggested the need for resourcefulness in his urban life which relied on mobility and the ability to move on.[43]

Alan moved from Flora's place to a bedsit of his own. His landlady there disapproved of his new black boyfriend and 'I said "that's it, moonlight flit"' and again moved on. 'It was easy, very easy' to find places to stay, he said. Alan describes queer, drug, prostitution and Afro-Caribbean counter cultures coming together in the bedsits, flats, streets, shebeens and cafes of Notting Hill. It seemed, he said, 'to gel' and was 'very supportive'. The black guys 'knew our camp names' and 'a lot of the landladies [...] were on the game':

> I remember walking down the road one day when there were police cars around and all that [...] This girl was running past me, saw me with my hair and goodness knows what else, grabbed hold of me by the arm, dragged me down the steps of a basement in through the door [...] and there I was staying the night with all these prostitutes around me [...] running around in their blinking' bras and knickers.

What Alan described was a climate in Notting Hill of sexual openness and liberalism, which was not only live-and-let-live but felt to him more actively supportive.

Whilst Rex measures his sense of home and belonging against the period before he moved to London, for Alan it was Notting Hill in the 1950s that was his main reference point in interview. He contrasted this with the Portsmouth of his youth and with the Hackney of his middle and older age. He articulated the dullness of life in Portsmouth and the loneliness and sense of insecurity he felt in east London. Talking about Notting Hill was in part a way of explaining what felt wrong to him in Hackney.[44] The day I interviewed Alan he had been watching *Tales of the City* – the adaptation of the first of Armistead Maupin's novels about a boarding house in San Francisco in the 1970s. 'It did remind me of my time in Notting Hill', he said.

Alan's feeling of support and safety in Notting Hill supersede other ways that he might have talked about life in the area in this period. Aside from the brief reference to the racist landlady, he didn't mention Teddy Boy animosity and attacks which culminated in race riots of 1958 and gave the area a fresh notoriety.[45] The absence of those feelings of belonging and safety for him later in Hackney perhaps meant that local tensions and socio-economic realities there came into sharper focus. They were also of course more immediate and local and so to the fore. Neither did Alan dwell on the upset of relationships ending or any sense of dislocation in moving, often without notice, from room to room, or being made (in his words) 'homeless' at least twice. Indeed the transitory nature of housing in Notting Hill for him reflected and was the practical result of the way his relationships worked and worked out – something he seems to have accepted. Home for Alan at that time was not associated with lifelong partnership, nor with particular flats, houses or rooms, but rather with a local area and a counterculture. This resonates with historian Eric Hobsbawm's reflection on the meanings of home for exiles and emigrants in New York where there was often 'no sharp distinction between house, neighbourhood and town'.[46]

This is a feature of Carl's narrative too: he described in his memoir a similar ease of movement and the acceptance or a least surface toleration he found in the different places he lived. Carl was (in the title he gave to his memoir) 'Betty's Bastard' and though there is little mention of Betty (his mother), the sense of his having cut lose from her and having made his own home and family in London pervades the memoir he began writing after he became more and more housebound through ill health in the late 1990s. His London home and queer family life were out of reach of, and formed in opposition to, his troubled childhood homes and experiences. He arrived in London in 1958 doubly outlawed – 'a[n army] deserter and a poofta' – and began to remake himself in the capital. He did this not least with a change of name from Geoff Marshall to Carl Christian in 1959 (and officially by deed poll in 1969; he subsequently and selectively started using Marshall again in his later years – which is why I use it primarily here too). Despite the instability of accommodation for him, the city supported a sense of who he felt he was and wanted to be. In his first weeks, Carl found beds for the night by picking up men in central London – around Speakers Corner in Hyde Park initially – before being taken in by two rent boys with a flat on Leicester Square ('real rough diamonds who looked after me and took it in turns to fuck me').[47] He moved on to a two bedroomed flat in Swiss Cottage which another lover shared with his mother and her boyfriend. There was a sufficient ease in this household for the couple to sometimes take a third man home with them for sex. From here, and after serving a sentence for his desertion from the army in 1959, Carl found through a friend a basement room in a large Victorian house in Highbury in central north London. The landlord had 'turned a house of eight rooms into a house of twenty four rooms […] each had at least two walls of hardboard, a bed, a sink and a gas meter'. Carl was 'one of the

Figure 14 Carl Marshall in 2005
© Andy and Carol McEwan.

fortunate ones in having only one hardboard wall between me and my next door neighbour'.[48] In the front basement room three or four Irish labourers shared (one of whom he had sex with); upstairs lived Simone, a French woman in her 50s and sometimes her boyfriend Reg.

In these and in several subsequent bedsits and flats, alone or shared with lovers, Carl describes an intimacy with neighbours – either cultivated or enforced because of the lack of sound-proofing. 'One of the irritations of living in a boarding house was the other boarders – particularly the two [queer] men living above me [in Highbury] who banged on the ceiling every time I played the piano.'[49] There was in all this an informal meshing of men and women (though largely men) living with little money and finding through each other places to live, friendships, sex, relationships, and some sense of belonging.

Carl described the places he lived and visited in incredible detail. 'I got [a room] in Gloucester Terrace, Bayswater', he wrote: 'a small back room on the ground floor containing a single bed, chair, gas ring, gas fire and a wash basin with hot and cold water. My window looked out onto a brick wall'. It was in this period, he went on, that he met a new lover, Michael:

> He never took me back to his place, it was usually to a room in a punter's flat in Mayfair or Cheyne Walk [home ground for Oscar Wilde and architect Charles Ashbee fifty years earlier], a flat with antique furniture and a long table covered in eighteenth and nineteenth century cookery books.[50]

'Going into a house', he wrote, 'I would scan through the bookshelves. You can read so much into the person's mind by the books they own'.[51] On another occasion he visited a pornographer in Cleveland Street. 'It was a small flat on the third floor of a tall Victorian/Edwardian house' – perhaps not unlike the Cleveland Street male brothel sensationally exposed in 1889.[52] 'The door of that flat opened on to one of the rooms; sparsely furnished, a table, divan bed, a couple of chairs, a small photographic screen by the door, walls and woodwork in need of a coat of paint and a door leading to another room, unseen'. There is an air of a theatrical set to this – especially in that final 'unseen', offstage space of promise or danger. In each of these instances Carl took in the surroundings in detail to 'read' the inhabitant; to assess, perhaps, the sexual set-up, and possibly to check how to get out if he needed to. Such scene setting suggests Carl's mobility between classes and levels of wealth – a particular and defining feature of queer urban life and sociability in this period.[53] Some contemporary commentators discussed earlier may have seen in all this a rootless, fragmented queer existence.[54] However, such detailed remembrance – of these and other places such as the Colherne Pub in Earls Court (part of a burgeoning leather scene in the later 1960s) and a close friend's house in Highbury – might instead signal a sense of home and being at home in the city.

Domestic dangers

Despite the possibilities associated with home for each of these men, there were also dangers. The bedsit in Camden is described as a place of relative safety for Tom and Michael in Rex's novel in terms especially of their landlady and neighbours, but that safety is punctured when the phone rings in the corridor, when letters arrive, and when the police finally come knocking. Tom and Michael's (Rex and John's) domestic habits were shaped in part through such potential intrusion. Rex describes changing gender in signing off letters and of destroying photographs (as Ashley had failed to do: it was partly such evidence that had incriminated him). In the novel Tom feels his heart sink when he spots a physique magazine on the table while the police are interviewing him. He felt, meanwhile, that reaching for his pipe acted as a decoy. These were the day-to-day conventions of domestic caution for homosexual men in the 1950s. It was essential to be carefully attuned to supposedly tell-tale signs and also to keep the landlord or landlady onside. 'I seldom seem to be off my guard', wrote one of Schofield's case studies:

> Even living with my friend – and neither of us go chasing others – I realise I'm in danger. It can happen in many ways. Perhaps a quarrel with the landlord and so he reports us to the police. The law must have an effect on all friendships and will hinder their development. If a person is on his guard, or feels insecure, he will be more difficult to live with.[55]

Rex and John's sex life came to a halt during the period of Ashley's arrest, trial and ultimate imprisonment.

The press underscored the dangers, and though most arrests and prosecutions related to cottaging offences, police did sometimes search homes. Coloured slides found at a St George's Square flat in Pimlico in 1963 led to the arrest of ten men aged between 32 and 54 who had 'behaved obscenely' at another flat in Stockwell. This kind of evidence – taken in private in a sexualized spin on home movies and the family album – was repeatedly at stake in court cases once photographic and cine cameras had become commonplace.[56] Such cases were a reminder that however permissive their milieu and immediate neighbours, queer men still needed to take care to avoid police interference, arrest and prosecution. It is also true that this mattered more to some than others. Rex was fearful in part because of his family; his brush with the law stayed with him all his adult life and led him to write his novel. Carl and Alan who were at a distance from their families of origin were more cavalier in the face of the law.

There were other dangers aside from the police. Carl was threatened with a knife after having sex with one of the Irish labourers from the neighbouring bedsit in Highbury: 'I turned around and he was standing on the other end of the kitchen table with a sharp kitchen knife in his hand saying "I'm going to cut your cock off "'.[57] Other interviewees describe further risks. 'Terry' was robbed on a number of occasions by casual pick-ups from Hampstead Heath whom he took to his nearby home.[58] 'Daniel' described older richer men who would lock their doors to prevent younger guests escaping – their clutches or with their possessions perhaps; either way there was on both sides suspicion and a sense of danger.[59]

Given the dangers and tensions that could accrue to the rooms where they lived, each of my interviewees described other places they retreated to. Rex and John 'escaped' to a high Anglican church and to the fantastical Astoria cinema at Finsbury Park with its Moorish foyer and auditorium styled as an Andalucian village. At the cinema Rex would 'walk through the swing doors and [be] transported to another world [...] escape was at hand'.[60] For Carl in the 1960s it was the Coleherne that provided respite from domestic tensions and a place to be himself, while for 'Terry' Hampstead Heath was his anchor point. '"Home" somehow is out in the green', he said.[61] These non-domestic spaces fulfilled some aspects of idealized home culture for these men.[62]

Ideal homes

A sense of privacy and safety was what Rex and John aspired to. In their own home in East Dulwich from 1957, 'one was safe [...] because it was private, it was our home we were living in'.[63] This move to south-east London marked the end of their troubles with the law, the close of the 1950s and the end of Rex's novel. What Rex and John sought in their new home was the space to conduct their relationship without standing out from those around them. They 'just wanted to be accepted in the new street'. The two felt a sense of local community and belonging which did not stop at a bedsit next door. 'It was very much a south London working-class street', he said. Within a week 'half a dozen bread puddings' had arrived from neighbours who doubted the ability of two men to look after themselves, and they were subsequently invited to local parties together. Deliberately or not, their home was not flamboyantly different from those of other 'normal' post-war couples who had limited disposable income. 'All the furniture when we moved in was second hand, pre-war', Rex said. They bought *Homes and Gardens*, ripped out the Victoriana ('it was old fashioned, past a joke: you did not take it seriously'), covered a door with orange formica, the new wonder substance (now removed; fashions change), and like others of their generation did not only use the parlour for 'best'. But these innovations were part of a broader modernising domestic fashion. Though their décor linked to what has been identified as a queer taste in the modern,[64] theirs was not the kind of queer departure in interior décor I described earlier.[65] Whatever local knowledge there was about Rex and John remained tacit, and only in 1967 – a full ten years after they had moved in – did they buy a double bed. 'That was a hell of a statement to make! Because everybody would know what came in [...] We never had any comment about it [...] we just wanted to fit in with the street, and we were accepted'.

Aside from continuities with the local community, there were ongoing connections with Rex's Dorset home and village. The East Dulwich house belonged to a family friend who had moved back to Dorset, so allowing Rex and John to move in. This wasn't only a piece of good fortune but a sign of the way family networks might work (rather like Carl's network of close friends). That Rex had this connection might also have helped in the couple's integration into the neighbourhood; there was a sense of continuity. Maps of his home county still hang on the wall, and these west country links embraced both Rex and John. Once, when Rex visited Dorset alone, his mother berated him for not bringing John with him: 'he IS family', she had said, 'and don't you ever do that again'. Terry was similarly reprimanded for not bringing one of his long-term boyfriends 'home'.

While we can draw some obvious divisions between rural and urban life, and between the parental, bedsitter, and East Dulwich homes, what is striking in Rex's testimony (as opposed to Carl and Alan's) is the *lack* of disjunction and rather the emotional continuities between these different spaces. They each in different ways provided a sense of safety and reassurance, and the domestic served as a lodestone for Rex in these respects. It consolidated, articulated, and partially 'normalised' Rex's relationship with John. They were the kind of couple addressed by the Wolfenden recommendations and the Sexual Offences Act of 1967 (relating to the permissibility of sex between two men over 21 in private) and they fitted into a refashioned postwar domestic culture which was seeing more and more (though far from all) couples living independently together. This was 'a more distinct and privatised version of homosexual identity' than had been apparent, common or possible before – especially for men without much money.[66] Rex observed that 'the great thing moving here [to East Dulwich] was you had a house you could make a home out of, I think that was it, we found somewhere we could make a home. We didn't discuss it but I'm sure we felt we were both making a home'. What other oral histories and Joe Ackerley and Schofield's work in the 1950s also highlight is the aspiration to this kind of independent coupledom for many men in this period even if it was an actual or seeming impossibility. 'Sometimes', Schofield wrote:

> The contacts have become resigned to living alone because for social reasons it would be difficult or impossible to live with another man. A man who holds a position where he is expected to entertain business associates in his home would be in a difficult situation if he shared a flat with another man. A man would require courage to set up house with another who has any mannerisms, or who is known to have been arrested for homosexual offences. A man living with his parents would find it difficult to explain why he wishes to leave and share a flat with another man. Above all, the gossip of neighbours, of friends, and of people at work discourages many homosexuals from pairing up.[67]

The broader shift towards expectations (if not the realities) of companionate marriage and domestic togetherness informed the hopes of homosexual men and the presumptions of commentators more than ever before. This had the effect of creating single status or living alone as part of the queer tragedy while quiet coupledom and domesticity was the marker of success, happiness and normalisation. Alan and Carl meanwhile testify more positively to the pleasures of being single and the separation of sexual, relationship and domestic lives.

Remembering home

The men I've discussed certainly frequented central London and the few queer bars there in the 1950s and 1960s, but whereas that 'scene' is often the start of analysis of queer life, what is striking in these cases is the extent to which they spent most of their time in the areas where they lived. Their nostalgia was for these other places. Alan's profound sense of loss was to do with his move from Notting Hill to council housing in Hackney and a feeling of a lack of safety and neighbourliness there. He experienced theft and homophobic abuse, and ultimately opted to live in sheltered accommodation. He didn't find a sense of community there and so (for him) a sense of home: 'they know I'm gay and they are all very friendly, we have a laugh and a joke. But it's not the same thing; I should be with my own'. Alan's hankering for Notting Hill was for a particular area and milieu, but also for a sense of self, identity and community forged in his youth. Alan hoped to rediscover that sense of belonging. 'I do not suffer in silence', he said:

> I went to a meeting last week and [we talked about] what LGBT people would like to find in Hackney, [so that it is] a better place to grow old in [...] I remember way back the Porchester Drag Queen Balls [in the 1970s and 1980s at Porchester Hall in Queensway] I thought we could do something [like that] here. I would like to see something like that come back, it is part of gay history.

Alan's search for community was in part a desire to bind the past into the present, to recoup a sense of a queer London to which he felt he belonged. Part of the sadness for him perhaps was that that milieu had shifted: the particular countercultures and countercultural crossovers he enjoyed were not part of street and home life in Hackney or now gentrified Notting Hill.

For Rex home was about his partnership with John. They marked their fortieth anniversary in 1990 with a stained-glass window set into their front door and so into the fabric of the home they had shared for 30 years. The dates are there, the names are not. Only those in the know can understand their significance and when Rex gave me permission to photograph it he asked that I did not include the door number for fear someone might come and smash the glass. In *Rid England of this Plague* Rex fictionalised his story, rendered it in the third person, and used pseudonyms. He thus preserved a distance between himself and the events he described. In this he replayed what was a felt necessity for many men in the 1950s. Schofield initially wrote under the alias Gordon Westwood. Rex's narrative choices differentiate his work from the confessional 'coming out' stories and AIDS memoirs of the 1970s, 1980s and early 1990s in which the first person 'I' was politically and personally crucial. His choices also resonate with the novel's themes of caution and (non) revelation. Rex himself describes not having the language to describe himself or the subcultural 'type' he encountered as a younger man whilst at the same time 'knowing' what he wanted and was. He didn't 'come out' to neighbours or his parents, but they knew about him and exercised those values of discretion, and propriety which were prized by many in the postwar generation.[68]

Carl moved in the mid-1980s to a flat in Kennington and lived there until his death in 2010. He shared with a boyfriend for a while but a letter from that man describing the 1980s and his own AIDS diagnosis indicates the tensions and fears the virus could bring domestically. 'I'm afraid my relationship with Carl has diminished', he wrote in 1987. 'He is just emotionally exhausted, very scared of the big A and sees me as a scapegoat; he hasn't spoken to me for two months. I'm hoping to get a new flat and the hospital are trying to pull strings'.[69] Carl himself contracted the virus in the late 1980s and was diagnosed with emphysema in 1999. The flat needed adjusting so he could live more easily with these conditions. He also arranged it around his photographic work: of the four rooms one was turned into a photographic darkroom, another into a studio/store. Though the earlier places he lived were also marked by his creativity (not least in the piano that went with him from place to place), his medical diagnoses, like his move to London, marked a new phase in his domestic life:

> My cock had ruled my head for most of my life. Unfortunately cock won most of the time. [...] Now at the age of 65 [...] I have finally controlled my cock. Perhaps having two terminal illnesses – HIV and emphysema – has a lot to do with it. I know if I don't use my talent now I will regret it on my deathbed.[70]

This later, more domestically orientated and creatively focussed period of his life was also marked by a reconnection of sorts with his family. Carl's family story is one of repeated rejections, abuse and of deep unhappiness, and he left them behind when he joined the army. But in his last years he began to write about them in his memoir, revisiting difficult times that he had blocked out. In that later writing he found shades of his mother in himself and traced his sexual history through her in ways that are resonant with Joe Ackerley's sexual genealogy.[71] He had no affection for her, but he recounts how his aunt had told him he 'would end up in the gutter like my mum'. 'I'm dying from a sexual disease which has at the moment no cure. Mum probably died from one as well, liking cock so much. Like I do. [...] I took after mum in my sexual life and my unknown father the artistic side'.[72] 'She knew how to charm the pants off a man', he wrote: 'like mother like son'. Like him, she had also 'escaped' to London.[73] The city was not only a queer draw.

Each of these three men conceived of their queer desires and associated identities in different ways and in relation to camp and effeminacy, to a nascent respectability and the couple 'norm', and to SM and promiscuity. In doing so they also articulated differing relationships with home as an idea, a memory and a material place. For Rex it remained tightly bound by the four walls within which he lived, and yet was linked as tightly to memories of a former family home. Home was for Rex a place of safety, a connection to a wider cultural and social imperative, and a building block and communicative tool in his relationship. It provided a connection to the outside world and a mode of achieving legitimacy within it, and yet also functioned as a place of retreat. These understandings intersect and run together in Rex's final comments in my interview with him. 'Well', he said, 'you can't buy a home, you've got to make it, [...] and I think home means to me a place you can be together and you feel not cut off from the world outside but you are part of it and that great mass can do what they want outside'. In his new relationship Rex has followed what sociologist Sasha Roseneil has identified as a new trend: Rex spends much of the week with his new partner John, chiefly in the East Dulwich house, but they do not live together; choosing instead to 'live together apart'.[74]

For Alan home seemed at first elusive – in an interview specifically about home and domesticity he veered continually into the streets of Notting Hill. His sense of home, I've suggested, related as much to that area as it did to where he actually slept. When I asked him what home meant to him at the end of the interview he very clearly differentiated it from his current place. 'I think home would be where I would feel comfortable, where I could have people of my choice coming to stay or visit. A place where I have my own furniture, belongings etc. which I can't have here. Basically that'. That he did not have his things around him, that he didn't have the easy sense of people coming and going that he had had before, meant he was no longer at home. This for Alan was accompanied by a feeling of isolation. Despite living in sheltered housing, his sexual difference meant for him that he did not have the companionship there that he had enjoyed earlier in his life. The experiences he described are not unusual for elderly people in general,[75] but are especially common for elderly gays and lesbians.[76]

I didn't interview Carl and didn't ask him this direct question, but the places where he lived anchored and structured his narrative and are described in detail alongside similar accounts of pick-ups, cruising, and sex. Carl's sense of home seems to have been about the fabric of the city and what it facilitated for him in terms of an escape from a past and associated expectations. It was in this sense about distance from his childhood homes. But it was more positively about the sexual, social and artistic networks he formed and was part of in adulthood, and about how they intersected with the places he and his lovers and friends lived and socialised. Carl and Rex both described the past haunting the houses they lived or stayed in. Rex's Camden bedsit 'had once been the home of a prosperous family with the servants housed in the semi basement', he said; his family home in war-time Dorset was a constant reference point in his subsequent life in London. Carl talks about houses he stayed in being literally haunted by ghosts of the past. He experienced in his friend's Highbury home a feeling of a fatal struggle at the top of the stairs – in an echo perhaps of the circumstances surrounding his grandmother's death when he was a teenager. These past homes and family relationships within them were gathered into Rex and Carl's accounts of their youth in London and their lives since. The queer domestic present is often haunted by vestiges of homes long gone.

6
Homes Fit for Homos: Joe Orton's Queer Domestic

Geoffrey Fisher, the new post-war Archbishop of Canterbury, called on Britons to reject 'war time morality' and return to living 'Christian lives'.[1] His words encapsulate a rearguard attempt to awaken supposed pre-war moral certainties in the quest for national renewal. The war, though, had changed things irrevocably. Men and women had seen and experienced things which accelerated social, cultural and attitudinal shifts already underway in the interwar period.[2] Postwar demographics provided further impetus: there was a sharp rise (of 20 per cent) in the number of teenagers in the late 1950s and 1960s as the baby boomer generation came of age.[3] This fed a growing and more visible youth culture shaking up apparently established and establishment attitudes and widening the generation gap.[4] Single mothers, those living 'in sin', homosexuals and prostitutes, were still judged harshly, and many felt terrible isolation.[5] There was nevertheless a sense of things changing.[6] The 1950s and 1960s saw a determined push for homosexual law reform voiced in film and literature, in some landmark sociology (like Michael Schofield's), in the work of the Homosexual Law Reform Society (from 1958), and in the recommendations of the Church of England (1954) and of the Wolfenden Committee (1957).[7] Though many homosexual men certainly experienced the 1950s as an especially harsh decade,[8] there was not the broad moral consensus that has often been assumed. Men like Rex Batten, Alan Louis and Carl Marshall (whom we met in the last chapter) often found a live-and-let-live permissiveness in the city. As the decade progressed, and more particularly from the early 1960s, such shifts were widely discussed in the print and broadcast media. There was a sense of the country entering a new and different era as the austerity of the war and immediate postwar years eased with economic recovery, as the first generation not to have lived through the war came of age, and as vestiges of that war – rationing and national service – ended (in 1954 and 1960 respectively). There was irreverence for the old and for tradition in art and architecture. Artists experimented with different forms and materials, tower blocks replaced terraces in new Utopian models of living, and iconic nineteenth-century buildings like Euston Station were razed in favour of new architecture.[9] London was re-imagined as 'one of the most cosmopolitan cities in the world' a 'swinging' capital of a liberalising country.[10] The latter part of the decade saw the partial legalisation of abortion (1967) and the introduction of no-fault divorce (1969) – measures of huge practical and symbolic significance. Homosexual sex between two men over 21 in private was decriminalised in 1967. The measure only legitimised those conducting their sexual and relationship lives in certain domesticated ways, and some (Joe Orton included) saw it as an irrelevance. It was nevertheless a turning point in the lives and minds of others; this was the moment at which Rex and his partner John finally felt able to buy a double bed.

Fashions, music, and clubs altered the ways in which some – especially young – people socialised, and also changed the look and feel of parts of the capital, most famously the Kings Road in Chelsea and Carnaby Street in Soho.[11] Queer bars with dance floors like the Candy Lounge and Le Duce in Soho provided alternatives to the pubs and more exclusive clubs like the A and B where no dancing was allowed. This all seemed more democratic and more widely accessible, and there now seemed to be more scope to participate in a growing counter culture and grass roots protest, inspired in part by CND (Campaign for Nuclear Disarmament) and from the USA the anti-Vietnam and Civil Rights movements. Different – and certainly more widely used – recreational drugs marked a further separation of the generations. Indeed drug use started to be seen as a pronounced social problem in London especially – signalled by the tightening of drugs law in 1964.[12] For Angus, one of my interviewees, they were nevertheless 'an abiding social force' for his Notting Hill milieu in that decade, drawing together hippies, punks, musicians and artists who were women and men, queer and normal.[13]

Angus' experience was by no means everyone's. Derek Jarman, for example, found little to be excited about in London in the sixties, and the swinging city largely passed Rex and John by in East Dulwich too.[14] Whether the city was lived on a day-to-day basis in these new ways depended very much on where and in what circumstances you lived, on the people you met and mixed with, and on the money you had. The effects of the much hyped sixties 'swing' were equivocal, partial and localised – but in the wide coverage of new music, art, theatre, fashion and mores, there was an least a suggestion of the scope to do things differently, something the capital seemed to foster.[15] And prominent in this coverage of the rising generation from the mid-1960s was the playwright Joe Orton.[16]

Orton was the third of four siblings in a working-class family from Leicester in the midlands. In the context of some difficult family dynamics he threw himself into amateur dramatics before moving to London in 1951 and taking up a scholarship place at RADA (the Royal Academy of Dramatic Art) at the same time as Rex Batten. There he met his lifelong partner, Kenneth Halliwell. He was seven years Joe's senior and had moved to London after losing his parents. For both men, and somewhat like Carl Marshall and Alan Louis in the last chapter, the move to the capital can been seen partly as leaving family behind. Joe and Kenneth moved into a flat in West Hampstead which they shared initially with two other students. Later they were alone and lived an intensely insular life there and subsequently in Islington on Halliwell's inheritance and joint wages from various menial jobs. They read, wrote and made collages – most notoriously from prints cut from library books, vandalism for which the pair were imprisoned in 1962. From the 1960s the couple's dynamic began to change as Orton's profile as a playwright grew. His radio play *The Ruffian on the Stair* was broadcast by the BBC in 1964, just as his stage play *Entertaining Mr Sloane* was winning plaudits. He came joint first in *Variety* magazine's critics poll for best new play, and second for most promising playwright. *Entertaining Mr Sloane* was soon being staged internationally (in New York, Australia and Spain) and reworked for film and TV. His subsequent play, *Loot*, had a shaky start, but in its 1966 incarnation received enthusiastic reviews and more awards. Orton was by then working on a number of other projects – including *What the Butler Saw*, which was first staged posthumously in 1969. In this period Orton became a public figure: his plays were discussed, feted and criticised and he was profiled and interviewed repeatedly in the press and on chat shows. He was also locked into the stories of London told by some of the men I discuss in this book. One of my interviewees recalls having sex with him in a cottage (or public toilet) in Holloway;[17] Rex visited him and Halliwell in their first flat in West Hampstead; Carl Marshall made a point of noting in his memoir that one of his pick-ups made an appearance in the 1969 version of *Entertaining Mr Sloane*; and Derek Jarman remembers seeing him around Islington in 1967 when he was living there too.[18] That was just shortly before Halliwell murdered Orton and then committed suicide in their bedsit on 9 August 1967 – days after the Sexual Offences Act partially legalising sex between men had passed into law.

Since his death, Orton has been characterised as a queer urban iconoclast who parodied and seemed deliberately to trounce ideas about home and family which retained their power but were also increasingly challenged in the 1960s. He was an exemplar of what historian Matt Houlbrook identifies as a new urban type.[19] He differentiated himself from other working-class 'types' (the camp queans or the sexually flexible men Joe Ackerley and Alan Louis took as their lovers) and also from circulating ideas of the respectable middle-class homosexual. He was 'neither a quean [sic] nor normal' and struck a pose as a man living out his homosexual life in the city unapologetically.[20] In exploring the dimensions of this persona, one that in its strident self-confidence prefigured ideas of the post-liberation gay man, I suggest that home was again key – and was as important to him as the city streets or cottages. There are continuities in this with the testimonies I discussed in the last chapter. With them, however, I sought out the place of London and of home in the 1950s and the early 1960s in memory and so also the way home as a place and idea in this period was figured in Rex, Alan and Carl's enduring sense of themselves. Orton provides a different perspective: his diaries and plays were of his present. We do not get with Orton the critical reflective distance that was an important part of those other testimonies. Instead we get Orton – or rather the Orton he chose to depict to his contemporary audience – unmediated by the intervening period. This, we'll see, changes the nature of the story that can be told – not least because his violent death is writ large in the way he was described and analysed subsequently. The sixties were his decade because he rose to fame then but did not live beyond them.

Orton parodied and poked fun at English priggishness and small-mindedness. 'Being married', he quipped on the Eamonn Andrews TV chat show in 1967, 'is like being a baby and having to play with the same rattle always'.[21] In this light it is hardly surprising that literary critic Randall Nakayama describes him 'continually and self-consciously formulating his identity in terms of opposition'.[22] Joe Orton's diaries and plays apparently underscore his position as sexual, familial and domestic outlaw. In this he was seen as indicative of other queer lives. Orton in some ways cultivated this image. Aside from the diaries, his plays were populated by confident young men who had no family and sometimes no home: Wilson in *The Ruffian on the Stair* (1964) and Sloane in *Entertaining Mr Sloane* (1964) are both parentless and ostensibly seeking lodgings. Their arrival disrupts and forces a reconfiguration of the established domestic set-ups in each play – though importantly each of these set-ups is a little skewed from convention in the first place. John Lahr's biography of Orton also suggests the playwright's distance from domestic and family life – a distance which literary critic Simon Shepherd suggests Lahr uses to account for the couple's demise: crudely put, they could not survive beyond conventions of home and family.[23] Though Shepherd angrily rebuts what he sees as Lahr's subtext, however, he does not really qualify the core features of this depiction as far as home and family goes. To Shepherd, Orton's estrangement from these things was part of what made him distinctively and defiantly queer. What both biographers do implicitly or explicitly is to underscore the heterosexual/homosexual, familial/anti-familial, domestic/anti-domestic binaries, fixing these formulations and our historical gaze – and especially our historical gaze at the postwar period – in ways which do not quite work. Rather than the oppositional relationship Lahr, Shepherd, and some commentators on the 'homosexual problem' in the 1950s and 1960s envisage, I show in this chapter some more subtle negotiations and accommodations on Orton's part. I explore these complexities with a more singular focus than in the last. This chapter moves more fully into the sixties and looks more at interiors and domestic relationships – Orton's own and those he conjured in his plays. In so doing I make an argument about the continuing malleability and fragility of concepts of home and family – as well as the care that queer men like Orton took in sustaining them.

At home with Joe and Ken

There is precious little to go on in reconstructing Orton's domestic life with Halliwell.[24] While his candour about the sex he had in public toilets is infamous, Orton is evasive about his time at home. One unpublished diary – written when he was at RADA in 1951 – tails off tantalizingly four days after he moved in with Halliwell in West Hampstead.

> June 16 Move into Ken's flat
> June 17 Well!
> June 18 Well!!
> June 19 Well!!!
> The rest is silence.[25]

Orton was playing here with the ideas of secrecy and revelation that attended queer life and there is a mock prudery at what might go on behind the couple's closed doors. However ironic he was being, however, 'the rest' was indeed 'silence' – at least until Orton resumed his diary in December 1966 at the suggestion of his agent Peggy Ramsay. For the intervening 15 years we know very little about the couple's home life together. There are the insights of occasional visitors interviewed by Lahr after the couple's deaths,[26] there are Rex's vague memories of tea at the West Hampstead flat, and there are also some letters from Peggy Ramsay recounting Orton's comments on these years (of which more of later). From this and other material it would be difficult to persuasively domesticate Orton in 1950s and 1960s terms. What is also true, though, is that Orton and Halliwell did live an intensely insular and domestic life together. Like Schofield's case study couple whom we met in the introduction to this part of the book, they were 'seldom apart', took no part in London's organised queer scene,[27] and were 'content' to stay at home. We know they pooled their resources, took menial jobs to get by, and spent time together reading and writing, defacing and rewriting the cover blurbs of library books and cutting out images to create elaborate collages. Orton's almost complete silence about his domestic life in early adulthood is certainly not easy to analyse, but this silence, in itself and in what lay behind it, remains highly significant to our understanding of the playwright, and also of wider queer dynamics surrounding home and home life in this period.

Orton's 'silence' was not unusual for queer men. For all the freedoms of bedsitter living in London,[28] home could be a tricky place to conduct relationships or to have sex. There was the need to quickly assess the permissiveness and safety of a particular area or domestic set-up, or to establish the kind of queer who was in residence. Carl Marshall remembered and wrote about places he had sex or felt at home in incredible detail, signalling a particular emotional or erotic investment in them. Orton's wry and highly detailed domestic observations in his diaries and anecdotes resonate with these descriptions. In one entry he described sex in a bedsit in Highbury, for example:

> A room on the ground floor of a large house. The place was damp, not lived in. A smell of dust. He didn't live there. He rented it for sex. There was a table covered in grime. Bits of furniture. A huge mantelpiece with broken glass ornaments on it. All dusty. There was a double bed with grayish sheets. A torn eiderdown. He pulled the curtain which seemed unnecessary because the windows were so dirty. He had a white body. Not in good condition. Going to fat.

Very good sex though, surprisingly. [...] As I lay on the bed looking upwards, I noticed what an amazing ceiling it was. Heavy moulding, a centrepiece of acorns and birds painted blue. All cracked now.[29]

The description reads like a stage direction for a theatre set, ready for the action that ensues. The dirty, unkempt room seems to provide an appropriate frame for the man's body, which is 'out of condition' and 'going to fat'. Together they suggest a double life, a particular attitude to sex, a distance, perhaps, from a queer scene, subculture and identification. In telling the story Orton suggests he himself was a different sort of man and homosexual, and one who was more attentive to both his body and room. It comes as a further example of the conflation of home, sex and physique in writing and commentary by and about queer men.[30]

Orton describes another type of queer man via an anecdote about a pick-up which he related to his actor friend Kenneth Williams (who was friends too with Oliver Ford).[31] The pick-up claimed that rich men could be found in a particular area. 'They're not all effeminate either', said the man, 'some of them are really manly and you'd never dream that they were queer, not from the look of 'em. But I can tell because they've all got LPs of Judy Garland'.[32] These records and other domestic ephemera took on particular meanings which could then be read back to the inhabitant and/or used as a means of affirmation or revelation to others who (like this pick-up) were 'in the know'.[33]

Carl Marshall and Orton's careful observation of places and people was about 'reading' their hosts and also sometimes about distinguishing themselves from them. Orton and Halliwell were not slovenly in their bedsit like the man in the first example and if they had Judy Garland LPs they didn't advertise the fact (though their neighbours reported that the pair played rather camp musicals almost exclusively).[34] Despite his posture of indifference, Orton was acutely aware of how the domestic spoke of others, of himself and of his relationship with Halliwell. Firstly, Orton directly opposed the aspirational middle-class domestic. The bedsit in Noel Road in Islington was a set-up not unlike that of many working-class individuals, couples and families nearby (and indeed in the same building). If the bedsit was deployed after their death to signal the couple's queerness and 'the sterility and self destruction of homosexual love' after they died,[35] it was also 'a symbol of [Orton's] authentic working-class roots'.[36] In addition, though, Orton and Halliwell were part of an artistic, queer and middle-class trend for buying up cheap property as run-down central suburbs gentrified. They were among the first wave of owner-occupiers who contributed to the shift in Islington's demographic in the 1960s.[37] In 1961 the *Evening News and Star* reported that Carl Toms, a 'bachelor' interior designer who worked on Princess Margaret's apartment at Kensington Palace, had bought a house in Noel Road (Orton and Halliwell's street) and was busy 'converting [it] into an attractive and comfortable home'.[38] 'Demand for houses in Islington is greater today than at any time this century', an agent at the time was reported as saying. 'I have a long list on my books now of waiting purchasers, with many well-known folk in the artistic and social spheres amongst them'.[39] By 1966 Orton was parodying the new influx. In an interview with the *Daily Sketch* he observed that 'late at night you can hear car doors banging and people singing out "good night darling"'.[40] Two thirds of the population had moved away by 1961 – the place of the skilled working-class emigrants taken by 'a polarized population of middle class gentrifiers and unskilled workers'.[41] The influx of money did not lead to a general improvement in living conditions. In 1971, four years after Orton's death, 44 per cent of Islington households still did not have exclusive use of a bath or shower (the highest rate in the capital; the cross-London average was 25 per cent).[42] In Orton's time there, Noel Road was a mixed street (the Italian immigrant restaurateur Elena Salvoni was next door, downstairs the working-class Cordons) and one which seem to have accommodated Orton and Halliwell's relationship comfortably. If they have been depicted as isolated domestically they were also on friendly terms with others on the street. There were not the countercultural intimacies Alan Louis found in Notting Hill,[43] but there was a sense of people rubbing along in the day to day. Because Orton wrote at home and had such a seemingly intense domestic relationship with Halliwell, meanwhile, his interaction with the city was on different terms to those who went out to work. His accounts of going out pivoted instead on sex and cottaging, suggesting the ways in which non-domestic spaces in the city provided scope for something which was increasingly seen to belong at home.

Whatever the changing complexion of his home neighbourhood (and perhaps partly because of it), Orton was keen to distance himself from middle-class trappings. In his diary he sneered at the suburban Brighton home and family of *Loot* producer Oscar Lewenstein. He also related his attempt to shock the straight American couple at an adjoining table in Morocco by parodying queer and middle-class domestic acquisitiveness and fussiness (in an anecdote underpinned too by a casual racism in relation to the excitability and uncontrollability of Moroccan 'boys'):

> 'We've got a leopard skin rug in the flat and he wanted me to fuck him on that', I said in an undertone which was perfectly audible to the next table, 'only I'm afraid of the spunk, you see, it might adversely affect the spots on the leopard', adding loudly 'he might bite a hole in the rug, and I can't ask him to control his excitement'.[44]

Orton and Halliwell meanwhile pared down the excesses of the apartment they rented in Morocco (the same one in which queer American playwright Tennessee Williams wrote *Suddenly Last Summer* [1959]). 'We've locked the main salon of the flat', wrote Orton, 'which is enormous and gives an impression of millionaire elegance. We'll just pretend that the flat consists of the kitchen, bathroom, and two bedrooms'.[45] In the generally middle and upper-middle-class milieu of queer expatriates, Orton and Halliwell tried to preserve some domestic austerity and so signal their distance from the compatriots they bitchily deride.

Back at home they adopted this approach too. Their bedsit was functional: it had a desk, two chairs, two stools, two single beds. After their deaths a lawyer's letter to Orton's brother detailed the rest:

> Of the articles remaining in the flat it would appear that the most valuable are your brother's typewriter, two student-type table lamps which appear to be new, and a considerable number of gramophone records and books. There is also what appears to be a valuable hi-fi set. Copies of your brother's plays of course will eventually form part of his Estate, and all the paintings in the flat appear to have been collages done by Halliwell. There is a quantity of clothing in the flat including a great coat which Miss Ramsay has suggested you may care to keep. Apparently it was one which she gave to your brother.[46]

The room's simplicity resonates with a bachelor aesthetic emerging in the 1950s and which architect Joel Sanders argues was an 'attempt to showcase masculine austerity' in opposition to a supposedly frivolous decorative femininity.[47] The pair did not attempt to create a stylish 'home beautiful',[48] and despite the broader increase in and fashion for domestic consumption, they didn't accumulate mod cons either. The most expensive item amidst their otherwise minimal possessions was the hi-fi. In this we might see a reflection and production of Orton's working-class masculine 'swagger':[49] 'Men's domain' in this period, historian James Obelkevich writes, was 'limited to the car and audio equipment'.[50] The single beds preserved them (to an extent) from the conjectures of others, of course, but they also fostered a sense of equal and parallel masculinity and mateyness. 'Americans see homosexuality in terms of fag and drag', Orton wrote in a US production note for *Loot*. 'This isn't my vision of the universal brotherhood. They must be perfectly ordinary boys who happen to be fucking each other. Nothing could be more natural. I won't have the Great American Queen brought into it'.[51] Brotherhood and sexual versatility were more appealing for Orton than other models of homosexuality circulating during this period (like those modelled by Alan Louis or Rex Batten, for example). Because of the way home had been gendered and ideologically freighted, though, Orton had a fine line to tread in maintaining domestic life, masculinity, and the illusion of being one of 'two ordinary boys'.

Orton reviled what he saw as feminised roles which could structure queer encounters and relationships, and which also underpinned ideas of queer (and as we've seen elite) interior styling.[52] In July 1967, for example, he recounted an argument with Halliwell in his diary: 'I said "are you going to stand in front of the mirror all day?" He said "I've been washing your fucking underpants! That's why I've been at the sink!" He shouted it loudly and I said "please don't let the whole neighbourhood know you're a queen"'.[53] Though in his resentment of Halliwell's behaviour he signalled a desire for an alternative domestic model (one they perhaps shared before Orton's success), his discontent sinks back into a familiar misogyny and a fear of femininity.[54] He was concerned about what Halliwell's 'hysterical' outbursts, vanity and housework might say about him and them both. This had little to do with a fear of exposure, arrest and prosecution; Orton was after all cavalier in the face of the law. It was much more about protecting and constructing a particular masculinity which was for him also part of a reconstruction of homosexual style.[55] A letter in the Ramsay archive from a school peer of Orton's suggests that this was an image deliberately cultivated in his move to London. 'The other kids used to make fun of him', wrote the correspondent, 'they teased him unmercifully. He was very effeminate. Very shy and he had long eyelashes, very smooth skin and a girlish way of talking. [...] John was different and he felt it'.[56] If this school-mate is right, then it was not just a name that changed in Orton's move to London – from John, to Jack in his very first play, and then to Joe – but also his gendered persona. This was something his plays, his austere domestic set-up, and the clothes he wore all helped to shore up. The studied indifference in the diary is part of this and was a particular production of himself for the readership he and Ramsay envisaged. What it demanded also was a careful negotiation of the domestic and what it could signify to Orton and to the magazine audience looking at pictures of the rising playwright at home. If, with Orton's rise to fame, Halliwell was more home alone and focused on domestic work, and if (as Orton attests) the couple had largely ceased to have sex, then they were for the playwright no longer 'perfectly normal boys who happen to be fucking each other'.

Orton was also defensive about his association with the arts and theatre. 'I mean', he remarked in an *Evening Standard* interview, 'there's absolutely no reason why a writer shouldn't be as tough as a brick layer'.[57] He certainly had the artistic and cultural references to be part of a (queer) literary and artistic *avant garde* and lineage.[58] His debt to Ronald Firbank, Oscar Wilde, and Noel Coward is well documented; they all figure in the 'melting pot' of Orton's writing.[59] Orton refused, however, to wear these cultural and implicitly queer pretensions on his sleeve – something other men did as a means of 'coming out' in this period (in an avowed love of opera, for example).[60] For Orton behaving in this way would have made him a different sort of queer – one he in fact rather despised. In the bedsit there was thus no specially commissioned furniture, none of the latest styles or domestic fashions (aside from the Venetian blinds), no swags of plush velvet, no restrained Queen Anne designs (favoured by Oliver Ford at this time), and no embroidered cushions, such as those which, in an unpublished section of the diary, Orton derisively describes a group of 'queens' working on.[61]

The impulse to mark out a domestic difference was evident before the couple met and in their respective family homes. There were distinct continuities between their youthful and then adult styling. Orton had pulled up the lino of the room he shared with his brother in Leicester, painted the doors and floors, pinned up theatre programmes, and 'painted secret words' in the shorthand he had learned at secretarial college – hiving off for himself something private in that shared space. Alone after his father's suicide in 1949, Halliwell 'began to reclaim the family home, repainting much of it, including the furniture, the dining room collaged with images cut from art books and pasted directly on the walls. His bedroom became "light pink"'.[62] Mural collages were also a strident decorative statement on the walls of the later Noel Road bedsit, which Lahr describes as a 'wall of culture' between the couple and 'the mediocre world outside'.[63] It combined those markers of queer sensibility – Greek statuary and Renaissance art – but crucially presented them prosaically. The men had no miniature replica statues of a Greek

Figure 15 Joe Orton in the bedsit he shared with Kenneth Halliwell, c.1964
© Mirrorpix.

athlete or carefully placed reproduction of a Michelangelo. Instead these featured in a mural made with images cut from library books.[64] This technique and the use of 'found' materials linked the mural to London's Independent Group of artists, which had met at the Institute of Contemporary Art between 1952 and 1955 and whose interest in mass culture and the use of everyday objects and materials posed a challenge to fine art, modernism and notions of high culture.[65] These ideas and approaches were taken up more widely in the pop art emerging in the second half of the 1950s, later described by George Melly, the flamboyantly bisexual jazz musician, as a 'revolt into style' – one that often gave a kitsch, camp twist to art and the art world.[66] There is an association too back to the domestic murals of the 'amusing' stylists and Bloomsbury set and to Shannon and Ricketts' walls at Kenninton Park Road (see figure 2).[67] In Orton and Halliwell's bedsit the murals were a push against convention – a promiscuous mingling of faces and (often naked) torsos spreading across the walls and dominating the simply furnished room. The mural was excessive and unbounded in a sphere which others thought should be organised and tightly controlled.

The mural shrank over time, however. The two men – or one of them – removed or painted over blocks of it, so that by the summer of

1967, art historian Ilsa Colsell writes, 'there would be no collages pasted directly onto the walls of Noel Road. Halliwell's framed works [mentioned by the solicitor] and Orton's play posters the only adornment'.[68] If, as Colsell suggests, we take the murals on the walls of the bedsit in Noel Road to be chiefly Halliwell's work, then the couple had for years been immersed in Halliwell's aesthetic. As Orton's fame increased, there seems to have been a parallel erasure of the murals, making way (deliberately or not) for posters which indicated Orton's accelerating success. Next to the murals of largely pre-twentieth-century art, these playbills presented a contrast – introducing contemporary design and the new sexual subjectivities Orton both wrote into his plays and was himself attempting to embody. The playbills also forged a connection between the bedsit and London's theatreland which was barely 20 minutes away by bus. This aesthetic rebalancing and the 'diminishing murals' comes, Colsell argues, as 'a neat metaphor for Halliwell's own demise'.[69] If Halliwell was the main mural artist, however, Orton had certainly been involved in them – at least in stealing and cutting images from the library books that fed the growing art work. In that sense mural making was part of their domestic life together, even if the mural was reduced in the final months of their lives. Orton had certainly seen it as an appropriate frame within which to be viewed. He repeatedly had himself photographed in front of it, not least for publicity shots (see figure 15). The mural thus spoke of his queer difference and also (much more obliquely) of his togetherness with Halliwell.

Between the bedsit's ordered furnishing and this expansive and then gradually tamed mural, between the artistic references of that mural and the everyday materials used to compile it, between their London base as a couple and their childhood homes, Orton and Halliwell marked out their association with but also distance from domestic, artistic, youth and queer cultures. These tensions revealed something of their own trajectory as a couple. Peggy Ramsay summarised their working life and suggested the ways that it compelled, shaped and overlapped with their domestic life in a letter to Lahr in 1970. She wrote:

> Kenneth's family left him a little bit of money, which subsidised the two of them in a small room and all day they read the classics aloud to one another, and it was during that time that they studied Firbank and Wilde in such detail. Also, during that time, they wrote very bad novels together [...]. When they began running out of money, they used to work in the daytime and earn their living at night in an ice cream factory in order to save electric light. When Joe sent me

Entertaining Mr Sloane, he always spoke of the play as 'we', and after he'd visited me the first time, he always brought Kenneth with him afterwards, and Kenneth always attended rehearsals.[70]

Ramsay (presumably partly via Orton's own accounts of his life) described a financially, emotionally and intellectually interdependent couple playing out their relationship and work life in this 'small room'. Orton himself obliquely and romantically described it in *The Ruffian on the Stair* (1963) just after he and Halliwell had been separated for six months during their imprisonment for defacing Islington library books. In the play Wilson and his (now dead) brother 'had a little room'; they were 'happy', 'bosom friends': 'we had separate beds', he says, 'he was a stickler for convention, but that's as far as it went. We spent every night in each other's company. It's the reason we never got any work done'. 'I'm going round the twist with heartbreak', Wilson adds poignantly on his brother's death.[71] Domestic brotherhood here and elsewhere served as a model for sex and emotional attachment for Orton – as it had for some of the 'homogenic' romantic socialists in the early part of the century.[72] The sense of equality in such relationships might supersede the gender role playing in queer coupledom which Orton detested.

Though Ramsay notes how Orton and Halliwell went together to the rehearsal room, to her office and to the theatre, the bedsit was the chief setting for their relationship in the 1960s, and ironically in this home-based companionate coupledom they keyed into an aspect of wider post-war expectations of intimate relationships.[73] Comradeship had been ranked as fifth in a 1952 survey of the most important thing in marriage; by 1969 (two years after Orton and Halliwell died) it was first.[74] Such intimacy went to the heart of modern subjectivity.[75] As I've suggested, though, Orton and Halliwell's version of home and couple-dom was perhaps too undiluted – and unsustainable. Orton wrote of his relationship with Halliwell in 1967: 'I think it's bad that we live in each other's pockets 24 hours a day and 365 days a year'.[76] Their privacy and protection of the home space exceeded that of the middle-class homosexual couple Schofield described and whose domestic privacy was normalized by going out to work and having friends visit.[77] Orton and Halliwell's perceived domestic isolation, meanwhile, became part of their peculiarity and queerness. The gap between the pair's particular set-up on the one hand and expectations of what a (conventional) home and couple might be on the other, made the relationship difficult to judge, or perhaps easier to dismiss as neurotic, or unloving, or as only those things. After they died Ramsay was highly sensitive to what she saw as the misrepresentation of the partnership. In a letter about Lahr's dramatization of the diary (*Diary of a Somebody* – performed in 1987 and published two years later), she observed: 'they loved each other. There is no love in the play. I mean the kindliness of affection, the comradery of all their years together, and the fun they had'.[78] The manner of their deaths and their being *just* too distant from convention at home and in their conduct, made their relationship difficult to read, for Lahr and for others.

Families of choice

Having read the diaries, Orton's younger sister, Leonie, observed the different kind of home and family her brother had constructed in London. She wrote to Ramsay: 'I realize we were nothing to Joe. You and Kenneth were all the family he acknowledged. His natural family were just an embarrassment to him. I think I've always been aware of this but never admitted it before'.[79] Implicit in Leonie's account is the familiar story of the queer son and brother who leaves his family and reinvents himself through new bonds in a new city. Perhaps, though, it was not so clear-cut. Orton sought to sustain a connection with his family of origin and clearly saw these connections as significant if at one remove from his London life and lifestyle. Leonie observed later that her brother used to write to his mother, but she never wrote back; 'he kept writing and nobody answered'.[80] Joe also returned home (his use of the word) for two weeks every summer and Ramsay described to Leonie how 'warmly' he talked of her.[81] What emerges is not a simple 'either'/'or', but more of a 'this' *and* 'this'.[82]

Orton stayed close to home and family in terms of theme and setting in his plays, but explored different structures of loyalty and emotional and sexual connection. There are thus the cohabiting brothers/lovers in *The Ruffian on the Stair* (1963) while in *Entertaining Mr Sloane* (1964) we have the eponymous hero entering a time-sharing arrangement with sister and brother Kath and Ed, and the baby to come. Sloane veers between the roles of lover, son, and beyond the end of the play, father. In *The Good and Faithful Servant* (1965) Ray – another parentless young man – is told by his grandmother that things would have been easier 'if [his] fathers were alive'. Seeking an explanation for the plural, she explains: 'Your mother was a generous woman and your fathers – though one of them must surely have been your uncle – loved her dearly. You were the result'.[83]

In these configurations Orton deliberately refused to respect the sanctity of the 1950s family or the image of the effete or respectable middle-class homosexual.[84] Through Orton's 'knack of dialogue collage', he drew together 'the elegant, the crude and the ridiculous' to desentimentalise family life in his plays.[85] But rather than creating what literary critic J.E. Gardner calls 'alternative communities',[86] he played with an existing language, structure and set of relationships to create scenarios that were contingent and pragmatic – foreshadowing analysis of more recent family life.[87] The subversiveness of Orton's work lay not in the end result and the formation of a coherent alternative to the norm but rather in the suggestion that home and family were categories and relationships which were not fixed but which could shift shape. It was a lesson learned from the necessarily improvised intimacies of queer life in London in this period and also from the pragmatics and contingencies of his own early family life.

In this Orton offered a model of queer home and family formations which was more complex than that presented by Pauline Macaulay in her contemporaneous play *The Creeper*, which transferred from Nottingham to the West End stage in 1965 – the same year as Orton's *Loot* premiered in Cambridge. As with Orton's plays, *The Creeper's* setting was contemporary, but unlike his, it harked back: the elderly single bachelor Edward Kimberley has an impeccably designed livingroom tellingly furnished with antiques. He 'plays' with bows and arrows and children's toys there, an allusion perhaps to the supposed arrested development of queer men. Paid to play with him are successive non-sexual companions whom he seeks to control completely (rather as Dulcimer had sought to do with his adopted son Julian in Mordant Sharpe's 1932 play *The Green Bay Tree*).[88] If the amoral, criminal Maurice – Kimberley's current companion – parallels Orton's Mr Sloane in his arrival in an established and somewhat troubled home, in *The Creeper* there is no reforming of family. Having already murdered his effeminate predecessor, in the final moments of the play Maurice murders Kimberley too (with the bow and arrow). The young queen and the queer old 'creeper' are both dead and their domestic set-up is closed down. Orton's queer vision is more contingent than Macaulay's – and ultimately more hopeful. However cynical, however selfish his protagonists, family is opened out, given a queer twist, and pressed forward in Orton's plays.

Orton's preoccupation with home and family – in the elaborate mural, the orderly bedsit, and his intense domestic brotherly relationship – resonate with broader contemporary ideas, ideals and cultures associated with youth, class, masculinity, homosexuality, and the arts. The working-class but gentrifying area of London where he and Halliwell chose to live was also significant to the way he fashioned and presented himself. Orton's lifestyle was not compatible with the elusive domestic norm or with John Wolfenden's vision of respectable homosexual domesticity. Nor, given the public sex he had, would he have been any more legal under the 1967 Sexual Offences Act had he lived longer. What is clear, though, is that domestic spaces and familial bonds remained key to the ideas he had about himself and his sense of belonging in London. He might indeed exemplify a self-conscious opening out of family and domestic forms in this period – a prelude to the more overt politicisation of these things in the years that followed.

Part IV
Taking Sexual Politics Home

Introduction

In 1972 a group of Gay Liberation Front squatters wrote to the Notting Hill Housing Trust, which was attempting to evict them:

> We are one unmarried couple and a family of 12 gay men who decided to live together in a rented house in Brixton. There we were harassed by gangs of local queer bashers. [...] We came to Notting Hill principally because most of us had been squeezed out of rooms in the district in the first place. [...] Where must we go? Back into our cells in lonely bedsits?.[1]

The letter signals shifts in approach and consciousness amongst queer men. There was now a sense of rights, of a collective position, and of new possibilities (albeit here potentially curtailed) for living differently. We can certainly identify some of these things before – not least with Orton – but a fresh stridency was now palpable. In the years that followed the home lives of gay men were opened out in new ways, subject to fresh scrutiny on the part of the media, and fought over in local council committee-rooms as equality became a new watch word. AIDS and HIV meant changes to the ways many men lived out their home lives and also adjustments in welfare and housing policy. I have already discussed how the stereotype of the domestically stylish queer was elaborated in the late twentieth century and illustrated the new visibility and possibilities associated with gay fatherhood.[2] This introduction tracks the closely related politicization of issues of housing for gay men in these various contexts, while the two case-study chapters consider in part the impact of this politics on a group of squatters in

Brixton in the 1970s and on photographer Ajamu X (chapter 7), and on the film-maker Derek Jarman (chapter 8).

For many a decisive shift came with the activism and message of the Gay Liberation Front between 1970 and 1972.[3] The Front attempted to bring leftist, identity, and sexual politics together (though not altogether happily or straightforwardly),[4] and sought a sexual and social revolution that would reconfigure family, sexual, and emotional relations and 'abolish all forms of social oppression'.[5] Through various groups, campaigns, and direct actions (or 'zaps') men and women in the Front challenged bigotry and misinformation whilst also looking to their own behaviour and preconceptions through consciousness-raising and experiments in communal living. GLF communards tried to jettison notions of privacy, private property, and monogamy and to provide a counter to the idealized nuclear home and family which they saw embedding sexism, homophobia, and capitalism, and inhibiting self-expression and self-exploration.[6] The nuclear family was in these ways seen as dangerous and in any case, as a ubiquitous model, a myth: the 1971 census had shown that less than a third of households could be described in these terms and only one in ten had a male breadwinner and full-time housewife.[7] This 'traditional' organization had certainly been questioned before,[8] but there was now a more thoroughgoing politicisation of home, family and domesticity through writing associated with Gay and Women's Liberation, through a renewed interest in precedent experiments in living (on the part of Edward Carpenter, for example),[9] through a new radical psychiatry,[10] and through the direct experience and local visibility of radical squats and communes. Such ideas were rehearsed in the GLF magazine *Come Together*, in *Gay News* (from 1972) and in *Gay Left* (from 1975) – underscoring the connections between a politicised gay and politicised domestic life. One issue of *Come Together* was titled 'Fuck the Family' and suggested the ways true liberation depended on the jettisoning of family forms as most people had known them. It was, however, not the abolition but the reform of family that compelled many Gay and Women's Liberationists.[11] After a backlash against anti-family rhetoric in the mid-1970s, a trio of feminist sociologists argued that liberationists sought not to reject but to embrace the 'best' of the 'ideals' of family: 'intimacy, commitment, nurturance, collectivity and individual autonomy'.[12] The letter from gay communards cited earlier similarly retained the language and some of the associations of family: 'We are as close as any nuclear family', the letter went on, 'we hear so much about the plight of broken families, but we are surrounded on all sides by attempts to break our family'.[13]

The London GLF petered out during 1972 after a walk-out by many of the women and conflict over approaches and emphasis – especially between the leftist 'politicos' and those experimenting with radical drag, gender-bending and alternative living.[14] Though the GLF was short-lived, its impact was tangible in subsequent debates about family, campaigning around AIDS and Clause 28 in the 1980s and 1990s, and even in the legislative programme of the New Labour government from 1997.[15] More immediately men and women involved in or influenced by the GLF carried its perspectives and activism forward in local groups and in continuing and further experiments in living like the squats in Brixton. By reshaping ideas of sex and sexuality, Women's and Gay Liberation opened out new possibilities for sexual relations and domestic life. As a 'revolutionary' moment, though, it needs to be seen as both a new spur to action and lifestyle change and also as an articulation of changes already in process.[16] Moreover, if there were new voices and a fresh visibility, this was not a mass movement. Only a handful of gays and lesbians were directly involved in zaps and other activities. GLFers tended to be metropolitan and without the responsibilities of home, work and family that might require more caution and conformity. Squatting, communal living, experimental sex and coming out were still things that did not feel possible for most queer men and women. Others felt a loss in the new movement. Some counter cultural encounters from the fifties – in the cross-over identifications of queer men, prostitutes and new Afro-Caribbean immigrants in London's Notting Hill, for example – did not map easily onto the new identity politics.[17] Derek Jarman and Carl Marshall were, meanwhile, a little older than most GLFers and had already felt different or differently conceptualized freedoms arising out of 1960s youth and counterculture.[18] They had found other ways to live differently and without joining communes and squats. These were not the only ways of practising politics at home.

So while the liberationists and communards certainly had an impact in terms of setting an agenda and providing precedents for political organizing and action,[19] for many people this activism and lifestyle seemed peripheral. It is important to remember that many queer men continued to forge domestic lives which echoed those of previous generations. Moreover, sexual and social conservatism was sufficiently ingrained in broader attitudes and behaviours to encourage the championing by Margaret Thatcher's governments of (supposed) Victorian and family values from 1979 – ideas which took hold to an extent in the wider conservative backlash of the 1980s. This was a decade when the putative dangers of the permissive society were articulated forcefully by government and the media, and when Labour was pilloried for its 'loony' support of 'minorities'. A platform speaker at the 1985 Tory party proclaimed (to applause): 'if you want a queer for a neighbour, vote Labour'.[20] Gays, lesbians and single mothers especially were sharply criticised. The former were subject to the infamous Section 28 of the Local Government Act (1988) which stated that local authorities 'shall not [...] promote the teaching in any maintained school of the acceptability of homosexuality as a pretended family relationship'. There seemed to be a wider hardening of attitudes towards homosexuality. In 1983 62 per cent of people surveyed disapproved of gay relationships; by 1987 this had risen to 74 per cent. In the same year – and providing ammunition for the government in its pursuit of Section 28 – 93 percent per cent stated that gay adoption should be forbidden,[21] compared to 63 per cent in 1979.[22] As deaths from AIDS-related illnesses peaked at the end of the decade, prosecutions for consensual homosexual acts reached their highest level since records began – 3065 in 1989. This exceeded even the levels during the so-called witch-hunt against homosexuals in the mid-1950s.[23]

Partly as a result of previous organizing and consciousness raising, gays and lesbians campaigned as never before, entrenching the association between gay lives, a leftist and activist politics, and (in the wake of Section 28 especially) issues of family. Early Gay Pride marches had been passionate but relatively small in the 1970s and early 1980s, but Section 28 brought 40,000 people out in 1988. In 1990 the newspaper *Capital Gay* observed that the lesbian and gay movement had 'come of age': 'we have [...] taken to the streets in the biggest ever lesbian and gay demonstrations, the media coverage has been massive and the visibility of our community has rarely, if ever, been greater'.[24] It was through such mass public demonstrations and media and parliamentary confrontations, and also through private debate among family members, friends and neighbours that sexual difference was brought more fully into people's consciousness.[25] In this we can still mark the importance of Gay Liberation in the early 1970s but gesture also to a second vociferous wave of radicalism in the late 1980s relating specifically (and more narrowly) to issues of housing, Section 28, and HIV and AIDS.

Housing was highlighted as a central issue for gay men in this period in terms of prejudice in the private rental market, council-house allocation, and specialist provision for people with AIDS. The gay press was key in steering attention towards an issue which was seen to present particular challenges (though also possibilities) for gay men.[26] A feature in *Gay News* in 1972 investigated ongoing prejudice,[27] although the 'shock' results of an accommodation survey a few issues later suggested a more permissive rental market than had been assumed. 'Accommodation agencies have come out almost unanimously in favour of gays' on the 'grounds of their reliability and cleanliness', it said. Landlords contacted directly were slightly more equivocal, though only 3 out of 33 were totally opposed to having gay tenants. 'The flat hunting business in and around London just doesn't have the anti-gay drama that we first believed it did', the paper concluded.[28]

Personal ads in *Gay News* enlarged the possibility for finding gay and gay friendly landlords and tenants. Sometimes there was an implied or explicit deal on rent relating to sex, companionship or domestic chores, signalling a desire on the part of some men for more than a conventional lodging or sharing arrangement. A 'young man' in North London 'require[d] another to share my modern house N. London and form sincere friendship. Not camp but good looking. The right guy is more important than excessive rent'. In the same issue a 'slim, hairy' 50-year old sought a 'young person [...] non effeminate, no rent, no ties or restrictions. Photo appreciated slim, well-built [...] Genuine friendship needed'.[29] The limits of desirability and acceptability become clear in these ads. Around two in ten adverts in the run of *Gay News* sought non-effeminate non-camp house sharers or tenants in that by now familiar repudiation of femininity on the queer home front. This led others to seek rooms specifically on their own terms. 'Real gay brother (camp) and sister need a flat up to £15 prefer unfurnished' wrote one pair;[30] another, more despairing: 'unfurnished flat required London by two genuine gays early 1940s. Fed up with furnished rooms and prejudice, will understanding landlord please help'.[31] Alongside such ads, the paper flagged housing alternatives (like squats and communes) and sources of housing help and guidance (including Lesbian and Gay Switchboard).

Homelessness was by this time recognized as a particular problem among gay and lesbian young people, who, having come out, were obliged or felt the need to leave family homes. CHAR – the national campaign for single homeless people – observed in 1989 that 'harassment is one of the major causes of homelessness among lesbians and gay men', concluding that 11 per cent of young gay men and women were evicted by their parents.[32] A survey of callers to Lesbian and Gay Switchboard found that one in four attributed their particular housing problems to their sexuality.[33] Homeless charities, housing associations and co-ops began in the 1980s to include specific policy initiatives to support homeless gay men. Gay charity Stonewall Housing (launched in

1982), for example, opened a hostel in 1988 amidst much controversy.[34] The *ad hoc*, word-of-mouth housing solutions for queer men with limited resources of earlier in the postwar period endured, but there were now more formalized avenues of support and a greater visibility of different housing options – from gay house-shares flagged in the gay press to squats, co-ops, housing associations and council housing.

In the 1980s The Greater London Council (GLC) and left-wing local London Borough Councils (especially Lambeth, Islington, Hackney and Haringey) began tackling discrimination directly in their policy on housing. There were a number of reasons for council engagement with these issues at this time – including the rise of a new generation of Labour party activists schooled in liberationist and countercultural politics, a more visible gay constituency in the Labour Party, and a broader intellectual shift in left-wing politics away from class and towards broader notions of social justice.[35] Housing issues were increasingly examined as part of an equal-opportunities agenda, contributing to a broader shift in lesbian and gay politics away from GLF-style social revolution.[36] By 1986, 10 of the 36 London boroughs had an equal-opportunities policy statement for gays and lesbians,[37] and though action was uneven it was significant in bringing consideration of gay and lesbian needs on to agendas in the early to mid-1980s in terms especially of homelessness, abuse, and succession rights for gay couples in council property[38] – an urgent problem in the context of AIDS.

In 1985 central government had – seemingly inadvertently and without any direct reference to AIDS – laid the groundwork for a local council response to the housing crisis many men with AIDS found themselves in. The Homeless Persons Housing Act of 1985 outlined the situations in which single people might be assessed as being in priority need – that was either because of 'threats of violence' from another person in the same accommodation or because of 'vulnerability' 'as a result of handicap or physical disability or other special reason'.[39] While 39 per cent of local authorities nationally did not consider an AIDS diagnosis on its own to constitute a priority, in London where the problem was most acute almost all councils did.[40] Because many men with AIDS were relatively young, they had often not secured stable or permanent accommodation and frequently faced harassment or a lack of support from elsewhere.[41] The issue for councils, though, was the pressure on resources. Hammersmith and Fulham council reported that even as a priority, 40 per cent of people with AIDS died before being permanently housed. It had to use the private rental market to meet the extra demand.[42] This was all in the context of a sharp reduction in funding for local authority house building programmes and the right for tenants to buy their council homes, which, from 1980, shifted a significant amount of council housing into the private sector.[43]

In light of the new engagement with housing equality, the *Mail*, the *Express* and the *Evening Standard* especially ran stories on how local council measures encouraged homosexuality, placed young homosexuals at risk of abuse,[44] flouted the age of consent laws,[45] provided 'a queue jumpers' charter' for gays,[46] and placed 'normal' families at a disadvantage.[47] When Lambeth Council became the first nationally to designate homeless people with AIDS as in priority housing need there was 'outrage' in the *Express*. Under a banner headline 'AIDS Gays to Get Council Housing', the paper cited the fears of a local Tory councillor that the borough would be 'turn[ed] into a Mecca for these people, with Lambeth being flooded by gay men claiming they have AIDS and then demanding council housing'.[48] These press responses hinged on ideas of legitimacy and of who was within or beyond the purview of civic and state support.

The Conservative government meanwhile refused to include gay and lesbian couples in reform of council house succession rights in the Housing Acts of 1980 and 1985; it abolished the GLC and other metropolitan councils in 1986; and most directly, as we have seen, it introduced Section 28 to the Local Government Act of 1988.[49] A key issue in this measure, and again in the further adjustment to the Housing Act which in 1996 (which finally gave partnership succession rights in council property to all couples) was one of pretence. Section 28 alluded to the pretend families of homosexuals. The 1996 Act raised the apparent problem of determining 'whether a homosexual relationship is genuine'.[50] The status of two men living together was still causing more uncertainty than a man and a woman sharing (even though the latter might also be 'just friends'). The flood of 'AIDS gays' moving to Lambeth might, remember, only be 'claiming' to be ill.

Despite the press vitriol, this issue of pretence, and the practical difficulties of housing shortfalls for local councils, something significant had changed in a relatively short space of time and in response to a particular crisis. Gay men in need increasingly felt they could expect housing assistance and there was at least an attempt to meet that need by London councils and various housing associations and trusts. Gay men were no longer quite the outsiders in terms of council and charitable housing policy and provision that they had been in previous decades.

The period from the 1960s to the present covered by the coming two chapters is thus marked by a broad developing sense of the particularity of gay men in relation to home and family. They were a category in council housing equalities policy, and were often deemed to be in special housing need as a result of homelessness and AIDS. They were the subject of specific policies on the part of mortgage lenders, were touted in various forums as leaders in domestic taste, and were gaining visibility as fathers.[51] There was growing insistence on equality even as many gay men sought to mark out their distinction and difference with pride. These imperatives of equality and difference were often entwined and this braced a new politics of gay home-making from the 1970s. Taking up the stories of Brixton squatters, of Ajamu X and of Derek Jarman helps us to see how this played out in localized and particular circumstances.

7
'Gay Times': The Brixton Squatters

Soon after arriving from Ireland in the mid-1970s David got off the bus in Brixton, south London, and wandered along Railton Road.

> There was this group of black men standing around and I remember going up to them and saying 'excuse me, could you tell me where the Gay Centre is in Brixton'. This black man said 'sure, I'm just going home. I can take you up there'. [... I] waited there and about a minute or two afterwards this vision in purple and red and diamonds walked past. He flashed his eyes at me and swished around the corner and up the stairs. [...] It was Alistair. He took me to 159 Railton Road and it was liberation because I looked around at all these people who looked like me [...] we were going to change the world tomorrow – overnight and there as going to be gay liberation in a year's time. Marvellous. ('David', 1983)[1]

This was David's introduction to what became known as the Brixton Gay Community. The first house in this community – the one visited by David – was squatted in 1974; the gay centre he mentions opened in squatted premises just along the street at 79 Railton Road in the same year. Nine more houses were subsequently squatted on Railton Road (between 153 and 159) and the parallel Mayall Road (between 146 and 152), and were home for between 50 and 60 men for anything from a week to almost ten years. Several stayed on once the houses were converted into flats and absorbed as a gay enclave into the Brixton Housing Co-operative between 1982 and 1984. The South London Gay Centre was an important but short-lived focal point; it closed in 1976 and I talk about it only peripherally here, concentrating instead on the squats and the squatters' attempt to create home differently.

This relates to the histories of counter, leftist and gay radical culture in 1970s London and exemplifies some of the new meanings of gay identity, community and politics emerging in this period. Focusing on this local and particular housing solution alerts us to the contingencies of the domestic and everyday and the ways in which they shape political commitment and action. David's testimony immediately flags the significance of personal encounters, of the coincident Afro-Caribbean community, and of his own status as an outsider. Other accounts highlight the importance of local material circumstances, of jobs (or the lack of them), of local politics and political formations, and of the Brixton riots of 1981. They also illuminate the complex ways in which the unspoken and often unconscious imperatives associated with ethnicity, class, and the familial, social and cultural contexts of our upbringing get played out and mediated under new and changing local circumstances. This chapter thus considers the limits of identification for this group of men, the inclusions and exclusions associated with their community, and the continuities and discontinuities between that community, other Brixton counter cultures and broader expectations of home and family. It explores the desire for a form of domestic life which could reflect sexual difference and an associated politics. It also looks at the ways in which that was hard to achieve and sustain. However powerful the desire for collectivity, the individual's desire to shape space and to have some form of ownership of it was very strong. The ultimate decision by the majority of the squatters to divide the squatted houses into single occupancy flats when they were transferred to the Brixton Housing Co-op is suggestive in this respect.

My main sources are three sets of interviews. The first were gathered by Jamie Hall and Bill Thornycroft in Brixton in 1983 and 1984 (Jamie was one of the squatters; Bill lived – and still lives – nearby but was very much part of the community); the second by another former squatter, Ian Townson, in 1996 and 1997 for a history of the South London Gay Liberation Front, Gay Centre and Railton/Mayall Road squats.[2] In 2008 I conducted further interviews – including some with men who had previously participated in Jamie, Bill and Ian's projects. Taken together the three sets of interviews can show how memories and judgements shift with changing times and personal circumstances.[3] Alongside letters, diaries, newspaper articles and ephemera also held at the London School of Economics, they give multiple, partial and sometimes contradictory insights into Brixton in the 1970s and early 1980s. They permit reflections on the legacy of the squats – for the men themselves, for other later residents of the area, and for the wider stories we tell about gay identity, community and politics in the 1970s and since.

Contexts

Squatting has a long history, associated especially with the housing crises following the two world wars,[4] but it became more embedded in the urban landscape and took on additional counter and youth culture associations in the late 1960s and 1970s. Squatters' were, to one contemporary commentator, 'symbols of the age'.[5] Successive issues of *Alternative London* (from 1971) and the *Squatters Handbook* (from 1975) provided practical advice and outlined the political case for opposing private property and joining a collective struggle for personal autonomy.[6] In 1976 there were an estimated 30,000 squatters in London out of a total of around 50,000 nationally. For some gay men and lesbians especially it was a positive alternative to the restrictions and isolation they could feel in family homes, bedsits and other rented accommodation. In the wake of a much more visible gay politics post-Stonewall and post-GLF, some wanted to live without the kind of reserve often required in the private rental market. 'Couples in bed-sits will always be vulnerable to society's hostility in a way that a collective will not', announced GLF newspaper *Come Together*.[7] The infamous Cockettes communes in San Francisco,[8] and closer to home the GLF communes in Bounds Green, Brixton, Notting Hill and Bethnal Green meanwhile offered examples of how it might be possible to organize domestic lives differently.[9]

The level of vacant (often council) property in areas like Notting Hill, Camden, Islington and Brixton meant that space was available in the capital for just such experiments.[10] In the London Borough of Lambeth – which includes Brixton – 1.1 per cent of council housing stock was vacant in 1975, rising to 4.6 per cent by 1978. This put it in the top five of the 33 London boroughs in terms of vacancy rates. Much of this was dilapidated pre-1919 terrace housing like that in Railton and Mayall Roads.[11] The Brixton area had been through some significant demographic shifts. It was a relatively affluent middle-class Victorian suburb before becoming poorer and more working class in the first half of the twentieth century. During this time it was known for boarding houses popular with actors, giving the area a Bohemian slant.[12] A black student presence before World War Two expanded and became more established in the late 1940s and 1950s – largely because Brixton also had some of cheapest rents in the capital.[13] By the 1970s the area was associated with social deprivation.[14] It had a higher proportion of single people and immigrants (predominantly from the Caribbean) than any other inner London borough. Much of the population was also relatively new to the area; 48 per cent had lived in Brixton for less than five years.[15] Perhaps partly as a result, a local government survey of 1974 revealed a felt lack of 'community' or 'neighbourhood' compared with other areas of London. Only 33 per cent said it was an area they felt they belonged to, as opposed to 75 per cent in a similar survey in Hornsey in north London, and 78 per cent nationally.[16] This local vacuum arguably cleaved a space for countercultures to develop. Railton Road was already well squatted by the time the gay contingent arrived, providing a precedent radical/alternative network in housing that had only recently been saved from council demolition after a local campaign.[17] Ian remembers that 'Railton Road [was] littered with alternative political groups.' There was the People's News Service, and the anarchist bookshop; there were the two women's centres and also 'a lot of leftwing Labour councillors [including future Greater London Council Leader and London Mayor, Ken Livingstone] who were quite willing to support you' (Ian, 2008). In addition the area was now more accessible. The Victoria Line connected Brixton with the underground network and central London from 1971. All this, Ian observed, created a 'crucible in which [the gay squats] could happen', facilitating what he called a 'a moment of community' (Ian, 2008).

'Com[ing] together'

Most of the squatters were politically active in some way before they moved into the squats – through involvement in the British Communist Party, in other left-wing groups, in student activism, in the GLF, and, for the Australian contingent especially, in the anti-Vietnam war movement. Others, though, arrived with a looser politics and were drawn to friends, lovers or a 'certain mystique' associated with some squatters (Peter, 2008). Only a handful were from Brixton and the majority came from outside London – from elsewhere in the UK, from Ireland, other parts of Europe, and (as flights became cheaper and the backpacking tradition became more established) Australia.[18] This is key: the squatters had been and continued to be highly mobile, in terms of their daily lives in London and in terms of moving on to other places, nationally and internationally, temporarily and permanently.[19] This mobility marked them out from large sections of the local population who lived their lives largely in and around Brixton.[20] The squats were a pragmatic, practical solution and also an experimental space where men with a loosely shared politics, sexuality, and investment in youth and counterculture came together. The relative importance of these different factors varied from squatter to squatter but there was a consensus between those interviewed that the experience of living in the community was formative. It provided a new sense of belonging for some, a further or even heightened feeling of alienation for others. They were often frustrated by the difficulty of making the kind of individual mark that might be possible in other circumstances. For each of the men the experience of living in the squats nevertheless ushered in a new or reshaped political engagement, and a changed attitude to sexual identity, sex, relationships and friendships.

Between the Gay Centre and the squats there was 'always an immense amount of stuff happening' (Peter, 1983). South London GLF, the *Gay News* Defence Committee and SM gays met in the squats; the theatre troupe the Brixton Faeries wrote and rehearsed there; and banners and costumes were made for zaps, campaigns and community events. Two members of the *Gay Left* collective were closely associated with the squats which meant it also met there occasionally. In addition, Jem recalls, 'we'd do things like paint the ceilings, talk, make endless cups of tea, put graffiti on the walls – which was good. It was actually part of the breaking from old ideas' ('Jem', 1983). 'Some people', Mike observed, 'made a community within a house and others moved around and related to two or three houses. Everybody had different patterns of interaction' ('Mike', 1983). The communal garden (formed as squatters demolished dividing garden walls) and back doors left unlocked meant it was easy to drop in and out of the houses without going on to Mayall or Railton Roads themselves. This helped to cement a sense of community even as it also fostered a certain insularity – especially for those who weren't working. Once inside 'it was almost as though you never had to go out [...] it provided a whole lifestyle. [...] There was companionship and sex, discussion and good food and an endless stream of faces all under one roof' (Peter, 1983). As with the GLF, the squats could be all-consuming – shaping an idea of gay identity that was about much more than sexual object choice.

Houses developed particular reputations. In one, two men assembled 'all this detritus of 50s domestic objects and created a whole life out of it' (Don, 1997) – performing a camp twist on the iconic (if illusory) postwar home. Residents of 159 Railton Road keyed into personal growth and self-awareness, and the house became known as 'purity ashram'. To the disdain of 'hardliners' in other houses, some from 159 went on gay men's retreats to Laurieston Hall in Scotland. They left 'the

Figure 16 Tony Smith (r) and Alistair Kerr (l) in one of the Railton Road squats
© Ian Townson.

struggle' behind; 'it was ridiculous to go all the way up the country to eat oak leaves', they were told (Peter, 1983). In all this there are clear echoes of the GLF with its broad church of leftist political debate and argument, direct action, structured campaigning, consciousness raising, radical drag, and a general talkativeness and playfulness with – as well as serious thinking about – sex, family, home, drugs, identity, and lifestyle. There are echoes too of attendant tensions – between socialist and identity politics, between activist strategies, and in debate about the role of the individual in processes of social change and how in practice to live collectively.[21]

Given the diversity of opinion and the different levels and manner of political engagement, the degree of separation enforced by the small terraced houses perhaps allowed the community to endure – for considerably longer than the GLF communes, for example. Though bounds of acceptability were under constant negotiation in the squats, and though in the attempt to escape convention there may ironically have been 'a higher degree of social control' (as squatters monitored each others' behaviour and attitudes),[22] there was yet no initiating agreement for any particular model of living as there had been in GLF communes. 'One of the big dangers within big communal structures or co-ops is that you lose yourself to this wider theme', said Peter (2008). The separate houses in the Brixton squats lent themselves to an individualism which was nevertheless a disappointment to some – especially those who had lived communally before. With experience of the Brixton and Notting Hill GLF communes behind him, Julian encouraged fellow squatters to move into houses where couples had ended up living together in a 'parody' of heterosexuality (Julian, 1997). Don found in the squats an insufficient challenge to normalised domestic arrangements. There were, he said, 'no large spaces [...] in which communal eating could take place; communal washing could take place' (Don, 1997).[23]

Andreas did in fact create one such space by knocking down an internal wall in one of the houses to create an area for group meals. This for him, though, was not the radical departure Don might have seen it to be. Instead it reminded him of his childhood experiences in Cyprus, and allowed him to see the squatters as his 'new family' (Andreas, 2008). If group meals in the squats subverted traditional families, in some ways they replicated their function in fostering togetherness and also tacitly suggesting who was at the core of the community.[24] Such connections to the past were pertinent for other squatters too. Peter saw his life in the squat as a break with his 'narrow' past, for example, but also reflected on the ways in which his sense of comfort in an extended group and in down-at-heel conditions in Brixton came partly from his upbringing in a large and poor family in Australia. 'I just wouldn't have felt comfortable in a chic squat in Belgravia – and they did exist' (Peter, 2008).[25]

Despite these links to the past there was for most of the squatters a strong sense of disjuncture between the homes they had known as children and the different relationships and ethos of the squats. Robert saw the squats as an 'alternative to everything; alternative diet to my parents, alternative beliefs to my parents, alternative sexuality to my parents [...I] want[ed] to try my own form of expression in the world'

Figure 17 A communal meal – with (l to r) John Lloyd, Alistair Kerr and Julian Hows
© Ian Townson.

('Robert', 1997). Living this way was for Stephen 'a kind of rupture'. He remembers his mother telling him that his father 'was coming to get me out of that place'. 'It was shocking to them that I lived in those conditions', he went on. 'To them – who had grown up in the 30s and 40s – [it was like] everything was dissolving' (Stephen, 2008). The conjunction of London, squatting and homosexuality was 'very disappointing, frightening'. For Stephen and his fellow squatters, meanwhile, that conjunction suggested a new way of being in the world which potentially reinvented family and home beyond relations of production. Though historian John D'Emilio and others have shown gay identity and an associated individualism emerging out of capitalism,[26] the squatters saw their coming together in this context as a direct challenge to it. It evaded the rental market, mortgages, split roles of (feminine) homemaker and (masculine) provider, and allowed for experimentation with other forms of identification. 'No matter what the politics of the squats were, there was a reconstruction of gay men going on. There wasn't the constraints of careers, property to tie us down to social expectations. We were charting new territory' (Stephen, 1997). Sam had lived 'with a guy in Dulwich' ten years earlier. 'He didn't acknowledge it as a gay relationship. The term hadn't even been invented really in 1959. It was just two guys living together that liked each other' (rather as Joe Orton idealised queer co-residence).[27] The relationship ended, and Sam's experiences with other men became 'sort of furtive'; Earls Court in west London, was, he said, 'about the only gay scene'. The Brixton gay community provided something different: 'I liked the atmosphere. It was infinitely preferable to the straight gay scene because people were more politicized, there was a message, there was a cause'. In an echo of GLFers' memories of their first meeting,[28] he noted that: 'it was a wonderful feeling of having your own people' ('Sam', 1997). The Brixton community shaped Joe's sense of 'what it is to be gay' and his 'vision of what a gay community could be' ('Joe', 1997).[29] Former GLF communard Julian saw this domestic coming together as similarly pivotal: 'until you live with gay people, you haven't come out' (Julian, 1997).

This domestic coming together (if not coming out) had been important for earlier queer men. The association of this with a politicised gay community was new, though, and this novelty and distinctiveness was noted beyond the squats. In the furore about the Gay Centre's application for a council grant in 1975, Mrs Auld, a local pub landlady, disputed the squatters' 'homosexual' credentials in the local press. They were 'exhibitionists, not true homosexuals', she said. 'I saw one of them run outside dressed in women's underwear, black tights and a suspender belt' – while insisting she didn't mind 'what they did inside their own walls'.[30] An opinion piece in the *South London Press* denounced the protest by members of the community outside Mrs Auld's pub, The George, after men had been banned for kissing there. 'It is very doubtful whether the quieter breed of homosexuals – who form the majority – welcome this gay intrusion on their privacy'.[31] The letters' pages carried similar sentiments – supporting 'the unobvious happy homosexual', while condemning the unpalatable Brixton 'breed'.[32] When the Sexual Offences Act was passed less than a decade earlier in 1967 (decriminalising sex between two men over 21 in private), Lord Arran had asked homosexuals to show their thanks by conducting themselves 'quietly and with dignity'.[33] Mrs Auld and her supporters were rehearsing the same model of acceptability.

Such comments on the squats in the press helped to consolidate them as a distinctive and homogenous community of gay men existing in opposition to another (and, to some, more acceptable) homosexual type. This in part fostered a collective identity between the very different households, especially when they came under attack. Windows of one of the first houses Ian squatted were smashed and there was a serious attack later from another group of local squatters. The police were generally either unresponsive or slow to respond to these incidents, and there were also two police raids (one after the police had taken some decorative windmills in a squatters' window box as drug dealing code). If Andreas thought the squats looked fortified from the streets, it was, to Ian and others, for good reason given the periodic attacks and sense of danger from outside some squatters felt (Andreas, 2008; Ian, 2008).

By creating a deliberate distance from past (and enduring) cultures of homosexuality and of family and home, the men also underscored a difference from the wider local community. Many were determined nevertheless to live as part of that community rather than reproducing what they saw as the separatist mentality of the 'straight gay scene' (Sam, 1997).[34] They issued press releases about events and the police raids to raise awareness, wrote campaigning letters on various fronts, got involved in local community events, and toured old people's homes with shows and sing-a-longs. Their stance – again echoing that of the GLF – was engagement with the local community and other struggles. When Malcolm stood as a GLF candidate in the local elections in 1974 he pledged 'to fight for the right of all oppressed minority groups including black people, unmarried mothers and the single homeless'.[35] A massive banner unfurled across Railton Road in honour of Gay Pride welcomed 'anti-fascists' to the area, and several squatters took part in pickets of Brixton police station over racist harassment which they had sometimes witnessed literally on their doorsteps.

In and out

The sense of the squatting community being closed and insular and yet open and embracing played out in multiple ways. The attempt to 'work out a way of living' had 'different impacts in different houses' and also among different people (Ian, 2008). This sometimes related to class: 'I don't know if class is the right word but [you got] people of the same style living together in a house' (Tony, 2008). As Tony's hesitation suggests, it is difficult to roll out any simplistic class analysis in relation to the community. The way in which the men talk about class suggests that it functioned differently for them than for their parents or some of their straight contemporaries. This is about how gay identities were being conceptualized and articulated during this period – most particularly in relation to the postwar growth in higher education in the UK and to increasing social and geographic mobility. The university experience and the chance to move away from home allowed for some a more strident expression of sexual difference than if had they remained at or near their family homes. Those same moves and experiences might also have suggested a class shift, even though Gay Liberation, counter-cultural and local community politics sought to challenge class divisions and associated privileges and oppressions. The geography of London's housing market meanwhile meant that vacant property for squatting was largely situated in working-class areas like Brixton. For some squatters this all added up to a sense of being *déclassé* and distant from cultures of class, though we might instead observe a collision and/ or a coming together of various class identifications.[36]

These and related assumptions (especially when the men did not quite realize them) could be exclusive – of local queer working-class and Afro-Caribbean men, and of women and straight men. This was something several squatters directly and incisively mention in subsequent interviews and letters. Bill, for example, recalls local working-class gay men living in nearby squats whom

> we rudely called the 'nerds': [...] Local working class lad[s] who resented (and still resent!) us politicos and the college boy brown rice brigade. [The nerds] mostly did not live in what are now the gay houses but other buildings around and about Railton Road [...] But they were a part of the whole thing and are not reflected in the [interview] tapes.[37]

Most of the men in the Railton Road squats were university educated, and amongst those that worked many were teachers, musicians and artists. The tacit kudos working outside the private sector gave them made Don, who was waiting in restaurants in the West End, feel 'very very insecure'. 'I did not like the gay community in the squat at all. [...] [There was] a certain kind of Bohemian ease, an affected ennui about the place that I simply couldn't participate in' (Don, 1997). Ben, a local working class man who lived in a nearby gay squat at St George's Mansions before moving to one of the Railton Road houses, felt something similar:

> There are so many differences between what has just been lumped together as a gay community [...] It wasn't so much a subculture [as a subculture] within a subculture. It was split more along class lines and racial lines and all kind of things ('Ben', 1997).

Ben goes on to highlight a sense of difference in the later 1970s and early 1980s between Brixton gays and another element who brought different drugs and a certain cynicism to St George's Mansions, with knock-on effects for the Railton Road community because of the crossover of people:

> I think heroin use came about when more of the criminal element sub-culture part of the gay world moved in [...] Up until then [...] it had been dope and perhaps hallucinogenics. They were sort of expressive and exploratory and possibly even artistic. [...] I think the more criminal element [...] were coming from places like Earl's Court and Chelsea and Piccadilly. [...] Hard drugs moved in when the actual vision of gay liberation moved out (Ben, 1997).

In this Ben marks clear lines between West End and Brixton gay 'worlds', lines drawn in different ways by other squatters in their disdain for the central London 'straight gay scene'. In addition Ben suggests that intersecting drug and class cultures in part modulated a sense of who was 'in' and who was 'out' in these different places. This is especially true for the British squatters. It is noticeable that the Australian and Irish contingent mention class (and indeed drugs) less; their sense of difference perhaps arose less from these factors and more from their immigrant status.

The squats were conspicuously male. One woman lived for a while at 46 Mayall Road; two others at 159 Railton Road. Peter remembers that partly as a result 159 was 'a bit separate from other houses because [they were] living there' (Peter, 1997). It was specifically and deliberately a gay male community at a point when there was a considerable focus on what being gay meant. Though some of the men had relationships with women, and though there was discussion about and support for the Women's Liberation movement, there was also in practice a separatism – with the Railton Road and St George's Mansions squats and Gay Community Centre on the one hand, and, on the other, the Railton Road Women's Centres and a lesbian squatting community in nearby Bellefields Road. Though one of the Women's Centres helped and advised the gay squatters and there was some mutual support, the centres and the lesbian squats are mentioned rarely in interview and there seems to have been little cross-over between them.

This separatism was replicated with local straight male squatters – some of whom had also been practically helpful. Ben signals a distinct shift between the squatting period and the late 1990s when he was interviewed. 'I don't think the concept of being gay friendly was as well rooted then as it is now. [...] I think it was still kind of cut and dried' (Ben, 1997). Peter remembers that 'there were years when we never saw another straight man [...] The whole community seemed to be separatist in terms of heterosexual men [...] There was positive vetting' (Peter, 1997). Bill believes that this deliberate exclusion had an impact on wider political connections:

> A straight man had already squatted the Gay Centre before we had it. [...] He tried to be supportive until he was chased away by the heavy gang. You know, there were all the 'Men Against sexism' groups which I think had died by then because they were screamed at by gay men.[38]

Despite a commitment to fluid identities and open relationships between different genders and sexualities, in practice things were much more divided.

Relations between the squatters and the local Afro-Caribbean community were generally cordial. This was the experience of David who I cited at the start of this chapter, and Don remembers that the poet Linton Kwesi Johnson always 'tipped his hat and said good day in one of the most ceremonial of ways' (Don, 1997). If there was a cordiality, though, there was again a sense of distance. Liz, who lived in a black squat at 121 Railton Rd, remembers things being friendly enough, but also little interaction. There was no joint political organising, for example, partly, she suggests, because the gay squatters were focusing on different issues.[39]

Racial difference came into sharper focus with the riots of April 1981. The intense stop and search police activity that preceded and triggered the riots did not especially affect the gay squatting community. Few were subject to the kind of police harassment that black men in particular experienced under 'Operation Swamp' for five days from 6 April when nearly 1000 black people were stopped and searched by a force of over 100 plain clothes officers. Although among the squatters there was 'lots of feeling against the police' who were 'like an occupying force', there were also different issues at stake for them (Stephen, 2008). Several squatters watched the riots 'from the roof', feeling like spectators of the growing tension and then rioting (Ian, 2008). Australian Clive wrote: 'what I remember of my reaction to the riot was the desire to witness it'.

Such responses highlights the limits of identification, of identity-based politics, and of participation in parallel struggles. Ted Walker

Brown moved into an earlier GLF commune at Penge, south-east London, with his white boyfriend. His three years there and in subsequent communes at Bounds Green and Muswell Hill were 'the best' of his life, but he still found it difficult to engage fellow communards in debate about race because of a liberal cautiousness about causing offence. 'I tried to initiate a discussion about race', he said, 'but as I was the only black present it didn't work very well. It was just me lecturing everybody, and everybody, being very liberal and so on, they would just say yes to whatever I said and it didn't get anywhere'.[40]

If this sense of disengagement came partly from differing political priorities and also pressing differences in the way racism and anti-gay prejudice played out locally and more broadly, there were also other reasons why the squats remained almost exclusively white. Rhetorician Charles I. Nero observes that 'the controlling image of black gay men, which is produced by gays and straights, provides ideological support for the exclusion of black gay men from full participation in queer cultures'.[41] Certainly the experimental films of Derek Jarman and Ron Peck in London during the 1970s were populated by white men, and it was not until Isaac Julien's work in the late 1980s that a fuller exploration of distinctive queer black identities and experiences in Britain began to emerge on film. Ajamu describes a continuing invisibility as a black gay man in Brixton because of perceptions of what gay was and still is conceived to be; white and more effeminate friends get more trouble than he ever has, he said (Ajamu, 2010). For queer men in Brixton – within or beyond the squats – the fact that the gay community was white fitted expectations. There was clearly no lack of local knowledge about the existence of the community but the dimensions of gay identity as it was developing during this period meant that it might also feel inaccessible or unrelated to local black queer experience. Three black men stayed in the squats – two, from Portugal, very briefly; the other, from France, for longer. Significantly, though, these men had no other local ties.

Such separatism has been explained through the model of double exclusion for black gay men from family and community of origin on the one hand and from the gay scene on the other.[42] Sociologists Peter Keogh, Laurie Henderson and Catherine Dodds suggest something rather different. They conclude that Afro-Caribbean gay men in London effectively 'negotiate[d] their space within both [communities]'. 'This', they write, 'was done through a series of slow and subtle acceptances and rejections, disclosures and withholdings'. The immigrant culture of parents and family provided 'a vital sense of social and cultural situation':[43] there was too much at stake to execute the kind of rupture that formed part of several of the squatters' stories. Though we need to be extremely cautious about applying sociological research undertaken in the early 2000s to the 1970s, these conclusions may go some way to explaining why many black queer men were unwilling to make the kind of prioritising statements about their identities that most of the white squatters were prepared to do. There was a queer scene in Brixton that was predominantly black – a shebeen (or illegal bar) in Railton Road (run by a black artist called Pearl Allcock and visited regularly by some of the squatters) and a public sex culture (behind the station and in public toilets adjacent to the cinema).[44] But socialising or having sex in these places did not involve making the kind of explicit statements about sexual identity that visiting the Gay Centre or moving into the gay squatting community would have done. Keogh makes a useful comparison with Irish gay men in London in this respect.

> [Whereas] coming out for Black Caribbean men was defined by accommodation and mediation, [for] Irish men, it was about personal rupture and abrupt movement. [...] Any possible clash between gay identity and sociality and the structure of family, community and church was avoided not by careful accommodation and negotiation but by migration.[45]

It is perhaps not surprising, then, that the squats had a large and enduring Irish contingent; their negotiation of gay identity was markedly different from that of local Afro-Caribbean men whose homes were already there and who perhaps did not feel inclined to make a new (gayer) one on the doorstep.

What becomes clear through an examination of the squats is that gayness did not necessarily trump and certainly did not erase other consciously and less consciously felt and articulated identities and identifications. Men felt themselves to be part of or alienated from the community or sections of it because of class, education, politics, ethnicity, nationality, work, drugs, beliefs about family and many other factors.[46] If a particular and differentiated gay identity linked these men and informed their politics, the squatters' evidence also suggests the need to situate 'being gay' more carefully within a network of identities, identifications and associations which intersect with and modulate each other in different ways and at different times. The men I interviewed in 2008 each saw their sexual identity differently from the 1970s. If being 'gay' was then new, radical, experimental and overtly politicized through life in the squats, in the new century it had become for them a (more simply?) descriptive term.

Changing times

By the later 1970s many of the squatters had become tired of living in what several described as squalor, and in houses that were less and less cared for. Ian talks about a feeling of 'weariness' by this time – weariness both at the condition of some of the houses, but also the routine and growing abuse from outside (perhaps as awareness of the community and of gay life more broadly grew locally). It was, Ian said, 'hard work' living there (Ian, 2008). Jem felt 'everyone changed' over time; 'it got heavier in there. All sorts of power struggles going on' (Jem, 1983). Ben alludes to this too in the shift in drug cultures he identifies. 'People began selling keys to squats and selling drugs [...] There is a sort of illusion of camaraderie in the druggy subculture. But I say it is an illusion because it doesn't go very far beyond competing for the punter' (Ben, 1997). The 'heavier' atmosphere related partly to this, partly to a wider growing cynicism about what might be politically achievable after the riots and as Thatcher's Conservatives, riding high on the patriotism accompanying the Falklands war, united free market economics with a narrowing morality.[47] The riots represented 'the death knell' of the community for James. 'You see the thing that the riots taught everyone around here, if it taught them anything at all, was that revolutions actually change nothing' ('James', 1984). Railton Road was more than ever now a 'broken down' street. 'The same [community] could not happen again [...] the politics are different', James said in 1983. 'The sense of optimism has gone. There's a lot more cynicism and pessimism'.

Squatters often related the waning of the community chiefly to their personal trajectories and shifts in the group dynamics – and these are surely important. But as James and others suggest there were broader social, cultural and local factors that hastened a change and reflected a 'fad[ing] away' of 'broad-reaching political consciousness' in the late seventies.[48] Aside from a developing pessimism there was nationally (and of course only for some) a growth in disposable income, a more conspicuous culture of consumption, and (especially following the Housing Act of 1980 giving the 'right to buy' to council tenants) a rise in home ownership and further heightened expectations of what home should be.[49] Historian Laurance Black writes that in this period the citizen increasingly 'thought of himself [sic] as a consumer in all sorts of spheres [with...] the dominance of the individual and individual preferences in social mores and practices'.[50] If the GLF in its emphasis on self-fulfilment and realization was paradoxically part of that move to individualism,[51] GLFers had certainly not envisaged it relating to the kind of social and cultural transformation and privatisation of identity fostered by Thatcherism.

The politics of and options for housing had also shifted by the 1980s. A report on housing stress from the Department of the Environment in 1975 recommended that Lambeth Council allocate more housing to single people, childless couples, and non-manual and service workers needed by the London economy.[52] These recommendations took some time to filter through, but by the early 1980s a number of squatters who had put their names on the council's housing waiting list in the early 1970s were offered hard-to-let properties in the borough and moved away from the immediate community. In 1977, meanwhile, the Greater London Council's squatting amnesty had given 8000 squatters across the capital short-term licences to live in the properties they occupied. This encouraged the formation of housing co-operatives and associations to manage the licensing process, undertake negotiations, and seek funding for refurbishment.[53] The Brixton Housing Co-op was one of these, and between 1982 and 1984 the gay community squats were gradually absorbed as a gay subgroup of the organisation. The co-op undertook a refurbishment programme in consultation with the squatters, and the houses were subdivided into single occupancy units, with the communal garden retained. This coincided with council and central government initiatives to 'repair' Brixton after the riots, which led to the sprucing up of other houses in and around Railton Road and the equivocal and 'chaotic' process of gentrification in Brixton from the early 1980s.[54]

The return of the middle classes to central London from the 1960s onwards led to marked shifts in the later 1980s in the class make-up of some areas.[55] In Brixton this was partial and came later. Property values then rose, partly because of the proximity to central London, and local working-class and lower-income people found it increasingly difficult to enter the housing market. Brixton nevertheless remained relatively mixed compared with other gentrified areas.[56] People moved there not only for 'bargain Victoriana' but for 'new urban experiences' associated with its multiculturalism and countercultural reputation.[57] With a couple of exceptions, the squatters did not themselves invest in local property, but Brixton's gay squatting community and the wider counter and artistic culture of the 1970s did inform the particular trajectory of Brixton's subsequent gentrification. One of the women interviewed in a comparative study of three gentrified areas of south London in the late 1990s valued Brixton's 'very diverse population'; 'we don't stick out here as two women living together'. Another remarked that 'the best thing about living here is that it's an open community. [...] There's no norm'.[58] More broadly counter cultures 'soften up areas where risk averse capital, with a taste for selling simultaneous social frisson and personal security, might invest next'.[59] The 'individualist and creatively diverse atmosphere' and history of Brixton, the burgeoning local (and 'alternative') commercial gay scene, and the ease of access to 'gay' Soho and Vauxhall drew significantly higher numbers of 'gentrifying' gay men than the investigators' other case-study areas in which schools and social cohesion were bigger attractions.

Both the gay squatters in the 1970s and these later incomers were drawn by relatively cheap (for the latter) or free (for the former) accommodation and a particular local dynamic. Both lived out 'an apparent paradox of informal, voluntary segregation and the embracing of multiculturalism'.[60] They were each respectively 'in flight from normative aspects of social capital' and their successive moves to Brixton served to put the area on the gay map of the capital.[61] It did not, however, become a white and middle-class gay 'ghetto' like the Marigny in New Orleans or Cabbage Town in Toronto.[62] This is not to understate the impact of gentrification in Brixton – it was in many ways similar to that in other areas of the capital and in those other cities – but local circumstances nevertheless modulated the process. In a similar way, though the gay squatters were not divorced from wider gay liberation and countercultural politics and experiments in living (and indeed exemplify them), they had a distinctive experience because of what was particular about Brixton.

There was a real sense of loss for the squatters who remained in the area amidst all this. Max who had one of the newly refurbished flats had hoped it 'would still be a form of community living' despite these changes. After 15 years in the co-op, though, he felt disappointed.

> I think people have moved further and further apart and also more kind of self-centred perhaps. So I don't think today there's much communal spirit. I think what it seems to be today is a bunch of people, and we are neighbours and we are all gay and do more or less know each other. ('Max', 1997)

Max increasingly found support instead through the voluntary and professional AIDS networks that formed in and around Brixton from the mid to late 1980s, and which constituted a different form of community. Jonathan gives a slightly different account of the co-op flats; he hadn't lived in the squats but became involved in the housing co-op through his boyfriend, Nigel, who had. Jonathan echoes Max in observing that the commitment to alternative living waned as people who had squatted gradually moved away, but he also notes the way in which the co-op flats with their shared garden and also his relationship with Nigel ameliorated the sense of isolation he had felt previously in his east London flat and especially following his AIDS diagnosis. If the single occupancy units in the gay enclave can be linked to growing individualism, they also encouraged ongoing connection and accommodated the particular nature of Jonathan and Nigel's relationship. The two each have their own co-op flat in the same subdivided ex-squatted house. They visit each other for meals, sometimes sleep together, but also retain their own space for themselves.[63]

Squatters who moved away into council housing found the change more alarming than those who stayed on in the co-op – bringing what the community offered into sharper focus. For Ben: 'even though [the squatting community] was all fragmented – at least for a time there was the feeling of a sheltered haven. I wasn't totally at the mercy of the straight world and this illness' (Ben, 1997). This sense of loss in the dissolution of the squats was echoed in a number of interviews. There had been a particular conjunction of local circumstances, a shift in gay politics, a growth in squatting and counterculture, and chance encounters between particular individuals which had allowed the squatting community to form and endure for almost ten years. It allowed a gay identity and community to coalesce in specific and emphatic relation to domestic space as opposed to the burgeoning commercial 'straight' gay scene. Because this happened in squatted premises the men could conceive of themselves as not only evading 'compulsory heterosexuality' but also challenging a housing market which they saw as controlling, regimenting and commodifying relationships. In this sense and for a short period the gay identity they claimed and lived out seemed to represent a fusion (albeit incomplete and in various ways exclusionary) of sexuality, identity and anti-capitalist politics.[64]

By the 1980s the men involved were older, the dynamics in the squats had changed, local and national politics and culture had shifted, and housing co-ops were formalising makeshift housing solutions. A particular form of community had indeed been lost. There were new gay networks in the area, though, energized by wider social and cultural change, by different explorations of identity, and by shifts in local gay subcultures and circumstances partly related to the growing AIDS crisis. We can glimpse this in Max and Jonathan's testimony about life in the co-op. We also see it in that of black gay photographer Ajamu X who lived in a number of Brixton co-op houses around Railton Road after arriving in London from Leeds in 1987.

Ajamu X

Ajamu had been living in Leeds with a girlfriend before coming to London to the first black gay men's conference in Islington in 1987 and immediately moving in with his first boyfriend. '[He] was living with his current lover at that time. It was a horrible situation to be in [...] I had a friend [...] who was living at 171 Railton Road [and so] I moved to Brixton' (Ajamu X, 2010). This was a council-owned short-life shared property managed by the Brixton Housing Co-op. It had no bath, and so Ajamu used the bathroom of a friend living in one of the converted flats that had formerly been part of the gay squatting community.

> I had the impression [that the gay co-op community] was very very English [apart from a handful of people], and at this point there was

Figure 18 Ajamu, 2012
© Jane Standing.

lots of friction around being housed [because] some of the black members were not getting housed into where the white members [mostly the former squatters] were.

Ajamu became active in the co-op, forging friendships with members of that gay subgroup as well as with activists and journalists working on the radical anti-racist monthly *Race Today,* which had offices in the same building. He describes his artistic, black and gay identities, and his politics, developing in relation to each other partly through the physical proximity of these organisations, people and places – and his easy movement between them.

Ajamu was soon allocated a room in a co-op house with seven other black artists at 187 Railton Road – about a hundred yards along the street from the gay community. Here he describes engaging in a more productive debate about race and sexual identity than Ted Walker Brown had been able to find in the early 1970s. This may have been to do with a shift in local, London-wide, and national politics by the late-1980s. It may also have been about the need felt by Ajamu and his housemates to think about these issues directly because of the continuing dearth in representations of black gays and lesbians and because not all the housemates identified as gay. Ajamu describes the debate and experiences he had in this co-op house as key to his developing sense of himself, his art, and his politics. What helped too was that it took place in the context of wider Brixton networks. He talks about feeling anchored there by the housing co-op which succeeded the squats, the history of the immediate area (including the squatting community and the radical women's and black press working from Railton Rd), the growth of an alternative and more mixed commercial gay scene locally (including nights at the Fridge and Substation South), and finally (Ajamu argues strongly) the lasting local impact of the Greater London Council's work with artists and with gay and minority ethnic groups in the early 1980s (shaped in part by Ken Livingstone's experience as a local councillor in Brixton in the 1970s).[65] There was, finally, Lambeth's status as one of London's 'loony left' councils.[66] Brixton, Ajamu says, 'shaped my politics'; it attracted 'outsiderness': 'if you are black and gay they merge in Brixton' (Ajamu, 2010).

Ajamu moved into a smaller co-op flat in 1992 which he has shared with a (gay) flatmate (a life coach) since 2000. From there he ran parties for the Black Breakfast Club, Black Perverts Network ('where you're sat now this was the chill-out area, kitchen was bar area, downstairs was sex areas'), put on photographic exhibitions of his work in the main room (renamed the Parlour Gallery for that purpose), used the same space as part of a HIV testing campaign, and developed a black gay history archive, rukus!, which he sees as crucial underpinning to his politics.[67] His flatmate 'does not connect to it all on a political level, […] we cook separately, have a few shared friends but our networks are radically different. So basically my door shuts it's my space; when his door shuts it's his life coaching space. […] It works'. Influences from the preceding years come together here and, like the earlier squats, the flat had and continues to have several functions in Ajamu's sexual, artistic, social, cultural and political life. It was and is not only a privatized place of retreat, and there is a fluidity in the way he describes its uses. There are resonances here with the particular significance of home for African Americans that feminist, activist and theorist bell hooks describes. Home is, she says, a place of resistance, of politics, of renewal and self-recovery, a place where black people (and for hooks women in particular) could be 'subjects not objects'.[68] Given the objectification Ajamu had experienced in parts of the commercial gay scene, the last point is key – as is the sense of self-determination in shaping home space which some of the other squatters felt they had lacked in the Railton Road houses.

Family networks

Ajamu's grandparents moved from Kingston, Jamaica, first to Bradford then to work at the Vauxhall car plant in Luton; his parents settled in Huddersfield for jobs in a mill and a hospital respectively. He was christened Carlton Cockburn and brought up in a 'close knit' family of six siblings. He was, he joked, 'the first boy or third girl' – a joke also made by Peter McGraith and signalling the frequent feminisation of gay men in family rhetoric.[69] Growing up as 'the only identifiable black gay' in Huddersfield and experiencing white gay racism there meant that his family felt like an important resource: 'family plays key roles in protecting us [black gay men]. Families can be safe on one level', he said. 'Personally I [find] go[ing] back into the family network and reverting to Carlton Cockburn comforting'. '"Ajamu" is a particular kind of identity here – the artist here – the activist here'. His family's continued use of Carlton 'keeps me secure with that link'. Ajamu's name-switch roughly coincided with his move to London and his involvement with the Black Unity and Freedom Party, and he associates it with his life in the capital (his repetition of 'here' emphasising the point). Whereas Carl Marshall changed his name in a rupture from his family of origin,[70] for Ajamu it is different: his two names separate his family and London homes, but not to the exclusion of either.

Ajamu didn't invite his mother and family to visit at first 'because I was embarrassed living in a short-life house; it was basically if my mum came down she would be wondering "why am I living in a squat?" That's not her frame of reference; you have a nice house, nice things'. He invited her when he moved to his subsequent co-op house. 'And then the first thing she says was "you've got no net curtains" and took me to Brixton market to buy net curtains'. This he relates to 'black households' and a sense of respectability: 'it keeps people out, people can't see in but you can see out of net curtains'.

> She comes and stays here every so often, some of my friends come and visit and some of them are not the butchest boys on the block [...] but she is cool with that. For her it's not whether you are gay or straight it's whether you have manners and respect [...] I think it's a very kind of Afro-Caribbean frame of reference: manners and respect. (Ajamu, 2010)

For Ajamu there is a currency of comfort and security in his mother's conception of home and the endurance of family and family networks. Historian Mary Chamberlain finds 'family love' to be crucial in the Afro-Caribbean diaspora, with mothers 'principally responsible for maintaining the norms of reciprocity and care'.[71] There was less investment for the white squatters in their parents' versions of home – partly because there was less to be lost and more to be gained in moving away from them. Ajamu, meanwhile, emphasises mobility in the concept of home and the way he self-consciously holds together earlier and other experiences of it. 'Home is somewhere you go back to', he says, and in addition to Brixton he refers to Huddersfield and also Amsterdam as 'home'. These are places where 'my real family are or the real family that I have created because of my sexuality'. What Ajamu captures is a sense of home formed via a fusion of identifications which coalesce in Brixton but draw in other places too. In describing this he neatly junks the idea of real and pretended families – both are 'real'; both are also, Chamberlain suggests, important and part of 'survival strategies in migration'.[72]

Ajamu brings these notions of home and family to bear on the way he conceptualises his gay network in Brixton. Whereas the squatters a decade earlier talk of horizontal bonds, Ajamu draws in vertical attachments which bring with them a certain responsibility. Chamberlain notes how adults in the West Indies often assume 'avuncular and quasi parenting roles' and 'children, in turn, learn to defer to their "natural" authority'.[73]

Ajamu noted that 'with the black gay community [we have] kind of adoptive sons [to] look out for [...] [We're known as] dad, or grandma, we create a family frame of reference. The black community do this I'm not sure about other communities'. Notably, given both a historic queer tendency to feminise bonds of affections (most often as sisters) and the particular onus on mothers for Afro-Caribbean men and women, Ajamu talks of his (queer male) 'daughters' who live in Brixton, Streatham, and 'one [who] lives in the States now'. 'They spend time, come here and cook, so daughters might turn up: "hi mum how you are doing?" and just come and cook'. 'I was walking down Brixton escalator one day and one of my granddaughters came up and said "how are you doing Grandma?"' While such bonds resonate in some ways with the way George Ives describes his household relationships and his 'sons' in the first half of the century,[74] for Ajamu this relates to a specific sense of solidarity and care giving forged through black and gay identifications. These came together for him in Brixton. While by this point many of the squatters felt something had been lost, a different configuration of circumstances allowed the development of another, differently formulated, differently valuable, differently politicised 'moment of community' (Ian, 2008) which has held Ajamu in Brixton and made it 'home' for him for over 20 years.

Remembering and concluding

Brixton squatter and stalwart of 159 Railton Road, Colm Clifford, was closely involved in the making of *Nighthawks*, the landmark 1979 film of gay life in London by Ron Peck. The film follows the day and night life of gay teacher Jim, and Colm was filmed picking him up and taking him back to the Railton Road community. This section of the film was ultimately cut after the kind of extended debate and argument that often braced co-operative film making ventures. The scenes in the squat and with Colm were 'too alternative' and 'too political' for some; they gave 'the wrong impression' and were too stark a depiction of gay difference.[75] Jim's other multiple pickups in the film live alone in bedsits or flats across London. They do not stand out and their gay lives are shown to be separated from but fitting around 'regular' work and home lives. The scenes in the squats represented something more challenging. The squatters' homes and days did not follow a familiar rhythm and they paid much less attention to passing as straight. These were men who didn't fit in and who were self-consciously attempting to disrupt putative 'norms' – most especially in terms of where and how they lived. It was this that was deemed challenging in Peck's depiction of gay life.

In Peck's subsequent film, *Strip Jack Naked* (1991), he included these previously discarded scenes. The film begins with a tribute to Colm, who had died of an AIDS related illness in 1989, and replays the cut footage in an elegy of sorts. Peck's own voiceover to these and other cuts, reinvents his first full-length feature as his own story, detailing his search for love, his invigoration through the 1970s commercial gay scene, and his friendship and work with Colm and others. There was, he shows, a community in the making of *Nighthawks* which he tries to recover, honour and remember in *Strip Jack Naked*. The later film puts men lost and also communities lost (the squatting community, the film-making community) at the centre. It is more celebratory, elegiac and angry than *Nighthawks*. It pinpoints the battles still to be won in 1991 and – partially by reinstating the scenes in the squats – suggests the importance of a politics of difference, of living differently, and of collective action. The 1970s were ridiculed by the Thatcher government in their prescriptive quest for 'Victorian' and 'family' values. Peck suggests, meanwhile, that the very same decade might offer resources for and examples of dissidence and proud distinctiveness.[76]

The seventies retained their significance for the squatters themselves too. After collecting the first set of interviews and being cared for by former squatters at Bill's home in Herne Hill, Jamie died at the age of 35 in 1985. The AIDS crisis rendered visible powerful pre-existing bonds between gay friends which sometimes operated with the unconditionality of (some) families. Individual losses and indeed the broader sense of loss of a particular and particularly tight form of community underpinned the subsequent drive to remember and record the squatters' individually *and* collectively. When Ian began gathering material for a history of the Brixton gay community in the mid-1990s former community members were keen to share their stories with him in interviews and some lengthy letters. Their enthusiasm for the project suggests the continuing relevance of the squatting period to their lives. In the process they blur the boundaries between individualism and collectivity and underscore ongoing investments in collective formations in the past, however difficult they were at the time.[77] There is generally a striking loyalty between the former squatters in interview. They are, as we have seen, self-reflective and often self-critical. Criticism of others, at the same time, is cautious and careful, indicating an ongoing regard for and investment in those earlier bonds – even though most of the men have since grown apart. Reflection on experiences in the squats is laced with sadness, anger, humour, and sometimes a little embarrassment – humour and embarrassment to the fore in the latest round of interviews; anger and sadness in the first.

As we have seen, the squatters talked more and less explicitly about the ways in which their backgrounds and personal histories in the 1950s and 1960s modulated their subsequent experiences in Mayall and Railton Road, but they also describe how those experiences in turn informed later life choices and shaped their subsequent understandings of themselves and their relationships with others. Several of the squatters still live in and around Brixton and there is a loose friendship network between them. Ian met his partner Tony in the squats and they still live together in nearby Clapham. Jonathan and Nigel carried on living in the co-op. Stephen bought a property across the street and works as a psychotherapist – a professional move he associates with the squats, grief at losses to AIDS, and a sense of alienation relating to both. 'We couldn't mourn properly', he said, 'because we weren't real people; we weren't a real population; we didn't have the right to have those rituals' (Stephen, 2008). Peter lives in a house in Brixton he bought from the council. He works as a carpenter and furniture maker in an attached workshop, using skills he developed in the Railton Rd squats. He shares his home with a number of other gay men in a muted echo of earlier times. He notes the difference, though, between his own attitudes and those of his younger boyfriend and flat mates:

> I think that period has certainly shaped what I feel I need to be happy [...] I feel there needs to be an openness [...] I think that young people – including my boyfriend – [don't] allow [themselves] the same space to question what is possible, I think that's what that period gave us, which is very difficult now. (Peter, 2008)

Ajamu, though younger, feels something similar: 'I'm in my 40s and am probably artistic and leftfield [...]. Friends in their 20s – as far as they are concerned the battle has been won [...]. My younger friends have their own apartments, they don't live co-operatively'. The past is determinedly felt in the present by these men – and not only in their memories and the stories they tell but in the ways in which they live domestically now.[78]

Most of the interviews – as with Rex Batten and Alan Louis – feature this shuttling back and forth, comparing now with then, and reading one period off the other. Their memories of the 1970s come from the vantage point of changed personal, social, political and cultural contexts. The men were older by the second round of interviews in 1997, and those took place as new and promising treatments for AIDS were coming in. My interviews in 2008 followed equalities reform in relation to the age of consent, civil partnerships and adoption.[79] Many of the aspirations of the GLF were coming to pass by this time, though in a more assimilatory mode than GLFers and the Brixton squatters had hoped. Those aspirations seemed to be of another era; the collectivism, activism and challenge less relevant in these apparently more urbane and individualistic times. All this nostalgically reinflects memories of the earlier period and that past is in turn folded into the subsequent lives and politics of the squatters, into a local queer history of Brixton palpable to Ajamu, and even into the decisions of some 'gentrifiers' to move to this area.

8
Derek Jarman's Domestic Politics

Derek Jarman was, his biographer Tony Peake suggests, 'acutely sensitive to changes in the fabric of society':

> On many levels, his life is a litmus paper which reflects the major stages of Britain's social history in the second half of the twentieth century, from post-war austerity to the dying days of Thatcherism. The despairing and angry mood of the mid seventies, of a country facing economic recession, virtual war with the IRA and an uncertain post-imperial future – a mood epitomized by punk – awakened Jarman's passion and instinct for keeping abreast of the times.[1]

Jarman was himself cited in and drawn into the bigger debates and controversies about (homo)sexuality, and his obituaries clearly suggested his status as both pariah and saint by the time of his death in 1994.[2] In published diaries, interviews and some of his films he laid out his domestic life for public consumption and gave a vivid sense of how art, London counterculture, sexual radicalism, love, and friendship were woven through it.

Jarman was born in 1942 and had a peripatetic childhood as his father, Lance, moved between military postings – in Italy, in England, and, whilst he was at boarding school, in Pakistan. His mother, Elizabeth, spent much of her childhood in India, before studying dress design at Harrow Art School in London and working for the Queen's (queer) dress designer Norman Hartnell. The story of an apparently archetypical suburban middle-class nuclear family of the 1940s and 1950s – with two parents and their two children (daughter Gaye was born in 1943) – was shot through with the Raj, war and ongoing military service, and a certain stylish glamour. This perhaps suggested possibilities for Jarman himself in adulthood, while his fraught relationship with his father and isolation in boarding school added to his sense of separateness, independence and desire to make his own way. He studied literature, history and the history of art at Kings College, London, before turning to art at the Slade School. Like Charles Ricketts and Oliver Ford before him, he did some set-design work – his big break coming when film director Ken Russell asked him to design sets for what became Russell's landmark film, *The Devils* (1971). Thereafter, though, he mainly worked on his own films: he made 11 features and dozens of shorts, as well as music videos (including for the Sex Pistols in 1976 and for the Pet Shop Boys from 1987). He also published film diaries, memoirs and journals, and continued to paint and latterly (from 1989) to garden at his second home, Prospect Cottage at Dungeness on the Kent coast. Though he continued to shuttle to and from his tiny flat in the Charing Cross Road in London, it was the cottage which became synonymous with him and was much photographed, viewed and visited (especially after the posthumous publication of *Derek Jarman's Garden* in 1995).[3] This home was never private in a conventional way, but was instead part (a solid, material part) of Jarman's production of himself for himself and for an audience which extended well beyond queer counter culture. In this chapter I show how he used the cottage and also his London flats more or less self consciously to showcase his investment in home as a place and as an idea – and to show too how it could be given a queer twist and used confidently to articulate a radical politics and a sense of felt difference and endurance in 'sad times'.[4]

I draw this book to a close through Jarman's adult home life, showing how it was particular to him but also resonant with others I've discussed. We see the power of the personal past – of his family of origin, of his family homes, of class, of education – and of a distinctive queer heritage in his homes. Yet we also witness in this a desire for something new, for home and family conceived in different ways. There are tensions and hybridities between these things, which make it difficult to think of Jarman or any of the men I've discussed quite as insiders or outsiders. He and these others were embroiled in family and domestic cultures; they saw their value but also struggled against the dogma and convention associated with them. In multiple and different ways he, they, negotiated their desires – for love, for sex, for comfort, for safety, for a past and future, for new social and cultural ways of being – to a significant degree through the idea and material reality of home. 'Normal' men and women struggled to do these things too, but the case studies I've explored suggest that queer men were often more self-conscious than most in the face of legal incursion, particular and particularly simplistic caricatures and stereotypes, and the ebb and flow of wider knowledge, understanding, support and vitriol. Tracing these particular lives through home has signalled the importance of that space and idea for queer men across four generations, and has brought distinctive perspectives on twentieth-century London and change over time there. Housing, immigration, gender, class, legal change and subjectivities related to these things look different when viewed through the lens of these queer men and their everyday home lives.

Jarman was nine years younger than Orton and around ten years older than most of the squatters. Tracing his homes from the early 1960s onwards gives us a connective sweep across the decade in which Orton gained his fame and notoriety and the squatters made their way in Brixton; across years before and after the partial decriminalisation of homosexual acts (1967) and Gay Liberation (from 1970). Jarman gives us a glimpse at other ways of living queerly in the capital in these years. He also brings AIDS into sharper focus: he vividly depicts its impact on his own home life and uses it to reflect back his anger, frustration, and resilience. Home, I argue, was a place of work, rest and retreat for Jarman and a tool in his politics and activism. As for the other men I've discussed in this book, home had a distinctive place in his queer life and was part of how he marked out that queerness.

London life

Modern Nature (1991) – Jarman's diary of 1989–1990 – loops back repeatedly to his early years in London. He describes his first shared homes there as an independent adult and touches on a shift in attitudes and a sense of departure for that generation.[5] At Witley Court, Bloomsbury, in central London from 1962 he and his straight student flat-mates

> began to redefine our living space [...] we were very aware of the look of our rooms, after those of our suburban parents [...] white paint blotted out the past. The fifties fad of painting every wall a different colour was obliterated in these rooms [...]. We had a few objects picked up early in Bermondsey Market or from the far end of Portobello.[6]

What Jarman describes was part of a broader impulse to mark a distance in perspective from the preceding generation.[7] Jarman saw this not only in the redecoration of Witley Court but in the move to central London itself. The suburbs were, for him, determinedly straight. 'A suburban child', Jarman wrote, 'I was inexperienced and insecure, my upbringing designed to protect me from life'.[8] As for Rex Batten, Carl Marshall, and Alan Louis, finding home in the centre of London also meant finding himself. Collecting bric-à-brac from street markets like Bermondsey and Portobello – which saw a revival in the 1960s as a result of emerging gentrification in some parts of the city[9] – was part of this departure too: a way of making an eclectic, even subcultural style at odds with what was on the high street and so supposedly in suburban homes.[10] There is a sense of this in Neil Bartlett's domestic bricolage and also the serious, eclectic collecting of Charles Ricketts, Charles Shannon, and Oliver Ford.

Although 'at Witley Court, London could hardly be said to swing', Jarman and his friends 'met in each others flats, at parties or at college'.[11] This domestic social circuit was arty and student. This was where Jarman found the space to 'come out' as 'homosexual', 'gay' or 'queer' – the terminology shifted each time he described the event – whimsically in *Dancing Ledge* (1984), much more angrily in his polemic *At Your Own Risk* (1992).[12] In 1967, the year when homosexuality was partially decriminalized in England and Wales, Jarman graduated from art school and moved to a shared house and studio in Islington. It had 'the air of a commune' about it,[13] and the experience opened out his sense of what home might be and brought domestic and creative activity into a single space. In the same year he was also given keys to a flat above Sloane Square tube station belonging to his older friend, the playwright Anthony Harwood. The flat was 'a virtual temple to Harwood's taste', and a literal reflection of himself and his guests: 'everywhere you turned, you saw your reflection in the grey glass of the mirrored walls'.[14] For Jarman it was 'a vital extension to my life'. There 'he could properly and finally come into his own' with swinging, arty and rather queer Kings Road on his doorstep (Ives felt something similar when he moved into Albany on Piccadilly in the 1890s).[15] He lived there on and off until Harwood's death in 1976. Various court cases followed, leading ultimately to Jarman's eviction – an event he marked with a party at which he and his friends stripped the flat completely and covered the walls with graffiti (more anarchic signs of the self than the mirrors had been).[16] During this same period and beyond (1968–1979) he was using a series of three warehouse studios along the South Bank (at Upper Ground, near Blackfriars Bridge, at Bankside and finally from 1973 at Butler's Wharf) to work and 'to establish my own idiosyncratic mode of living'.[17] These he sublet for periods until the mid 1970s to help with his precarious finances but he also lived in them intermittently and more permanently in the later 1970s.[18] Today fashionable and expensive, the South Bank was then run down and barely residential, its warehouses empty following the decline of shipping and the docks which had altered London's economy and the way the river and its banks were used. There was a sense of living in the gritty heart of the city and yet on the edge – of the Thames and of respectability. For much of this period Jarman was flitting between these and other places across the city (tracking him is dizzying), disrupting ideas of permanence and settled domesticity that are so attached to ideas of home. As for Carl Marshal, this related to a positively conceived promiscuity which was key to his queer identity.

At the Bankside studio (from 1970) he installed a bath without partitions (a middle-class transgression, though not a working class one: tin baths in kitchens had until recently been normal for many families). He slept in a green-house in the middle of the vast room for warmth. This was partly pragmatic but also prefigured the coming fashion for open-plan living and alluded to the iconic 'Glass House' that queer architect Philip Johnson designed and built for himself in New Canaan in Connecticut in the USA in 1949, and which Jarman had visited with Harwood in 1969.[19] The warehouse was a light-filled space, an antidote to the closet, a paean to visibility and openness.[20] This warehouse and the two subsequent ones became spaces for creativity, for a new kind of home movie making with his Super 8 camera,[21] for sex, for love affairs, for parties, and for socializing in more relaxed, less conventional and more mixed ways than he had experienced in his family home. 'We had studio shows and the most extraordinary crowds – no one thought twice when Lord Goodman [chair of the Arts Council 1965–1972] came. I suppose we thought it the norm then'.[22] As for the squatters in Brixton, such events and the other things that went on in the warehouses challenged ideas about separated spheres of domestic activity. It was home functioning in a very different mode from that of his parents and was part of a non-commercial artistic and gay network – before the wider acknowledgment of the power of the pink pound and the advent of a more overtly consumerist gay scene in the capital. Jarman's eye for design meant that in 1972 the Bankside warehouse appeared in *Italian Vogue* (as part of the publicity for his work on *The Devils*) and more tellingly perhaps in *Underground Interiors: Decorating for Alternative Lifestyles* in 1973.[23] There were echoes in this of Andy Warhol's warehouse work and living in New York.[24] Jarman was certainly in control of these spaces aesthetically (as Warhol was too) and the design emanated from what was produced there and found nearby. There was a reach here for a sense of belonging that Jarman articulated later and even more clearly at Prospect Cottage in Dungeness.

In multiple ways, then, Jarman's South Bank studios were part of a sexual and artistic reinvention of himself. They articulated a social and political engagement very different from that of Oliver Ford, who, in the same period, was consolidating a more conservative queerness through his London and country homes.[25] In this way, and then in the autobiographical drive of his written and filmic work, Jarman made an example of himself. 'Steps forward came by the example of our lives', he wrote later, 'one David Hockney in 1960 was worth more than the 1967 act and did more to change our lives. The aim is to open up discourse and with it broaden our horizons; that can't be legislated for'.[26] The law had not legalized Jarman's sexual life which was not confined to private space nor to one person at a time. Multiplying subcultural representations of gay lives yet proposed the affirmative possibilities of sexual experimentation, advertised still further London's queer co-ordinates, and underscored the city's status as the 'obvious' home for gay men.

Jarman encouraged friends to become neighbours and neighbours friends, and in this way an alternative community formed. If Jarman's life on Bankside was in some ways akin to the experimental squats we saw in the last chapter, he did not sign up in any enthusiastic way to the liberationist rhetoric and action of those Brixton, Bethnal Green and Notting Hill gays. He may well have struggled with the dilution of a singular aesthetic vision that came with communal living. Jarman attended GLF meetings in the early 1970s and found ideas resonant with his own, and yet, a little older than most, he carried a different set of experiences with him. He had 'come of age' in the youth and artistic counter culture of London in the sixties rather than at the liberationist moment of the early 1970s. He had, he wrote, 'already gone through the struggle and was already beyond it [...] [The GLF] seemed so backwards in its censoriousness [...] I disliked these well-meaning rather lonely people laying down the law [...] there was an element of joylessness to it'.[27] Carl Marshall articulated something similar.[28] Age and generation, he and Jarman remind us, modulated the response to and investment in politics and action.

Jarman decided to stop running what he called a 'gay Butlin's' on Bankside in 1979, and just as Thatcher came to power he rented a small flat in Phoenix House on Charing Cross Road and a studio nearby. Jarman separated work and home again in an era others have suggested was marked by a fresh privatization of identity and the domestic

('"Mummy, what did you do in the 1980s?", Jarman wrote in parody of that decade: "bought a house in deep suburbia, bought some clothes in Covent Garden, bought a Porsche and mobile phone" ').[29] Many of the warehouses on the South Bank were mysteriously gutted by fire around this time – a prelude to redevelopment and some vast profits for developers. In the West End, meanwhile, a gay scene was establishing itself with large clubs like Bang (from 1976) inspired by Studio One in Los Angeles, and soon after Heaven and Subway (with its vast darkroom about which Jarman waxed lyrical). They represented a new era of gay liberation as men partied on vast dance-floors with hundreds or thousands of others rather than in small basement clubs. These venues represented and promoted a new social, sexual and subcultural confidence.[30] Jarman's flat continued to have a stream of visitors – it was, Jarman's care-partner Keith Collins (HB) said, 'like another West End coffee shop for people with no money'.[31] With less space and the West End literally on the doorstep, eating and drinking as often took place at Comptons, Presto Italian Restaurant or French patisserie Maison Bertaux; dancing and fucking at clubs nearby or on Hampstead Heath, a bus or taxi ride away. Though Jarman's own perspective might not have changed, this was indicative of a broader pattern. By the 1980s more was happening on an increasingly diverse gay scene and this seems to have encouraged more men to socialize out rather than at home. There was in this way a partial shift in London from the kind of home-based creative and social life enjoyed by Jarman, the squatters and the GLF communards, towards a greater separation of home and social lives.[32]

While he was living at Phoenix House, Jarman took part in a documentary in 1986 on 'Andy the Furniture Maker' for Channel 4's *Six of Hearts* series on lesbian and gay lives (part of the new channel's commitment to broadening representation and audiences). Jarman talked there of how he 'rescued' Andy from a remand centre. He had given Andy his telephone number at a club, who had then passed it to a social worker. Andy subsequently stayed with Jarman at the Bankside warehouse while Jarman helped him look for work and encouraged him in his furniture making. His style and approach spoke to Jarman who filled the Phoenix House flat with his pieces (the bed, now at Prospect Cottage, is enormous). Andy made anything from torture furniture for sex workers to tables and beds 'which don't creak when you fuck in them'.[33] Jarman's friend Christopher Hobbs described Andy's work as a 'fight against respectable furniture', while Jarman characteristically placed it in a 'true tradition of British furniture' – in a lineage extending from William Morris. It was made of found materials and salvaged wood, and each piece had its own story to tell. This idea of authenticity, of stripping back, and of the significance of craftsmanship reached back to Charles Ashbee and Edward Carpenter who associated these things with an honesty in desire.[34] There was something a little queer in this aesthetic which Andy and Jarman both drew out and built on. Andy harked back to his rent boy days when he talked in the documentary about how he worked on a furniture commission. 'I don't size up the punter I price them up', he said.[35]

Jarman's support of Andy (amongst other young artists) was part perhaps of a relationship which had something paternal or avuncular to it. I argued earlier that such ties constituted a queer remodelling of family and associated ideas of responsibility. This relates to sexual liberation and a rethinking of the meanings and formations of family in that context. It also touches an older tradition of support and patronage of younger men (as of Glyn Philpot and Vivian Forbes by Charles Shannon and Charles Ricketts)[36] which was most visible in queer networks until the 1960s, a little less so thereafter.[37] Such pre-liberationist resonances can also be observed in Jarman's keen interest in a queer lineage and iconography. Jarman deliberately gestured to figures and modes of life that predated the GLF. In the diaries he refers to those ancient Theban bands which had so compelled George Ives, for example;[38] in his films about *Sebastiane* (1976), *Caravaggio* (1986), and *Edward II* (1991)[39] he drew out queer threads from the past that could eroticize and politicize the present and suggest a pre-existing if differently expressed queer radical spirit and solidarity (rather as Bartlett is still doing in his work and in his home in Brighton).[40] It was also a means for Jarman to cleave a queer space in English culture and tradition for himself and others. This cultural improvisation and the gathering together of histories and traditions which could speak to him and his sense of difference underpin the way he made his home and garden at Dungeness. There was, he suggested, a deeper history and texture to sexual change and revolution than was commonly appreciated by a younger generation of gay men who tended to look to the 1970s and to the USA, or by Thatcher and her government who were busy associating 'degenerate' contemporary mores with the 1960 and 1970s, and so again a more recent past.

Prospects

Jarman's early films – *Sebastiane* and *Jubilee* – were a celebration of counterculture, of homoeroticism, and of sexual difference, and were controversial from the first. But Jarman's own diagnosis with the HIV virus in

1986 unleashed a rage and more direct radicalism. He declared his status soon after and joined in a more direct, urgent politics. Jarman's films and writing became more clearly autobiographical from this time on.[41] His experience of home changed too. He fell in love with 21-year-old Keith Collins (or HB – Hinney Beast – as Jarman called him, and as Keith continues to call himself), who moved into Phoenix House with him in 1987. Though HB described himself as a 'bad gay' (a neat prelude to the 'queer' Jarman soon reclaimed) in his native Newcastle, he brought some order to Jarman's flat. Jarman had rarely cooked; his clothes washing consisted of dumping them in the bath with Lux flakes and then transferring them to a tumble drier for hours. If the Phoenix House flat was Jarman's home, he was not domesticated there in terms of cooking and cleaning.[42] HB took up these tasks and acted, he said jokingly, as the younger 'catamite domestic' to the 'artistic genius' who held court in the main room while he was in the kitchen (HB, 2012). Neither HB nor Jarman saw this role in passive or feminised terms – terms which many of the men I've discussed worked hard to evade. In Jarman's diaries there is a sense of equality, respect and intense mutual love and care in a relationship where both partners also retained sexual and social independence. Sex, in fact, was not part of their domestic life and relationship together. 'We were well-matched to survive together in that tiny space', HB observed.[43]

Around the same time, Jarman began to feel increasingly embattled by the vitriol levelled at him. There were new, less welcome incursions into his home. Abuse and even death threats came via the phone and through the post to Phoenix House. He was also more in demand: 'Back home at the flat in Charing Cross Road', he wrote, 'another enormous pile of letters blocked the door: would I write? Judge? Give advice? Attend? Approve? Help? – The phone rings till I find myself running. What happiness has this cacophony bought?'[44] With the ongoing stream of casual callers, these increasing work and AIDS-related demands on his time, and the new hatred levelled at him, Phoenix House felt anything but that retreat from the world home was commonly supposed to be.

The changes at Phoenix House in part motivated his purchase of a second home outside London – a small fisherman's cottage on the Kent coast at Dungeness which he and Collins came across by chance. A legacy from his father, who died in 1987, enabled Jarman to knock on the door and to offer cash (£32,000). Jarman positioned Prospect Cottage as 'the last of a long line of "escape houses" I started building as a child at the end of the garden: grass houses of fragrant mowings [...]; sandcastles; a turf hut, hardly big enough to turn round in; another of scrap metal and twigs'.[45] Prospect 'stood', wrote Peake, 'at the still centre of Jarman's

Figure 19 Derek Jarman and HB (Keith Collins) at Phoenix House
© The Estate of Derek Jarman. Courtesy of Keith Collins.

embattled world'.[46] It provided an escape and seems – in the diaries – to have fulfilled practically and symbolically this core function of home. In HB's account Prospect was more often a work place, and one where Jarman was seldom alone. Friends were omnipresent wherever Jarman lived; HB labelled some of the frequent visitors here 'the Dungenettes'. Moving to Prospect Cottage nevertheless put a distance between him and London and came to represent endurance against the odds. In the opening entry of *Modern Nature* Jarman describes 'the waves' which 'one stormy night many years ago [...] roared up to the front door threatening to swallow it' and later writes of the great storm of 1988: 'my Prospect Cottage never seemed so dear, beaten like a drum in the rushing wind that assaulted it and flew on howling for other prey'. In a riff on *The Wizard of Oz* (which Jarman returns to repeatedly), '[Prospect] stood firm on its foundation, unlike the farm in Kansas'.[47] If in some ways beautiful to Jarman, the looming nuclear power-station was also enviasaged as a constant threat which he and the little cottage endured. The garden he planted in the infertile ground meanwhile blossomed.

In the diary Prospect prompts memories of early homes and especially gardens, and he gathers these and memories of childhood into his present (as others of my case studies did too). On Monday 6 February

1989 he recalls the expansive gardens of the Villa Zuassa by Lake Maggiore – requisitioned for the family while Jarman's father served as Commandant of the Rome airfield and witness at the Venice war trials.[48] 'In this Eden', Jarman writes, 'my sister and I walked arm-in arm, naked, along a jetty submerged in the waters of the lake'. It was there too, he remembers, that he met his 'first love' – Davide, the 18-year-old nephew of the housekeeper. On Monday 13 February 1989 Jarman was recalling the Borghese Gardens in Rome where they moved to another requisitioned flat in the same year. 'Years later, in 1972, I returned to the Borghese Gardens with a soldier I met in the Cinema Olympia. He had thrown his arms around me in the gods; later we made love under the stars of my Eden'.[49] In the same diary entry Jarman recounts the return to England, now aged six, and the 'Nissen hut' family home on an army base near Cambridge, surrounded with barbed wire.[50] Jarman drew these past places vividly into his present, signalling for us and for himself the deeper resonances, the romanticism, of his current home and garden. 'I find it mysterious', he wrote

> that all the years that have passed should lead to Prospect Cottage – perhaps it is the tin roof which reminds me of the Nissen huts of an RAF childhood in the forties [...] maybe it is the flower bed which runs in front of the house – it has the same lumps of concrete from some long demolished fortification as those in Abingdon and Kidlington.[51]

There was a connection to Italy at Prospect too: with the watery aspect, a garden whose boundaries 'are the horizon', and where, as at Zuassa, he found love and, as at Borghese, sex. This looping back to childhood homes is a common motif in post-liberation gay fiction and autobiography – as in testimonies before that period, as we've seen. It is often used to mark a distance travelled and to accentuate a sense of rupture – experienced by some of the squatters, for example. But as we saw with Rex Batten, this looping back can also comfortably recoup those spaces of childhood at moments of crisis.[52]

Alongside the links to a personal history, Jarman connects Prospect mythically to Eden and Gethsemane in his film, *The Garden* (1990).[53] He also links in here to an English tradition and passion for gardening which in the interwar years especially developed and became more widespread.[54] In *The Garden* he laid claim to wider myths, stories and traditions, and asserted a right to use them as he liked, to re-form them and make them 'mean' different things. Like Charles Shannon and

Charles Ricketts at the Keep of Chilham Castle (also in Kent and around 30 miles from Prospect), Jarman's home and garden appeared in that quintessentially English magazine: *Country Life* (June 1993). Jarman, though, gardened differently. He worked hard at it – entry after entry in *Modern Nature* details new plants and sculptural additions – but he did not protect it by enclosing it. It was unfenced and open, and thus refused to exclude or contain as a 'traditional' (Victorian domestic) English garden 'should'. There was perhaps instead an allusion to the eighteenth-century landscape tradition: aristocrats used the ha-ha (a kind of ditch) to suggest grounds stretching into the distance.[55] Ralph Lamprell and Oliver Ford's fondness for eighteenth-century interiors was about creating a related sense of light and space: the century's domestic aesthetics perhaps represented queer hope more than did Victorian gardens and cluttered interiors. 'My garden's boundaries are the horizon', Jarman wrote, and so encompassed the entire land and seascape. It was also open to and unshielded from that world beyond.[56] He pitched this conceptually against 'the castle of heterosex' with its 'walls of tears and dungeons of sadness'.[57] The limitations and tragedies of 'heterosex' and 'heterosoc' were thus represented by Jarman in enclosing architectural terms.

In these various ways the cottage and garden were given a depth of meaning which extended their reach beyond that particular place and moment – and at a point in time when Jarman himself was directly facing his own mortality.[58] He lived at Prospect for less than five years but he embedded himself there – giving himself a sense of endurance and the cottage an enduring association with him. Though HB inherited it, and though he has tended the garden for five times as long as Jarman did, 'it will', he said, always be 'Derek Jarman's garden' not 'HB's'. HB's comment replays that sense he had and has of doing the behind the scenes (and literal) spade work to support the 'artistic genius'.

Home comforts

Jarman describes Prospect Cottage in some detail in the diary – evoking very precisely, as Carl Marshall and Joe Orton also did, the dimensions of places significant to them.

> Prospect Cottage has four rooms. I call this room the Spring room; it is my writing room and bedroom, 12ft × 10 of polished tongue and groove with a single window facing the sea. In front of the window

is my desk: a simple 18th century elm table. On it is a reading lamp of tarnished copper, two pewter mugs full of stamps, loose change, paperclips [...], an iron spittoon used as an ashtray; in the centre a lead tobacco box in the shape of a little Victorian cottage, in which I keep my cheque book and money. To the left and right against the walls are two Red Cross medicine chests from an army surplus store; here I keep my clothes. A large oak chest dominates the room: it has 15th century panels [...] I keep my bedding in it. Next to it is a teak and khaki canvas campaign chair. On the wall are three paintings [two by Jarman, one by John Maybury] [...]. In the four corners of the room are driftwood staffs crowned with garlands of stone and polished bone [...]. Purple curtains shut out the winter stars'.[59]

Later he writes of his (other) front room:

In the four corners of the [other] room are sentinel posts, driftwood from the seashore, hung with necklaces of pierced stones, dedicated to the Hinney Beast. On the walls are several more driftwood pieces [...]. The furniture is warehouse packing case, mostly from skips and derelict buildings [...] oh and lastly on either side of the fireplace are diamond paned Tudorbethan doors brought here from a scrapyard in London, covering alcoves packed with books.[60]

As he describes the room he makes his own presence felt in the immediacy of his prose ('I call this the Spring room', he writes as if we were there with him; 'here I keep my clothes'). *The Garden* includes a scene of Jarman with his head on the desk in this room. In these instances and others he opens the rooms out to his audiences and invites them to read him through them and through their contents. He indicates again his impulse to adapt, re-use, and salvage, and to have things about him that had some particular story to tell (rather as Shannon, Ricketts, Ford and Bartlett did and do). Again the rooms are rooted in place and context. Like the garden beyond, driftwood and found objects are integrated into the house. If there are associations with London (the salvaged doors, for example), the contents of the house also bind him to Dungeness.

One fleeting comment alone undermines this sense of belonging on the Kent coast amongst people whose families had lived there for generations. 'Am I a sightseer', he wrote, 'or do I live here? A hobo in a ruined coat trudging in circles'.[61] Like the Brixton squatter who felt like a 'sightseer' during the riots in 1987, this comment casts light on the uncertainty of belonging and home. Jarman links to that longer association of homosexuality with homelessness with which the first part of this book opened. There is perhaps a sense that he still didn't quite belong. The deliberateness and particularity with which Jarman and some of the other men I have discussed made home (and also the detail with which they describe it) speaks of some insecurity, and so a determination to seize and hold on to home space and find permanence and stability there.

Jarman certainly made his presence felt at Prospect, and from the art which hangs on the walls to the props and film memorabilia on the shelves, he was and is inescapable. Jarman and his home are one and the latter sustained and represented him before and also after his death. It protected and protects him. Prospect Cottage proved itself robust against sea and wind and possible nuclear fall-out while inside sentinels guarded each room. HB added to these. Jarman wrote on 23 May 1991: 'in the cereal packet are glow-in-the-dark monsters that [he] has stuck all over the bedroom wall to protect me from the curious who drop by each day to see the garden'.[62] In this Prospect Cottage performs a classic function of home for Jarman – though additional sentinel reinforcements were needed, installed theatrically in each corner of the room and multiplying over the walls.

HB was at Prospect a lot and was honoured in those 'sentinel posts [...] hung with necklaces of pierced stones'. But this was Jarman's home. The diaries seem to associate HB more with Phoenix House, meanwhile – though the flat too was Jarman's first and had mainly his things in it. There was, writes Peake, 'a form of domestic schizophrenia' as 'Phoenix House became primarily the domain of Collins, Prospect Cottage that of Jarman'.[63] HB's domestic work at Phoenix House and the adaptations he undertook, though, were largely for Jarman's sake in the context of his deteriorating health. 'In the middle of the day', Jarman wrote, '[HB] knocked down the wall between the bathroom and the living room, to make a bathroom cupboard so I don't hit my head on the shelves again'.[64] Their contentedness in often living together apart is a reflection of what seems to have been their unflinching confidence in their relationship – one which in broader cultural terms was suspect or considered impermanent: on account of being between two men, and between men of very different ages and different classes. Their two domestic bases meanwhile allowed them to organise their relationship as they wished and in defiance of such broader cultural expectations. 'HB is shut up in Phoenix House with his M&S [Marks and Spencers] oven-ready meal', Jarman wrote at Christmas 1992. 'Why do we spend our Christmases apart? Perhaps it confirms the need to reject family at this time' (as some of the squatters had also sought to do).[65]

There was growing acknowledgement of the importance of friendship networks in the 1980s and 1990s. They were part of a drive to self-determination and individuation beyond families of origin, and developed as 'coming out' from the 1970s and AIDS and HIV from the 1980s brought new affiliations into focus and sometimes created familial rifts.[66] Jarman's diary gives a flavour of the extent of his own friendship network; a shelf of carefully compiled albums at Prospect is full of photos of friends. Putting together such albums (rather like his use of the home-movie genre) gathered together the people featured 'as family' – and a family decimated by loss. As I looked through the albums HB pointed out that many of these people were now dead. Like the scrapbooks of newspaper clippings, photographs, and ephemera Ives compiled, there is a sense of a queer assemblage in this; a skewed and differently revealing version of the usual family album.[67]

Prospect and its garden accommodated this 'family of choice', while his film *The Garden*, made in the aftermath of the introduction of Section 28, insists on such expansive versions of family and intimacy. One sequence, for example, shows a gay couple bathing a child; in another the lone 'mother Mary' cares for her baby against the backdrop of the unbounded Dungeness land and sea-scape. He writes around the same time in his diary of the 'house of cards called the Family' which could, he suggests, come tumbling down. An interviewer from the *Guardian* newspaper was, Jarman noted, 'unable to understand that we [gay men] had children and families' too.[68] Jarman very deliberately deploys his own home for this particular politics, and uses it too as a space for celebratory, protective and memorial rituals of queer love and death which were being given little credence elsewhere. 'My garden', he wrote

> is a memorial, each circular bed and dial a true lover's knot – planted with lavender, helichryssum and santolina. *Santolina ... resisteth poison, putrefaction, and heals the bites of venomous beasts.* Whilst a sprig of lavender held in the hand or placed under the pillow enables you to see ghosts, travel to the land of the dead.[69]

He evokes repeatedly the mythic meanings of plants and flowers and through them conjures dead friends and what his friend, the writer Oscar Moore, described as a 'fraternity of sickness' – those unexpected bonds forged through the experience of a virus and 'tales of hell and high water in the pursuit of temporary relief'.[70] The garden witnessed Jarman's ordination as a queer saint (St Derek of Dungeness of the Order of Celluloid Knights in September 1991), and some queer marriages: 'today is the day of the marriage', he wrote on 22 June 1993:

> Sven has worked hard in the garden and also polished the floors so the cottage looks smart. Emma and Anna arrived for the wedding at four. Great excitement [...]. We all walked to the sea, where I married them[...]. I know that Anna's and Emma's decision to get married was an important event, lesbians and gay men have no way of sanctioning their relationships.[71]

As for Ajamu X and the Brixton squatters, home for Jarman served multiple functions in his own life and the lives of others, and also symbolized a wider political battle. It could not be a private retreat, a secluded Eden for a queer family, and this meant there might also be unwelcome incursions. In *The Garden* he depicted the press and assorted homophobes invading. Prospect itself meanwhile drew increasing number of tourists. Because the house and garden had these broader associations, because it had been represented relatively widely, and because it was linked so closely to this public figure, there was a sense of open invitation. However benign in intent, this could be intrusive in practice. An extension to the cottage in 1992 included a ceiling to floor window which looks directly out onto the unfenced garden. In that room there was and is a feeling of being on show. Perhaps this was part of what HB describes as Jarman's 'showmanship'. The simple black pitch cottage, like others along that stretch of coast, was marked out by Jarman with bright yellow woodwork, and on its side he had John Donne's poem *The Sun Rising* mounted in black lettering. 'If Derek had had his way it would have been in neon', HB said. The transcription of the poem faces out, seemingly addressing those visitors who come to look at the garden, and gives a sense once more of Jarman's home being at once private and public. The poem captures the paradox. It opens with a resentment of intrusion: 'Busie old foole, unruly Sunne,/ Why dost thou thus,/ Through windowes and through curtaines call on us?' It ends with an arrogant invitation: 'To warme the world,/ That's done in warming us./ Shine here to us, and thou art everywhere;/ This bed thy center is, these walls thy spheare'.

The idea that home was private was always a fallacy. As I observed at the outset it was the scene of a broader politics of sexuality, gender and family and there were rhetorical invocations and economic and architectural inducements to structure these things in particular ways domestically. These imperatives, these ways of doing things, came to be seen as obvious and common sense, but Jarman, like the GLF communards and squatters, gave the lie to this. Jarman used his home polemically, showing how intimately it related to his sense of himself and his personal history, to his difference and his politics. In so doing, of course, he was hooking into some prevailing ideas about home's capacity to reflect and produce the individual. But then Jarman did not reject circulating mythologies and traditions. Rather he seized them and gave them that queer twist we have seen some other of my case studies execute too.

Home help

Jarman's use of the diary form means that he emphasizes the day-to-day, and he also talks about the rhythms established by the seasons, by the gardening calendar, by the roster of film festivals and events he attended, and increasingly by the vicissitudes of his health. The last part of his diary, published posthumously as *Smiling in Slow Motion* (2000), focuses on daily struggle, resolve, and sometimes a sense of defeat. 'I've noticed', he writes, 'that the diary is sinking under the weight of illness'. He remained extraordinarily active with other things nevertheless – with work, with friends, with film festivals and events, with breakfasts at Maison Bertaux in Soho. Remembering this activity is vital. As novelist Edmund White reminds us, men with AIDS were and are not reducible to their illness or death: 'there is more to gay culture than disease'.[72] Nevertheless Jarman follows domestic detail and routine more closely in his later entries. And these things become more significant in the context of his failing eyesight and energy (both AIDS related). 'My only panic is my morning shave. I couldn't bear anyone else to touch my face as my skin is so irritating, even when I do it I hold my breath', he writes.[73] He details the bouts of night sweats ('a pile of a dozen wet t-shirts wringing wet at my bedside') and of diarrhoea. 'The day started with a disaster: my stomach went in Camisa so I staggered back dripping shit from my trouser bottoms. Sweet HB bathed me and put my clothes into the machine. You just have to put yourself into accepting it all'.[74] There is a constant vigilance of chest, stomach, sleep and temperatures and of the impact these things have. The health diary kept by Carl Marshall details such daily shifts too – indicating the contingency of the day-to-day. 'My life is a minefield', Carl wrote, 'something could go wrong at any second, [...] I step out of bed in the morning and I could step on one'.[75] Increasingly a tight circle of friends stepped up for Carl and in his diaries he notes kindnesses and errands run. 'My friends are the family I didn't have and are important, without them I would be very lonely', he wrote.[76] Later he noted his desire to adjust his will so it is not only 'straight people' who benefit but also his queer family. In this Carl signals a broader consequence of AIDS and the early deaths it caused: individuals thought earlier and carefully about their legacy and who should benefit. This was often not only families of origin but families of friends; sometimes it was just the latter. As we saw with Ives, such legacies can be indicative of a queerer organization of love and affection.[77]

Jarman also paid tribute to friends and to neighbours; 'I am blessed in my neighbours', he wrote. HB, though, is especially praised: 'he is my lifeline in this crisis, as day-by-day the aches and pains drive in'.[78] He has an acute awareness of the effect he has on HB's sleeping and waking hours. 'I slept so badly again last night, HB very uncomfortable, he usually takes a sleeping pill to survive these nights', Jarman wrote in June 1991.[79] And later: 'he's worried about going to Newcastle at the weekend, but I insist that I can admit myself to hospital'.[80] HB took on the role of carer (he described himself as Jarman's 'care partner'; the kitchen became his 'office' as he cooked and washed clothes and dishes: 'he protects the space against my intrusion [...] and guards the washing up like I guard my papers'.[81] 'HB cleans and polishes so constantly [...] He says because he lives in the most public AIDS household in England it "wouldn't do" if someone came round and the toilet wasn't "...hygienic"'. HB had a point: journalists would not have been beyond publishing a piece on Jarman's 'squalid AIDS house'.

The illness imposed its own domestic discipline and routines (not least in terms of the timings and extent of the drug regime) and as Jarman weakened so potentially shared tasks shifted to HB. Jarman yet wondered whether 'if he wasn't a drudge to me he'd be a drudge for himself'.[82] There was in this a different way of knowing and experiencing the home which was – and is – common in the context of ill health. HB said Phoenix House sometimes looked like a hospital room. This association was a familiar one for men who shuttled frequently between home and hospital, often laden with medical equipment. At Carl Marshall's flat in Kennington, for example, oxygen was installed. Oscar Moore described changes in his home that with the onset of his AIDS related blindness: 'at busy times', he writes, 'my flat fairly hums with the clutter of talking watches, calculators, kitchen scales, bathroom scales [...] and all manner of bleeping, whistling and ringing timers, detectors and measures'.[83] There were other new and sometimes unwanted intrusions. Medical interventions, well-wishers, the need for carers and a feeling of being unable to cope or to be in control could make the familiar strange, or, to use Freud, unhomely (*'unheimlich'*).[84] 'Home – ha!', wrote Moore in his *Guardian* column:

> A refuge, a sanctuary, a bolt-hole. Frankly I bolted the hole as fast as I could. It wasn't so much the milling well-wishers whose faces I could not discern and whose concerns I could not face. It was the fact that when someone brought me a pot of tea and a cup, I carefully poured the tea out on to the table next to the cup, scalding my legs and chilling my mind. I felt stupid, desperate, alone and scared.[85]

Moore's regular hospital ward (the Broderip at the Middlesex Hospital), 'his second London address', sometimes felt more comforting.[86] As for Ricketts when Shannon's health failed, home took on different meanings and was experienced differently.[87] Photographs and objects around the house could yet still gesture to more robust times.

Sociologist Judith Stacey writes that 'the AIDS epidemic subjected gay male sexuality to extraordinary levels of collective scrutiny and debate. And it incited gay men to perform Herculean levels of caretaking outside default family form'.[88] This created what she describes as 'postmodern' urban families, involving existing friends, men from that 'fraternity of sickness', professional care givers, and volunteers. We have seen how Marshall, Moore and Jarman mentioned their friends and the support they brought; the latter two talked about their families of origin too. Jarman's sister Gaye and Moore's parents were frequent visitors. There are terrible stories of families rejecting sick sons, or caring for them but excluding partners and friends from discussion of treatment or the planning of funeral services and inheritance. This might sometimes have been deliberate, at other times associated with a lack of comprehension of queer intimacies, bonds and connections that might differ from the parents' experience of friendship.[89] For some, the fear that their son's sexuality and cause of death might have been revealed to extended family or communities made it feel imperative to foreclose on such gay friends at a time of intense agony for all. The art historian Simon Watney remembers a friend's parents who felt 'condemned to silence, to euphemism [...] in this the most devastating moment of their lives as parents'. For Watney at the funeral 'the irony of the difference between the suffocating life of the suburbs where we found ourselves, and our knowledge of the world in which Bruno had actually lived, as a magnificently affirmative and life-enhancing gay man, was all but unbearable'.[90]

Such accounts, reactions and experiences can underscore the distance that is often presumed to stand between gay men and their families – and again we get the suburban/urban dichotomy that has run through this book. Other accounts show the reverse. If AIDS caused many familial ruptures, it could also unite families in the struggle to cope. Telling family of an AIDS diagnosis for some involved coming out and connecting gay and kin circles unevenly – integrating formerly separate parts of a life. Patrick Gale wrote of his novel *The Facts of Life* (1995):

> I wanted to put the gay characters with AIDS firmly back in the family context – once again to show perspective; to say: 'he's dying from AIDS, but ultimately he's just dying'. People die of all manner of things. Families have a way of coping. The structure of family will extend around and beyond a death.[91]

While some families did not manage to do this, it is also true that in many cases families did come together in new and unexpected ways in the context of AIDS. The separation from family Oscar Moore depicts in his thinly veiled autobiographical novel *A Matter of Life and Sex* (1991) is no longer apparent in the testimony he gave in his *Guardian* columns – the reverse in fact. The point here is that the AIDS crisis and the losses it brought with it have been met with multiple responses which are not reducible to a simple rejection on the part of birth family nor necessarily a parallel stepping up of gay 'families of choice' (Carl Mashall complained of a lack of consideration and care from some friends, for example). For everyone dealing with AIDS there was some shift in home life. For Jarman it meant spending more time there and an even more home-orientated work and social life. It also meant a gradual or uneven reinflection and amplification of what home meant in terms of comfort, retreat, care and safety. AIDS forced Jarman to renegotiate his queer domestic life and like many others and against many odds he did that with considerable verve and agency.

* * *

Derek Jarman was canonized at Prospect Cottage. It was also from here that he was carried after his death to a very English church and graveyard

Figure 20 Derek Jarman and HB
© The Estate of Derek Jarman. Courtesy of Keith Collins.

to be buried under a very English yew tree. These two events help to crystallize an argument I have made in this chapter. Jarman's experience and radical articulation of art, of sex, of family (in an expansive sense), of love, and of AIDS, were crucially modulated by his Englishness, by his class, by his commitment to art history and cultural myth and tradition, and by those clinching symbols of English life: home and garden. Tracking some of the ways in which these things intersected for him reminds us that changing times are experienced in particular ways depending on desire, sexuality, age, generation, class, ethnicity, nationality, and the particular homes it is practically possible to make. That Jarman's ultimate home was in England, but on its very edge, and in a landscape open but dominated by the ominous nuclear-power station, speaks of his sense of himself in relation to English culture. It characterizes a wider cultural climate in the 1980s and early 1990s in which vile and vivid homophobia was met with a stubborn insistence upon visibility, difference and the right to sexual expression. This was far from abstract in the context of AIDS. The era demanded friendship, care and mutual support and ushered in some angry activism. Jarman was almost completely blind on his final birthday – his 52nd. HB and friends gathered at Prospect; the actress Tilda Swinton sat beside Jarman to describe the fireworks launched on the beach in his honour. It was precisely such circles of love and care that he was seeking to assert and defend. Prospect Cottage served as a symbol of presence and defiance; it was from here that he wrote and fired off his polemics on queer love and liberation. It was also a place for working, remembering lost friends, and enjoying companionship in the present.

When I visited HB at Prospect Cottage in June 2012 I found that Jarman's descriptions of the rooms were exact. 'It's only stuff', HB said when I commented. But as anthropologist Daniel Miller notes, such household 'stuff' resonates with the people who have had and held it, with its previous owners or the places it came from. It gives, he argues, some comfort to those who hold and have it after.[92] We saw this in Neil Bartlett's collection, and tacitly HB is doing something similar in keeping the furniture, the photos of film shoots in the hall, the book case full of Jarman's albums, books and objects which seem always to have a story, to relate to some friend, some film, some particular place. Light-fingered mourners at the funeral and the damaging ultra-violet light at Dungeness pushed HB to have the shelves enclosed – preserving behind glass, more museum-like than before, these objects and their associated memories (in an echo of the ultimate shift of Shannon and Ricketts collection to the Fitzwilliam Museum in Cambridge). In this, though, HB meets a sense of responsibility he has – to his late partner, to the many visitors who come to see the garden, and to those who come to grieve lost sons, brothers and friends in a place associated not only with Jarman but also a generation of men Jarman himself mourned there. Three people's ashes (two with permission, one without) are scattered here.

Prospect is freighted so richly with Jarman, with what he did there, with his things, with his garden, that it isn't home for HB. He has bought another cottage not far away, and has left the flat at Phoenix House and bought another, in Pimlico, which he shares with flatmates. The new flat is, he says, more fully his home than Prospect or Phoenix House were or could ever be. His flat – along with his work since 1994 (chiefly as a fisherman at Dungeness) – perhaps gives him an anchor for a sense of self which is separate from Jarman. This is something that matters especially given Jarman's fame and the potency of his presence at Prospect. HB comes and goes with just a bag. He doesn't keep many of his own things there (though, as he notes, and unlike his late partner), he 'doesn't have many things'.

That HB is committed to maintaining the cottage and the garden gives a sense of what a home can come to mean. In addition to all the echoes of other places and times, real and imagined, that Jarman found there, it stands now as a place of remembrance for him and for many others. It is part, loosely, queerly, of a heritage house and garden tradition – outside the domain of the National Trust or English Heritage (though in some respects it could belong with them).[93] Less obviously than it should be, Prospect is also testament to the relationship between Jarman and HB, and to the care HB took of Jarman before his death in 1994 and has continued to take of the cottage and garden since. Miller is right in noting the 'comfort of things' – Shannon and Ricketts, Ives, Ford and Bartlett all felt it; Alan Louis and some of the squatters felt the lack of it. In Jarman's case the cottage and garden come to materialise grief, and in ways other than what he called that 'horrible [AIDS] quilt'.

'What bits of cast-off clothing would be sewn into mine?', he asked, conjecturing on what a panel dedicated to him might contain. 'Old taxi receipts to Hampstead and a membership to the Subway [a 1970s/80 fuck club]?'[94] The quilt has been said to domesticate queerness: quilts are associated with home and with family.[95] With its taxi receipts and fuck-club membership card, Jarman rejected such domestication in his imagined panel. Yet he domesticated queerness in other ways. His multiple homes had long been the focus of his 'queer' life before he reached Prospect and through them and through his representation of them he queered home and family – and queered himself in the process. Prospect Cottage and garden are tangible residues of that process. The queer domestic lives I have examined in this book cannot be reduced to the standardized dimensions of a quilted panel. They were too multiple, shifting, richly textured, and interwoven with other ideas and identifications for that. Yet for those who made panels for the quilt and went to view it as a whole, it could suggest remembrance, comfort, connection, community, visibility, politics, and action. It connected the intimate, personal, domestic and familial with the public and activist. It perhaps seemed to Jarman to mute raw anger, grief and a vivid sense of difference. Yet the quilt also represented those things – just as it represented the multiplicity of gay lives and also paradoxically homogenized them in those regularized squares.

I have not located a singular mode of queer domesticity in this book. I don't think it's possible to do that. I have suggested some connecting threads in the ways that queer men have thought about home and family. I have shown how this arises from the way those men were positioned socially, culturally and politically, and from the way they themselves had to negotiate self-consciously their place within, local, urban and national cultures. Many felt the need to move away from family and homes of origin and to start again, creating resonant but also somewhat different homes and families of their own. These cultures and processes have been a bind and binding, a way to fit in and to be different. That eclectically panelled quilt perhaps after all serves as an apt metaphor for queer domesticities.

Notes

Introduction

1. http://www.fritzhaeg.com/schoolhouse/projects/queer-home-ec.html (Accessed 1 June 2012).
2. http://www.southbankcentre.co.uk/whatson/alternative-fairytales-alternative-families-70813 (Accessed 12 July 2013).
3. Collected in: Oscar Moore, *PWA: Looking AIDS in the Face* (London: Picador, 1996).
4. For a flavour see: Amy Brandzel, 'Queering Citizenship? Same-sex Marriage and the State', *GLQ: A Journal of Lesbian and Gay Studies* 11, no. 2 (2005): 171–204; Jeffrey Weeks, Brian Heaphy, and Catherine Donovan, *Same Sex Intimacies: Families of Choice and Other Life Experiments* (London: Routledge, 2001); Michael Warner, *The Trouble With Normal: Sex, Politics and the Ethics of Queer Life* (New York: Free Press, 1999); Lisa Duggan, 'The New Heteronormativity: The Sexual Politics of Neo-Liberalism', in *Materializing Democracy: Toward a Revitalized Cultural Politics*, ed. Russ Castronovo and Dana D. Nelson (Durham: Duke University Press, 2002); S. Roseneil and S. Budgeon, 'Cultures of Intimacy and Care Beyond "the Family": Personal Life and Social Change in the Early 21st Century', *Current Sociology* 52, no. 2 (2004): 135–159; A. Gorman-Murray, 'Contesting Domestic Ideals: Queering the Australian Home', *Australian Geographer* 38, no. 2 (2007): 195–213; Stephen Hicks, *Lesbian, Gay and Queer Parenting: Families, Intimacies, Genealogies* (Basingstoke: Palgrave Macmillan, 2011).
5. On this point see: Carol Smart, *Personal Life: New Directions in Sociological Thinking* (Cambridge: Polity, 2007), 21.
6. Sharon Marcus, 'At Home with the Other Victorians', *South Atlantic Quarterly* 108, no. 1 (Winter 2009): 120–145.
7. Hilde Heynen and Gulsum Baydar, eds., *Negotiating Domesticity: Spatial Productions of Gender in Modern Architecture* (London: Routledge, 2005), intro, 2.
8. Cited in: Matt Houlbrook, *Queer London: Perils and Pleasures in the Sexual Metropolis, 1918–1957* (Chicago: University of Chicago Press, 2005), 110.
9. John Osborne, 'Diary of a Somebody', *The Spectator*, 29 November 1986.
10. On home in relation to Englishness see especially: Deborah Cohen, *Household Gods: The British and Their Possessions* (New Haven: Yale University Press, 2006), xii; Alison Ravetz, *The Place of Home: English Domestic Environments, 1914–2000* (London: Spon, 1995).
11. Deborah Cohen and Sharon Marcus are notable exceptions in this regard. Cohen, *Household Gods*; Deborah Cohen, *Family Secrets: Living with Shame from the Victorians to the Present Day* (London: Viking, 2013); Sharon Marcus, *Between Women: Friendship, Desire, and Marriage in Victorian England* (Princeton: Princeton University Press, 2007); Marcus, 'At Home'.
12. As Kath Weston has it. Kath Weston, *Families We Choose: Lesbians, Gays, Kinship* (New York: Columbia University Press, 1991), 22.

13. For foundational arguments on the power of these discourses see especially: Jeffrey Weeks, *Coming Out: Homosexual Politics in Britain from the Nineteenth Century to the Present* (London: Quartet Books, 1977); Michel Foucault, *History of Sexuality Volume 1: An Introduction*, trans. Robert Hurley (London: Allen Lane, 1979); Mary McIntosh, 'The Homosexual Role', *Social Problems* 16, no. 2 (1968): 182–192.
14. Jordon Goodman, 'History and Anthropology', in *Companion to Historiography*, ed. Michael Bently (London: Routledge, 1997), 794; on this approach see also: Judy Giles, *The Parlour and the Suburb: Domestic Identities, Class, Femininity and Modernity* (Oxford: Berg, 2004), 24.
15. On this point see: Scott Bravmann, *Queer Fictions of the Past: History, Culture, and Difference* (Cambridge: Cambridge University Press, 1997), 127.
16. On the usefulness of stereotype in analysis see: David M. Halperin, *How to be Gay* (Cambridge: Harvard University Press, 2012), 91.
17. I borrow this idea of 'composure' from Graham Dawson who uses it to describe the effect of giving a testimony and creating a narrative of the self. See: Graham Dawson, *Soldier Heroes: British Adventure, Empire, and the Imagining of Masculinities* (London: Routledge, 1994), intro.
18. As Joe Ackerley has it in: J.R. Ackerley, *My Father and Myself* (New York: NYRB Classics, 2006), 239.
19. See: Sally Ledger, *The New Woman: Fiction and Feminism at the Fin de Siècle* (Manchester: Manchester University Press, 1997), chap. 4; On this see especially: Laura Doan, 'Woman's Place in the Home', in *Sapphic Modernities: Sexuality, Women and National Culture*, ed. J. Garrity and L. Doan (Basingstoke: Palgrave Macmillan, 2006); Martha Vicinus, *Intimate Friends: Women Who Loved Women, 1778–1928* (Chicago: University of Chicago Press, 2004); for a flavour in sexology, see: Havelock Ellis and John Addington Symonds, *Sexual Inversion*, ed. Ivan Crozier (Basingstoke: Palgrave Macmillan, 2008), chap. 4.
20. George Cruikshank, *Sinks of London Laid Open* (London: J. Duncombe, 1848).
21. Charles Ricketts, *Self-Portrait: Taken from the Letters and Journals*, ed. T. Sturge Moore and C. Lewis (London: Peter Davies, 1939), 341.
22. George Orwell, *Down and Out in Paris and London* (London: Penguin Books, 2003), 203.
23. Paul Sieveking, *Man Bites Dog: The Scrapbooks of and Edwardian Eccentric* (London: Jay Landesman, 1980), preface, 5.
24. Ackerley, *My Father*, 239.
25. Cited in: Simon Shepherd, *Because We're Queers: The Life and Crimes of Kenneth Halliwell and Joe Orton* (London: Gay Mens Press, 1989), title page.
26. Derek Jarman, *Smiling in Slow Motion* (London: Century, 2000), 10.
27. Historian of consciousness Teresa de Lauretis reputedly coined the term 'queer theory' at a lesbian and gay studies conference at the University of California, Santa Cruz, in 1990. She, Eve Sedgwick and Judith Butler were key to the development of associated concepts in the first part of the 1990s.
28. Mary Douglas, 'The Idea of a Home: a Kind of Space', *Social Research* 58, no. 1 (1991): 287–307.
29. For a vivid sense of the difference class can make see: Joanna Bourke, *Working Class Cultures in Britain 1890–1960: Gender, Class, and Ethnicity* (London: Routledge, 1994), chap. 2 & 3; Ross McKibbin, *Classes and Cultures: England, 1918–1951* (Oxford: Oxford University Press, 1998), chap. 5 & 8.

30. Zvi Razi, 'The Myth of the Immutable English Family', *Past and Present* 140, no. 1 (1993): 3–44; L. Davidoff, 'The Family in Britain', *The Cambridge Social History of Britain, 1750–1950* 2 (1993): 71–129; Tamara K. Hareven, 'The Home and the Family in Historical Perspective', *Social Research* 58, no. 1 (1991): 253–285.
31. Cohen, *Family Secrets*; Laura Doan, *Disturbing Practices: History, Sexuality, and Women's Experience of Modern War* (Chicago: University of Chicago Press, 2013).
32. John Tosh, *A Man's Place: Masculinity and the Middle-Class Home in Victorian England* (New Haven: Yale University Press, 1999), 4. There is now a large literature on the gender and sexual dynamics of domestic life. Aside from works cited elsewhere in this introduction I have found the following especially suggestive: Calvin Smith, 'Men Don't Do That Sort of Thing', *Men and Masculinities* 12 (October 1998): 138–172; Peter Williams, 'Constituting Class and Gender: A Social History of the Home, 1700–1901', in *Class and Space: The Making of Urban Society*, ed. N.J Thrift and Peter Williams (London: Routledge, 1987); Tony Chapman, *Gender and Domestic Life* (Basingstoke: Palgrave, 2002); Juliet Kinchin, 'Interiors: Nineteenth Century Essays on the "Masculine" and "Feminine" Room', in *The Gendered Object*, ed. Pat Kirkham (Manchester: Manchester University Press, 1996); Heynen and Baydar, *Negotiating Domesticity*; Clare Cooper Marcus, *House as a Mirror of Self: Exploring the Deeper Meaning of Home* (Berkeley: Conari Press, 1995); Nikolas Rose, *Governing the Soul: The Shaping of the Private Self* (London: Routledge, 1990).
33. Giles, *The Parlour and the Suburb*, 4; see also Cohen, *Household Gods*, 138; S.I. Benn and G.F. Gaus, eds., 'The Liberal Conception of the Public and the Private', in *Public and Private in Social Life* (London: Croom Helm, 1983), 31–65; Linda McDowell, *Gender Identity and Place: Understanding Feminist Geographies* (Cambridge: Polity Press, 1999); Marcus, *House as a Mirror*; Kenneth Plummer, *Intimate Citizenship: Private Decisions and Public Dialogues* (Seattle: University of Washington Press, 2003); Rose, *Governing the Soul*; J.A. Holstein and J.F. Gubrium, 'Deprivatization and the Construction of Domestic Life', *Journal of Marriage and the Family* 57, no. 4 (1995): 894–908.
34. Freud's understanding of the uncanny (or 'unheimlich'/unhomely) has been helpful to my thinking here. Sigmund Freud, *The Uncanny*, trans. David McLintock (London: Penguin, 2003).
35. Morag Shiach, 'Modernism, the City and the "Domestic Interior" ', *Home Cultures* 2, no. 3 (2005): 251–268.
36. On the potency of desire in this respect see, for example: A. Blunt, 'Home and Identity: Life Stories in Text and Person', in *Cultural Geography in Practice*, ed. Alison Blunt, P. Gruffudd, J. May, Miles Ogborn, and D. Pinder (London: Arnold, 2003); Adrian Forty, *Objects of Desire: Design and Society, 1750–1980* (London: Thames and Hudson, 1986).
37. See: Aaron Betsky, *Building Sex: Men, Women, and the Construction of Sexuality* (New York: William Morrow, 1995); Aaron Betsky, *Queer Space: Architecture and Same-Sex Desire* (New York: William Morrow, 1997); and essays in: Beatriz Colomina, ed., *Sexuality & Space* (New York: Princeton Architectural Press, 1992).
38. There is a large literature describing this process; see, for example: Charles Rice, *The Emergence of the Interior: Architecture, Modernity, Domesticity* (London: Routledge, 2007); Mary Poovey, *Uneven Developments: The*

Ideological Work of Gender in Mid-Victorian England (Chicago: University of Chicago Press, 1988); Tosh, *A Man's Place*; Erika Diane Rappaport, *Shopping for Pleasure: Women in the Making of London's West End* (Princeton: Princeton University Press, 2000); Cohen, *Household Gods*; Marcus, *Between Women*.

39. Cohen, *Household Gods*, chap. 4; J. Tosh, 'Imperial Masculinity and the Flight from Domesticity in Britain 1880–1914', in *Gender and Colonialism*, ed. Timothy P. Foley (Galway: Galway University Press, 1995), 72–85.
40. Amanda Vickery, for example, suggests the importance of the eighteenth century in this division. Amanda Vickery, *Behind Closed Doors: At Home in Georgian England* (New Haven: Yale University Press, 2009).
41. On this point see: John D' Emilio, 'Capitalism and Gay Identity', in *Families in the US: Kinship and Domestic Politics*, ed. Karen Hansen and Anita Garey (Philadelphia: Temple University Press, 1998).
42. Matt Cook, *London and the Culture of Homosexuality, 1885–1914* (Cambridge: Cambridge University Press, 2003), chap. 1 & 2; see also: Sean Brady, *Masculinity and Male Homosexuality in Britain, 1861–1913* (London: Palgrave Macmillan, 2005); H.G. Cocks, *Nameless Offences: Homosexual Desire in the Nineteenth Century* (London: I.B. Tauris, 2003).
43. Ed Cohen, *Talk on the Wilde Side: Towards a Genealogy of a Discourse on Male Sexualities* (London: Routledge, 1992); Neil Bartlett, *Who Was That Man: A Present for Mr Oscar Wilde* (London: Serpent's Tail, 1988).
44. Ravetz, *The Place of Home*, 41, 61–63; chap. 2 & 3; Sharon Marcus, *Apartment Stories: City and Home in Nineteenth-Century Paris and London* (Berkeley: University of California Press, 1999), 84.
45. Sara Ahmed, *The Cultural Politics of Emotion* (Edinburgh: Edinburgh University Press, 2004), 154; Marcus, *Apartment Stories*, 4.
46. Marcus, *Apartment Stories*, 93.
47. Cook, *London*.
48. See also: Cocks, *Nameless Offences*; Morris B. Kaplan, *Sodom on the Thames: Sex, Love, and Scandal in Wilde Times* (Ithaca: Cornell University Press, 2005); Houlbrook, *Queer London*.
49. On this point see: Catherine Robinson, 'I Think Home is More Than a Building: Young Home(Less) People on the Cusp of Home, Self and Something Else', *Urban Policy and Research* 20, no. 1 (2002): 27–38.
50. Carlo Ginzberg, 'Microhistory: Two or Three Things That I Know About It', *Critical Inquiry* 20, no. 1 (1993): 10–35, 33; for more on the use of case studies as indicative rather than representative see: Eve Kosofsky Sedgwick, *Epistemology of the Closet* (London: Harvester Wheatsheaf, 1991), 29; Michael Quinn Patton, *Qualitative Research & Evaluation Methods*, 3rd ed. (London: Sage, 2002).
51. Mary Chamberlain and Paul Thompson, *Narrative and Genre* (London: Routledge, 1998), 13; see also and especially: Jean Baudrillard, *The System of Objects* (London: Verso, 1996), 8; Judy Attfield, *Wild Things: The Material Culture of Everyday Life* (Oxford: Berg, 2000), chap. 2 & 5; Smart, *Personal Life*, chap. 7; Daniel Miller, ed., 'Possessions', in *Home Possessions: Material Culture Behind Closed Doors* (Oxford: Berg, 2001); Daniel Miller, *Material Cultures: Why Some Things Matter* (London: UCL Press, 1997), intro; Forty, *Objects of Desire*.

254 *Notes*

52. Judy Giles makes a related argument about women. Giles, *The Parlour and the Suburb*, 14.
53. Richard Dyer and David Halperin both pursue this argument in relation to a queer appreciation of the arts. See: Richard Dyer, *Culture of Queers* (London: Routledge, 2001); Halperin, *How to be Gay*.
54. Chamberlain and Thompson, *Narrative and Genre*, 1.
55. Raphael Samuel and Paul Thompson, *The Myths We Live By* (London: Routledge, 1990), 8.
56. Kenneth Plummer, *Telling Sexual Stories: Power, Change, and Social Worlds* (London: Routledge, 1994), 203; see also: Lynn Jamieson, *Intimacy: Personal Relationships in Modern Societies* (Cambridge: Polity Press, 1998), 10–13.
57. On this see especially: Joan W. Scott, 'The Evidence of Experience', *Critical Inquiry* 17, no. 4 (July 1991): 773–797; Bravmann, *Queer Fictions of the Past*, intro.
58. For a survey of some of those myths and fantasies (and the way they relate to everyday lives) see especially: John R. Gillis, *A World of Their Own Making: Myth, Ritual, and the Quest for Family Values* (New York: Basic Books, 1996).
59. Marcus observes the domestic pulse in all of Wilde's work. Marcus, 'At Home', 140.
60. Peter Parker, *Ackerley: A Life of J.R. Ackerley* (London: Constable, 1989), 261.
61. Derek Jarman, *Modern Nature: The Journals of Derek Jarman* (London: Century, 1991), 18.
62. Samuel and Thompson, *The Myths We Live By*, 10.
63. Ibid., 2. See also Ginzberg, 'Microhistory', 33.
64. Ibid., 5.
65. On this point see especially: Poovey, *Uneven Developments*.
66. James W. Cook, Lawrence B. Glickman, and Michael O'Malley, eds., *The Cultural Turn in U.S. History: Past, Present, and Future* (Chicago: University of Chicago Press, 2008), 25; see also: Matt Cook, 'Squatting in History: Queer Pasts and the Cultural Turn', in *Social Research After the Cultural Turn*, ed. Sasha Roseneil and Stephen Frosh (Basingstoke: Palgrave, 2012).
67. Bryant Keith Alexander, *Performing Black Masculinity: Race, Culture, and Queer Identity* (Lanham: Rowman & Littlefield, 2006), xx; see also: Kath Weston, *Render Me, Gender Me: Lesbians Talk Sex, Class, Color, Nation, Studmuffins* (New York: Columbia University Press, 1996), 5.
68. Seth Koven makes this point beautifully in: Seth Koven, *Slumming: Sexual and Social Politics in Victorian London* (Princeton: Princeton University Press, 2004), intro.
69. Weeks, Heaphy and Donovan, *Same-Sex Intimacies*; Weston, *Families We Choose*

Part I Beautiful Homes: Introduction

1. Cited in: John Potvin, '*Askesis* as Aesthetic Home: Edward Perry Warren, Lewes House, and the Ideal of Greek Love', *Home Cultures* 8, no. 1 (2011): 71–89.
2. Colin Cruise, *Love Revealed: Simeon Solomon and the Pre-Raphaelites* (London: Merrell, 2005), 9.
3. Rupert Croft Cooke, *Feasting with Panthers a New Consideration of Some Late Victorian Writers* (London: W.H. Allen, 1967), 42.
4. Cruise, *Love Revealed*, 11.

5. Simon Reynolds, *The Vision of Simeon Solomon* (Stroud: Catalpa Press, 1984), 89.
6. Cooke, *Feasting with Panthers*, 61.
7. Reynolds, *The Vision*, 90.
8. Ibid., 89.
9. Matt Houlbrook, *Queer London: Perils and Pleasures in the Sexual Metropolis, 1918–1957* (Chicago: University of Chicago Press, 2005), 120.
10. See especially: Daniel Pick, *Faces of Degeneration: A European Disorder, C.1848–c.1918* (Cambridge: Cambridge University Press, 1989); Gareth Stedman Jones, *Outcast London: A Study in the Relationship Between Classes in Victorian Society* (Oxford: Clarendon Press, 1972), chap. 16.
11. On the 1880s see: Jones, *Outcast London*; Seth Koven, *Slumming: Sexual and Social Politics in Victorian London* (Princeton: Princeton University Press, 2004), chap. 4; Michelle Allen, *Cleansing the City: Sanitary Geographies in Victorian London* (Ohio: Ohio University Press, 2008), chap. 4; of the 1930s Juliet Gardiner notes that 16,911 people were sleeping in casual wards nationally in 1932 as against 3188 in 1920. Juliet Gardiner, *The Thirties: An Intimate History* (London: Harper Press, 2010); see also: Jerry White, *London in the Twentieth Century: A City and Its People* (London: Vantage, 2008), 30, 203, 208, 221.
12. See: Koven, *Slumming*, chap. 1; Anthony Wohl, ed., 'Sex and the Single Room: Incest Among the Victorian Working Classes', in *The Victorian Family: Structures and Stresses* (London: Croom-Helm, 1977); P. Gurney, '"Intersex" and "Dirty Girls": Mass-Observation and Working-Class Sexuality in England in the 1930s', *Journal of the History of Sexuality* 8, no. 3 (1997): 256–290.
13. See, for example: Octavia Hill, 'The Influence of Model Dwellings on Character', in *The Life and Labour of the People of London*, ed. Charles Booth, vol. 3 (London: Macmillan, 1892).
14. *The Daily Telegraph*, 6 April 1895: 4; see also: Pick, *Faces of Degeneration*, chap. 1; Harry Cocks, *Nameless Offences: Homosexual Desire in the Nineteenth Century* (London: I.B. Tauris, 2003), chap. 2.
15. Cocks, *Nameless Offences*, chaps. 1 & 2; Pick, *Faces of Degeneration*, chap. 2; G. Chauncey, 'Privacy Could Only Be Had in Public: Gay Uses of the Streets', in *Stud: Architectures of Masculinity*, ed. J. Sanders (New York: Princeton Architectural Press, 1996), 224–267.
16. Cited by: Koven, *Slumming*, 47.
17. Havelock Ellis and John Addington Symonds, *Sexual Inversion*, ed. Ivan Crozier (Basingstoke: Palgrave Macmillan, 2008), 296.
18. Ibid.; see also: Koven, *Slumming*, 73.
19. Ellis and Symonds, *Sexual Inversion*, 300.
20. For a discussion of the act and this connection see: Koven, *Slumming*, 70–74; Matt Cook, *London and the Culture of Homosexuality, 1885–1914* (Cambridge: Cambridge University Press, 2003), chap. 2.
21. George Orwell, *Down and Out in Paris and London* (London: Penguin Books, 2003), 203.
22. See the introduction to this book for a brief queer etymology.
23. Anthony Grey, 'Homes for Homosexuals', *Social Action* (May 1969): 4.
24. Houlbrook, *Queer London*, 119.
25. Ibid., 121.
26. Orwell, *Down and Out in Paris and London*, 161.
27. Houlbrook, *Queer London*, 229.

28. White, *London in the Twentieth Century*, 124; Gardiner, *The Thirties*, 266, 262–263.
29. Cyril Donson and Armand Georgês, *Lonely-Land and Bedsitter-Land* (Bala: Bala Press, 1967); for further discussion of this association see the introduction to part III and also: Mark Armstrong, 'A Room in Chelsea: Quentin Crisp at Home', *Visual Culture in Britain* 12, no. 2 (2011): 155–169.
30. Deborah Cohen, *Family Secrets: Living with Shame from the Victorians to the Present Day* (London: Viking, 2013), 125.
31. For an overview see: Alison Ravetz, *The Place of Home: English Domestic Environments, 1914–2000* (London: Spon, 1995), chap. 3; 202–204.
32. Gardiner, *The Thirties*, 260.
33. Ibid., 275.
34. Judy Giles, *Women, Identity and Private Life in Britain, 1900–50* (Basingstoke: Macmillan, 1995), 22, 28; Judy Giles, '"Playing Hard to Get": Working-Class Women, Sexuality and Respectability in Britain, 1918–40', *Women's History Review* 1, no. 2 (1992): 239–255; Jill Greenfield, Sean O'Connell, and Chris Reid, 'Fashioning Masculinity: Men Only, Consumption and the Development of Marketing in the 1930s', *Twentieth Century British History* 10, no. 4 (1 January 1999): 457–476.
35. Sharon Marcus, *Apartment Stories: City and Home in Nineteenth-Century Paris and London* (Berkeley: University of California Press, 1999), 93; Gardiner, *The Thirties*, 261.
36. White, *London in the Twentieth Century*, 118; Houlbrook, *Queer London*, 134; Marcus, *Apartment Stories*, 93.
37. H. Montgomery Hyde, *The Trials of Oscar Wilde* (New York: Dover, 1973), 178; see also: Houlbrook, *Queer London*, 20; Marcus, *Apartment Stories*, 93.
38. Less than half of the households in Deptford Katherine Holden examined were composed of just husband, wife and children or a couple alone; most had additional residents. Katherine Holden, *The Shadow of Marriage: Singleness in England, 1914–60* (Manchester: Manchester University Press, 2010), 57; Tamara K. Hareven, 'The Home and the Family in Historical Perspective', *Social Research* 58, no. 1 (1991): 253–285.
39. Gardiner, *The Thirties*, 278.
40. Edward Carpenter, *Towards Democracy* (1883–1902; London: GMP, 1985), 325.
41. See especially: Houlbrook, *Queer London*, part 3.
42. Ibid., 134; Frank Mort, *Capital Affairs: London and the Making of the Permissive Society* (New Haven: Yale University Press, 2010), 156.
43. Richard Dennis, '"Babylonian Flats" in Victorian and Edwardian London', *The London Journal* 33, no. 3 (1 November 2008): 243.

1 Domestic Passions: Unpacking the Homes of Charles Shannon and Charles Ricketts

1. Christopher Hussey, 'The Keep, Chilham Castle, Kent. A Residence of Mr Charles Shannon, R.A. and Mr Charles Ricketts, A.R.A', *Country Life* (21 June 1924).
2. On the legendary friendship of this couple see: Robert Aldrich, *Gay Life Stories* (London: Thames & Hudson, 2012), 47.
3. Hussey, 'The Keep'.

4. Ricketts to Thomas Lewinsky, 18 November 1918 cited in: Charles Ricketts, *Self-Portrait: Taken from the Letters and Journals*, ed. T. Sturge Moore and C. Lewis (London: Peter Davies, 1939), 306.
5. Ricketts to R.N.R. Holst, 13 June 1919, in Ricketts, *Self-Portrait*, 317.
6. Ricketts to Gordon Bottomley, 23 March 1919, in Ricketts, *Self-Portrait*, 341.
7. Deborah Cohen, *Household Gods: The British and Their Possessions* (New Haven: Yale University Press, 2006), x–xi; Judy Neiswander, *The Cosmopolitan Interior: Liberalism and the British Home 1870–1914* (New Haven: Yale University Press, 2008), 161.
8. Neiswander, *The Cosmopolitan Interior*, 33.
9. Ibid., 33.
10. Ibid., 40.
11. On this point see, for example: Cohen, *Household Gods*, chap. 1; Nicholas Cooper, *The Opulent Eye: Late Victorian and Edwardian Taste in Interior Design* (London: Architectural Press, 1976); Jane Hamlett, *Material Relations: Families and Middle-Class Domestic Interiors in England, 1850–1910* (London: I.B. Taurus, 2009); Helen Long, *The Edwardian Home: The Middle-Class Home in Britain 1880–1914* (Manchester: Manchester University Press, 1993); David Dewing, *Home and Garden: Paintings and Drawings of English, Middle-Class, Urban Domestic Spaces, 1675–1914* (London: Geffrye Museum, 2003).
12. See: Neiswander, *The Cosmopolitan Interior*, 87; Cohen, *Household Gods*, chap. 4; Penny Sparke, *As Long as It's Pink: The Sexual Politics of Taste* (London: Pandora, 1995), pt. 1.
13. See: Note 65.
14. J. Tosh, 'Imperial Masculinity and the Flight from Domesticity in Britain 1880–1914', in *Gender and Colonialism*, ed. Timothy P. Foley (Galway: Galway University Press, 1995), 72–85.
15. Aldrich, *Gay Life Stories*, 47.
16. J.G. Paul Delaney, *Charles Ricketts: A Biography* (Oxford: Clarendon, 1990), 7, 19.
17. See: Chapter 2.
18. Catherine Hall, Keith McClelland, and Jane Rendall, *Defining the Victorian Nation: Class, Race, Gender and the British Reform Act of 1867* (Cambridge University Press, 2000), chap. 2.
19. Charles Booth's map of Kennington is at: http://booth.lse.ac.uk/cgi-bin/do.pl?sub=view_booth_only&b.l=1&b.d.l=4&b.p.x=13871&b.p.y=12541&b.p.w=500&b.p.h=309&b.p.l=2&b.move.right.x=4&b.move.right.y=7&b.t.w=128&b.t.h=96 (Accessed 7 October 2012).
20. For a wonderful account of the mythology and putative distinctiveness of Bohemians and Bohemias see: Elizabeth Wilson, *Bohemians: The Glamorous Outcasts* (London: I.B. Tauris, 2000).
21. On the artistic reputation of particular areas of London in the period see Giles Walkley, *Artists' Houses in London 1764–1914* (Aldershot: Scolar Press, 1994), chap. 4 & 5; Caroline Dakers, *The Holland Park Circle: Artists and Victorian Society* (New Haven: Yale University Press, 1999), 2.
22. See Charles Booth's poverty map of Chelsea at: http://booth.lse.ac.uk/cgi-bin/do.pl?sub=view_booth_and_barth&m.l=1&m.d.l=2&m.p.x=6283&m.p.y=9207&m.p.w=500&m.p.h=309&m.p.l=1&m.move.left.x=7&m.move.left.y=5&m.t.w=128&m.t.h=80&b.p.x=10192&b.p.y=13311&b.p.w=500&b.p.h=309&b.p.l=2 (Accessed 7 October 2012).
23. Cited in: White, *London in the Twentieth Century*, 16.

24. Neiswander, *The Cosmopolitan Interior*, 50; Walkley, *Artists' Houses*, 158.
25. Delaney, *Charles Ricketts*, 2.
26. Ibid., 22.
27. Ibid., 24–25.
28. Jason Edwards and Imogen Hart, eds., *Rethinking the Interior, c.1867–1896: Aestheticism and Arts and Crafts* (Farnham: Ashgate, 2010), 5. See also John Potvin, 'The Aesthetics of Community: Queer Interiors and the Desire for Intimacy', in *Rethinking*, ed. Edwards and Hart, 181.
29. Sharon Marcus, 'At Home with the Other Victorians', *South Atlantic Quarterly* 108, no. 1 (Winter 2009): 139.
30. On the femininity of diary writing see: Matt Cook, 'Sex Lives and Diary Writing: The Journals of George Ives', in *Life Writing and Victorian Culture*, ed. David Amigoni (Farnham: Ashgate, 2006), 199; Jennifer Sinor, *The Extraordinary Work of Ordinary Writing: Annie Ray's Diary* (Iowa City: University of Iowa Press, 2002), 47.
31. Delaney, *Charles Ricketts*, 389.
32. Eve Sedgwick, *Tendencies* (London: Routledge, 1994), 79.
33. Alan Bray, *The Friend* (Chicago: University of Chicago Press, 2003); Edward Carpenter, ed., *Ioläus. An Anthology of Friendship* (London: Swan Sonnenschein, 1902); Jeffrey Weeks, Brian Heaphy, and Catherine Donovan, *Same Sex Intimacies: Families of Choice and Other Life Experiments* (London: Routledge, 2001); Sasha Roseneil, 'Why We Should Care About Friends: An Argument for Queering the Care Imaginary in Social Policy', *Social Policy and Society* 3, no. 4 (2004): 409–419; P. Nardi, 'That's What Friends Are For: Friends as Family in the Gay and Lesbian Community', in *Modern Homosexualities: Fragments of Lesbian and Gay Experience*, ed. K. Plummer (New York: Routledge, 1992); Kath Weston, *Families We Choose: Lesbians, Gays, Kinship* (New York: Columbia University Press, 1991).
34. Related arguments about what might constitute a queer life can be found in: Sedgwick, *Tendencies*; Mo Moulton, 'Bricks and Flowers: Unconventionality in Katherine Everett's Life Writing', in *British Queer History*, ed. Brian Lewis (Manchester: Manchester University Press, 2013); Diana Maltz, '"Baffling Arrangements": Vernon Lee and John Singer Sargent in Queer Tangier', in *Rethinking*, ed. Edwards and Hart (Ashgate: Farnham, 2010).
35. Maltz, 'Baffling Arrangements', 207.
36. Delaney, *Charles Ricketts*, 15.
37. For a beautifully illustrated account of the concept see: Charlotte Gere, *The House Beautiful: Oscar Wilde and the Aesthetic Interior* (London: Lund Humphries, 2000).
38. Michael Hatt, 'Space, Surface, Self: Homosexuality and the Aesthetic Interior', *Visual Culture in Britain* 8, no. 1 (2007): 111.
39. On this see especially: Dennis Denisoff, *Aestheticism and Sexual Parody 1840–1940* (Cambridge: Cambridge University Press, 2006), chap. 4.
40. Franny Moyle shows the extent to which Tite Street was a joint project for the couple. Franny Moyle, *Constance: The Tragic and Scandalous Life of Mrs. Oscar Wilde* (London: John Murray, 2012), 127.
41. Max Beerbohm and Charles Hirsch cited in: Cook, *London*, 97.
42. Hatt, 'Space, Surface, Self'.
43. Marcus, 'At Home', 140.

44. Hatt, 'Space, Surface, Self'.
45. Anon, *Teleny, or the Reverse of the Medal* (Cosmopoli, 1893), 114; for more on the representation of home in the novel see: Cook, *London*, 111–115; Marcus, 'At Home'; Hatt, 'Space, Surface, Self'.
46. Hyde, *The Trials of Oscar Wilde*, 178; Ed Cohen, *Talk on the Wilde Side: Towards a Genealogy of a Discourse on Male Sexualities* (London: Routledge, 1992), 180.
47. Charles Ricketts, *Oscar Wilde* (London: Nonesuch Press, 1932), 35.
48. Ibid., 33.
49. Ricketts, *Self-Portrait*, 22; for comparative values see the Economic History Association website at http://eh.net/hmit/.
50. Sparke, *As Long as It's Pink*, 37; Joseph Bristow, *Effeminate England: Homoerotic Writing after 1885* (New York: Columbia University Press, 1995); Alan Sinfield, *The Wilde Century: Effeminacy, Oscar Wilde and the Queer Moment* (London: Cassell, 1994).
51. Neil Bartlett, *Who Was That Man: A Present for Mr Oscar Wilde* (London: Serpent's Tail, 1988), chap.2 'Flowers'.
52. Letter to William Pye, May 1906, in Ricketts, *Self-Portrait*, 134.
53. Cited in: Delaney, *Charles Ricketts*, 97.
54. On this sense of queer superiority and natural aristocracy see: David M. Halperin, *How to be Gay* (Cambridge: Harvard University Press, 2012), 226.
55. Delaney, *Charles Ricketts*, 97.
56. Ricketts, *Oscar Wilde*, 2; see also: John Potvin, 'Collecting Intimacy One Object at a Time: Material Culture, Aestheticism, and the Spaces of Aesthetic Companionship', in *Material Cultures, 1740–1920: The Meanings and Pleasures of Collecting*, ed. John Potvin and Alla Myzelev (Farnham: Ashgate, 2009), 196; Jason Edwards, 'The Lessons of Leighton House: Aesthetics, Politics, Erotics', in *Rethinking*, ed. Edwards and Hart.
57. Lewis, in Ricketts, *Self-Portrait*, ix.
58. Cohen, *Household Gods*, 156, 165.
59. Neiswander, *The Cosmopolitan Interior*, 55.
60. Potvin, 'Collecting Intimacy', 197.
61. Sparke, *As Long as It's Pink*, 50.
62. Lewis, in Ricketts, *Self-Portrait*, ix.
63. On the Victorian trend for eclecticism, see Cohen, *Household Gods*, 84; on the need for more nuanced readings of eclecticism, see Jason Edwards and Imogen Hart, 'Introduction: The Victorian Interior' in *Rethinking*, ed. Edwards and Hart, 12–14.
64. See: Chapter 2 and Cohen, *Household Gods*, chap. 7.
65. Ricketts, *Self-Portrait*, vii.
66. Ricketts, *Oscar Wilde*, 40.
67. Potvin, 'Collecting Intimacy', 203.
68. Ricketts, *Self-Portrait*, vii.
69. Jacques-Émile Blanche, *Portraits of a Lifetime: The Late Victorian Era, the Edwardian Pageant 1870–1914* (London: Dent, 1937), 130. The depiction of Leighton's bedroom was somewhat erroneous, Edwards suggests. See Edwards, 'Lessons'.
70. Potvin, '*Askesis*', 73, 86.
71. Marcus, 'At Home', 120, 138.
72. Ibid., 138; see also: Potvin, 'Collecting Intimacy', 182.

73. Edwards, 'Lessons', 97, 105.
74. Michael Camille, 'Editor's Introduction', *Art History* 24, no. 2 (April 2001): 163.
75. Barrett Kalter, *Modern Antiques: The Material Past in England, 1660–1780* (Lewisburg: Bucknell University Press, 2011), chap. 6; Aaron Betsky, *Queer Space: Architecture and Same-Sex Desire* (New York: William Morrow, 1997), 63–78.
76. Cohen, *Household Gods*, 160; Will Fellows, *A Passion to Preserve: Gay Men as Keepers of Culture* (Madison: University of Wisconsin Press, 2004), 22.
77. Ricketts, *Self-Portrait*, 165.
78. Susan Pearce, *On Collecting: An Investigation into Collecting in the European Tradition* (London: Routledge, 1995), 22; see also essays in: Anthony Shelton, ed., *Collectors: Expressions of Self and Other* (London: Horniman Museum and Gardens, 2001).
79. On this see: Tirza Latimer, 'Balletomania: A Sexual Disorder?', *GLQ: A Journal of Lesbian and Gay Studies* 5, no. 2 (1999): 173–197; Martha Vicinus, 'Male Impersonation and Lesbian Desire', in *Borderlines: Genders and Identities in War and Peace, 1870–1930*, ed. Billie Melman (London: Routledge, 1998).
80. Ricketts, *Self-Portrait*, 320.
81. Cook, *London*, 127–129.
82. Warren's biographers Osbert Burdett and E.H. Goddard, cited by Potvin, '*Askesis*', 77; Delaney, *Charles Ricketts*, 26.
83. Claire Wintle, 'Career Development: Domestic Display as Imperial, Anthropological, and Social Trophy', *Victorian Studies* 50, no. 2 (Winter 2008): 280.
84. Jonathan Katz Ned, 'The Art of Code: Jasper Johns and Robert Rauchenberg', in *Significant Others: Creativity & Intimate Partnership*, ed. Whitney Chadwick and Isabelle de Courtivron (London: Thames & Hudson, 1993), 197.
85. Laurel Brake, *Print in Transition, 1850–1910: Studies in Media and Book History* (Basingstoke: Palgrave, 2001), 110–144.
86. Ibid.
87. Marcus, 'At Home', 129.
88. John Addington Symonds, *The Memoirs of John Addington Symonds* (London: Hutchinson, 1984), 63.
89. Max Nordau, *Degeneration* (1895; Lincoln: University of Nebraska Press, 1993), 7; see: Cook, *London*, 79–80; Potvin, 'Collecting Intimacy', 199.
90. Phyllis Grosskurth, *John Addington Symonds: A Biography* (New York: Arno Press, 1975), 63.
91. Sedgwick, *Tendencies*, 66; Laurence Dreyfus, *Wagner and the Erotic Impulse* (Cambridge: Harvard University Press, 2012), chap. 5.
92. Ricketts, *Self-Portrait*, 12.
93. See: Marcus, 'At Home', 121; John Tosh, *A Man's Place: Masculinity and the Middle-Class Home in Victorian England* (New Haven: Yale University Press, 1999), 7; G.K. Behlmer, *Friends of the Family: The English Home and Its Guardians, 1850–1940* (Standford: Stanford University Press, 1998).
94. See: Vicinus, 'Male Impersonation and Lesbian Desire'; Cook, *London*, 28–29; for more on the iconic queer status of the Ballets Russes see: Latimer, 'Balletomania', 102–106; Christopher Reed, *Bloomsbury Rooms: Modernism, Subculture, and Domesticity* (New Haven: Yale University Press, 2004), 102.
95. For discussion see: Cook, *London*, 96–97.
96. Charles S. Ricketts, *Michael Field* (Edinburgh: Tragara Press, 1976), 1.

97. Ricketts, *Oscar Wilde*, 45.
98. Ricketts, *Self-Portrait*, vii.
99. Cited in: Delaney, *Charles Ricketts*, 177.
100. Ibid., 279.
101. Potvin, '*Askesis*', 84.
102. See the introduction to this section.
103. Ricketts, *Oscar Wilde*, 33.
104. Cited in: Delaney, *Charles Ricketts*, 279.
105. Blanche, *Portraits of a Lifetime*, 166.
106. Delaney, *Charles Ricketts*, 160.
107. Ibid., 220.
108. On this point, see also Potvin, 'Collecting Intimacy', 195.
109. Potvin, '*Askesis*', 75.
110. Delaney, *Charles Ricketts*, 220.
111. Ricketts, *Self-Portrait*, 96.
112. Delaney, *Charles Ricketts*, 220.
113. Ibid., 305.
114. Ricketts, *Self-Portrait*, 22.
115. Ibid., 78; Freud to Jung, 2 November 1911 Sigmund Freud and Karl Jung, *The Freud–Jung Letters*, ed. William McGuire, trans. Ralph Mannheim and R.F.C. Hull (London: Hogarth and Routledge, 1974), 453–454.
116. Delaney, *Charles Ricketts*, 123.
117. Ibid., 334.
118. Ricketts, *Self-Portrait*, 107.
119. On this point, see Edwards and Hart, 'Introduction: The Victorian Interior', in *Rethinking*, ed. Edwards and Hart, 9.
120. Delaney, *Charles Ricketts*, 334. On this point, see Potvin, 'Collecting Intimacy', 201–202.
121. Walkley, *Artists' Houses*, 218; Delaney, *Charles Ricketts*, 49.
122. Potvin, 'Aesthetics of Community', 174.
123. Ricketts, *Oscar Wilde*, 44.
124. Marcus, 'At Home', 137.
125. Lewis in the preface to Ricketts, *Self-Portrait*, v–vi.
126. Delaney, *Charles Ricketts*, 58.
127. Ibid., 55.
128. Ricketts, *Oscar Wilde*, 36–37.
129. Dakers, *The Holland Park Circle*, 2; see also: Martina Droth, 'Sculpture and Aesthetic Intent in the Late-Victorian Interior', in *Rethinking*, ed. Edwards and Hart, 226.
130. Delaney, *Charles Ricketts*, 55.
131. Both men worked with Wilde on various books; Ricketts designed Symonds' *In the Key of Blue* (1893) and Gray's *Silverpoints* (1893); Gray was supposedly the model for Dorian Gray and Shannon for Basil Hallward in Wilde's novel.
132. Delaney, *Charles Ricketts*, 314.
133. Emphasis mine. Lewis in Ricketts, *Self-Portrait*, viii. On the queer significance of uncles, see: Eve Sedwick, 'Tales of the Avunculate', in *Tendencies*, ed. Sedgwick; Eileen Cleere, *Avuncularism: Capitalism, Patriarchy, and Nineteenth-Century English Culture* (Stanford: Stanford University Press, 2004).

134. Potvin, *'Askesis'*, 72, 82; on changing queer interaction see especially: John Grube, '"Native and Settlers": An Ethnographic Note on Early Interaction of Older Homosexual Men with Younger Gay Liberationists', *Journal of Homosexuality* 20, no. 3 (1990): 119–136.
135. Delaney, *Charles Ricketts*, 314.
136. 'Diary', 12 May 1905, in Charles S. Ricketts, *Letters from Charles Ricketts to 'Michael Field' (1903–1913)* (Edinburgh: Tragara, 1981), 17.
137. 'Diary', 5 December 1900, in Ricketts, *Self-Portrait*, 49–50.
138. Ricketts, *Letters*, 5; Delaney, *Charles Ricketts*, 88.
139. Ricketts, *Letters*, 5.
140. 'Diary', 20 May 1901, in Ricketts, *Self-Portrait*, 34.
141. Potvin, *'Askesis'*, 81.
142. See: Part IV.
143. Marcus, 'At Home', 121.
144. On queer heterosociality see especially: Marc Stein, *City of Sisterly and Brotherly Loves: Lesbian and Gay Philadelphia, 1945–1972* (Philadelphia: Temple University Press, 2004); Maltz, 'Baffling Arrangements'; Terry Castle, *Noel Coward and Radclyffe Hall: Kindred Spirits* (New York: Columbia University Press, 1996).
145. Ricketts, *Self-Portrait*, 12.
146. Ibid., 411.
147. Delaney, *Charles Ricketts*, 389.
148. Ricketts, *Self-Portrait*, 415.
149. Delaney, *Charles Ricketts*, 383.
150. Ricketts to Gordon Bottomley, 16 September 1922, in Ibid., 342.
151. Ricketts to John Gray, cited in: Delaney, *Charles Ricketts*, 389.
152. Ibid., 388.
153. Ricketts, *Self-Portrait*, 343.
154. Neiswander, *The Cosmopolitan Interior*, 147.
155. Ravetz, *The Place of Home*, chap. 9.
156. Neiswander, *The Cosmopolitan Interior*, 148; see also: Alison Light, *Forever England: Femininity, Literature and Conservatism between the Wars* (London: Routledge, 1991); Ravetz, *The Place of Home*, chap. 2.
157. Cited in: Delaney, *Charles Ricketts*, 310–312.
158. See: Chapter 3.
159. Simon Garfield, *Our Hidden Lives: The Everyday Diaries of a Forgotten Britain, 1945–1948* (London: Ebury, 2004); Cohen discusses B. Charles under the pseudonym Anatole James in: Cohen, *Household Gods*, chap. 5.
160. See: Chapter 6.
161. See: Daniel Farson, *Gilbert and George: A Portrait* (London: Harper Collins, 1999).
162. See the epilogue to this section.

2 Queer Interiors: C.R. Ashbee to Oliver Ford

1. For accounts of Ashbee's childhood see: Alan Crawford, *C.R. Ashbee: Architect, Designer & Romantic Socialist* (New Haven: Yale University Press, 1985), 2–10; John Tosh, *A Man's Place: Masculinity and the Middle-Class Home in Victorian England* (New Haven: Yale University Press, 1999), 185.

2. C.R. Ashbee, 'Memoirs' (unpublished), cited in Jonathan Rose, *The Edwardian Temperament, 1895–1919* (Athens: Ohio University Press, 1986), 65.
3. Edward Carpenter, *The Intermediate Sex* (London: Swan Sonnenschein, 1908).
4. Ibid.; Judith Walkowitz, *City of Dreadful Delight: Narratives of Sexual Danger in Late-Victorian London* (Chicago: University of Chicago Press, 1992), 59; see also: Asa Briggs, *Toynbee Hall: The First Hundred Years* (London: Routledge, 1984).
5. Aaron Betsky, *Queer Space: Architecture and Same-Sex Desire* (New York: William Morrow, 1997), 86.
6. Fiona MacCarthy, *The Simple Life: C.R. Ashbee in the Cotswolds* (London: Lund Humphries, 1981), 23.
7. C.R.Ashbee, 'Journal', 1 Oct. 1898; 'Journal', 1898 – 1899 CRA/1/5, Library, King's College, Cambridge.
8. For a less idealised account of Carpenter's household see: Sheila Rowbotham, *A Life of Liberty and Love* (London: Verso, 2008).
9. 'The New Magpie and Stump – A Successful Experiment in Domestic Architecture', *The Studio* 5 (May 1895): 72.
10. Crawford, *Ashbee*, 280, 306; Judy Neiswander, *The Cosmopolitan Interior: Liberalism and the British Home 1870–1914* (New Haven: Yale University Press, 2008), 187; for an overview of design history in this period see: Adrian Forty, *Objects of Desire: Design and Society, 1750–1980* (London: Thames and Hudson, 1986).
11. Laurel Brake, *Print in Transition, 1850–1910: Studies in Media and Book History* (Basingstoke: Palgrave, 2001), 127; Matt Cook, *London and the Culture of Homosexuality, 1885–1914* (Cambridge: Cambridge University Press, 2003), 128.
12. See, for example: 'The Nude in Photography', *The Studio: An Illustrated Magazine of Fine and Applied Arts* 1, no. 2 (June 1893): 104–107.
13. 'The New Magpie and Stump', 68.
14. On this see chapter 1; and Cook, *London*, chap. 5.
15. Neiswander, *The Cosmopolitan Interior*, 38.
16. Crawford, *Ashbee*, 207.
17. The conceptual dimensions of these links are discussed by: Judy Attfield, *Wild Things: The Material Culture of Everyday Life* (Oxford: Berg, 2000), chap. 2.
18. Michael Hatt, 'Space, Surface, Self: Homosexuality and the Aesthetic Interior', *Visual Culture in Britain* 8, no. 1 (2007), 125.
19. Ibid., 125.
20. Crawford, *Ashbee*, 72.
21. Hatt, 'Space, Surface, Self', 120, 124.
22. 'The New Magpie and Stump', 74.
23. Hatt, 'Space, Surface, Self', 122 & 124.
24. Christopher Reed, *Bloomsbury Rooms: Modernism, Subculture, and Domesticity* (New Haven: Yale University Press, 2004).
25. Crawford, *Ashbee*, 75.
26. Matt Houlbrook, 'Soldier Heroes and Rent Boys: Homosex, Masculinities, and Britishness in the Brigade of Guards, Circa 1900–1960', *Journal of British Studies* 42, no. 3 (July 2003): 351–388.
27. Crawford, *Ashbee*, 161.
28. Ibid., 75.
29. MacCarthy, *The Simple Life*, 146; Felicity Ashbee, *Janet Ashbee: Love, Marriage, and the Arts & Crafts Movement* (Syracuse: Syracuse University Press, 2002).

30. For an account of the development of (and challenges to) these ideas across the twentieth century see: Marcus Collins, *Modern Love: An Intimate History of Men and Women in Twentieth-Century Britain* (London: Atlantic, 2003).
31. Hatt, 'Space, Surface, Self', 125.
32. On the latitude often enjoyed by the avant garde see: Susan Suleiman, *Subversive Intent: Gender, Politics, and the Avant-Garde* (Cambridge, MA and London: Harvard University Press, 1990); Virginia Nicholson, *Among the Bohemians: Experiments in Living 1900–1939* (London: Viking, 2002).
33. Jeffrey Weeks, *The World We Have Won: The Remaking of Erotic and Intimate Life* (London: Routledge, 2007), 36–38; Hera Cook, *The Long Sexual Revolution: English Women, Sex, and Contraception, 1800–1975* (Oxford: Oxford University Press, 2004), 179.
34. J. Sanders, 'Curtain Wars: Architects, Decorators, and the 20th-Century Domestic Interior', *Harvard Design Magazine* 16 (2002): 14.
35. Penny Sparke, *As Long as It's Pink: The Sexual Politics of Taste* (London: Pandora, 1995), 148; see also: Anna Massey, *Interior Design Since 1900* (London: Thames & Hudson, 2008), 123.
36. Mary Eliza Haweis, *The Art of Decoration* (London: Chatto & Windus, 1881); Rhoda Garrett and Agnes Garrett, *Suggestions for House Decoration* (London: Macmillan, 1876); Jane Ellen Panton, *From Kitchen to Garret.* (London: Ward & Downey, 1888); Charlotte Talbot Coke, *The Gentlewoman at Home.* (London: Henry & Co, 1892); see also: Juliet Kinchin, 'Interiors: Nineteenth-Century Essays on the "Masculine" and "Feminine" Room', in *The Gendered Object*, ed. Pat Kirkham (Manchester: Manchester University Press, 1996).
37. Deborah Cohen, *Household Gods: The British and Their Possessions* (New Haven: Yale University Press, 2006), 105.
38. On the way de Wolfe and other interior designers 'queer[ed] modernism' see: Betsky, *Queer Space*, 98–102.
39. Sparke, *As Long as It's Pink*, 150.
40. See: Chapter 1.
41. For more on this association see: Tirza Latimer, 'Balletomania: A Sexual Disorder?', *GLQ: A Journal of Lesbian and Gay Studies* 5, no. 2 (1999); Martha Vicinus, *Independent Women: Work and Community for Single Women: 1850–1920* (London: Virago, 1985); Richard Dyer, *Culture of Queers* (London: Routledge, 2001); David M. Halperin, *How to Be Gay* (Cambridge: Harvard University Press, 2012).
42. Lady Cadbury, 'Mr Ronald Fleming', *The Times*, 9 November 1968.
43. See the 1958 feature on Ronald Fleming, 'The Luxury Touch', *The Queen*, 28 October 1958, 86–87.
44. Katherine V. Snyder, *Bachelors, Manhood, and the Novel, 1850–1925* (Cambridge: Cambridge University Press, 1999); Katherine Holden, *The Shadow of Marriage: Singleness in England, 1914–60* (Manchester: Manchester University Press, 2010).
45. Ronald Fleming, 'AA Talk on Decoration' (1931), in Ronald Fleming Archive, V&A Archive of Art and Design, AAD/2013/1/1.
46. Christopher Reed, 'Design for (Queer) Living: Sexual Identity, Performance, and Decor in British Vogue, 1922–1926', *GLQ: A Journal of Lesbian and Gay Studies* 12, no. 3 (2006): 377.

47. Osbert Sitwell, *Noble Essences* (1950) cited in: Reed, *Bloomsbury Rooms*, 236.
48. 'Unity in Diversity', *Vogue* 1924, cited in Reed, 'Design for (Queer) Living', 390–391.
49. Snyder, *Bachelors, Manhood, and the Novel, 1850–1925*, 34.
50. John Babuscio, 'Camp and Gay Sensibility', in *Camp Grounds: Style and Homosexuality*, ed. David Bergman (Amherst: University of Massachusetts Press, 1993), 24.
51. This playfulness with interiors was celebrated in the pages of *Vogue* in the 1920s. See: Reed, 'Design for (Queer) Living', 379–380.
52. Fleming, 'A Talk on Decoration'; Ronald Fleming, 'New and Old in Decoration' (1932), in Ronald Fleming Archive, AAD/2013/1/1; Fleming, 'The Luxury Touch'.
53. On this see: Cecil Beaton, *The Glass of Fashion* (London: Weidenfeld & Nicolson, 1954), 2–3; Fleming, 'A Talk on Decoration'.
54. Fleming, 'A Talk on Decoration'.
55. See: Sanders, 'Curtain Wars'.
56. Sparke, *As Long as it's Pink*, 102.
57. Fleming, 'New and Old in Decoration'.
58. James Gardiner, *Who's a Pretty Boy, Then?: One Hundred & Fifty Years of Gay Life in Pictures* (London: Serpent's Tail, 1997), 130.
59. Juliet Gardiner, *The Thirties: An Intimate History* (London: Harper Press, 2010), 358; E. Darling, *Re-forming Britain: Narratives of Modernity Before Reconstruction* (Taylor & Francis, 2006), chap. 5.
60. Lanchester revealed her husband's homosexuality in: Elsa Lanchester, *Elsa Lanchester Herself* (New York: St Martins Press, 1983).
61. Around half the 132 Queen Anne Mansions apartments were single occupancy according to the 1901 census. Richard Dennis, ' "Babylonian Flats" in Victorian and Edwardian London', *The London Journal* 33, no. 3 (1 November 2008): 233, 243; Matt Houlbrook, *Queer London: Perils and Pleasures in the Sexual Metropolis, 1918–1957* (Chicago: University of Chicago Press, 2005), 113–114.
62. 'Goings On', *Weekend Review*, 4 February 1933.
63. Mordant Sharpe, 'The Green Bay Tree', in *Gay Plays*, ed. Michael Wilcox (London: Methuen, 1984), 55.
64. Ibid., 64.
65. Ibid., 71.
66. Halperin, *How to Be Gay*, 238.
67. Gardiner, *The Thirties*, chap. 12.
68. Ibid.
69. Richard Hornsey, *The Spiv and the Architect: Unruly Life in Postwar London* (Minneapolis: University of Minnesota Press, 2010), 210.
70. Ibid.
71. Rodney Garland, *The Heart in Exile* (1953; Brighton: Milliveres, 1995), 47; for further analysis of the novel see: Hornsey, *The Spiv*, 29, 192; Chris Waters and Matt Houlbrook, 'The Heart in Exile: Detachment and Desire in 1950s London', *History Workshop Journal* 62 (Autumn 2006): 142–163.
72. See: Chapter 6.
73. See: Chapter 8.
74. Philippa Toomey, 'Oliver Ford', *The Times*, 7 July 1976.

75. Oliver Ford Archive (AAD/1994/20/36), V&A Archive of Art and Design.
76. As Fellows has it. Fellows, *A Passion to Preserve*.
77. Diaries 1954–1990, Oliver Ford Archive, V&A (AAD/1994/20/22).
78. Oliver Ford Archive, V&A (AAD/1994/20/37).
79. Oliver Ford Archive, V&A (AAD/1994/20/19).
80. Oliver Ford Archive, V&A (AAD/1994/20/33).
81. Unreferenced scrapbook clipping, Oliver Ford Archive, V&A (AAD/1994/20/19).
82. Halperin, *How to be Gay*, 228.
83. Willa Petschek, 'Oliver Ford: A Cushion of Elegance', *International Herald Tribune*, 16 July 1981.
84. Snyder, *Bachelors, Manhood, and the Novel, 1850–1925*, 18; See also: Massey, *Interior Design*, 123.
85. Toomey, 'Oliver Ford'.
86. On this point see: Sanders, 'Curtain Wars'.
87. 'Oliver Ford', *International Herald Tribune*, 16 July 1981.
88. 'Appointment Diary' (1968) and diaries (1954–1990), Oliver Ford Archive (AAD/1994/20/22).
89. 'Desk Diary', Oliver Ford Archive (AAD/1994/20/23).
90. 'Director Fined £700 in Guardsman Case', *Nottingham Guardian Journal*, 7 May 1968.
91. 'Interior Designer Fined £700', *Blackpool Evening Gazette*, 6 May 1968.
92. 'Director Fined for Indecency with Guards', *The Guardian*, 7 May 1968.
93. Houlbrook, 'Soldier Heroes'.
94. 'Director Fined', *The Guardian*.
95. 'Director is Fined £700 in Guards Case', *Liverpool Echo*, 6 May 1968.
96. 'Interior Designer Fined', *Blackpool Evening Gazette*.
97. 'Director is Fined', *Liverpool Echo*.
98. 'Man in Vice Case with Guards is Fined £700', *Daily Express*, 7 May 168.
99. Letter to Oliver Ford, 28 November 1969, Oliver Ford Archive (AAD/1994/20/33).
100. John Tudor Rees, ed., *They Stand Apart. A Critical Survey of the Problems of Homosexuality* (London: Heinemann, 1955).
101. 'Obituary: Oliver Ford', *The Independent*, 21 October 1992.
102. Ibid.
103. http://opencharities.org/charities/1026551 (Accessed 13 August 2013).

Epilogue

1. 'A Neat Solution', *The Independent*, 14 July 2004.
2. Jerry White, *London in the Twentieth Century: A City and Its People* (London: Vantage, 2008), 156; see also John R. Short, *Housing in Britain: The Post-War Experience* (London: Methuen, 1982), 232.
3. James Obelkevich, 'Consumption', in *Understanding Post-War British Society*, ed. James Obelkevich and Peter Catterall (London: Routledge, 1994), 143.
4. In 1961 one in six shared a bedroom; by 1991 the figure was one in 20. By the end of the century 29 per cent of households were single occupancy. White, *London in the Twentieth Century*, 239, 56; Weeks, *The World We Have Won*, 139.
5. White, *London in the Twentieth Century*, 309; see also Alison Ravetz, *The Place of Home: English Domestic Environments, 1914–2000* (London: Spon, 1995), 3–4.

6. H.G. Cocks, *Classified: The Secret History of the Personal Column* (London: Random House Books, 2009), 183; see also: Weeks, *The World We Have Won*, 160. On the impact of the internet in this, see: E.R. Merkle and R.A. Richardson, 'Digital Dating and Virtual Relating: Conceptualizing Computer Mediated Romantic Relationships', *Family Relations* 49, no. 2 (2000): 187–192; G. Valentine, 'Globalizing Intimacy: The Role of Information and Communication Technologies in Maintaining and Creating Relationships', *Women's Studies Quarterly* 34 (2006): 365–393.
7. See: R. Hennessy, 'Queer Visibility in Commodity Culture', *Cultural Critique* 29 (1994): 31–76.
8. *The Economist*, 23 January 1982.
9. 'Life Insurance for Gays', *Financial Times*, 3 August 1991. See also: Weeks, *The World We Have Won*, 186.
10. See: Tim Butler and Garry Robson, 'Social Change, Gentrification and Neighbourhood Change in London: A Comparison of Three Areas of South London', *Urban Studies* 38 (2001): 2145–2162.
11. *Sunday Times*, 19 December 1982.
12. White, *London in the Twentieth Century*, 65.
13. Deborah Bright, 'Shopping the Leftovers: Warhol's Collecting Strategies in Raid the Icebox I', *Art History* 24, no. 2 (April 2001): 278–291; see also: R. Meyer, 'Mapplethorpe's Living Room: Photography and the Furnishing of Desire', *Art History* 24, no. 2 (2001): 292–311.
14. White, *London in the Twentieth Century*, 65; on New York loft living – and the shift from 'arts production to housing market' – see: Sharon Zukin, *Loft Living: Culture and Capital in Urban Change* (Baltimore: Johns Hopkins University Press, 1982), chap. 3 – 5.
15. Fellows, *A Passion to Preserve*, 27; Richard L. Florida, *Cities and the Creative Class* (London: Routledge, 2005); Richard L. Florida, *The Rise of the Creative Class* (New York: Basic Books, 2002); Halperin, *How to Be Gay*, 10.
16. Around half the 132 Queen Anne Mansions apartments were single occupancy according to the 1901 census. Dennis, 'Babylonian Flats', 233, 243; Houlbrook, *Queer London*, 113–114.
17. A Mayfair flat was used by 'homosexual' spies Burgess and Maclean in 1951, for example, and in the same year a BBC official, 43-year-old Arthur Birley and 23-year-old Trooper George Baldwin (who lived at the Hyde Park Barracks) were watched by police and military officials through the window of Birley's Curzon Street flat. 'Flat was Watched from Fire Escape', *News of the World*, 18 May 1951.
18. 'Pink Pound Powers Gay Housing Boom', *The Sunday Times*, 10 August 1997.
19. Ibid.; see also: J. Binnie, 'Quartering Sexualities: Gay Villages and Sexual Citizenship', in *City of Quarters: Urban Villages in the Contemporary City*, ed. David Bell and Mark Jayne (Aldershot: Ashgate, 2004), 163–172.
20. See: A. Collins, 'Sexual Dissidence, Enterprise and Assimilation: Bedfellows in Urban Regeneration', *Urban Studies* 41, no. 9 (2004): 1789; the trend for central loft living was identified in the early 1980s. See, for example: Zukin, *Loft Living*.
21. 'Pink Pound', *The Sunday Times*.

22. 'Queer Eye for the Perfect Flat', *The London Paper*, 14 September 2007.
23. See: Part IV.
24. See: K.P.R. Hart, 'We're Here, We're Queer – and We're Better Than You: The Representational Superiority of Gay Men to Heterosexuals on Queer Eye for the Straight Guy', *The Journal of Men's Studies* 12, no. 3 (2004): 241–253; E.M. Ramsey and G. Santiago, 'The Conflation of Male Homosexuality and Femininity in Queer Eye for the Straight Guy', *Feminist Media Studies* 4, no. 3 (2004): 353–355; Andrew Gorman-Murray, 'Queering Home or Domesticating Deviance?', *International Journal of Cultural Studies* 9, no. 2 (1 June 2006): 227–247; K. Pearson and N.M. Reich, 'Queer Eye Fairy Tale: Changing the World One Manicure at a Time', *Feminist Media Studies* 4, no. 2 (2004): 229–231; on this sense of queer superiority see also: Halperin, *How to be Gay*, 226.
25. Buck Clifford Rosenberg, 'Masculine Makeovers: Lifestyle Television, Metrosexuals and Real Blokes', in *Exposing Lifestyle Television: The Big Reveal*, ed. Gareth Palmer (Aldershot: Ashgate, 2008).
26. For an indicative sense of the debate on this see: Lisa Duggan, 'The New Homonormativity: The Sexual Politics of Neoliberalism', in *Materializing Democracy: Toward a Revitalized Cultural Politics*, ed. Russ Castronovo and Dana D. Nelson (London: Duke University Press, 2002); Steven Seidman, *Beyond the Closet: The Transformation of Gay and Lesbian Life* (London: Routledge, 2003), chap. 4 & 5; Michael Warner, *The Trouble With Normal: Sex, Politics and the Ethics of Queer Life* (New York: Free Press, 1999); S. Reimer and D. Leslie, 'Identity, Consumption, and the Home', *Home Cultures* 1, no. 2 (2004): 187–208; Hennessy, 'Queer Visibility in Commodity Culture'.
27. See: G.A. Dunne, S. Prendergast, and D. Telford, 'Young, Gay, Homeless and Invisible: A Growing Population?', *Culture, Health & Sexuality* 4, no. 1 (2002): 103–115; S. Prendergast, G.A. Dunne, and D. Telford, 'A Story of "Difference", a Different Story: Young Homeless Lesbian, Gay and Bisexual People', *International Journal of Sociology and Social Policy* 21, no. 4/5/6 (2001): 64–91.
28. See: Part III.
29. As Daniel Miller has it: Daniel Miller, *The Comfort of Things* (Cambridge: Polity, 2008).
30. Neil Bartlett, interview 14 June 2012. Unless otherwise indicated, all ensuing quotation is from this interview.
31. On the concept of the uncanny and of the familiar made strange see: Sigmund Freud, *The Uncanny*, trans. David McLintock (London: Penguin, 2003).
32. Martin F. Manalansan, *Global Divas: Filipino Gay Men in the Diaspora* (Durham: Duke University Press, 2003), 3.
33. Neil Bartlett, *Who Was That Man: A Present for Mr Oscar Wilde* (London: Serpent's Tail, 1988); Alan Sinfield, *The Wilde Century: Effeminacy, Oscar Wilde and the Queer Moment* (London: Cassell, 1994), 11; Dick Hebdige, 'Subculture: The Meaning of Style', in *The Subcultures Reader*, ed. Ken Gelder (London: Routledge, 2005).
34. See: Chapter 8.
35. See: Meyer, 'Mapplethorpe's Living Room', 292–311, 309.

Part II Queer Families: Introduction

1. Dir. Adrian Goycoolea, *Uncle Denis*, 2009.
2. Adrian Goycoolea, Programe notes on *Uncle Denis*, 'Beautiful Things' collection, British Film Institute.
3. Goycoolea, *Uncle Denis*.
4. Goycoolea, *Uncle Denis*.
5. Ibid.
6. Adrian Goycoolea to Matt Cook, e-mail, 18 October 2012.
7. Deborah Cohen, *Family Secrets: Living with Shame from the Victorians to the Present Day* (London: Viking, 2013), 143.
8. 'Exiles from kin' is a phrase used by Kath Weston. See: Kath Weston, *Families We Choose: Lesbians, Gays, Kinship* (New York: Columbia University Press, 1991), 22.
9. Havelock Ellis and John Addington Symonds, *Sexual Inversion*, ed. Ivan Crozier (Basingstoke: Palgrave Macmillan, 2008), 213.
10. Iwan Bloch, *The Sexual Life of Our Time in Its Relations to Modern Civilization* (London: Rebman, 1908), 510. Bloch was citing his forerunner Magnus Hirschfeld in this.
11. Auguste Forel, *The Sexual Question: a Scientific, Psychological, Hygienic and Sociological Study for the Cultured Classes* (London: Rebman, 1908), 446.
12. Charles Féré, *The Evolution and Dissolution of the Sexual Instinct* (Paris: Charles Carrington, 1904), 309; Richard von Krafft-Ebing, *Psychopathia Sexualis* (London: Rebman, 1893), 321.
13. Friedrich Engels, *The Origin of the Family, Private Property and the State* (Chicago: C.H. Kerr, 1902).
14. John D'Emilio, 'Capitalism and Gay Identity', in *Families in the US: Kinship and Domestic Politics*, ed. Karen Hansen and Anita Garey (Philadelphia: Temple University Press, 1998).
15. On this point see: Joseph Bristow, *Effeminate England: Homoerotic Writing after 1885* (New York: Columbia University Press, 1995), 133.
16. Bloch, *Sexual Life*, 534.
17. M.D. O'Brien, *Socialism and Infamy: The Homogenic or Comrade Love Exposed: An Open Letter in Plain Words for a Socialist Prophet* (Sheffield: Privately Published, 1909), 21, cited in: Sean Brady, *Masculinity and Male Homosexuality in Britain, 1861–1913* (London: Palgrave Macmillan, 2005), 46.
18. Bloch, *Sexual Life*, 405; Rictor Norton, *Mother Clap's Molly House: Gay Subculture in England 1700–1830* (London: GMP, 1992).
19. Ellis and Symonds, *Sexual Inversion*, intro.
20. Weston, *Families We Choose*, 22.
21. A notable exception was the play discussed in the last chapter – Mordant Sharpe's *The Green Bay Tree* (1934).
22. See: Leonore Davidoff and Catherine Hall, *Family Fortunes: Men and Women of the English Middle Class 1780–1850* (London: Hutchinson, 1987).
23. Eileen Cleere, *Avuncularism: Capitalism, Patriarchy, and Nineteenth-Century English Culture* (Stanford: Stanford University Press, 2004), 7.
24. Cohen, *Family Secrets*, 110.
25. Sixty-three per cent of deaths were in the under sixties between 1911 and 1915 compared to 12 per cent for the period 1991–1995, for example. Joe Hicks and Graham Allen, 'A Century of Change: Trends in UK Statistics

270 Notes

since 1900', *Research Papers* 99/111 (2 December 1999) (London: Social and General Statistics Section, House of Commons Library, 1999): 9. http://www.parliament.uk/commons/lib/research/rp99/rp99-111.pdf.
26. Katherine Holden, *The Shadow of Marriage: Singleness in England, 1914–60* (Manchester: Manchester University Press, 2010), 141; Jenny Keating, *A Child for Keeps: The History of Adoption in England, 1918–45* (Basingstoke: Palgrave Macmillan, 2009).
27. On this role see: Edward Carpenter, *The Intermediate Sex* (London: Swan Sonnenschein, 1908); Cleere, *Avuncularism*, 7, 10; Craig Owens, 'Outlaws: Gay Men in Feminism', in *Men in Feminism*, ed. Alice Jardine and Paul Smith (New York: Methuen, 1987); Holly Furneaux, *Queer Dickens: Erotics, Families, Masculinities* (Oxford: Oxford University Press, 2009); on the frequency with which unmarried uncles appear in children's fiction see: Holden, *The Shadow of Marriage*, 17.
28. Holden, *The Shadow of Marriage*.

3 George Ives, Queer Lives and the Family

1. George Ives, 'Diary', vol. 70, 21 May 1917, 118, George Cecil Ives Papers, Harry Ransom Humanities Research Center, University of Texas at Austin.
2. Ives, 'Diary', vol. 103, 24 February 1939, 206.
3. Ives, 'Diary', vol. 78, 14 January 1921, 14.
4. For more on Ives' diary see: Matt Cook, 'Sex Lives and Diary Writing: The Journals of George Ives', in *Life Writing and Victorian Culture*, ed. David Amigoni (Farnham: Ashgate, 2006).
5. Ibid.
6. Ives, 'Diary', vol. 100, 19 March 1935, 11.
7. Her dementia was suggested in letters to Ives from nuns who cared for her in Oxfordshire until her death in 1935. I am grateful to Brian Lewis for this information.
8. On this point see especially: John Tosh, *A Man's Place: Masculinity and the Middle-Class Home in Victorian England* (New Haven: Yale University Press, 1999).
9. Ives, 'Diary', vol. 109, 1 April 1943, 62.
10. Arthur Brittan, *Masculinity and Power* (Oxford: Basil Blackwell, 1989), 41.
11. Ives, 'Diary', vol. 9, 6 December 1890, 66.
12. Roy Porter, *London: a Social History* (Cambridge: Harvard University Press, 1998), 282.
13. Alan Crawford, *C.R. Ashbee: Architect, Designer & Romantic Socialist* (New Haven: Yale University Press, 1985), 4, 185.
14. Ives, 'Diary', vol. 17, 26 October 1893, 129.
15. 'London Bachelors and their Mode of Living', *Leisure Hour* 35 (1886): 413–416, 415.
16. Cited in: Karl E. Beckson, *London in the 1890s: A Cultural History* (New York and London: Norton, 1993), 210.
17. Cited in the in-house booklet: *Albany* (Albany, 2003).
18. Ives, 'Diary', vol. 17, 28 October 1893, 119.
19. 'Ben' (not his real name), interview, January 2012.

20. Henry James Forman, *London: An Intimate Portrait* (1913) cited in: Jerry White, *London in the Twentieth Century: A City and Its People* (London: Vantage, 2008), 17.
21. On the correspondence of household and family see: Michael Gilding, *The Making and Breaking of the Australian Family* (North Sydney, NSW: Allen & Unwin, 1991), 2–4; G.K. Behlmer, *Friends of the Family: The English Home and Its Guardians, 1850–1940* (Standford: Stanford University Press, 1998), 26; T.M. McBride and P. McCandless, 'The Domestic Revolution: The Modernisation of Household Service in England and France 1820–1920', *History: Reviews of New Books* 4, no. 10 (1976): 16; Tosh, *A Man's Place*, 196.
22. I am grateful to Brian Lewis for this observation.
23. Ives, 'Diary', vol. 113, 20 November 1944, 32.
24. Cited in Behlmer, *Friends of the Family*, 6.
25. Ives, 'Diary', vol. 78, 20 January 1921, 25.
26. Ives, 'Diary', vol. 74, 9 May 1919, 30.
27. Ives, 'Diary', vol. 85, 1 August 1923, 46.
28. Ives, 'Diary', vol. 78, 13 January 1921, 12.
29. Ives, 'Diary', vol. 78, 20 January 1921, 27.
30. Ives, 'Diary', vol. 76, 2 October 1920, 49.
31. Ives, 'Diary', vol. 103, 25 March 1939, 229.
32. Ives, 'Diary', vol. 85, 23 July 1923, 31.
33. Ives, 'Diary', vol. 76, 29 September 1920, 43.
34. Matt Houlbrook observes a similar inclusiveness in some of his case studies. Matt Houlbrook, *Queer London: Perils and Pleasures in the Sexual Metropolis, 1918–1957* (Chicago: University of Chicago Press, 2005), 185.
35. Ives, 'Diary', vol. 76, 20 January 1921, 25.
36. Ives, 'Diary', vol. 78, 16 January 1921, 17.
37. Michael Roper, 'Maternal Relations: Moral Manliness and Emotional Survival in Letters Home during the First World War', in *Masculinities in Politics and War: Gendering Modern History*, ed. S. Dudink, K. Hagemann, and J. Tosh (Manchester: Manchester University Press, 2004), 295–315.
38. As Ralph LaRossa and others observe, see: Ralph LaRossa, *The Modernization of Fatherhood: A Social and Political History* (Chicago: University of Chicago Press, 1996), 15; Eva Paulina Bueno, Terry Caesar, and William Hummel, *Naming the Father: Legacies, Genealogies, and Explorations of Fatherhood in Modern and Contemporary Literature* (Lanham: Lexington Books, 2000), intro, 8.
39. See: Chapter 2.
40. The classes ran between c.1900 and 1907. See Kate Bradley, 'Poverty and Philanthropy in East London, 1918–1959: The University Settlements and the Urban Working Classes' (unpublished doctoral thesis, Institute of Historical Research, London, 2006), 78–79.
41. Tim Fisher, 'Fatherhood and the British Fathercraft Movement, 1919–1939', *Gender & History* 17 (2005): 441–462.
42. Tosh, *A Man's Place*, 4.
43. See: Alison Light, *Mrs Woolf and the Servants: The Hidden Heart of Domestic Service* (London: Fig Tree, 2007).
44. See, exceptionally, Ives, 'Diary', vol. 78, 5 February 1921, 56.
45. Judy Giles, *Women, Identity and Private Life in Britain, 1900–50* (Basingstoke: Macmillan, 1995), 8.

46. Cited in: Brady, *Masculinity*, 161.
47. Paul Sieveking, *Man Bites Dog: The Scrapbooks of and Edwardian Eccentric* (London: Jay Landesman, 1980), preface, 5. The scrapbooks are now held by the Beinecke Library at Yale University.
48. Ives, 'Diary', vol. 68, 13 September 1917, 123.
49. Jeffrey Weeks, Brian Heaphy, and Catherine Donovan, *Same Sex Intimacies: Families of Choice and Other Life Experiments* (London: Routledge, 2001), 9.
50. For more on this see: Cook, 'Sex Lives and Diary Writing'.
51. On this point see: Sharon Marcus, *Between Women: Friendship, Desire, and Marriage in Victorian England* (Princeton: Princeton University Press, 2007), 13.
52. Other examples include Reginald Brett, the second Lord Esher, and the writer Edmund Gosse. See: Morris B. Kaplan, *Sodom on the Thames: Sex, Love, and Scandal in Wilde Times* (Ithaca: Cornell University Press, 2005), 161; Ann Thwaite, *Edmund Gosse: A Literary Landscape 1849–1928* (London: Secker & Warburg, 1984).
53. See Felicity Ashbee, *Janet Ashbee: Love, Marriage and the Arts and Crafts Movement* (Syracuse: Syracuse University Press, 2002); Crawford, *C.R. Ashbee*.
54. Kaplan, *Sodom on the Thames*, 161.
55. Matt Cook, *London and the Culture of Homosexuality, 1885–1914* (Cambridge: Cambridge University Press, 2003), 59.
56. Ives, 'Diary', vol. 108, 4 September 1942, 90.
57. Ives, 'Diary', vol. 96, 2 January 1932, 139.
58. Kaplan, *Sodom on the Thames*, 208. Henry's brother Arthur was implicated in the Cleveland Street male brothel scandal of 1889–1890 and also went into exile.
59. There is evidence that people were increasingly exercising this choice: family sizes were declining in the interwar period, and in 1930 40 per cent of middle-class couples and 28 per cent of working-class couples were thought to be using some form of contraception. See: Holden, *The Shadow of Marriage*, 89; Juliet Gardiner, *The Thirties: An Intimate History* (London: Harper Press, 2010), 563.
60. Ives, 'Diary', vol. 100, 11 April 1935, 27.
61. I am grateful to Brian Lewis for making the connection between Hayes and the 'certain girl' Ives evasively refers to.
62. Ives, 'Diary', vol. 76, 14 September 1920, 20.
63. Ives, 'Diary', vol. 101, 15 April 1936, 34.
64. Ives, 'Diary', vol. 94, 10 March 1930, 108.
65. Ives, 'Diary', vol. 114, 13 June 1945, 19.
66. See Lucy Bland, *Banishing the Beast: English Feminism and Sexual Morality 1885–1914* (London: Penguin, 1995), chap. 1 & 4.
67. Tosh, *A Man's Place*, 182–185.
68. Lynn Jamieson, *Intimacy: Personal Relationships in Modern Societies* (Cambridge: Polity Press, 1998), 27, 43; Brady, *Masculinity*, 37.
69. Lynn Hunt, *The Family Romance of the French Revolution* (London: Routledge, 1992); Joseph Bristow, '*Fratrum Societati*: Forster's Apostolic Dedications', in *Queer Forster*, ed. Robert K. Martin and George Piggford (Chicago: University of Chicago Press, 1997); H. Cocks, 'Calamus in Bolton: Spirituality and Homosexual Desire in Late Victorian England', *Gender & History* 13, no. 2 (2002): 191–223.

70. See the 'Service of Initiation' (1899) and 'Order Rules' (1933) in box 5, folder 11, George Cecil Ives Papers, HRHRC.
71. Derek Jarman, *Modern Nature: The Journals of Derek Jarman* (London: Century, 1991), 63.
72. Ives, 'Diary', vol. 101, 15 April 1936, 34.
73. Edward Shorter, *The Making of the Modern Family* (New York: Basic Books, 1975), 26.
74. See, for example, Ives, 'Diary', vol. 60, 5 May 1914, 87.
75. Jacques Derrida, *Politics of Friendship*, vol. 5 (London: Verso, 2005), 306.
76. Ibid., vii.
77. A.T. Fitzroy, *Despised and Rejected* (London: C.W. Daniel, 1918); Radclyffe Hall, *The Well of Loneliness* (Paris: Pegasus, 1928).
78. Ives told Janet early on of his 'tastes'. Ives and Janet Ashbee, 4 April 1902, 'Ashbee Journals: 1902, January – July', C.R. Ashbee Collection, King's College, Cambridge, CRA/1/11.
79. This sense of rhetorical restriction was theorised in relation to the chartist movement by Gareth Stedman-Jones. See: Gareth Stedman-Jones, ed., 'Rethinking Chartism', in *Languages of Class* (Cambridge: Cambridge University Press, 1983).
80. 'The Last Will of George Cecil Ives', 1 December 1939 (date of death 4 June 1950; executed 15 November 1950), Probate Registry, London.
81. Daniel Monk, 'E.M. Forster's Will: An Overlooked Posthumous Publication', *Legal Studies*, 33, 4 (2013): 572–597, early view online. I am extremely grateful to Daniel for discussion on these points.
82. 'The Last Will of George Cecil Ives'.
83. Carol Smart, *Personal Life: New Directions in Sociological Thinking* (Cambridge: Polity, 2007), 167.
84. I am grateful to Brian Lewis for making this connection.
85. On these issues see: Janet Finch, *Passing On: Kinship and Inheritance in England* (London: Routledge, 2001).
86. 'The Last Will and Testament of Joe Randolph Ackerley', 25 May 1965 (date of death 4 June 1967; executed 18 December 1967); Probate Registry, London.

4 Joe Ackerley's 'Family Values'

1. Deborah Cohen, *Family Secrets: Living with Shame from the Victorians to the Present Day* (London: Viking, 2013), 154. See also: Chris Waters, 'Havelock Ellis, Sigmund Freud and the State: Discourses of Homosexual Identity in Interwar Britain', in *Sexology in Culture: Labelling Bodies and Desires*, ed. Lucy Bland and Laura L. Doan (Cambridge: Polity, 1998).
2. Susan McHugh, 'Marrying My Bitch: J.R. Ackerley's Pack Sexualities', *Critical Inquiry* 27, no. 1 (Autumn 2000): 21–41.
3. Peter Parker, *Ackerley: A Life of J.R. Ackerley* (London: Constable, 1989), 10–11.
4. J.R. Ackerley, *My Dog Tulip* (New York: New York Review Books, 1999), back cover.
5. J.R. Ackerley, *The Letters of J.R. Ackerley*, ed. Neville Braybrooke (London: Duckworth: Duckworth, 1975), 15 July 1954, 102.

6. On this point see the Introduction to Part III and also: Chris Waters and Matt Houlbrook, 'The Heart in Exile: Detachment and Desire in 1950s London', *History Workshop Journal* 62 (Autumn 2006): 142–163.
7. Esther Saxey, *Homoplot: The Coming Out Story as Sexual Identity Narrative* (University of Sussex PhD, 2003).
8. See the epilogue to this part and the Introduction to Part IV.
9. J.R. Ackerley, *My Father and Myself* (New York: NYRB Classics, 2006), 153.
10. Ackerley, *My Father*, 83.
11. Cited in: Juliet Gardiner, *The Thirties: An Intimate History* (London: Harper Press, 2010), 577.
12. Parker, *Ackerley*, 211–212.
13. P.N. Furbank, *E.M. Forster: A Life* (London: Cardinal, 1988), 212.
14. Parker, *Ackerley*, 215.
15. Ackerley, *My Father*, 239.
16. Ibid., 240.
17. Cited in: Parker, *Ackerley*, 103.
18. Ibid., 113.
19. Jerry White, London in the Twentieth Century: A City and Its People (London: Vintage, 2008), 39.
20. Quentin Crisp, *The Naked Civil Servant* (Glasgow: Fontana Collins, 1977), 155.
21. Havelock Ellis and John Addington Symonds, *Sexual Inversion*, ed. Ivan Crozier (Basingstoke: Palgrave Macmillan, 2008), 182.
22. Cohen, *Family Secrets*, 159.
23. Ellis and Symonds, *Sexual Inversion*, 141.
24. Ibid., 135.
25. See 'Tales of the Avunculate', in Eve Kosofsky Sedgwick, *Tendencies* (London: Routledge, 1994); Katherine Holden, *The Shadow of Marriage: Singleness in England, 1914–60* (Manchester: Manchester University Press, 2010), 166.
26. John Addington Symonds, *The Memoirs of John Addington Symonds* (London: Hutchinson, 1984), 38.
27. Edmund Gosse, *Father and Son*, ed. Michael Newton (1907; Oxford: Oxford University Press, 2004).
28. Parker, *Ackerley*, 11.
29. Ackerley, *My Father*, 252.
30. Joseph Bristow, *Effeminate England: Homoerotic Writing after 1885* (New York: Columbia University Press, 1995), 150.
31. John Byng-Hall, 'Family Myths', in *The Myths We Live By*, ed. Raphael Samuel and Paul Thompson (London: Routledge, 1990).
32. Ackerley, *My Father*, 243.
33. Ibid., 259.
34. Ibid., 32.
35. Ibid., 33.
36. Ibid., 34.
37. Ibid., 39.
38. Ibid.
39. Ibid., 56.
40. Diana Petre, *The Secret Orchard of Roger Ackerley* (London: Phoenix, 1993).
41. Holden, *The Shadow of Marriage*, 134.
42. Parker, *Ackerley*, 169.

43. Ackerley, *My Father*, 154.
44. Ibid., 257.
45. Joseph Bristow highlights some of these acutely in Bristow, *Effeminate England*, 146–153.
46. Parker, *Ackerley*, 53.
47. Ackerley, *My Father*, 211.
48. Ibid., 102.
49. On this point see: Bristow, *Effeminate England*, 152.
50. Ackerley, *My Father*, 108.
51. Ibid., 190.
52. Ibid., 255.
53. Parker, *Ackerley*, 82.
54. Bristow, *Effeminate England*.
55. On the potency and significance of such silences see: Harry Cocks, *Nameless Offences: Homosexual Desire in the Nineteenth Century* (London: I.B. Tauris, 2003), intro; Eve Kosofsky Sedgwick, *Epistemology of the Closet* (London: Harvester Wheatsheaf, 1991); Carol Smart, *Personal Life: New Directions in Sociological Thinking* (Cambridge: Polity, 2007), chap. 5.
56. Ackerley, *My Father*, 71.
57. Ibid., 145.
58. Ibid.
59. Katie Hindmarch-Watson, 'Male Prostitution and the London GPO: Telegraph Boys' "Immorality" from Nationalization to the Cleveland Street Scandal', *Journal of British Studies* 51, no. 3 (July 2012): 594–617; H. Montgomery Hyde, *The Cleveland Street Scandal* (London: W.H. Allen, 1976).
60. Ackerley, *My Father*, 161.
61. Ibid., 186.
62. Peter Stallybrass and Allon White, *The Politics and Poetics of Transgression* (London: Methuen, 1986), chap. 4; Lucy Delap, *Knowing Their Place: Domestic Service in Twentieth-Century Britain* (Oxford: Oxford University Press, 2011).
63. 'Clergyman's ex-Valet', *News of the World*, 21 September 1959.
64. Derek Jarman, *Modern Nature: The Journals of Derek Jarman* (London: Century, 1991), 11; Nigel Slater, *Toast: The Story of a Boy's Hunger* (London: Fourth Estate, 2003), 13–14.
65. B. Osgerby, 'The Bachelor Pad as Cultural Icon: Masculinity, Consumption and Interior Design in American Men's Magazines, 1930–65', *Journal of Design History* 18, no. 1 (2005): 99; Katherine V. Snyder, *Bachelors, Manhood, and the Novel, 1850–1925* (Cambridge: Cambridge University Press, 1999), 26–27; Holden, *The Shadow of Marriage*.
66. Ackerley, *My Father*, 166.
67. Parker, *Ackerley*, 274.
68. Jeffrey Weeks, *The World We Have Won: The Remaking of Erotic and Intimate Life* (London: Routledge, 2007), 46.
69. J.R. Ackerley, *My Sister and Myself: The Diaries of J.R. Ackerley* (London: Hutchinson, 1982), 9 January 1949, 92.
70. Ibid., 12 February 1949, 121; 9 July 1957, 206.
71. Ibid., Francis King, 'Introduction', 12.
72. Ibid., 23 February 1949, 125–126.

73. On this point see especially: Leonore Davidoff, *Thicker than Water: Siblings and their Relations, 1780-1920* (Oxford: Oxford University Press, 2012); Prophecy Coles, ed., *Sibling Relationships* (London: Karnac, 2006); Juliet Mitchell, *Siblings: Sex and Violence* (Oxford: Polity, 2003).
74. Ackerley, *My Father*, 102.
75. On this point see: Edmund Bergler, *Counterfeit-Sex* (New York: Grune & Stratton, 1958), 185; Alex Comfort, *Sex in Society* (London: Duckworth, 1963), 131-132; Waters, 'Havelock Ellis'; Nikolas Rose, *Governing the Soul: The Shaping of the Private Self* (London: Routledge, 1990); Edgar Jones and Simon Wesseley, 'The Impact of Total War on British Psychiatry', in *In the Shadow of Total War: Europe, East Asia and the United States, 1919-1939*, ed. R. Chickering and S. Forster (Cambridge: Cambridge University Press, 2003).
76. Eileen Cleere, *Avuncularism: Capitalism, Patriarchy, and Nineteenth-century English Culture* (Stanford: Stanford University Press, 2004), 5.
77. Talcot Parsons and Robert Bales, *Family, Socialisation and Interaction Process* (Glencoe: Free Press, 1955).
78. Michael Schofield, *A Minority: A Report on the Life of the Male Homosexual in Great Britain* (London: Longmans, 1960), 65.
79. 'Consenting Adults: The Men', *Man Alive*, BBC2, 7 June 1967.
80. Elizabeth Hodgkinson, 'Homosexuality: What Mothers Should Know', *Modern Mother and Baby*, October 1972. *Mother and Baby* repeated the theory in 1977: homosexuals came from unhappy homes with inappropriate close relationships with their mothers and a distance from their fathers. 'Could My Child Be Gay?', *Mother and Baby*, January 1977.
81. Ackerley, *The Letters of J.R. Ackerley*, Appendix F, 339.
82. On pets in personal life see: B. Tipper, 'Pets and Personal Life', in *Sociology of Personal Life*, ed. Vanessa May (Houndmills: Palgrave Macmillan, 2011); Donna Jeanne Haraway, *The Companion Species Manifesto: Dogs, People, and Significant Otherness* (Chicago: Prickly Paradigm, 2003).
83. Parker, *Ackerley*, 257.
84. See: E.M. Forster's *Maurice* (1914), Noel Coward *Private Lives* (1930), Mordant Sharpe's *The Green Bay Tree* (1936), and Evelyn Waugh's *Brideshead Revisited* (1945). Postwar it gets retold in the films *Oscar Wilde* and *The Trials of Oscar Wilde* (both 1960), *Victim* (1961), and *The Family Way* (1966, based on Bill Naughton's play *All in Good Time* of 1964); on stage in Joe Orton's *Entertaining Mr Sloane* (1964); and on the small screen in the John Mortimer's BBC drama *Bermondsey* (1972).
85. See Alkarim Jivani, *It's Not Unusual: A History of Lesbian and Gay Britain in the Twentieth Century* (London: Michael O'Mara, 1997), 66; Emma Vickers, 'The Good Fellow: Negotiation, Remembrance and Recollection – Homosexuality in the British Armed Forces, 1939-1945', in *Brutality and Desire: War and Sexuality in Europe's Twentieth Century*, ed. Dagmar Herzog (Basingstoke: Palgrave, 2009).
86. Ackerley, *My Father*, 77.
87. Ibid., 194.
88. Ibid., 169.
89. Parker, *Ackerley*, 93.
90. Ackerley, *My Sister*, 1 May 1949, 150-151.

91. Gardiner, *The Thirties*, 580; Matt Houlbrook, *Queer London: Perils and Pleasures in the Sexual Metropolis, 1918–1957* (Chicago: University of Chicago Press, 2005), 211.
92. Anthony Giddens, *The Transformation of Intimacy: Sexuality, Love and Eroticism in Modern Societies* (Cambridge: Polity, 1992); Silvia Silva and Carol Smart, eds., *The New Family?* (London: Sage, 1998); Smart, *Personal Life*.
93. Ackerley, *My Father*, 173.
94. Ibid., 168.
95. Houlbrook, *Queer London*, 173.
96. Ibid.; Holden, *The Shadow of Marriage*, 99.
97. Ackerley, *My Father*, 166.
98. Ives, 'Diary', vol. 57, 14 July 1912, 100.
99. John R. Gillis, *A World of Their Own Making: Myth, Ritual, and the Quest for Family Values* (New York: Basic Books, 1996), xv.

Epilogue

1. Bruce Voeller and James Walters, 'Gay Fathers', *The Family Coordinator* 27, no. 2 (1978): 149–157.
2. On the sexologists see introduction to this part of the book.
3. Susanne Bösche, *Jenny Lives with Eric and Martin* (London: Gay Men's Press, 1983).
4. John Osborne, 'The Diary of a Somebody', *Spectator* (29 November 1986): 3. For further discussion of Osborne's comments in relation to John Lahr's editing of the Orton's diaries see: Matt Cook, 'Orton in the Archives', *History Workshop Journal* 66 (2008): 163–180.
5. Osborne, 'Diary', 3.
6. See, for example: Jeffrey Bernard, 'My Fathers', *Spectator*, 14 January 1977; Gay Gaye, 'Letter: Multiple Parenting', *Private Eye*, 17 June 1981.
7. *Re D (An Infant) Adoption: Parents Consent* 1977 AC 602, House of Lords.
8. 'Homosexual Father and Consent to Adoption', *Daily Telegraph*, 10 February 1976.
9. Ibid. See also David Bradley, 'Homosexuality and Child Custody in English Law', *International Journal of Law Policy Family* 1, no. 2 (1987): 155–205.
10. 'Lord's Attacked Over Gay Father's Rights', *Guardian*, 14 March 1977; see also 'Father's Consent to Adoption', *Solicitors Journal*, 4 February 1977; 'Rights of Natural Parents', *New Law Journal*, 10 March 1977, 236.
11. D. Rivers, ' "In the Best Interests of the Child": Lesbian and Gay Parenting Custody Cases, 1967–1985', *Journal of Social History* 43, no. 4 (Summer 2010); Weeks, *The World We Have Won*, 185; Sarah Beresford, ' "Get Over Your (Legal) Self": A Brief History of Lesbians, Motherhood and Law', *Journal of Social Welfare and Family Law* 30, no. 2 (June 2008): 95–106.
12. 'Judge Opposes Care in Gay Homes', *Express and Star*, 22 July 1982.
13. H. Reece, 'Subverting the Stigmatisation Argument', *Journal of Law and Society* 23, no. 4 (1996): 484–505; H. Reece, 'The Paramountcy Principle Consensus or Construct?', *Current Legal Problems* 49, no. 1 (1996): 267–304.
14. Voeller and Walters, 'Gay Fathers'.
15. 'Can Two Men Take the Place of a Mother?' *Woman's Worlds*, May 1978.

16. For a discussion of formerly married gay fathers more recently see especially: Gillian Dunne, 'The Lady Vanishes? Reflections on the Experiences of Married and Divorced Non- Heterosexual Fathers', *Sociological Research Online* 6 (2001): http://ideas.repec.org/a/sro/srosro/2001-39-2.html.
17. 'Council Invite Gays to Adopt', *Evening Standard*, 7 January 1985; 'A Loony Lot', *Sun*, 9 January 1985; 'A Foolish Move', *Daily Express*, 9 January 1985, 'Ridiculous to Place Children with Gays', 12 February 1985.
18. 'Homosexuals Need Not Apply', *Kentish Times*, 20 June 1985; 'Town Hall Strike Threat Over Homosexual Foster Parents', *Wandsworth Borough News*, 27 September 1991.
19. 'Outrage as Gays Adopt Girl', *Sun*, 6 April 1992; on ongoing concern and debate about what constitutes family see especially: J. McCandless and S. Sheldon, 'The Human Fertilisation and Embryology Act (2008) and the Tenacity of the Sexual Family Form', *The Modern Law Review* 73, no. 2 (2010): 175–207.
20. 'The Child Comes First', *Daily Telegraph*, 22 April 1993.
21. 'Now Gays Can Adopt Children', *Daily Mirror*, 30 December 1993; 'Row on Adoption by Homosexuals', *Daily Telegraph*, 30 December 1993.
22. See, for example: Kath Weston, *Families We Choose: Lesbians, Gays, Kinship* (New York: Columbia University Press, 1991); Christopher Carrington, *No Place Like Home: Relationships and Family Life Among Lesbians and Gay Men* (Chicago: University of Chicago Press, 1999); R. Goss and A.A.S. Strongheart, eds., *Our Families, Our Values: Snapshots of Queer Kinship* (New York: Harrington Park Press, 1997).
23. 'Two Gay Couples Share a Toddler', *Daily Express*, 7 May 1996; 'Gay Couples Timeshare Son', *Daily Mail*, 7 May 1996; 'Toddler Can Stay With Gay Couple', *The Herald Glasgow*, 8 May 1996.
24. 'A Harsh Judgement on Home Affairs', *Scotland on Sunday*, 12 May 1996.
25. 'Adoption Ban on Gays Overturned', *Scotsman*, 27 July 1996; 'Gay Male Nurse to Adopt Boy', *New Law Journal*, 2 August 1996.
26. 'Surrogate Mother Gives Gay Men a Baby', *Mail on Sunday*, 1 September 1996; 'Joy for Gay Couple after Surrogacy', *Sunday Express*, 1 September 1996; 'Storm as Gay Men Buy a Baby Daughter', *Sunday Mirror*, 1 September 1996.
27. 'Gay Couple's Surrogate Child Angers Tory MPs', *The Observer*, 1 September 1996.
28. Holden, *The Shadow of Marriage*, 216.
29. Daniel Monk, 'Re G (Children) (Residence: Same-Sex Partner) – Commentary', in *Feminist Judgments: From Theory to Practice*, ed. R. Hunter, C. McGlynn, and E. Rackley (Durham: Hart, 2010).
30. Smart, *Personal Life*, 27.
31. Stephen Hicks, 'Lesbian and Gay Foster Care and Adoption: a Brief UK History', *Adoption & Fostering Journal* 29, no. 3 (2005): 42–56.
32. Weeks, *The World We Have Won*, 65; see also: Zygmunt Bauman, *Liquid Love: On the Frailty of Human Bonds* (Cambridge: Polity Press, 2003); Rosemary Hennessy, *Profit and Pleasure: Sexual Identities in Late Capitalism* (London: Routledge, 2000).
33. Simon Duncan and Darren Smith, *Individuation Versus the Geography of 'New' Families* (London: South Bank University, June 2006), http://www.lsbu.ac.uk/ahs/downloads/families/familieswp19.pdf.

34. On the diversity of the Victorian family see the introduction to this part. On its subsequent narrowing with more uniform family size, rising rates of marriage and greater life expectancy see: Cohen, *Family Secrets*; Holden, *The Shadow of Marriage*.
35. Weeks, *The World We Have Won*, 8; see also: Jane Lewis, *The End of Marriage?: Individualism and Intimate Relations* (Cheltenham: Elgar, 2001); Fiona Williams, *Rethinking Families* (London: Calouste Gulbenkian Foundation, 2004); Carol Smart, 'Changing Landscapes of Family Life: Rethinking Divorce', *Social Policy and Society* 3, no. 4 (2004): 401–408.
36. Smart, *Personal Life*, 27; Paul Ridley, Preface to Williams, *Rethinking Families*, 5.
37. Weeks, *The World We Have Won*, 64; Hera Cook, *The Long Sexual Revolution: English Women, Sex, and Contraception, 1800–1975* (Oxford: Oxford University Press, 2004), chap. 12 & 15.
38. Including the Divorce Law Reform Act (1969), the Family Law Act (1987) and the Children Act (1989).
39. Weeks, *The World We Have Won*, 15, 10. For debate on the implications of artificial insemination between 1945 and 1959 in the press and elsewhere see the 'Artificial Insemination' folder at The Women's Library, London. 3AMS/B/09/09.
40. Ibid., 114, 165.
41. 'Britain 2008: A Nation in Thrall to Thatcherism', *Independent*, 23 January 2008.
42. See: Part IV.
43. Rupert Haselden, 'Gay Abandon', *Guardian*, 7 September 1991, 20.
44. Cohen, *Family Secrets*, 253.
45. Lisa Duggan, 'The New Heteronormativity: The Sexual Politics of Neo-Liberalism', in *Materializing Democracy: Toward a Revitalized Cultural Politics*, ed. Russ Castronovo and Dana D. Nelson (Durham: Duke University Press, 2002).
46. Lee Edelman, *No Future: Queer Theory and the Death Drive* (Durham: Duke University Press, 2004).
47. Bruce Bawer, *A Place at the Table : The Gay Individual in American Society* (London: Poseidon Press, 1993).
48. Weeks, *The World We Have Won*.
49. Peter McGraith, interview, June 2012.
50. On this point see; Penny Sparke, *As Long as It's Pink: The Sexual Politics of Taste* (London: Pandora, 1995).
51. Email Peter McGraith to Matt Cook 9 January 2013.
52. See: Chapter 2.

Part III   Outsiders Inside: Finding Room in the City

1. James Obelkevich, 'Consumption', in *Understanding Post-War British Society*, ed. James Obelkevich and Peter Catterall (London: Routledge, 1994), 144.
2. Judy Giles, *Women, Identity and Private Life in Britain, 1900–50* (Basingstoke: Macmillan, 1995), 28.
3. Katherine Holden, *The Shadow of Marriage: Singleness in England, 1914–60* (Manchester: Manchester University Press, 2010), 27.
4. David Kynaston, *Family Britain, 1951–1957* (New York: Walker & Co, 2009), 165; Dagmar Herzog, ed., *Brutality and Desire: War and Sexuality in Europe's*

Twentieth Century (Basingstoke: Palgrave Macmillan, 2009); Chris Harris, 'The Family in Post-War Britain', in *Understanding*, ed. Obelkevich and Catterall, 144.
5. Ronald Fleming, 'The Interior of One's Home' (1949), Ronald Fleming Archive (AAD/2013/1/1), V&A Archive of Art and Design.
6. On these points see especially: Sophie Leighton, *The 1950s Home* (Oxford: Shire, 2009); Shirley Echlin, *At Home in the 1950s* (Harlow: Longman, 1983).
7. See Richard Hornsey, *The Spiv and the Architect: Unruly Life in Postwar London* (Minneapolis: University of Minnesota Press, 2010), 77.
8. Obelkevich, 'Consumption'; Alistair Davies and Peter Saunders, 'Literature, Politics and Society', in *Society and Literature*, ed. Alan Sinfield (London: Methuen, 1983), 21.
9. Matt Houlbrook, *Queer London: Perils and Pleasures in the Sexual Metropolis, 1918–1957* (Chicago: University of Chicago Press, 2005), 192.
10. Jonathan Dollimore, 'The Challenge of Sexuality', in *Society and Literature*, ed. Alan Sinfield (London: Methuen, 1983), 60–61; Lesley Hall, *Sex, Gender and Social Change in Britain since 1880* (Basingstoke: Macmillan, 2000).
11. For the significance of 'home' in the formation of the Victorian middle class, for example. See especially: G.K. Behlmer, *Friends of the Family: The English Home and Its Guardians, 1850–1940* (Standford: Stanford University Press, 1998); Leonore Davidoff and Catherine Hall, *Family Fortunes: Men and Women of the English Middle Class 1780–1850* (London: Hutchinson, 1987); John Tosh, *A Man's Place: Masculinity and the Middle-Class Home in Victorian England* (New Haven: Yale University Press, 1999).
12. Peter J. Kalliney, *Cities of Affluence and Anger: A Literary Geography of Modern Englishness* (Charlottesville: University of Virginia Press, 2006), 122.
13. Simon Shepherd, *Because We're Queers: The Life and Crimes of Kenneth Halliwell and Joe Orton* (London: Gay Men's Press, 1989), 137.
14. Frank Mort, 'Scandalous Events: Metropolitan Culture and Moral Change in Post-Second World War London', *Representations* 93 (1 January 2006): 106–137; Hornsey, *The Spiv*, 83; Kynaston observes the 'anti-Victorianism' of postwar society: Kynaston, *Family*, 96; Jeffrey Weeks, *The World We Have Won: The Remaking of Erotic and Intimate Life* (London: Routledge, 2007), 42.
15. Rex Batten, *Rid England of This Plague* (London: Paradise, 2006), 95.
16. On this point see Matt Cook, ed., *A Gay History of Britain: Love and Sex between Men since the Middle Ages* (Oxford: Greenwood World, 2007), 167–171; see also: P. Higgins, *Heterosexual Dictatorship: Male Homosexuality in Postwar Britain* (London: Fourth Estate, 1996).
17. Dollimore, 'Challenge', 76.
18. Deborah Cohen, *Family Secrets: Living with Shame from the Victorians to the Present Day* (London: Viking, 2013), 110.
19. Carolyn Steedman, *Landscape for a Good Woman: A Story of Two Lives* (London: Virago, 1986); Penny Summerfield, 'Women in Britain since 1945: Companionate Marriage and the Double Burden', in *Understanding*, ed. Obelkevich and Catterall; Kynaston, *Family*, 46, 104, 152–153.
20. Paul Addison, *No Turning Back: The Peacetime Revolutions of Post-War Britain* (Oxford: Oxford University Press, 2010), 96; see also: Frank Mort, *Capital*

Affairs: London and the Making of the Permissive Society (New Haven: Yale University Press, 2010), 109; Kynaston, *Family*, 46, 54–55; Cohen, *Family Secrets*, 197.
21. Addison, *No Turning Back*, 340.
22. John Tudor Rees, ed., *They Stand Apart: A Critical Survey of the Problems of Homosexuality* (London: Heinemann, 1955).
23. Michael Schofield, *A Minority: A Report on the Life of the Male Homosexual in Great Britain* (London: Longmans, 1960), 178.
24. Rees's subtitle flagged 'the problems of homosexuality'. Rees, *They Stand Apart*.
25. J.E. Gardner, 'A Normal Family: Alternative Communities in the Plays of Joe Orton', in *Joe Orton: a Casebook*, ed. Francesca Coppa (London: Routledge, 2003), 79.
26. Schofield, *A Minority*, 93.
27. See: Chapter 2.
28. Michael Schofield, *Society and the Homosexual* (London: Victor Gollancz, 1952), 132.
29. Hornsey, *The Spiv*, 202.
30. Liz Stanley, *Sex Surveyed, 1949–1994: From Mass-Observation's 'Little Kinsey' to the National Survey and the Hite Reports* (London: Taylor & Francis, 1995), 199–203.
31. On youth culture see: Addison, *No Turning Back*, 181; Stuart Hall, *Resistance through Rituals: Youth Subcultures in Post-War Britain* (London: Routledge, 2007); David Fowler, *Youth Culture in Modern Britain, c. 1920–1970: From Ivory Tower to Global Movement – A New History* (Basingstoke: Palgrave Macmillan, 2008); Arthur Marwick, *The Sixties: Cultural Revolution in Britain, France, Italy, and the United States, C.1958–1974* (Oxford: Oxford University Press, 1998); Stanley Cohen, 'Symbols of Trouble', in *The Subcultures Reader*, ed. Ken Gelder (London: Routledge, 2005); Gillian Freeman, *The Leather Boys* (London: New English Library, 1972).
32. Schofield, *Society*, 139–140.
33. 'In Terror of Phone', *London Evening Standard*, 9 January 1959.
34. 'What About the Victim if the Blackmailed Can't Sleep', *News of the World*, 11 September 1955; 'Went to Soho', *News of the World*, 10 November 1957.
35. Houlbrook, *Queer London*; Hornsey, *The Spiv*.
36. Schofield, *A Minority*, 181.
37. Schofield, *A Minority*, 181.
38. Mort, *Capital Affairs*, 86–87; on some of the roots of youth culture and this generation gap see: Jerry White, *London in the Twentieth Century: A City and Its People* (London: Vantage, 2008), 268.
39. Houlbrook, *Queer London*, 118.
40. White, *London in the Twentieth Century*, 22, 27, 146.
41. Mort, *Capital Affairs*, 109.
42. White, *London in the Twentieth Century*, 95.
43. Ibid., 53.
44. Mark Armstrong, 'A Room in Chelsea: Quentin Crisp at Home', *Visual Culture in Britain* 12, no. 2 (2011): 158.
45. See for example, *Up the Junction* (1968) and *The L-Shaped Room* (1962), and the Salford set play and film *A Taste of Honey* (1958/1961).

46. J. Wynne-Tyson, *Accommodation Wanted: A Short Guide to the 'Bed-Sitter'* (London: Britannicus Liber, 1951); Cyril Donson with Armand Georges, *Lonely-Land and Bedsitter-Land* (Bala: Bala Press, 1967); Armand Georges, *The Bed-Sitter Tribe* (London: Jackson, 1959).
47. Hornsey, *The Spiv*, 6; Mort, *Capital Affairs*, 102.
48. Jack Miller, 'Murders in a Half World', *News of the World*, 25 February 1962.
49. Ibid.
50. Ibid.
51. Ibid.
52. Norman Lucas, 'I Escape Wardrobe Killer', *Daily Pictorial*, 3 March 1962.
53. Holden, *The Shadow of Marriage*, 46.
54. White, *London in the Twentieth Century*, 146.
55. Schofield, *A Minority*, 178.
56. Cited in Juliet Gardiner, *The Thirties: An Intimate History* (London: Harper Press, 2010), 295n.
57. Kynaston, *Family*, 55.
58. White, *London in the Twentieth Century*, 32.
59. Kynaston, *Family*, 55; White, *London in the Twentieth Century*, 44.
60. Kynaston, *Family*, 63; White, *London in the Twentieth Century*, 34.
61. Michael, Interview, 2008.
62. Armstrong, 'A Room in Chelsea'.
63. See: Epilogue to Part II and: Martin Dines, *Gay Suburban Narratives in American and British Culture: Homecoming Queens* (Basingstoke: Palgrave, 2010); and: Martin Dines, 'Bringing the Boy Back Home: Queer Domesticity and Egalitarian Relationships in Postwar London Novels', *The Literary London Journal*, vol.10, no.4 (Autumn 2013); Online at: http://www.literarylondon.org/london-journal/autumn2013/dines.html (Accessed on 3/3/2014).
64. Hornsey, *The Spiv*, 83.
65. White, *London in the Twentieth Century*, 324.
66. Mort, *Capital Affairs*, 102.

5 Remembering Beddsitteland: Rex Batten, Carl Marshall and Alan Louis

1. Rex Batten, Interview, 2010.
2. J.W. Scott, 'The Evidence of Experience', *Critical Inquiry* 17, no. 4 (1991): 773–797.
3. See: Elizabeth A. Kensinger, *Emotional Memory across the Adult Lifespan* (New York: Taylor and Francis, 2008).
4. 'Terry', Interview, 2010. Inverted commas indicates the use of a pseudonym.
5. Heather Murray, *Not in this Family: Gays and the Meaning of Kinship in Postwar North America* (Philadelphia: University of Pennsylvania Press, 2010); see also: Carol Smart, *Personal Life: New Directions in Sociological Thinking* (Cambridge: Polity, 2007).
6. Batten, *Rid England*, 65.
7. Ibid.
8. See: Part I.
9. See: Chapter 2.

10. Batten, *Rid England*, 74–75.
11. Ibid., 76.
12. B. Charles mass observation diary in: Simon Garfield, *Our Hidden Lives: The Everyday Diaries of a Forgotten Britain, 1945–1948* (London: Ebury, 2004), 214, 400, 406, 409–410, 414; 'B.Charles' is 'Anatole James' in Cohen, *Family Secrets*.
13. Garfield, *Our Hidden Lives*, 409–410.
14. See: Part I.
15. See: Chapter 2. Hornsey, *The Spiv*, 208–210.
16. Batten, *Rid England*, 80.
17. Matt Cook, *London and the Culture of Homosexuality, 1885–1914* (Cambridge: Cambridge University Press, 2003), chap.2.
18. Batten, *Rid England*, 80.
19. Hornsey, *The Spiv*, 99–101; Mort, *Capital Affairs*, 86.
20. Houlbrook, *Queer London*; F. Mort, 'Social and Symbolic Fathers and Sons in Postwar Britain', *Journal of British Studies* 38, no. 3 (1999): 353–384.
21. Batten, *Rid England*, 82.
22. See: Summerfield, 'Women in Britain', 60; Ronald Fletcher, *Britain in the Sixties: The Family and Marriage* (Harmondsworth: Penguin, 1962).
23. Batten, *Rid England*, 116.
24. Ibid., 108.
25. Ibid., 116.
26. Ibid., 123.
27. Ibid., 168.
28. From Rex's comments on a draft of this chapter (March 2011).
29. Batten, *Rid England*, 168.
30. Douglas Warth, 'Evil Men', *Sunday Pictorial*, 25 May 1952, 6, 15.
31. See: Chapter 2.
32. Andrew Salkey, *Escape to an Autumn Pavement* (Leeds: Peepal Tree, 2009), 150.
33. Ibid., 211.
34. Schofield, *A Minority*, 181.
35. Ibid.
36. Ibid.
37. Batten, Interview, 2010.
38. Schofield, *A Minority*, 175; White, *London in the Twentieth Century*, 116–117.
39. Batten, *Rid England*, 140.
40. Alan Louis, interview, 2010.
41. Weeks, *The World We Have Won*, 46.
42. Ibid.; Mort, *Capital Affairs*, 132–136.
43. They testify to what Hornsey describes as 'an active and ongoing form of composite self creation and one emphatically opposed to the stable interiority [...] on which sanctioned homosexual respectability was becoming based'. Hornsey, *The Spiv*, 259.
44. On this point see: Marianne Hirsch and Valerie Smith, 'Feminism and Cultural Memory: An Introduction', *Signs* 28, no. 1 (Fall 2002): 1–1912.
45. Robert Miles, 'The Riots of 1958: Notes on the Ideological Construction of "Race Relations" as a Political Issue in Britain', *Immigrants and Minorities* 3, no. 3 (1984): 252–275.
46. Eric Hobsbawm, 'Introduction', *Social Research* 58, no. 1 (Spring 1991): 65–68.

47. Carl Marshall, 'Betty's Bastard 1955–1958', 21. Carl's handwritten memoir was typed up by his friend and mine, Tony Wilburn, in 2009–2010. It is the typescript that I cite here. I am extremely grateful to Tony and Carl's executors for loaning me both typescript and the original endnotes.
48. Marshall, 'Betty's Bastard, 1958–1958', 49.
49. Marshall, 'Betty's Bastard 1952–1962', 21.
50. Marshall, 'Betty's Bastard 1955–1958', 27.
51. Marshall, 'Betty's Bastard 1965–1968', 10.
52. Cook, *London*, 50–51.
53. See introduction to this section.
54. Ibid.
55. Schofield, *A Minority*, 147.
56. David Bell, 'Pleasure and Danger: The Paradoxical Spaces of Sexual Citizenship', *Political Geography* 14, no. 2 (February 1995): 139–153; on the ubiquity of photographs in the 1950s queer novel see: Hornsey, *The Spiv*, 150.
57. Marshall, 'Betty's Bastard, 1956–1958', 51
58. 'Terry', Interview, 2010.
59. 'Daniel', interview, 2010.
60. Batten, *Rid England*, 259.
61. 'Terry', Interview, 2010.
62. On the significance of non-domestic spaces as 'home' see especially: Les Moran, 'The Poetics of Safety: Lesbians, Gay Men and Home', in *Crime and Insecurity: Governance and Safety in Europe*, ed. Adam Crawford (Devon: Willan, 2002); G. Chauncey, 'Privacy Could Only Be Had in Public: Gay Uses of the Streets', in *Stud: Architectures of Masculinity*, ed. J. Sanders (New York: Princeton Architectural Press, 1996), 224–267.
63. Batten, Interview.
64. Hornsey, *The Spiv*, 212–213.
65. See: Part I.
66. Mort, *Capital Affairs*, 17.
67. Schofield, *A Minority*, 115–116, 178.
68. Murray, *Not in this Family*; Cohen, *Family Secrets*, 148–149.
69. Letter Alexander to Steve, 16 April 1987, Carl Marshall's papers.
70. Marshall, 'Betty's Bastard 1962–1965', 13.
71. See chapter 4.
72. Marshall, 'Health Diary', vol. 4, 31 May 1998, 9.
73. Marshall, 'Health Diary', vol. 4, 26 June 1998, 75.
74. See: Sasha Roseneil, 'On Not Living with a Partner: Unpicking Coupledom and Cohabitation', 30 September 2006, http://www.socresonline.org.uk/11/3/roseneil.html.
75. J. Percival, 'Domestic Spaces: Uses and Meanings in the Daily Lives of Older People', *Ageing and Society* 22, no. 6 (2002): 729–749.
76. In their report for SIGMA research, Peter Keogh and his colleagues found that Lambeth's 'LGBT' people were more than twice as more to live alone. Twenty per cent said they had no one to call on in a crisis (ten times higher than the general population). Keogh, P., R. Reid, and P. Weatherburn, *Lambeth LGBT Matters: the needs and experiences of lesbians, gay men, bisexual and trans men and women in Lambeth* (London: Project SIGMA, 2006), 11.

6 Homes Fit for Homos: Joe Orton's Queer Domestic

1. Alkarim Jivani, *It's Not Unusual: A History of Lesbian and Gay Britain in the Twentieth Century* (London: Michael O'Mara, 1997), 89.
2. Ibid.; see also: Nick Thomas, 'Will the Real 1950s Please Stand up? View of a Contradictory Decade', *Cultural and Social History* 5, no. 2 (2008): 227–236; Lesley Hall, *Sex, Gender and Social Change in Britain since 1880* (Basingstoke: Macmillan, 2000), chap. 5; Frank Mort, *Capital Affairs: London and the Making of the Permissive Society* (New Haven: Yale University Press, 2010), intro.
3. Jeffrey Weeks, *The World We Have Won: The Remaking of Erotic and Intimate Life* (London: Routledge, 2007), 23.
4. Anna Clark, *Desire: A History of European Sexuality* (London: Routledge, 2008), 205; on British youth culture see: Adrian Horn, *Juke Box Britain: Americanisation and Youth Culture, 1945–60* (Manchester: Manchester University Press, 2009); David Fowler, *Youth Culture in Modern Britain, c. 1920–1970: From Ivory Tower to Global Movement – A New History* (Basingstoke: Palgrave Macmillan, 2008); Arthur Marwick, *The Sixties: Cultural Revolution in Britain, France, Italy, and the United States, C.1958–1974* (Oxford: Oxford University Press, 1998); on the impact on interior design see: Penny Sparke, *As Long as It's Pink: The Sexual Politics of Taste* (London: Pandora, 1995), 188.
5. Steedman, Rowbotham and Segal give a powerful sense of this in their memoirs. See: Carolyn Steedman, *Landscape for a Good Woman: A Story of Two Lives* (London: Virago, 1986); Sheila Rowbotham, *Promise of a Dream: Remembering the Sixties* (London: Allen Lane, 2000); Lynne Segal, *Making Trouble: Life and Politics* (London: Serpent's Tail, 2007); see also: Elizabeth Wilson, *Only Halfway to Paradise: Women in Postwar Britain 1945–1968* (London: Tavistock, 1980).
6. Weeks, *The World We Have Won*, 58; Helen McCarthy, 'Gender Equality', in *Unequal Britain: Equalities in Britain Since 1945*, ed. Pat Thane (London: Continuum, 2010). Aside from the increasing presence of women in the workforce, there was the Equal Pay Act of 1955 for women in public service and – more arcane but nevertheless symbolic – the Life Peers Act of 1958 which allowed women as well as men to be created as Life Peers in the House of Lords.
7. Matt Cook, *A Gay History of Britain: Love and Sex Between Men Since the Middle Ages* (Oxford: Greenwood World, 2007), chap. 5.
8. There is no evidence of such a co-ordinated operation, however: Matt Houlbrook, *Queer London: Perils and Pleasures in the Sexual Metropolis, 1918–1957* (Chicago: University of Chicago Press, 2005); Patrick Higgins, *Heterosexual Dictatorship: Male Homosexuality in Postwar Britain* (London: Fourth Estate, 1996).
9. On these shifts see especially: Fowler, *Youth Culture*; Marwick, *The Sixties*; Lisa Tickner and David Peters Corbett, eds., *British Art in the Cultural Field, 1939–69* (Chichester: Wiley-Blackwell, 2012).
10. Jerry White, *London in the Twentieth Century: A City and Its People* (London: Vantage, 2008), 137, 341.
11. Ibid., 137.
12. Ibid., 350.
13. Angus, interview, 2010.

286 Notes

14. Derek Jarman, *Modern Nature: The Journals of Derek Jarman* (London: Century, 1991), 113.
15. White, *London in the Twentieth Century*, 142, 144.
16. On this see: Michael Billington, *State of the Nation: British Theatre Since 1945* (London: Faber, 2007), chap. 5; Alan Sinfield, *Out on Stage: Lesbian and Gay Theatre in the Twentieth Century* (New Haven: Yale University Press, 1999), chap. 14.
17. Michael, interview, 2009.
18. Derek Jarman, *Dancing Ledge* (London: Quartet, 1984), 130.
19. Houlbrook, *Queer London*, 193; see also: Chris Waters and Matt Houlbrook, 'The Heart in Exile: Detachment and Desire in 1950s London', *History Workshop Journal* 62 (Autumn 2006): 142–163.
20. Houlbrook, *Queer London*, 193.
21. Joe Orton on the BBC's Eamonn Andrews show, 23 April 1967, Beautiful Things Collection, British Film Institute Mediatheque.
22. R.S. Nakayama, 'Domesticating Mr. Orton', *Theatre Journal* 45, no. 2 (1993): 185–195.
23. John Lahr, *Prick up Your Ears* (Bloomsbury Publishing, 2002); Simon Shepherd, *Because We're Queers: The Life and Crimes of Kenneth Halliwell and Joe Orton* (London: Allen Lane, 1978).
24. On this point see also David Van Leer, 'Saint Joe: Orton as Homosexual Rebel', in *Joe Orton: A Casebook*, ed. Francesca Coppa (London: Routledge, 2003), 112.
25. Joe Orton, 'Diary', 1951, Leicester University (LU) MS 237/21/1.
26. Van Leer rightly criticizes Lahr for failing to position the interviewees in this way: Orton and Halliwell's deaths necessarily coloured how they were remembered. See Van Leer, 'Saint Joe'.
27. For an autobiographical account of the Soho scene in the 60s see: Peter Burton, *Parallel Lives* (London: GMP, 1985), esp. 45.
28. See: Chapter 5.
29. Joe Orton, *The Orton Diaries*, ed. John Lahr (London: Methuen, 1986), 30 December 1967, 45.
30. See: Epilogue to Part I.
31. See: Chapter 2.
32. Cited in: Alan Sinfield, 'Is There a Queer Tradition and Is Orton in It?', in *Joe Orton*, ed. Coppa, 91.
33. See: M. Finn, 'Men's Things: Masculine Possession in the Consumer Revolution', *Social History* 25, no. 2 (2000): 133–155.
34. I am very grateful to Ilsa Colsell for this information.
35. Colin MacInnes was writing in *Encounter* 21 (August 1963). Cited by Jonathan Dollimore, 'The Challenge of Sexuality', in *Society and Literature*, ed. Alan Sinfield (London: Methuen, 1983), 78.
36. Richard Hornsey, *The Spiv and the Architect: Unruly Life in Postwar London* (Minneapolis: University of Minnesota Press, 2010), 244.
37. White, *London in the Twentieth Century*, 63–64; on the national rise in home ownership in the 1950s, see: James Obelkevich, 'Consumption', in *Understanding Post-War British Society*, ed. James Obelkevich and Peter Catterall (London: Routledge, 1994), 144.
38. Louis Wulff, 'They All Like Islington', *Evening News and Star*, 13 December 1961.

39. Ibid.
40. Cited in Shepherd, *Because*, 85.
41. White, *London in the Twentieth Century*, 72.
42. Ibid., 235.
43. See: Chapter 5.
44. Orton, *The Orton Diaries*, 25 May 1967, 187.
45. Ibid., 8 May 1967, 159.
46. Laurence Harbottle to Douglas Orton, 16 August 1967, British Library (BL), Deposit 9635: Peggy Ramsay papers, b.37, f.13. I am grateful to the trustees of Peggy Ramsay Foundation for permission to quote from this archive.
47. Joel Sanders, ed., *Stud: Architectures of Masculinity* (New York: Princeton Architectural Press, 1996), 18.
48. See: Chapter 1.
49. Francesca Coppa, ed., *Joe Orton: A Casebook* (New York: Routledge, 2003), intro, 4.
50. Obelkevich, 'Consumption', 149.
51. Lahr, *Prick*, 248.
52. David M. Halperin, *How to Be Gay* (Cambridge: Harvard University Press, 2012), 238, 334.
53. Orton, *The Orton Diaries*, 17 July 1967, 243.
54. Shepherd, *Because*, 130.
55. See: Chapter 5 and also: Van Leer, 'Saint Joe', 32, 109.
56. Letter to John Lahr (1 September 1987), b.37, f.1, BL.
57. Lahr, *Prick*, 152.
58. See: Sinfield, 'Is There a Queer Tradition and Is Orton in It?'.
59. See: Simon Shepherd, 'A Colored Girl Reading Proust', in *Joe Orton*, ed. Coppa; Leonie Orton and John Alderton, 'A Conversation', in *Joe Orton*, ed. Coppa, 157.
60. Richard Dyer, *Culture of Queers* (London: Routledge, 2001), 16.
61. Orton, 'Diary', 30 April 1967, Howard Gotlieb Archival Center at Boston University (BU), John Lahr Collection. For discussion of the status of the diary held at BU, and for citation and discussion of this particular section see: Cook, 'Orton', 174.
62. Lahr, *Prick*, 106.
63. Ibid., 138.
64. Around 1653 of them. Maurice Charney, *Joe Orton* (London: Macmillan, 1984), 7.
65. David Robbins, ed., *The Independent Group: Postwar Britain and the Aesthetics of Plenty* (Cambridge: MIT Press, 1990); Anne Massey, *The Independent Group: Modernism and Mass Culture in Britain, 1945–59* (Manchester: Manchester University Press, 1995).
66. Tickner and Corbett, *British Art in the Cultural Field*; Richard Leslie, *Pop Art: A New Generation of Style* (New York: Todtri, 1997); Marco Livingstone, *Pop Art* (London: Royal Academy of Arts, 1991); George Melly, *Revolt into Style: The Pop Arts in Britain* (Harmondsworth: Penguin, 1972).
67. See: Chapters 2 & 3.
68. Ilsa Colsell, *Malicious Damage: The Defaced Library Books of Kenneth Halliwell and Joe Orton* (London: Donlon, 2013), 52.
69. Ibid., 53.

70. Peggy Ramsay to John Lahr, 29 May 1970, Peggy Ramsay collection, BL, deposit 9635, b.37, f.17.
71. Joe Orton, 'The Ruffian on the Stair', in *Orton: The Complete Plays*, ed. John Lahr (London: Methuen, 1976), 49–50.
72. See: Chapter 2.
73. Penny Summerfield, 'Women and Britain since 1945: Companionate Marriage and the Double Burden', in *Understanding*, ed. Obelkevich and Catterall, 59.
74. Ibid.
75. Tamara K. Hareven, 'The Home and the Family in Historical Perspective', *Social Research* 58, no. 1 (1991): 253–285.
76. Lahr, *Orton Diaries*, 30 April 1967, 146.
77. Michael Schofield, *Society and the Homosexual* (London: Victor Gollancz, 1952), 132. For further discussion see the introduction to this part of the book.
78. Ramsay to Dan Crawford, 12 May 1987, BL Deposit 9635, b.37, f.17.
79. Leonie Orton to Peggy Ramsay, 19 October 1986, BL Deposit 9635, b.37, f.13.
80. Lahr, *Prick*, 88.
81. Ramsay to Leonie Orton, 22 October 1986, BL Deposit 9635, b.37, f.13.
82. On the need for flexible understandings of kinship in our approach to the past see: Robert Nye, 'Kinship, Male Bonds and Masculinity in Comparative Perspective', *American Historical Review* 105 (2000): 1658.
83. Joe Orton, 'The Good and Faithful Servant', in *Orton*, ed. Lahr, 166–167.
84. J.E. Gardner, 'A Normal Family: Alternative Communities in the Plays of Joe Orton', in *Joe Orton*, ed. Coppa.
85. Edmund White, 'The Importance of Being Joe', *Sunday Times*, 23 November 1986.
86. Gardner, 'A Normal Family', 76; see also: Randall Nakayama, 'Sensation and Sensibility: Joe Orton's Diaries', in *Joe Orton*, ed. Coppa.
87. See: Part II, Epilogue.
88. See: Chapter 2.

Part IV   Taking Sexual Politics Home: Introduction

1. Cited Chris Holmes, *The Other Notting Hill* (Studley: Brewin, 2005), 25.
2. See the epilogues to Parts I & II.
3. For detailed accounts of the formation, activism and legacy of the GLF see: Jeffrey Weeks, *Coming Out: Homosexual Politics in Britain from the Nineteenth Century to the Present* (London: Quartet Books, 1977); Lucy Robinson, *Gay Men and the Left in Post-War Britain: How the Personal Got Political* (Manchester: Manchester University Press, 2007); Lisa Power, *No Bath but Plenty of Bubbles: An Oral History of the Gay Liberation Front, 1970–1973* (London: Cassell, 1995); Bob Cant and Susan Hemmings, eds., *Radical Records: Thirty Years of Lesbian and Gay History, 1957–1987* (London: Routledge, 1988).
4. Robinson, *Gay Men*.
5. GLF principles reprinted in: Power, *No Bath but Plenty of Bubbles*, 36.
6. 'Gay Liberation Manifesto' (London, 1971); and the GLF Newspaper *Come Together* – especially issues 2 (carrying the Principles of the GLF), 11 ('Fuck the Family'), and 15 (compiled by the Notting Hill GLF Commune).

7. Michèle Barrett and Mary McIntosh, *The Anti-Social Family* (London: Verso, 1991), 33.
8. Most famously by: Friedrich Engels, *The Origin of the Family, Private Property and the State* (Chicago: C.H. Kerr, 1902); for a critique see: Barrett and McIntosh, *The Anti-Social Family*, 16–17.
9. See, for example: Barrett and McIntosh, *The Anti-Social Family*; Lynne Segal, ed., *What is to Be Done About the Family?* (Harmondsworth: Penguin, 1983); Michael Gordon, *The Nuclear Family in Crisis: The Search for an Alternative* (New York, London: Harper and Row, 1972); Sheila Rowbotham and Jeffrey Weeks, *Socialism and the New Life: The Personal and Sexual Politics of Edward Carpenter and Havelock Ellis* (London: Pluto Press, 1977).
10. See especially: David Cooper, *The Death of the Family* (Harmondsworth: Penguin, 1972); Robert Boyers, *R.D. Laing & Anti-Psychiatry* (New York: Octagon Books, 1974); R.D. Laing, *The Politics of the Family, and Other Essays* (London: Routledge, 1999).
11. On this point see: Deborah Cohen, *Family Secrets: Living with Shame from the Victorians to the Present Day* (London: Viking, 2013), 234.
12. Wini Breines, Margaret Cerullo, and Judith Stacey, 'Social Biology, Family Studies and Anti-Feminist Backlash', *Feminist Studies* 4, no. 1 (1978): 43.
13. Cited in: Holmes, *The Other Notting Hill*, 25.
14. Robinson, *Gay Men*, 86.
15. For more on this longer legacy see: Matt Cook, ed., *A Gay History of Britain: Love and Sex between Men since the Middle Ages* (Oxford: Greenwood World, 2007), chap. 6.
16. Cook, *A Gay History of Britain*, 183–184.
17. On Notting Hill see: Frank Mort, *Capital Affairs: London and the Making of the Permissive Society* (New Haven: Yale University Press, 2010); Holmes, *The Other Notting Hill*.
18. Carl Marshall, 'Betty's Bastard 1963–1965', ts of handwritten memoir (collection of Matt Cook) 5; Tony Peake, *Derek Jarman* (London: Abacus, 2001), 60.
19. Cook, *A Gay History of Britain*, 182.
20. David Rayside, *On the Fringe: Gays and Lesbians in Politics* (Ithaca: Cornell University Press, 1998), 23.
21. Jeffrey Weeks, *The World We Have Won: The Remaking of Erotic and Intimate Life* (London: Routledge, 2007).
22. 'Gallup-ing Forward', *Gay News*, 19 November 1979.
23. Cook, *A Gay History of Britain*, 206.
24. Cited in Alkarim Jivani, *It's Not Unusual: A History of Lesbian and Gay Britain in the Twentieth Century* (London: Michael O'Mara, 1997), 199.
25. On this multilayered shift see: Weeks, *The World We Have Won*, intro.
26. See: Epilogue to Part I.
27. 'No Gay Roof over our Heads', *Gay News*, 21, March 1972.
28. *Gay News*, 27, June 1972.
29. *Gay News*, 46, March 1973.
30. *Gay News*, 31, August 1972.
31. *Gay News*, 25, April 1972.
32. Sara Cookson, *Housing for Lesbians and Gay Men: Report of a Conference Held on 1st October, 1988* (CHAR, 1989); Ross Fraser, *Filling the Empties: Short Life Housing and How to Do It* (London: Shelter, 1986), 5.

33. 'Review of London's Needs', report prepared for the London Boroughs Grants Committee, 12 November 1986, 84, LSE, ref.421, f.2196.
34. 'Secret Move to Set Up Gays' Hostel', *The Standard*, 21 January 1985.
35. Davina Cooper, 'Off the Banner and onto the Agenda: The Emergence of a New Municipal Lesbian and Gay Politics, 1979 – 1986', *Critical Social Policy* 36 (1992): 22.
36. Ibid., 24.
37. Stephen Jeffery-Poulter, *Peers, Queers and Commons: The Struggle for Gay Law Reform from 1950 to the Present* (London: Routledge, 1991), 204; Cooper, 'Off the Banner', 35.
38. Cooper, 'Off the Banner'.
39. Chris Yates, *Building for Immunity: Housing People with HIV Disease and AIDS* (London: National Federation of Housing Associations, 1991), 6.
40. London had between 70 and 90 per cent of the UK's 'AIDS Sufferers' at this time. 'Review of London's Needs', 63–64.
41. Terry Cotton and Vijay Kumari, 'Local Authorities and HIV-Related Illness', in *AIDS: Individual, Cultural and Policy Dimensions*, ed. Peter Aggleton, Peter Davies, and Graham Hart (London: Falmer Press, 1990), 218.
42. Yates, *Building*.
43. Nick Raynsford, *Housing is an AIDS Issue* (London: National AIDS Trust, 1989).
44. 'Hostel for Gays Set Up in Secret', *The Standard*, 22 January 1985.
45. 'Council Housing to Under Age Gays', *Daily Mail*, 4 May 1982.
46. 'A Gay Way to Jump the Housing Queue', *Daily Express*, 25 June 1986.
47. 'Anger at Homes for Gays Plan', *Evening Standard*, 30 November 1984.
48. 'A Gay Way to Jump the Housing Queue', *Daily Express*.
49. See: Epilogue to Part II.
50. 'Gays Press for Lovers to Inherit Council Flats', *The Times*, 14 January 1993.
51. See: Epilogues to Parts I and II.

7 'Gay Times': The Brixton Squatters

1. Interview transcript, 'David', 1983, LSE Library, Townson Collection, HCA/ Townson/13. The names of interviewees have been changed unless explicit permission was granted. The use of pseudonyms is indicated in the use of inverted commas in the first reference. Because of the number of men interviewed I have used in-text bracketed references for clarity.
2. Held in the LSE, Townson Collection, HCA/Townson.
3. On the different interviewer/interviewee dynamics see: Matt Cook, 'Squatting in History: Queer Pasts and the Cultural Turn', in *Social Research After the Cultural Turn*, ed. Sasha Roseneil and Stephen Frosh (Basingstoke: Palgrave Macmillan, 2012); Michael Frisch, *A Shared Authority: Essays on the Craft and Meaning of Oral and Public History* (Albany: State University of New York Press, 1990); see also Lorraine Sitzia, *Seeking the Enemy* (London: Working Press, 2002).
4. Nick Anning, Nick Wates, and Christian Wolmar, *Squatting: the Real Story* (London: Bay Leaf, 1980); Gordon, *The Nuclear Family in Crisis*; James

Hinton, 'Self-Help and Socialism: the Squatters' Movement of 1946', *History Workshop* 25 (April 1988): 100–126; Alison Ravetz, *The Place of Home: English Domestic Environments, 1914–2000* (London: Spon, 1995), 109–112.
5. A. Sherman, 'Squatters and Socialism: Symbols of an Age', *Local Government Review* 139, no. 45 (15 November 1975): 763.
6. Nicholas Saunders, *Alternative London* (London: Wildwood House, 1978).
7. Aubrey Walter, ed., *Come Together: The Years of Gay Liberation (1970–73)* (London: Gay Men's Press, 1980), 158.
8. Benjamin Shepard, 'Play as World Making: From the Cockettes to the Germs, Gay Liberation to DIY Community Building', in *The Hidden 1970s: Histories of Radicalism*, ed. Dan Berger (New Brunswick: Rutgers University Press, 2002); dir. David Weissman and Bill Weber, *The Cockettes*, 2002.
9. Outlined, for example in: Gordon, *The Nuclear Family in Crisis*.
10. Andy Beckett, *When the Lights Went Out: Britain in the Seventies* (London: Faber, 2009), 245.
11. Josephine Schuman, *Empty Dwellings in Greater London: A Study of the Vacancy Question* (London: The Council, 1981), 14, 18–19.
12. Paul Addison, *No Turning Back: The Peacetime Revolutions of Post-War Britain* (Oxford: Oxford University Press, 2010), 121.
13. Jerry White, *London in the Twentieth Century: A City and Its People* (London: Vantage, 2008), 135.
14. Shankland Cox Partnership, *Lambeth Inner Area Study: People, Housing District* (London: Department of the Environment, 1974), 41.
15. Ibid., 8–9, 11.
16. Ibid., 48.
17. White, *London in the Twentieth Century*, 67.
18. Carl Bridge, Robert Crawford, and David Dunst, eds., *Australians in Britain: The Twentieth Century Experience* (Clayton: Monash University Press, 2009), 6.
19. For more on the importance of mobility and of globalisation to gay identity and community see: Weeks, *The World We Have Won*, 217; William L. Leap and Tom Boellstorff, eds., *Speaking in Queer Tongues: Globalisation and Gay Language* (Urbana: University of Illinois Press, 2003); Martin F. Manalansan, *Global Divas: Filipino Gay Men in the Diaspora* (Durham: Duke University Press, 2003).
20. White, *London in the Twentieth Century*, 160.
21. Power, *No Bath but Plenty of Bubbles*, 247; Robinson, *Gay Men*, 86–87.
22. Tony Chapman, 'Daring to Be Different?: Choosing an Alternative to the Ideal Home', in *Ideal Homes? Social Change and the Experience of the Home*, ed. Tony Chapman and Jennifer Hockey (London: Routledge, 1999), 196.
23. Don made similar arguments prior to moving into the squats in: Don Milligan, *The Politics of Homosexuality* (London: Pluto, 1973).
24. On the significance of meals and mealtimes see: Daniel Miller, ed., *Home Possessions: Material Culture Behind Closed Doors* (Oxford: Berg, 2001), into, 9; Elia Petridou, 'The Taste of Home', in *Home Possessions: Material Culture Behind Closed Doors*, ed. Daniel Miller (Oxford: Berg, 2001); Ravetz, *The Place of Home*, 212; see also: Michael Roper, *The Secret Battle:*

Emotional Survival in the Great War (Manchester: Manchester University Press, 2009), 15.
25. For an account of a central London squat in Piccadilly in the late 1960s see: Phil Cohen, *Reading Room Only: Memoir of a Radical Bibliophile* (Nottingham: Five Leaves Press, 2013).
26. John D'Emilio, 'Capitalism and Gay Identity', in *Powers of Desire: The Politics of Sexuality*, ed. Ann Snitow (New York: Monthly Review Press 1983); Amy Gluckman and Betsy Reed, eds., *Homo Economics: Capitalism, Community, and Lesbian and Gay Life* (New York: Routledge, 1997).
27. See: Chapter 6.
28. Power, *No Bath but Plenty of Bubbles*, 21–23.
29. 'Joe' letter to Ian Townson, 1997, LSE, HCA/Townson/box 13.
30. 'No Money for Male Homosexual Centre', *Streatham News*, 7 November 1975.
31. *South London Press*, 14 September 1975.
32. *South London Press*, 3 October 1975.
33. Weeks, *Coming Out*, 176.
34. Carl Whitman, 'A Gay Manifesto', in *We Are Everywhere*, ed. Mark Blasius and Shane Phelan (London: Routledge, 1997), 386–387.
35. 'Out to Help Oppressed Minorities', *South London Press*, 30 April 1974.
36. On these points see: Alan Berube, 'Intellectual Desire', *GLQ: A Journal of Lesbian and Gay Studies* 3, no. 1 (1996): 139–157; Stephen Valocchi, 'The Class-Inflected Nature of Gay Identity', *Social Problems* 46 (1999): 207; David Halperin, *How to Do the History of Homosexuality* (Chicago: University of Chicago Press, 2004), 19.
37. Bill Thornycroft, letter to Matt Cook, 2008.
38. Bill's comment came during his interview with Peter in 1983.
39. See: http://rememberolivemorris.wordpress.com/category/squatting/ (Accessed 20 August 2011).
40. GLF 40th Anniversary Conference, transcript (0.345.32), LSE; see also: Power, *No Bath but Plenty of Bubbles*, 213.
41. Charles I. Nero, 'Why Are Gay Ghettoes White?', in *Black Queer Studies*, ed. E. Patrick Johnson and Mae Henderson (Durham: Duke University Press, 2005), 238; see also: Alan Sinfield, 'The Production of Gay and the Return to Power', in *De-Centring Sexualities: Politics and Representations Beyond the Metropolis*, ed. Richard Phillips, Diane Watt, and David Shuttleton (London: Routledge, 2000), 31–33.
42. Peter Nevins, 'The Making of a Radical Blackgay Man', in *High Risk Lives: Lesbian and Gay Politics after the Clause*, ed. Tara Kaufmann and Paul Lincoln (Bridport: Prism, 1991).
43. Peter Keogh, Catherine Dodds, and Laurie Henderson, *Ethnic Minority Gay Men: Redefining Community, Restoring Identity: Research Report* (London: Sigma Research, 2004); Elijah Ward found something similar in his work on the relationship between gay men and the US black church. See: Elijah Ward, 'Homophobia, Hypermasculinity and the US Black Church', *Culture, Health & Sexuality* 7, no. 5 (2005): 493–504.
44. Ajamu X, Interview, 2010.
45. Keogh, Dodds, and Henderson, *Ethnic Minority Gay Men*, 33.
46. On this point see: Scott Bravmann, *Queer Fictions of the Past: History, Culture, and Difference* (Cambridge: Cambridge University Press, 1997), 127.

47. Robinson, *Gay Men*, 95.
48. Gluckman and Reed, *Homo Economics*, xv.
49. Beckett, *When the Lights Went Out*, 419–420.
50. Jeremy Black, *Britain since the Seventies: Politics and Society in the Consumer Age* (London: Reaktion, 2004), 11.
51. On the individualist strand in GLF thinking see: Power, *No Bath but Plenty of Bubbles*, 6; for an argument about the overlaps between counter and consumer cultures from the 1960s see: Joseph Heath and Andrew Potter, *The Rebel Sell: How the Counterculture Became Consumer Culture* (Toronto: Harper Collins, 2005).
52. Shankland Cox Partnership, *Lambeth Inner Area Study*, 36.
53. Boroughs Association London, *The Future of London's Housing* (London: London Boroughs Association, 1980), 48; Ravetz, *The Place of Home*, 112–116.
54. George Mavromatis, 'Stories from Brixton: Gentrification and Different Differences', *Sociological Research Online* 16 (2011) http://www.socresonline.org.uk/16/2/12.html; Tim Butler and Garry Robson, 'Social Change, Gentrification and Neighbourhood Change in London: A Comparison of Three Areas of South London', *Urban Studies* 38, no. 12 (2001): 2145–2162.
55. Ruth Glass, *London: Aspects of Change*, vol. 3 (London: MacGibbon and Kee, 1964), intro; Chris Hamnett, 'Gentrification and the Middle-Class Remaking of Inner London, 1961–2001', *Urban Studies* 40, no. 12 (2003): 2401–2426.
56. Butler and Robson, 'Social Change'.
57. Ibid., 2156.
58. Ibid.
59. Rowland Atkinson, 'Introduction: Misunderstood Saviour or Vengeful Wrecker? The Many Meanings and Problems of Gentrification', *Urban Studies* 40, no. 12 (2003): 2343–2350; see also: Addison, *No Turning Back*, 185.
60. Butler and Robson, 'Social Change', 2157.
61. Ibid.
62. Laurence Knopp, 'Gentrification and Gay Neighbourhood in New Orleans: a Case Study', in *Homo Economics: Capitalism, Community and Lesbian and Gay Life*, ed. Amy Gluckman and Betsy Reed (New York: Routledge, 1997); Anne-Marie Bouthillette, 'Gentrification by Gay Male Communities: a Case Study of Toronto's Cabbagetown', in *The Margins of the City: Gay Men's Urban Lives*, ed. Stephen Whittle (Aldershot: Ashgate, 1994); Nero, 'Why Are Gay Ghettoes White?'.
63. Sasha Roseneil, 'On Not Living with a Partner: Unpicking Coupledom and Cohabitation', *Sociological Research Online* 11, no. 3 (2006), http://www.socresonline.org.uk/11/3/roseneil.html.
64. Robinson, *Gay Men*, 75.
65. Robinson, *Gay Men*, 141; see also: White, *London in the Twentieth Century*, 387.
66. See introduction to this part of the book.
67. See http://www.rukus.co.uk/. The archive is now at the London Metropolitan Archive.
68. bell hooks, *Yearning: Race, Gender, and Cultural Politics* (Boston: South End Press, 1990), 49, 43, 42.
69. See: Epilogue to Part II.
70. See: Chapter 5.

294 Notes

71. Weeks, *The World We Have Won*, 176; see also: Mary Chamberlain, *Family Love in the Diaspora: Migration and the Anglo-Caribbean Experience* (London: Transaction, 2006); Tracey Reynolds and A. Jones, *Caribbean Mothers: Identity and Experience in the UK* (London: Tufnell Press, 2005).
72. Mary Chamberlain, 'Brothers and Sisters, Uncle and Aunts: A Lateral Perspective on Caribbean Families', in *The New Family?*, ed. Silvia Silva and Carol Smart (Thousand Oaks: Sage, 1998), 133.
73. Chamberlain, 'Brothers and Sisters'.
74. See: Chapter 3.
75. Dir. Ron Peck, *Strip Jack Naked*, 1991.
76. Peck, *Strip*.
77. On this point see: David Middleton, *The Social Psychology of Experience: Studies in Remembering and Forgetting* (London: Sage, 2005).
78. On this point see: Paul Connerton, *How Societies Remember* (Cambridge: Cambridge University Press, 1989); Mary Evans, *Missing Persons: The Impossibility of Auto/Biography* (London: Routledge, 1998); Mieke Bal, Leo Spitzer, and Jonathan V. Crewe, eds., *Acts of Memory: Cultural Recall in the Present* (Hanover: University Press of New England, 1999).
79. Cook, *A Gay History of Britain*, 211–212; Weeks, *The World We Have Won*.

8 Derek Jarman's Domestic Politics

1. Tony Peake, *Derek Jarman* (London: Abacus, 2001), 243.
2. The *Daily Mail* and the *Sun* published deeply negative obituaries: Christopher Tookey, 'How Can They Turn This Man into a Saint?', *Daily Mail*, 23 February 1994; 'Movies Jarman Dies from AIDS', *Sun*, 21 February 1994. Others were more positive, for example: John Taylor, 'Jarman's Heroism Leaves a Prolific Lyrical Legacy', *The Times*, 21 February 1994; Simon Garfield, 'Gay Icon Courage was Awesome', *Independent*, 21 February 1994.
3. Derek Jarman and Howard Sooley, *Derek Jarman's Garden* (London: Thames & Hudson, 1995).
4. Derek Jarman, *At Your Own Risk: A Saint's Testament* (London: Hutchinson, 1992), 134.
5. See: Introduction to Chapter 6.
6. Derek Jarman, *Modern Nature: The Journals of Derek Jarman* (London: Century, 1991), 196.
7. Richard Hornsey, *The Spiv and the Architect: Unruly Life in Postwar London* (Minneapolis: University of Minnesota Press, 2010).
8. Jarman, *Modern Nature*, 192.
9. See: Chapter 7; Jerry White, *London in the Twentieth Century: A City and Its People* (London: Vantage, 2008), 248.
10. On the subcultural dimensions of street markets see Angela McRobbie, 'The Role of the Ragmarket', in *The Subcultures Reader*, ed. Ken Gelder (London: Routledge, 2005).
11. Jarman, *Modern Nature*, 191.
12. Matt Cook, 'Words Written Without Any Stopping', in *Derek Jarman: A Portrait*, ed. Roger Wollen (London: Thames & Hudson, 1996).
13. Peake, *Derek Jarman*, 127.

14. Ibid., 122.
15. Derek Jarman, *Dancing Ledge* (London: Quartet, 1984), 78; Peake, *Derek Jarman*, 125. On Ives see: Chapter 3.
16. Peake, *Derek Jarman*, 234.
17. Jarman, *Dancing Ledge*, 96.
18. Peake, *Derek Jarman*, 239.
19. On Johnson's house see: Alice Friedman, *Women and the Making of the Modern House: A Social and Architectural History* (New Haven: Yale University Press, 2006), chap. 4; Aaron Betsky, *Queer Space: Architecture and Same-Sex Desire* (New York: William Morrow, 1997), 114–117.
20. Peake, *Derek Jarman*, 239.
21. Collated posthumously as 'Glitterbug' (1994).
22. Derek Jarman, *Smiling in Slow Motion* (London: Century, 2000), 260.
23. Peake, *Derek Jarman*, 168.
24. Deborah Bright, 'Shopping the Leftovers: Warhol's Collecting Strategies in Raid the Icebox I', *Art History* 24, no. 2 (April 2001): 289.
25. See: Chapter 2.
26. Jarman, *Smiling*, 43.
27. Peake, *Derek Jarman*, 60.
28. See: Chapter 5.
29. Jarman, *Smiling*, 259; for an incisive account of this privatisation process see: Jeremy Black, *Britain since the Seventies: Politics and Society in the Consumer Age* (London: Reaktion, 2004).
30. Peter Burton, *Parallel Lives* (London: GMP, 1985), 52.
31. Keith Collins (HB), interview, 2012. Hereafter references are in-text.
32. See: Chapter 5 and Matt Cook, *A Gay History of Britain: Love and Sex between Men Since the Middle Ages* (Oxford: Greenwood World, 2007), chap. 6.
33. 'Andy the Furniture Maker', *Channel 4*, 29 November 1986.
34. See: Part I.
35. 'Andy the Furniture Maker', *Channel 4*.
36. See: Chapter 1.
37. John Grube, '"Native and Settlers": An Ethnographic Note on Early Interaction of Older Homosexual Men with Younger Gay Liberationists', *Journal of Homosexuality* 20, no. 3 (1990): 119–136.
38. Jarman, *Modern Nature*, 63.
39. For a detailed examination of each of Jarman's films see: Rowland Wymer, *Derek Jarman* (Manchester: Manchester University Press, 2006).
40. See: Epilogue to Part I.
41. Cook, 'Words Written'.
42. Peake, *Derek Jarman*, 280–281.
43. For more on Collins and his relationship with Jarman see: Ibid., 390–394.
44. Jarman, *Modern Nature*, 17.
45. Ibid., 276.
46. Peake, *Derek Jarman*, 427.
47. Jarman, *Modern Nature*, 19.
48. Ibid., 10.
49. Ibid.
50. Ibid., 15.
51. Jarman, *Smiling*, 107.

52. See: Chapter 5.
53. On the religious resonances of the film see: Wymer, *Derek Jarman*, chap. 10.
54. Juliet Gardiner, *The Thirties: An Intimate History* (London: Harper Press, 2010), 312.
55. Alison Ravetz, *The Place of Home: English Domestic Environments, 1914–2000* (London: Spon, 1995), chap. 9.
56. Jarman, *Modern Nature*, 3.
57. Ibid., 102.
58. On Jarman's garden and these issues of temporality see especially: Daniel O'Quin, 'Gardening, History and the Escape from Time: Derek Jarman's *Modern Nature*', in *October*, 89 (1999): 113–126.
59. Jarman, *Modern Nature*, 32.
60. Ibid., 71.
61. Jarman, *Smiling*, 302.
62. Ibid., 8.
63. Peake, *Derek Jarman*, 402.
64. Jarman, *Smiling*, 382.
65. Ibid., 278.
66. Sasha Roseneil, 'Why We Should Care About Friends: An Argument for Queering the Care Imaginary in Social Policy', *Social Policy and Society* 3, no. 4 (2004): 409–419; Robert B. Hays, Sarah Chauncey, and Linda A. Tobey, 'The Social Support Networks of Gay Men with AIDS', *Journal of Community Psychology* 18, no. 4 (1990): 374–385; Barry Adam, 'Sex and Caring Among Men: Impacts of AIDS on Gay People', in *Modern Homosexualities: Fragments of Lesbian and Gay Experiences*, ed. Kenneth Plummer (London: Routledge, 1992).
67. On Ives' scrapbooks see: Matt Cook, 'Sex Lives and Diary Writing: The Journals of George Ives', in *Life Writing and Victorian Culture*, ed. David Amigoni (Farnham: Ashgate, 2006). On family photo albums see: Annette Kuhn, *Family Secrets: Acts of Memory and Imagination* (London: Verso, 1995).
68. Jarman, *Smiling*, 110.
69. Jarman, *Modern Nature*, 55.
70. Oscar Moore, *PWA: Looking AIDS in the Face* (London: Picador, 1996), 62.
71. Jarman, *Smiling*, 363.
72. Edmund White, 'Esthetics and Loss', in *Personal Dispatches: Writers Confront AIDS*, ed. John Preston (New York: St. Martin's, 1989).
73. Jarman, *Smiling*, 190.
74. Ibid., 373.
75. Carl Marshall, 'Health Diary', vol. 3, 19 April 1998, 29.
76. Ibid., 10 April 1998, 17.
77. I am grateful to Daniel Monk for his insights on the potency of wills in this respect.
78. Jarman, *Smiling*, 248.
79. Ibid., 18.
80. Ibid., 195.
81. Ibid.
82. Ibid., 287.
83. Moore, *PWA*, 182.

84. Sigmund Freud, *The Uncanny*, trans. David McLintock (London: Penguin, 2003).
85. Moore, *PWA*, 153.
86. On the idea of hospital as home in the context of HIV and AIDS see: Stephen Mayes and Lyndall Stein, eds., *Positive Lives: Responses to HIV: A Photodocumentary* (London: Cassell, 1993), 128.
87. Rob Imrie, 'Disability, Embodiment and the Meaning of the Home', *Housing Studies* 19, no. 5 (2004): 745–763.
88. Judith Stacey, 'The Families of Man: Gay Male Intimacy and Kinship in a Global Metropolis', *Signs: Journal of Women in Culture and Society* 30, no. 3 (2005): 1914.
89. Neil Bartlett writes movingly about this in: Neil Bartlett, 'That's What Friends are For', in *High Risk Lives 2: Writings on Sex, Death and Subversion*, ed. May Scholar and Ira Silverberg (London: Serpent's Tail, 1994), 87–90.
90. Simon Watney, *Policing Desire: Pornography, AIDS and the Media* (London: Comedia, 1986), 7.
91. Interview with Patrick Gale in: Richard Canning, *Gay Fiction Speaks: Conversations with Gay Novelists* (New York: Columbia University Press, 2000), 425.
92. Daniel Miller, *The Comfort of Things* (Cambridge: Polity, 2008).
93. Alison Oram, 'Going on an Outing: The Historic House and Queer Public History', *Rethinking History* 15, no. 2 (June 2011): 189–207.
94. Jarman, *Smiling*, 26; Eve Sedgwick had problems with the quilt too. See her essay: Eve Sedgwick, ed., 'White Glasses', in *Tendencies* (London: Routledge, 1994).
95. Richard Maguire, 'The Last of the Queer Romantics: Mourning and Melancholia in Gay Men's Autobiography' (PhD, King's College, London, 2011), 52–55.

Bibliography

Ackerley, J.R. *My Dog Tulip*. New York: New York Review Books, 1999.
——. *We Think the World of You*. New York: New York Review of Books, 2000.
——. *My Father and Myself*. New York: NYRB Classics, 2006.
——. *My Sister and Myself: The Diaries of J.R. Ackerley*. London: Hutchinson, 1982.
——. *The Letters of J.R. Ackerley*. Edited by Neville Braybrooke. London: Duckworth, 1975.
Addison, Paul. *No Turning Back: The Peacetime Revolutions of Post-War Britain*. Oxford: Oxford University Press, 2010.
Aggleton, Peter, Peter Davies, and Graham Hart, eds. *AIDS: Individual, Cultural and Policy Dimensions*. London: Falmer Press, 1990.
Ahmed, Sara. *The Cultural Politics of Emotion*. Edinburgh: Edinburgh University Press, 2004.
Aldrich, Robert. *Gay Life Stories*. London: Thames & Hudson, 2012.
Alexander, Bryant Keith. *Performing Black Masculinity: Race, Culture, and Queer Identity*. Lanham: Rowman & Littlefield, 2006.
Allen, Michelle. *Cleansing the City: Sanitary Geographies in Victorian London*. Ohio: Ohio University Press, 2008.
Anning, N., N. Wates, and C. Wolmar. *Squatting: The Real Story*. London: Bay Leaf, 1980.
Anon. *Teleny, or the Reverse of the Medal*. Cosmopoli, 1893.
Armstrong, Mark. 'A Room in Chelsea: Quentin Crisp at Home.' *Visual Culture in Britain* 12, no. 2 (2011): 155–169.
Ashbee, Felicity. *Janet Ashbee: Love, Marriage, and the Arts & Crafts Movement*. Syracuse: Syracuse University Press, 2002.
Atkinson, R. 'Introduction: Misunderstood Saviour or Vengeful Wrecker? The Many Meanings and Problems of Gentrification.' *Urban Studies* 40, no. 12 (2003): 2343–2350.
Attfield, Judy. *Wild Things: The Material Culture of Everyday Life*. Oxford: Berg, 2000.
Bal, Mieke, Leo Spitzer, and Jonathan V. Crewe, eds. *Acts of Memory: Cultural Recall in the Present*. Hanover: University Press of New England, 1999.
Barrett, Michèle, and Mary McIntosh. *The Anti-Social Family*. London: Verso, 1991.
Bartlett, Neil. 'That's What Friends Are For.' In *High Risk LIves 2: Writings on Sex, Death and Subversion*, edited by May Scholar and Ira Silverberg. London: Serpent's Tail, 1994.
——. *Who Was That Man: A Present for Mr Oscar Wilde*. London: Serpent's Tail, 1988.
Batten, Rex. *Rid England of This Plague*. London: Paradise, 2006.
Baudrillard, Jean. *The System of Objects*. London: Verso, 1996.
Bauman, Zygmunt. *Liquid Love: On the Frailty of Human Bonds*. Cambridge: Polity Press, 2003.
Bawer, Bruce. *A Place at the Table: The Gay Individual in American Society*. London: Poseidon Press, 1993.

Beaton, Cecil. *The Glass of Fashion*. London: Weidenfeld & Nicolson, 1954.
Beckett, Andy. *When the Lights Went Out: Britain in the Seventies*. London: Faber, 2009.
Beckson, Karl E. *London in the 1890s: A Cultural History*. London: Norton, 1993.
Behlmer, G.K. *Friends of the Family: The English Home and Its Guardians, 1850–1940*. Standford: Stanford University Press, 1998.
Bell, David. 'Pleasure and Danger: The Paradoxical Spaces of Sexual Citizenship.' *Political Geography* 14, no. 2 (February 1995): 139–153.
Benkov, Laura. *Reinventing the Family: The Emerging Story of Lesbian and Gay Parents*. New York: Crown, 1994.
Benn, S.I., and G.F. Gaus. 'The Liberal Conception of the Public and the Private.' In *Public and Private in Social Life*, edited by S.I. Benn and G.F. Gaus. London: Croom Helm, 1983, 31–65.
Beresford, Sarah. 'Get Over Your (Legal) "Self": A Brief History of Lesbians, Motherhood and Law.' *Journal of Social Welfare and Family Law* 30, no. 2 (June 2008): 95–106.
Bergler, Edmund. *Counterfeit-Sex*. New York: Grune & Stratton, 1958.
Bergman, David. *Camp Grounds: Style and Homosexuality*. Amherst: University of Massachusetts Press, 1993.
Berube, Alan. 'Intellectual Desire.' *GLQ: A Journal of Lesbian and Gay Studies* 3, no. 1 (1996): 139–157.
Betsky, Aaron. *Building Sex: Men, Women, and the Construction of Sexuality*. New York: William Morrow, 1995.
———. *Queer Space: Architecture and Same-Sex Desire*. New York: William Morrow, 1997.
Billington, Michael. *State of the Nation: British Theatre since 1945*. London: Faber, 2007.
Binnie, J. 'Quartering Sexualities: Gay Villages and Sexual Citizenship.' In *City of Quarters: Urban Villages in the Contemporary City*, edited by David Bell and Mark Jayne. Aldershot: Ashgate, 2004, 163–172.
Black, Jeremy. *Britain since the Seventies: Politics and Society in the Consumer Age*. London: Reaktion, 2004.
Blanche, Jacques-Emile. *Portraits of a Lifetime: The Late Victorian Era, the Edwardian Pageant 1870–1914*. London: Dent, 1937.
Bland, Lucy. *Banishing the Beast: English Feminism and Sexual Morality 1885–1914*. London: Penguin, 1995.
Bloch, Iwan. *The Sexual Life of Our Time in Its Relations to Modern Civilization*. London: Rebman, 1908.
Blunt, A. 'Home and Identity: Life Stories in Text and Person.' In *Cultural Geography in Practice*, edited by Alison Blunt, Pyrs Gruffudd, Jon May, Miles Ogborn, and David Pinder. London: Arnold, 2003.
Bösche, Susanne. *Jenny Lives with Eric and Martin*. London: Gay Men's Press, 1983.
Bourke, Joanna. *Working Class Cultures in Britain 1890–1960: Gender, Class, and Ethnicity*. London: Routledge, 1994.
Bouthillette, Anne-Marie. 'Gentrification by Gay Male Communities: A Case Study of Toronto's Cabbagetown.' In *The Margins of the City: Gays Men's Urban Lives*, edited by Stephen Whittle. Aldershot: Ashgate, 1994.
Boyers, Robert. *R.D. Laing & Anti-Psychiatry*. New York: Octagon Books, 1974.
Brady, Sean. *Masculinity and Male Homosexuality in Britain, 1861–1913*. London: Palgrave Macmillan, 2005.

Brake, Laurel. *Print in Transition, 1850–1910: Studies in Media and Book History*. Basingstoke: Palgrave, 2001.
Brandzel, Amy. 'Queering Citizenship? Same-Sex Marriage and the State.' *GLQ: A Journal of Lesbian and Gay Studies* 11, no. 2 (2005): 171–204.
Bravmann, Scott. *Queer Fictions of the Past: History, Culture, and Difference*. Cambridge: Cambridge University Press, 1997.
Bray, Alan. *The Friend*. Chicago: University of Chicago Press, 2003.
Breines, Wini, Margeret Cerullo, and Judith Stacey. 'Social Biology, Family Studies and Anti-Feminist Backlash.' *Feminist Studies* 4, no. 1 (1978): 43–67.
Bridge, Carl, Robert Crawford, and David Dunst, eds. *Australians in Britain: The Twentieth Century Experience*. Clayton: Monash University Press, 2009.
Briggs, Asa. *Toynbee Hall: The First Hundred Years*. London: Routledge, 1984.
Bright, Deborah. 'Shopping the Leftovers: Warhol's Collecting Strategies in Raid the Icebox I.' *Art History* 24, no. 2 (April 2001): 278–291.
Bristow, Joseph. *Effeminate England: Homoerotic Writing after 1885*. New York: Columbia University Press, 1995.
Brittan, Arthur. *Masculinity and Power*. Oxford: Basil Blackwell, 1989.
Bueno, Paulino, Terry Caesar, and Hummel Hummel. *Naming the Father: Legacies, Genealogies, and Explorations of Fatherhood in Modern and Contemporary Literature*. Lanham: Lexington Books, 2000.
Burton, Peter. *Parallel Lives*. London: GMP, 1985.
Butler, Tim, and Garry Robson. 'Social Change, Gentrification and Neighbourhood Change in London: A Comparison of Three Areas of South London.' *Urban Studies* 38, no. 12 (2001): 2145–2162.
Byng-Hall, John. 'Family Myths.' In *The Myths We Live By*, edited by Raphael Samuel and Paul Thompson. London: Routledge, 1990.
Camille, Michael. 'Editor's Introduction.' *Art History* 24, no. 2 (April 2001): 163.
Canning, Richard. *Gay Fiction Speaks: Conversations with Gay Novelists*. New York: Columbia University Press, 2000.
Cant, Bob, and Susan Hemmings, eds. *Radical Records: Thirty Years of Lesbian and Gay History, 1957–1987*. London: Routledge, 1988.
Carpenter, Edward, ed. *Ioläus. An Anthology of Friendship*. London: Swan Sonnenschein, 1902.
———. *The Intermediate Sex*. London: Swan Sonnenschein, 1908.
———. *Towards Democracy*. 1883–1902; London: GMP, 1985.
Carrington, Christopher. *No Place Like Home: Relationships and Family Life Among Lesbians and Gay Men*. Chicago: University of Chicago Press, 1999.
Castle, Terry. *Noel Coward and Radclyffe Hall; Kindred Spirits*. New York: Columbia University Press, 1996.
Castronovo, Russ, and Dana D. Nelson, eds. *Materializing Democracy: Toward a Revitalized Cultural Politics*. London: Duke University Press, 2002.
Chamberlain, Mary. 'Brothers and Sisters, Uncle and Aunts: a Lateral Perspective on Caribbean Families.' In *The New Family?*, edited by Silvia Silva and Carol Smart. Thousand Oaks: Sage, 1998.
———. *Family Love in the Diaspora: Migration and the Anglo-Caribbean Experience*. London: Transaction, 2006.
Chamberlain, Mary, and Paul Thompson. *Narrative and Genre*. London: Routledge, 1998.

Chapman, Tony. 'Daring to Be Different?: Choosing an Alternative to the Ideal Home.' In *Ideal Homes? Social Change and the Experience of the Home*, edited by Tony Chapman and Jennifer Hockey. London: Routledge, 1999.

———. *Gender and Domestic Life*. Basingstoke: Palgrave, 2002.

Charney, Maurice. *Joe Orton*. London: Macmillan, 1984.

Chauncey, G. 'Privacy Could Only Be Had in Public: Gay Uses of the Streets.' In *Stud: Architectures of Masculinity*, edited by J. Sanders. New York: Princeton Architectural Press, 1996, 224–267.

Clark, Anna. *Desire: A History of European Sexuality*. London: Routledge, 2008.

Cleere, Eileen. *Avuncularism: Capitalism, Patriarchy, and Nineteenth-Century English Culture*. Stanford: Stanford University Press, 2004.

Cocks, H.G. 'Calamus in Bolton: Spirituality and Homosexual Desire in Late Victorian England.' *Gender & History* 13, no. 2 (2002): 191–223.

———. *Nameless Offences: Homosexual Desire in the Nineteenth Century*. London: I.B. Tauris, 2003.

Cohen, Deborah. *Family Secrets: Living with Shame from the Victorians to the Present Day*. London: Viking, 2013.

———. *Household Gods: The British and Their Possessions*. New Haven: Yale University Press, 2006.

Cohen, Ed. *Talk on the Wilde Side: Towards a Genealogy of a Discourse on Male Sexualities*. London: Routledge, 1992.

Cohen, Phil. *Reading Room Only: Memoir of a Radical Bibliophile*. Nottingham: Five Leaves Press, 2013.

Coke, Charlotte Talbot. *The Gentlewoman at Home*. London: Henry & Co, 1892.

Coles, Prophecy, ed. *Sibling Relationships*. London: Karnac, 2006.

Collins, A. 'Sexual Dissidence, Enterprise and Assimilation: Bedfellows in Urban Regeneration.' *Urban Studies* 41, no. 9 (2004): 1789.

Collins, Marcus. *Modern Love: An Intimate History of Men and Women in Twentieth-Century Britain*. London: Atlantic, 2003.

Colomina, Beatriz, ed. *Sexuality & Space*. New York: Princeton Architectural Press, 1992.

Colsell, Ilsa. *Malicious Damage: The Defaced Library Books of Kenneth Halliwell and Joe Orton*. London: Donlon, 2013.

Comfort, Alex. *Sex in Society*. London: Duckworth, 1963.

Connerton, Paul. *How Societies Remember*. Cambridge: Cambridge University Press, 1989.

Cook, Hera. *The Long Sexual Revolution: English Women, Sex, and Contraception, 1800–1975*. Oxford: Oxford University Press, 2004.

Cook, James W., Lawrence B. Glickman, and Michael O'Malley, eds. *The Cultural Turn in U.S. History: Past, Present, and Future*. Chicago: University of Chicago Press, 2008.

Cook, Matt, ed. *A Gay History of Britain: Love and Sex between Men Since the Middle Ages*. Oxford: Greenwood World, 2007.

———. *London and the Culture of Homosexuality, 1885–1914*. Cambridge: Cambridge University Press, 2003.

———. 'Orton in the Archives.' *History Workshop Journal*, 66 (2008): 163–180.

———. 'Sex Lives and Diary Writing: The Journals of George Ives.' In *Life Writing and Victorian Culture*, edited by David Amigoni. Farnham: Ashgate, 2006.

———. 'Squatting in History: Queer Pasts and the Cultural Turn.' In *Social Research after the Cultural Turn*, edited by Sasha Roseneil and Stephen Frosh. Basingstoke: Palgrave, 2012.
Cookson, Sara. *Housing for Lesbians and Gay Men: Report of a Conference Held on 1st October, 1988*. CHAR, 1989.
Cooper, David. *The Death of the Family*. Harmondsworth: Penguin, 1972.
Cooper, Davina. 'Off the Banner and onto the Agenda: The Emergence of a New Municipal Lesbian and Gay Politics, 1979–1986.' *Critical Social Policy* 36 (1992): 20–39.
Cooper, Nicholas. *The Opulent Eye: Late Victorian and Edwardian Taste in Interior Design*. London: Architectural Press, 1976.
Coppa, Francesca, ed. *Joe Orton: A Casebook*. New York: Routledge, 2003.
Crawford, Adam. *Crime and Insecurity: Governance and Safety in Europe*. Devon: Willan, 2002.
Crawford, Alan. *C.R. Ashbee: Architect, Designer & Romantic Socialist*. New Haven: Yale University Press, 1985.
Crisp, Quentin. *The Naked Civil Servant*. Glasgow: Fontana/Collins, 1997.
Croft-Cooke, Rupert. *Feasting with Panthers a New Consideration of Some Late Victorian Writers*. London: W.H. Allen, 1967.
Cruikshank, George. *Sinks of London Laid Open*. London: J. Duncombe, 1848.
Cruise, Colin. *Love Revealed: Simeon Solomon and the Pre-Raphaelites*. London: Merrell, 2005.
D'Emilio, John. 'Capitalism and Gay Identity.' In *Families in the US: Kinship and Domestic Politics*, edited by Karen Hansen and Anita Garey. Philadelphia: Temple University Press, 1998.
———. *Making Trouble: Essays on Gay History, Politics, and the University*. London: Routledge, 1992.
Dakers, Caroline. *The Holland Park Circle: Artists and Victorian Society*. New Haven: Yale University Press, 1999.
Davidoff, Leonore. 'The Family in Britain.' *The Cambridge Social History of Britain, 1750 - 1950* 2 (1993): 71–129.
———. *Thicker Than Water: Siblings and Their Relations, 1780–1920*. Oxford: Oxford University Press, 2012.
Davidoff, Leonore, and Catherine Hall. *Family Fortunes: Men and Women of the English Middle Class 1780–1850*. London: Hutchinson, 1987.
Davies, Alistair, and Peter Saunders. 'Literature, Politics and Society.' In *Society and Literature*, edited by Alan Sinfield. London: Methuen, 1983.
Dawson, Graham. *Soldier Heroes: British Adventure, Empire, and the Imagining of Masculinities*. London: Routledge, 1994.
Delaney, J.G. Paul. *Charles Ricketts: A Biography*. Oxford: Clarendon, 1990.
Delap, Lucy. *Knowing their Place : Domestic Service in Twentieth-Century Britain*. Oxford: Oxford University Press, 2011.
Denisoff, Dennis. *Aestheticism and Sexual Parody 1840–1940*. Cambridge: Cambridge University Press, 2006.
Dennis, Richard. '"Babylonian Flats" in Victorian and Edwardian London.' *The London Journal* 33, no. 3 (1 November 2008): 233–247.
Derrida, Jacques. *Politics of Friendship*, vol. 5. London: Verso, 2005.
Dewing, David. *Home and Garden: Paintings and Drawings of English, Middle-Class, Urban Domestic Spaces, 1675–1914*. London: Geffrye Museum, 2003.

Dines, Martin. *Gay Suburban Narratives in American and British Culture: Homecoming Queens*. Basingstoke: Palgrave, 2010.
Doan, Laura. *Disturbing Practices: History, Sexuality, and Women's Experience of Modern War*. Chicago: University of Chicago Press, 2013.
Dollimore, Jonathan. 'The Challenge of Sexuality.' In *Society and Literature*, edited by Alan Sinfield. London: Methuen, 1983.
Donson, Cyril, and Armand Georgês. *Lonely-Land and Bedsitter-Land*. Bala: Bala Press, 1967.
Douglas, Mary. 'The Idea of a Home: A Kind of Space.' *Social Research* 58, no. 1 (1991): 287–307.
Dreyfus, Laurence. *Wagner and the Erotic Impulse*. Cambridge: Harvard University Press, 2012.
Droth, Martina. 'Sculpture and Aesthetic Intent in the Late-Victorian Interior.' In *Rethinking the Interior, c.1867 - 1896*, edited by Jason Edwards and Imogen Hart. Farnham: Ashgate, 2010.
Duggan, Lisa. 'The New Heteronormativity: The Sexual Politics of Neo-Liberalism.' In *Materializing Democracy: Toward a Revitalized Cultural Politics*, edited by Russ Castronovo and Dana D. Nelson. Durham: Duke University Press, 2002.
Duncan, Simon, and Darren Smith. *Individuation Versus the Geography of 'New' Families*. London: South Bank University, June 2006. http://www.lsbu.ac.uk/ahs/downloads/families/familieswp19.pdf.
Dunne, G.A., S. Prendergast, and D. Telford. 'Young, Gay, Homeless and Invisible: A Growing Population?' *Culture, Health & Sexuality* 4, no. 1 (2002): 103–115.
Dunne, Gillian. 'The Lady Vanishes? Reflections on the Experiences of Married and Divorced Non- Heterosexual Fathers.' *Sociological Research Online* 6 (2001). http://ideas.repec.org/a/sro/srosro/2001-39-2.html.
Dyer, Richard. *Culture of Queers*. London: Routledge, 2001.
Echlin, Shirley. *At Home in the 1950s*. Harlow: Longman, 1983.
Edelman, Lee. *No Future: Queer Theory and the Death Drive*. Durham: Duke University Press, 2004.
Edwards, Jason. 'The Lessons of Leighton House: Aesthetics, Politics, Erotics.' In *Rethinking the Interior, c.1867 - 1896*, edited by Jason Edwards and Imogen Hart. Farnham: Ashgate, 2010.
Edwards, Jason, and Imogen Hart, eds. *Rethinking the Interior, c.1867–1896: Aestheticism and Arts and Crafts*. Farnham: Ashgate, 2010.
Ellis, Havelock, and John Addington Symonds. *Sexual Inversion*. Edited by Ivan Crozier. Basingstoke: Palgrave Macmillan, 2008.
Engels, Friedrich. *The Origin of the Family, Private Property and the State*. Chicago: C.H. Kerr, 1902.
Evans, Mary. *Missing Persons: The Impossibility of Auto/Biography*. London: Routledge, 1998.
Farson, Daniel. *Gilbert and George: A Portrait*. London: Harper Collins, 1999.
Fellows, Will. *A Passion to Preserve: Gay Men as Keepers of Culture*. Madison: University of Wisconsin Press, 2004.
Féré, Charles. *The Evolution and Dissolution of the Sexual Instinct*. Paris: Charles Carrington, 1904.
Finch, Janet. *Passing On: Kinship and Inheritance in England*. London: Routledge, 2001.
Finn, M. 'Men's Things: Masculine Possession in the Consumer Revolution.' *Social History* 25, no. 2 (2000): 133–155.

Fletcher, Ronald. *Britain in the Sixties: The Family and Marriage*. Harmondsworth: Penguin, 1962.
Florida, Richard L. *Cities and the Creative Class*. London: Routledge, 2005.
———. *The Rise of the Creative Class*. New York: Basic Books, 2002.
Forel, Auguste. *The Sexual Question: A Scientific, Psychological, Hygienic and Sociological Study for the Cultured Classes*. London: Rebman, 1908.
Forty, Adrian. *Objects of Desire: Design and Society, 1750–1980*. London: Thames and Hudson, 1986.
Foucault, Michel. *History of Sexuality Volume 1 : An Introduction*. Translated by Robert Hurley. London: Allen Lane, 1979.
Fowler, David. *Youth Culture in Modern Britain, c. 1920–1970: From Ivory Tower to Global Movement - A New History*. Basingstoke: Palgrave Macmillan, 2008.
Fraser, Ross. *Filling the Empties: Short Life Housing and How to Do It*. London: Shelter, 1986.
Freeman, Gillian. *The Leather Boys*. London: New English Library, 1972.
Freud, Sigmund. *The Uncanny*. Translated by David McLintock. London: Penguin, 2003.
Freud, Sigmund, and Karl Jung. *The Freud – Jung Letters*. Edited by William McGuire. Translated by Ralph Mannheim and R.F.C. Hull. London: Hogarth and Routledge, 1974.
Friedman, Alice. *Women and the Making of the Modern House: A Social and Architectural History*. New Haven: Yale University Press, 2006.
Frisch, Michael. *A Shared Authority: Essays on the Craft and Meaning of Oral and Public History*. Albany: State University of New York Press, 1990.
Furbank, P.N. *E.M. Forster: A Life*. London: Cardinal, 1988.
Furneaux, Holly. *Queer Dickens: Erotics, Families, Masculinities*. Oxford: Oxford University Press, 2009.
Gardiner, James. *Who's a Pretty Boy, Then?: One Hundred & Fifty Years of Gay Life in Pictures*. London: Serpent's Tail, 1997.
Gardiner, Juliet. *The Thirties: An Intimate History*. London: Harper Press, 2010.
Gardner, J.E. 'A Normal Family: Alternative Communities in the Plays of Joe Orton.' In *Joe Orton: A Casebook*, edited by Francesca Coppa. London: Routledge, 2003, 79.
Garfield, Simon. *Our Hidden Lives: The Everyday Diaries of a Forgotten Britain, 1945–1948*. London: Ebury, 2004.
Garland, Rodney. *The Heart in Exile*. Brighton: Milliveres, 1995.
Garrett, Rhoda, and Agnes Garrett. *Suggestions for House Decoration*. London: Macmillan, 1876.
Garrity, J., and L. Doan. *Sapphic Modernities: Sexuality, Women and National Culture*. Basingstoke: Palgrave Macmillan, 2006.
Gelder, Ken. *The Subcultures Reader*. London: Routledge, 2005.
Georgês, Armand. *The Bed-Sitter Tribe*. London: Jackson, 1959.
Gere, Charlotte. *The House Beautiful: Oscar Wilde and the Aesthetic Interior*. London: Lund Humphries, 2000.
Giddens, Anthony. *The Transformation of Intimacy: Sexuality, Love and Eroticism in Modern Societies*. Cambridge: Polity, 1992.
Gilding, Michael. *The Making and Breaking of the Australian Family*. North Sydney NSW: Allen & Unwin, 1991.

Giles, Judy. '"Playing Hard to Get": Working-Class Women, Sexuality and Respectability in Britain, 1918–40.' *Women's History Review* 1, no. 2 (1992): 239–255.

———. *The Parlour and the Suburb: Domestic Identities, Class, Femininity and Modernity*. Oxford: Berg, 2004.

———. *Women, Identity and Private Life in Britain, 1900–50*. Basingstoke: Macmillan, 1995.

Gillis, John R. *A World of Their Own Making: Myth, Ritual, and the Quest for Family Values*. New York: Basic Books, 1996.

Ginzberg, Carlo. 'Microhistory: Two or Three Things That I Know About It.' *Critical Inquiry* 20, no. 1 (1993): 10–35, 33.

Glass, Ruth. *London: Aspects of Change*, vol. 3. London: MacGibbon & Kee, 1964.

Gluckman, Amy, and Betsy Reed, eds. *Homo Economics: Capitalism, Community, and Lesbian and Gay Life*. New York: Routledge, 1997.

Goodman, Jordon. 'History and Anthropology.' In *Companion to Historiography*, edited by Michael Bently. London: Routledge, 1997.

Gordon, Michael. *The Nuclear Family in Crisis: The Search for an Alternative*. New York and London: Harper and Row, 1972.

Gorman-Murray, A. 'Contesting Domestic Ideals: Queering the Australian Home.' *Australian Geographer* 38, no. 2 (2007): 195–213.

———. 'Queering Home or Domesticating Deviance?' *International Journal of Cultural Studies* 9, no. 2 (1 June 2006): 227–247.

Goss, R., and A.A.S. Strongheart, eds. *Our Families, Our Values: Snapshots of Queer Kinship*. New York: Harrington Park Press, 1997.

Gosse, Edmund. *Father and Son*. Edited by Michael Newton. Oxford: Oxford University Press, 2004.

Greenfield, Jill, Sean O'Connell, and Chris Reid. 'Fashioning Masculinity: Men Only, Consumption and the Development of Marketing in the 1930s.' *Twentieth Century British History* 10, no. 4 (1 January 1999): 457–476.

Grey, Anthony. 'Homes for Homosexuals.' *Social Action*, (May 1969): 4–5.

Grosskurth, Phyllis. *John Addington Symonds: A Biography*. New York: Ayer Company Pub, 1975.

Grube, John. '"Native and Settlers": An Ethnographic Note on Early Interaction of Older Homosexual Men with Younger Gay Liberationists.' *Journal of Homosexuality* 20, no. 3 (1990): 119–136.

Gurney, P. '"Intersex" and "Dirty Girls": Mass-Observation and Working-Class Sexuality in England in the 1930s.' *Journal of the History of Sexuality* 8, no. 3 (1997): 256–290.

Hall, Catherine, Keith McClelland, and Jane Rendall. *Defining the Victorian Nation: Class, Race, Gender and the British Reform Act of 1867*. Cambridge University Press, 2000.

Hall, Lesley. *Sex, Gender and Social Change in Britain since 1880*. Basingstoke: Macmillan, 2000.

Hall, Stuart. *Resistance through Rituals: Youth Subcultures in Post-War Britain*. London: Routledge, 2007.

Halperin, David M. *How to Be Gay*. Cambridge: Harvard University Press, 2012.

———. *How to Do the History of Homosexuality*. Chicago: University of Chicago Press, 2004.

Hamlett, Jane. *Material Relations: Families and Middle-class Domestic Interiors in England, 1850 - 1910*. London: I.B. Taurus, 2009.
Hamnett, C. 'Gentrification and the Middle-Class Remaking of Inner London, 1961–2001.' *Urban Studies* 40, no. 12 (2003): 2401–2426.
Haraway, Donna Jeanne. *The Companion Species Manifesto: Dogs, People, and Significant Otherness*. Chicago: Prickly Paradigm, 2003.
Hareven, Tamara K. 'The Home and the Family in Historical Perspective.' *Social Research* 58, no. 1 (1991): 253–285.
Harris, Chris. 'The Family in Post-War Britain.' In *Understanding Post-War British Society*, edited by James Obelkevich and Peter Catterall. London: Routledge, 1994, 144.
Hart, K.P.R. 'We're Here, We're Queer—and We're Better Than You: The Representational Superiority of Gay Men to Heterosexuals on Queer Eye for the Straight Guy.' *The Journal of Men's Studies* 12, no. 3 (2004): 241–253.
Hatt, Michael. 'Space, Surface, Self: Homosexuality and the Aesthetic Interior.' *Visual Culture in Britain* 8, no. 1 (2007): 105–128.
Haweis, Mary Eliza. *The Art of Decoration*. London: Chatto & Windus, 1881.
Hays, Robert B., Sarah Chauncey, and Linda A. Tobey. 'The Social Support Networks of Gay Men with AIDS.' *Journal of Community Psychology* 18, no. 4 (1990): 374–385.
Heath, Joseph, and Andrew Potter. *The Rebel Sell: How the Counterculture Became Consumer Culture*. Toronto: Harper Collins, 2005.
Hennessy, Rosemary. *Profit and Pleasure: Sexual Identities in Late Capitalism*. London: Routledge, 2000.
———. 'Queer Visibility in Commodity Culture.' *Cultural Critique* 29 (1994): 31–76.
Herzog, Dagmar, ed. *Brutality and Desire: War and Sexuality in Europe's Twentieth Century*. Basingstoke: Palgrave Macmillan, 2009.
Heynen, Hilde, and Gulsum Baydar, eds. *Negotiating Domesticity: Spatial Productions of Gender in Modern Architecture*. London: Routledge, 2005.
Hicks, Stephen. 'Lesbian and Gay Foster Care and Adoption: A Brief UK History.' *Adoption & Fostering Journal* 29, no. 3 (2005): 42–56.
———. *Lesbian, Gay and Queer Parenting: Families, Intimacies, Genealogies*. Basingstoke: Palgrave Macmillan, 2011.
Higgins, Patrick. *Heterosexual Dictatorship: Male Homosexuality in Postwar Britain*. London: Fourth Estate, 1996.
Hill, Octavia. 'The Influence of Model Dwellings on Character.' In *The Life and Labour of the People of London*, vol. 3, edited by Charles Booth. London: Macmillan, 1892.
Hindmarch-Watson, Katie. 'Male Prostitution and the London GPO: Telegraph Boys' "Immorality" from Nationalization to the Cleveland Street Scandal.' *Journal of British Studies* 51, no. 3 (July 2012): 594–617.
Hinton, James. 'Self-Help and Socialism the Squatters' Movement of 1946.' *History Workshop* 25 (1 April 1988): 100–126.
Hirsch, Marianne, and Valerie Smith. 'Feminism and Cultural Memory: An Introduction.' *Signs* 28, no. 1 (Fall 2002): 1–19.
Hobsbawm, Eric. 'Introduction.' *Social Research* 58, no. 1 (Spring 1991): 65–68.
Holden, Katherine. *The Shadow of Marriage: Singleness in England, 1914–60*. Manchester: Manchester University Press, 2010.

Holmes, Chris. *The Other Notting Hill*. Studley: Brewin, 2005.
Holstein, J.A., and J.F. Gubrium. 'Deprivatization and the Construction of Domestic Life.' *Journal of Marriage and the Family* 57, no. 4 (1995): 894–908.
hooks, bell. *Yearning: Race, Gender, and Cultural Politics*. Boston: South End Press, 1990.
Horn, Adrian. *Juke Box Britain: Americanisation and Youth Culture, 1945–60*. Manchester: Manchester University Press, 2009.
Hornsey, Richard. *The Spiv and the Architect: Unruly Life in Postwar London*. Minneapolis: University of Minnesota Press, 2010.
Houlbrook, Matt. *Queer London: Perils and Pleasures in the Sexual Metropolis, 1918–1957*. Chicago: University of Chicago Press, 2005.
———. 'Soldier Heroes and Rent Boys: Homosex, Masculinities, and Britishness in the Brigade of Guards, Circa 1900–1960.' *Journal of British Studies* 42, no. 3 (July 2003): 351–388.
Hunt, Lynn. *The Family Romance of the French Revolution*. London: Routledge, 1992.
Hussey, Christopher. 'The Keep, Chilham Castle, Kent. A Residence of Mr Charles Shannon, R.A. and Mr Charles Ricketts, A.R.A.' *Country Life*, 21 June 1924.
Hyde, H. Montgomery. *The Cleveland Street Scandal*. London: W.H. Allen, 1976.
———. *The Trials of Oscar Wilde*. New York: Dover, 1973.
Imrie, R. 'Disability, Embodiment and the Meaning of the Home.' *Housing Studies* 19, no. 5 (2004): 745–763.
Jamieson, Lynn. *Intimacy: Personal Relationships in Modern Societies*. Cambridge: Polity Press, 1998.
Jarman, Derek. *At Your Own Risk: A Saint's Testament*. London: Hutchinson, 1992.
———. *Dancing Ledge*. London: Quartet, 1984.
———. *Modern Nature: The Journals of Derek Jarman*. London: Century, 1991.
———. *Smiling in Slow Motion*. London: Century, 2000.
Jarman, Derek, and Howard Sooley. *Derek Jarman's Garden*. London: Thames & Hudson, 1995.
Jeffery-Poulter, Stephen. *Peers, Queers and Commons: The Struggle for Gay Law Reform from 1950 to the Present*. London: Routledge, 1991.
Jivani, Alkarim. *It's Not Unusual: A History of Lesbian and Gay Britain in the Twentieth Century*. London: Michael O'Mara, 1997.
Jones, Edgar, and Simon Wessely. 'The Impact of Total War on British Psychiatry.' In *In the Shadow of Total War: Europe, East Asia and the United States, 1919–1939*, edited by R. Chickering and S. Forster. Cambridge: Cambridge University Press, 2003.
Kalliney, Peter J. *Cities of Affluence and Anger: A Literary Geography of Modern Englishness*. Charlottesville: University of Virginia Press, 2006.
Kalter, Barrett. *Modern Antiques: The Material Past in England, 1660–1780*. Lewisburg: Bucknell University Press, 2011.
Kaplan, Morris B. *Sodom on the Thames: Sex, Love, and Scandal in Wilde Times*. Ithaca: Cornell University Press, 2005.
Katz, Jonathan Ned. 'The Art of Code: Jasper Johns and Robert Rauchenberg.' In *Significant Others: Creativity & Intimate Partnership*, edited by Whitney Chadwick and Isabelle de Courtivron. London: Thames & Hudson, 1993.
Keating, Jenny. *A Child for Keeps: The History of Adoption in England, 1918–45*. Basingstoke: Palgrave Macmillan, 2009.

Kensinger, Elizabeth A. *Emotional Memory across the Adult Lifespan.* New York: Taylor and Francis, 2008.

Keogh, Peter, Catherine Dodds, and Laurie Henderson. *Ethnic Minority Gay Men: Redefining Community, Restoring Identity: Research Report.* London: Sigma Research, 2004.

Keogh, Peter, R. Reid, and P. Weatherburn, *Lambeth LGBT Matters: the needs and experiences of lesbians, gay men, bisexual and trans men and women in Lambeth.* London: SIGMA Research, 2006.

Kinchin, Juliet. 'Interiors: Nineteenth-Century Essays on the "Masculine" and "Feminine" Room.' In *The Gendered Object*, edited by Pat Kirkham. Manchester: Manchester University Press, 1996.

Kirkham, Pat. *The Gendered Object.* Manchester: Manchester University Press, 1996.

Knopp, Laurance. 'Gentrification and Gay Neighbourhood in New Orleans: A Case Study.' In *Homo Economics: Capitalism, Community and Lesbian and Gay Life*, edited by Amy Gluckman and Betsy Reed. New York: Routledge, 1997.

Koven, Seth. *Slumming: Sexual and Social Politics in Victorian London.* Princeton: Princeton University Press, 2004.

Annette Kuhn, *Family Secrets: Acts of Memory and Imagination.* London: Verso, 1995.

Kynaston, David. *Family Britain, 1951–1957.* New York: Walker & Co, 2009.

La Rossa, Ralph. *The Modernization of Fatherhood: A Social and Political History.* Chicago: University of Chicago Press, 1996.

Lahr, John. *Prick up Your Ears.* Bloomsbury Publishing, London: Allen Lane, 1978.

Laing, R.D. *The Politics of the Family, and Other Essays.* London: Routledge, 1999.

Latimer, Tirza. 'Balletomania: A Sexual Disorder?' *GLQ: A Journal of Lesbian and Gay Studies* 5, no. 2 (1999): 173–197.

Leap, William L., and Tom Boellstorff, eds. *Speaking in Queer Tongues: Globalisation and Gay Language.* Urbana: University of Illinois Press, 2003.

Ledger, Sally. *The New Woman: Fiction and Feminism at the Fin de Siècle.* Manchester: Manchester University Press, 1997.

Leighton, Sophie. *The 1950s Home.* Oxford: Shire, 2009.

Leslie, Richard. *Pop Art: A New Generation of Style.* New York: Todtri, 1997.

Lewis, Jane. *The End of Marriage?: Individualism and Intimate Relations.* Cheltenham: Elgar, 2001.

Light, Alison. *Forever England: Femininity, Literature and Conservatism between the Wars.* London: Routledge, 1991.

———. *Mrs Woolf and the Servants: The Hidden Heart of Domestic Service.* London: Fig Tree, 2007.

Livingstone, Marco. *Pop Art.* London: Royal Academy of Arts, 1991.

London, Boroughs Association. *The Future of London's Housing.* London: London Boroughs Association, 1980.

Long, Helen. *The Edwardian Home: The Middle-Class Home in Britain 1880–1914.* Manchester: Manchester University Press, 1993.

MacCarthy, Fiona. *The Simple Life: C.R. Ashbee in the Cotswolds.* London: Lund Humphries, 1981.

Maguire, Richard. 'The Last of the Queer Romantics: Mourning and Melancholia in Gay Men's Autobiography.' PhD, King's College, London, 2011.

Maltz, Diana. '"Baffling Arrangements": Vernon Lee and John Singer Sargent in Queer Tangier.' In *Rethinking the Interior, c.1867–1896*, edited by Jason Edwards and Imogen Hart. Ashgate: Farnham, 2010.

Manalansan, Martin F. *Global Divas: Filipino Gay Men in the Diaspora*. Durham: Duke University Press, 2003.
Marcus, Clare Cooper. *House as a Mirror of Self: Exploring the Deeper Meaning of Home*. Berkeley: Conari Press, 1995.
Marcus, Sharon. *Apartment Stories: City and Home in Nineteenth-Century Paris and London*. Berkeley: University of California Press, 1999.
———. 'At Home with the Other Victorians.' *South Atlantic Quarterly* 108, no. 1 (Winter 2009): 120–145.
———. *Between Women: Friendship, Desire, and Marriage in Victorian England*. Princeton: Princeton University Press, 2007.
Marwick, Arthur. *The Sixties: Cultural Revolution in Britain, France, Italy, and the United States, C.1958–1974*. Oxford: Oxford University Press, 1998.
Massey, Anna. *Interior Design since 1900*. London: Thames & Hudson, 2008.
Massey, Anne. *The Independent Group: Modernism and Mass Culture in Britain, 1945–59*. Manchester: Manchester University Press, 1995.
Mavromatis, George. 'Stories from Brixton: Gentrification and Different Differences.' *Sociological Research Online* 16, 2 (2011) http://www.socresonline.org.uk/16/2/12.html
May, Vanessa, ed. *Sociology of Personal Life*. Houndmills: Palgrave Macmillan, 2011.
Mayes, Stephen, and Lyndall Stein, eds. *Positive Lives: Responses to HIV: A Photodocumentary*. London: Cassell, 1993.
McBride, T.M., and P. McCandless. 'The Domestic Revolution: The Modernisation of Household Service in England and France 1820–1920.' *History: Reviews of New Books* 4, no. 10 (1976): 228–229.
McCandless, J., and S. Sheldon. 'The Human Fertilisation and Embryology Act (2008) and the Tenacity of the Sexual Family Form.' *The Modern Law Review* 73, no. 2 (2010): 175–207.
McDowell, Linda. *Gender Identity and Place: Understanding Feminist Geographies*. Cambridge: Polity Press, 1999.
McHugh, Susan. 'Marrying My Bitch: J.R. Ackerley's Pack Sexualities.' *Critical Inquiry* 27, no. 1 (Autumn 2000): 21–41.
McIntosh, Mary. 'The Homosexual Role.' *Social Problems* 16, no. 2 (1968): 182–192.
McKibbin, Ross. *Classes and Cultures: England, 1918–1951*. Oxford: Oxford University Press, 1998.
Melly, George. *Revolt into Style: The Pop Arts in Britain*. Harmondsworth: Penguin, 1972.
Meyer, R. 'Mapplethorpe's Living Room: Photography and the Furnishing of Desire.' *Art History* 24, no. 2 (2001): 292–311.
Middleton, David. *The Social Psychology of Experience: Studies in Remembering and Forgetting*. London: Sage, 2005.
Miles, Robert. 'The Riots of 1958: Notes on the Ideological Construction of "Race Relations" as a Political Issue in Britain.' *Immigrants and Minorities* 3, no. 3 (1984): 252–275.
Miller, Daniel, ed. *Home Possessions: Material Culture behind Closed Doors*. Oxford: Berg, 2001.
———. *Material Cultures: Why Some Things Matter*. London: UCL Press, 1997.
———. *The Comfort of Things*. Cambridge: Polity, 2008.
Miller, Jack. 'Murders in a Half World.' *News of the World*, 25 February 1962.
Milligan, D. *The Politics of Homosexuality*. London: Pluto, 1973.
Mitchell, Juliet. *Siblings: Sex and Violence*. Oxford: Polity, 2003.

Monk, Daniel. 'EM Forster's Will: An Overlooked Posthumous Publication.' *Legal Studies* (2013): *Studies*, 33, 4 (2013): 572–597.
———. 'Re G (Children) (Residence: Same-Sex Partner) – Commentary.' In *Feminist Judgments: From Theory to Practice*, edited by R. Hunter, C. McGlynn, and E. Rackley. Durham: Hart, 2010.
Moore, Oscar. *PWA: Looking AIDS in the Face*. London: Picador, 1996.
Mort, Frank. *Capital Affairs: London and the Making of the Permissive Society*. New Haven: Yale University Press, 2010.
———. 'Scandalous Events: Metropolitan Culture and Moral Change in Post-Second World War London.' *Representations* 93 (1 January 2006): 106–137.
———. 'Social and Symbolic Fathers and Sons in Postwar Britain.' *Journal of British Studies* 38, no. 3 (1999): 353–384.
Moulton, Mo. 'Bricks and Flowers: Unconventionality in Katherine Everett's Life Writing.' In *British Queer History*, edited by Brian Lewis. Manchester: Manchester University Press, 2013.
Moyle, Franny. *Constance: The Tragic and Scandalous Life of Mrs. Oscar Wilde*. London: John Murray, 2012.
Murray, Heather. *Not in This Family: Gays and the Meaning of Kinship in Postwar North America*. Philadelphia: University of Pennsylvania Press, 2010.
Nakayama, Randall. 'Domesticating Mr. Orton.' *Theatre Journal* 45, no. 2 (1993): 185–195.
———. 'Sensation and Sensibility: Joe Orton's Diaries.' In *Joe Orton: a Casebook*, edited by Francesca Coppa. London: Routledge, 2003.
Nardi, P. 'That's What Friends Are For: Friends as Family in the Gay and Lesbian Community.' In *Modern Homosexualities: Fragments of Lesbian and Gay Experience*, edited by K. Plummer. New York: Routledge, 1992.
Neiswander, Judy. *The Cosmopolitan Interior: Liberalism and the British Home 1870–1914*. New Haven: Yale University Press, 2008.
Nero, Charles I. 'Why Are Gay Ghettoes White?' In *Black Queer Studies*, edited by E. Patrick Johnson and Mae Henderson. Durham: Duke University Press, 2005.
Nevins, Peter. 'The Making of a Radical Blackgay Man.' In *High Risk Lives: Lesbian and Gay Politics after the Clause*, edited by Tara Kaufmann and Paul Lincoln. Bridport: Prism, 1991.
Nordau, Max. *Degeneration*. Lincoln: University of Nebraska Press, 1993.
Norton, Rictor. *Mother Clap's Molly House: Gay Subculture in England 1700 - 1830*. London: GMP, 1992.
Nye, Robert. 'Kinship, Male Bonds and Maculinity in Comparative Perspective.' *American Historical Review* 105 (2000): 1656–1666.
Obelkevich, James. 'Consumption.' In *Understanding Post-War British Society*, edited by James Obelkevich and Peter Catterall. London: Routledge, 1994.
O'Quin, Daniel. 'Gardening, History and the Escape from Time: Derek Jarman's *Modern Nature*'. In *October*, 89 (1999): 113–126.
Oram, Alison. 'Going on an Outing: The Historic House and Queer Public History.' *Rethinking History* 15, no. 2 (June 2011): 189–207.
Orton, Joe. *The Complete Plays*. Edited by John Lahr. London: Methuen, 1976.
———. *The Orton Diaries*. Edited by John Lahr. London: Methuen, 1986.
Orton, Leonie, and John Alderton. 'A Conversation.' In *Joe Orton: A Casebook*, edited by Francesca Coppa. London: Routledge, 2003.
Orwell, George. *Down and Out in Paris and London*. London: Penguin Books, 2003.

Osborne, John. 'Diary of a Somebody.' *The Spectator*, 29 November 1986.
Osgerby, B. 'The Bachelor Pad as Cultural Icon: Masculinity, Consumption and Interior Design in American Men's Magazines, 1930–65.' *Journal of Design History* 18, no. 1 (2005): 99.
Owens, Craig. 'Outlaws: Gay Men in Feminism.' In *Men in Feminism*, edited by Alice Jardine and Paul Smith. New York: Methuen, 1987.
Panton, Jane Ellen. *From Kitchen to Garret*. London: Ward & Downey, 1888.
Parker, Peter. *Ackerley: A Life of J.R. Ackerley*. London: Constable, 1989.
Parsons, Talcot, and Robert Bales. *Family, Socialisation and Interaction Process*. Glencoe: Free Press, 1955.
Patton, Michael Quinn. *Qualitative Research & Evaluation Methods*, 3rd ed. London: Sage, 2002.
Peake, Tony. *Derek Jarman*. London: Abacus, 2001.
Pearce, Susan. *On Collecting: An Investigation into Collecting in the European Tradition*. London: Routledge, 1995.
Pearson, K., and N.M. Reich. 'Queer Eye Fairy Tale: Changing the World One Manicure at a Time.' *Feminist Media Studies* 4, no. 2 (2004): 229–231.
Percival, J. 'Domestic Spaces: Uses and Meanings in the Daily Lives of Older People.' *Ageing and Society* 22, no. 6 (2002): 729–749.
Petre, Diana. *The Secret Orchard of Roger Ackerley*. London: Phoenix, 1993.
Petridou, Elia. 'The Taste of Home.' In *Home Possessions: Material Culture behind Closed Doors*, edited by Daniel Miller. Oxford: Berg, 2001.
Pick, Daniel. *Faces of Degeneration: A European Disorder, C.1848–C.1918*. Cambridge: Cambridge University Press, 1989.
Plummer, Kenneth. *Intimate Citizenship: Private Decisions and Public Dialogues*. Seattle: University of Washington Press, 2003.
———. *Modern Homosexualities: Fragments of Lesbian and Gay Experiences*. London: Routledge, 1992.
———. *Telling Sexual Stories: Power, Change, and Social Worlds*. London: Routledge, 1994.
Poovey, Mary. *Uneven Developments: The Ideological Work of Gender in Mid-Victorian England*. Chicago: University of Chicago Press, 1988.
Porter, Roy. *London: A Social History*. Cambridge: Harvard University Press, 1998.
Potvin, John. 'Askesis as Aesthetic Home: Edward Perry Warren, Lewes House, and the Ideal of Greek Love.' *Home Cultures* 8, no. 1 (2011): 71–89.
———. 'Collecting Intimacy One Object at a Time: Material Culture, Aestheticism, and the Spaces of Aesthetic Companionship.' In *Material Cultures, 1740–1920: The Meanings and Pleasures of Collecting*, edited by John Potvin and Alla Myzelev. Farnham: Ashgate, 2009.
Power, Lisa. *No Bath but Plenty of Bubbles: An Oral History of the Gay Liberation Front, 1970–1973*. London: Cassell, 1995.
Prendergast, S., G.A. Dunne, and D. Telford. 'A Story of "Difference", a Different Story: Young Homeless Lesbian, Gay and Bisexual People.' *International Journal of Sociology and Social Policy* 21, no. 4/5/6 (2001): 64–91.
Ramsey, E.M., and G. Santiago. 'The Conflation of Male Homosexuality and Femininity in Queer Eye for the Straight Guy.' *Feminist Media Studies* 4, no. 3 (2004): 353–355.
Rappaport, Erika Diane. *Shopping for Pleasure: Women in the Making of London's West End*. Princeton: Princeton University Press, 2000.

Ravetz, Alison. *The Place of Home: English Domestic Environments, 1914–2000*. London: Spon, 1995.
Raynsford, Nick. *Housing is an AIDS Issue*. London: National AIDS Trust, 1989.
Razi, Zvi. 'The Myth of the Immutable English Family.' *Past and Present* 140, no. 1 (1993): 3–44.
Reece, H. 'Subverting the Stigmatisation Argument.' *Journal of Law and Society* 23, no. 4 (1996): 484–505.
———. 'The Paramountcy Principle Consensus or Construct?' *Current Legal Problems* 49, no. 1 (1996): 267–304.
Reed, Christopher. *Bloomsbury Rooms: Modernism, Subculture, and Domesticity*. New Haven: Yale University Press, 2004.
———. 'Design for (Queer) Living: Sexual Identity, Performance, and Decor in British Vogue, 1922–1926.' *GLQ: A Journal of Lesbian and Gay Studies* 12, no. 3 (2006): 377.
Rees, John Tudor, ed. *They Stand Apart: A Critical Survey of the Problems of Homosexuality*. London: Heinemann, 1955.
Reimer, S., and D. Leslie. 'Identity, Consumption, and the Home.' *Home Cultures* 1, no. 2 (2004): 187–208.
Reynolds, Simon. *The Vision of Simeon Solomon*. Stroud: Catalpa Press, 1984.
Reynolds, T., and A. Jones. *Caribbean Mothers: Identity and Experience in the UK*. London: Tufnell Press, 2005.
Rice, Charles. *The Emergence of the Interior: Architecture, Modernity, Domesticity*. London: Routledge, 2007.
Ricketts, Charles. *Letters from Charles Ricketts to 'Michael Field' (1903–1913)*. Edinburgh: Tragara, 1981.
———. *Oscar Wilde*. London: Nonesuch Press, 1932.
———. *Self-Portrait: Taken from the Letters and Journals*. Edited by T. Sturge Moore and C. Lewis. London: Peter Davies, 1939.
Rivers, D. '"In the Best Interests of the Child": Lesbian and Gay Parenting Custody Cases, 1967–1985.' *Journal of Social History* 43, no. 4 (Summer 2010): 917–944.
Robbins, David, ed. *The Independent Group: Postwar Britain and the Aesthetics of Plenty*. Cambridge: MIT Press, 1990.
Robert, K. Martin, and George Piggford, eds. *Queer Forster*. Chicago: University of Chicago Press, 1997.
Robinson, Catherine. 'I Think Home is More than a Building: Young Home(Less) People on the Cusp of Home, Self and Something Else.' *Urban Policy and Research* 20, no. 1 (2002): 27–38.
Robinson, Lucy. *Gay Men and the Left in Post-War Britain: How the Personal Got Political*. Manchester: Manchester University Press, 2007.
Roper, Michael. 'Maternal Relations: Moral Manliness and Emotional Survival in Letters Home during the First World War.' In *Masculinities in Politics and War: Gendering Modern History*, edited by S. Dudink, K. Hagemann, and J. Tosh. Manchester: Manchester University Press, 2004, 295–315.
———. *The Secret Battle: Emotional Survival in the Great War*. Manchester: Manchester University Press, 2009.
Rose, Jonathan. *The Edwardian Temperament, 1895–1919*. Athens: Ohio University Press, 1986.
Rose, Nikolas. *Governing the Soul: The Shaping of the Private Self*. London: Routledge, 1990.

Rosenberg, Buck Clifford. 'Masculine Makeovers: Lifestyle Television, Metrosexuals and Real Blokes.' In *Exposing Lifestyle Television: The Big Reveal*, edited by Gareth Palmer. Aldershot: Ashgate, 2008.

Roseneil, Sasha. 'On Not Living with a Partner: Unpicking Coupledom and Cohabitation.' *Sociological Research Online* 11, no. 3 (2006). http://www.socresonline.org.uk/11/3/roseneil.html.

———. 'Why We Should Care About Friends: An Argument for Queering the Care Imaginary in Social Policy.' *Social Policy and Society* 3, no. 4 (2004): 409–419.

Roseneil, Sasha, and Shelley Budgeon. 'Cultures of Intimacy and Care Beyond "the Family": Personal Life and Social Change in the Early 21st Century.' *Current Sociology* 52, no. 2 (2004): 135–159.

Ross, Ellen. *Love and Toil: Motherhood in Outcast London, 1870–1918*. Oxford: Oxford University Press, 1993.

Rowbotham, Sheila. *Promise of a Dream: Remembering the Sixties*. London: Allen Lane, 2000.

Rowbotham, Sheila, and Jeffrey Weeks. *Socialism and the New Life: The Personal and Sexual Politics of Edward Carpenter and Havelock Ellis*. London: Pluto Press, 1977.

Salkey, Andrew. *Escape to an Autumn Pavement*. Leeds: Peepal Tree, 2009.

Samuel, Raphael, and Paul Thompson. *The Myths We Live By*. London: Routledge, 1990.

Sanders, Joel. 'Curtain Wars: Architects, Decorators, and the 20th-Century Domestic Interior.' *Harvard Design Magazine* 16 (2002): 1–19.

———. *Stud: Architectures of Masculinity*. New York: Princeton Architectural Press, 1996.

Saunders, Nicholas. *Alternative London*. London: Wildwood House, 1978.

Saxey, Esther. 'Homoplot: The Coming Out Story as Sexual Identity Narrative.' University of Sussex PhD, 2003.

Schofield, Michael. *A Minority: A Report on the Life of the Male Homosexual in Great Britain*. London: Longmans, 1960.

———. *Society and the Homosexual*. London: Victor Gollancz, 1952.

Schuman, Josephine. *Empty Dwellings in Greater London: A Study of the Vacancy Question*. London: The Council, 1981.

Scott, Joan W. 'The Evidence of Experience.' *Critical Inquiry* 17, no. 4 (July 1991): 773–797.

Sedgwick, Eve Kosofsky. *Epistemology of the Closet*. London: Harvester Wheatsheaf, 1991.

———. *Tendencies*. London: Routledge, 1994.

Segal, Lynne. *Making Trouble: Life and Politics*. London: Serpent's Tail, 2007.

———. *What is to Be Done about the Family?* Harmondsworth: Penguin, 1983.

Seidman, Steven. *Beyond the Closet: The Transformation of Gay and Lesbian Life*. London: Routledge, 2003.

Shankland Cox Partnership, *Lambeth Inner Area Study: People, Housing and District*. London: Department of the Environment, 1974.

Sharpe, Mordant. 'The Green Bay Tree.' In *Gay Plays*, edited by Michael Wilcox. London: Methuen, 1984.

Shelton, Anthony, ed. *Collectors: Expressions of Self and Other*. London: Horniman Museum and Gardens, 2001.

Shepard, Benjamin. 'Play as World Making: From the Cockettes to the Germs, Gay Liberation to DIY Community Building.' In *The Hidden 1970s: Histories*

Bibliography

of Radicalism, edited by Dan Berger. New Brunswick: Rutgers University Press, 2002.

Shepherd, Simon. 'A Colored Girl Reading Proust.' In *Joe Orton: A Casebook*, edited by Francesca Coppa. London: Routledge, 2003.

———. *Because We're Queers: The Life and Crimes of Kenneth Halliwell and Joe Orton*. London: Gay Mens Press, 1989.

Sherman, A. 'Squatters and Socialism: Symbols of an Age.' *Local Government Review* 139, no. 45 (15 November 1975): 763.

Shiach, Morag. 'Modernism, the City and the "Domestic Interior".' *Home Cultures* 2, no. 3 (2005): 251–268.

Short, John R. *Housing in Britain: The Post-War Experience*. London: Methuen, 1982.

Shorter, Edward. *The Making of the Modern Family*. New York: Basic Books, 1975.

Sieveking, Paul. *Man Bites Dog: The Scrapbooks of and Edwardian Eccentric*. London: Jay Landesman, 1980.

Silva, Silvia, and Carol Smart, eds. *The New Family?* London: Sage, 1998.

Sinfield, Alan. 'Is There a Queer Tradition and Is Orton in It?' In *Joe Orton: A Casebook*, edited by Francesca Coppa. London: Routledge, 2003.

———. *Out on Stage: Lesbian and Gay Theatre in the Twentieth Century*. New Haven: Yale University Press, 1999.

———. 'The Production of Gay and the Return to Power.' In *De-Centring Sexualities: Politics and Representations Beyond the Metropolis*, edited by Richard Phillips, Diane Watt, and David Shuttleton. London: Routledge, 2000.

———. *The Wilde Century: Effeminacy, Oscar Wilde and the Queer Moment*. London: Cassell, 1994.

Sinor, Jennifer. *The Extraordinary Work of Ordinary Writing: Annie Ray's Diary*. Iowa City: University of Iowa Press, 2002.

Sitzia, Lorraine. *Seeking the Enemy*. London: Working Press, 2002.

Slater, Nigel. *Toast: The Story of a Boy's Hunger*. London: Fourth Estate, 2003.

Smart, Carol. 'Changing Landscapes of Family Life: Rethinking Divorce.' *Social Policy and Society* 3, no. 4 (2004): 401–408.

———. *Personal Life: New Directions in Sociological Thinking*. Cambridge: Polity, 2007.

Smith, Calvin. 'Men Don't Do That Sort of Thing.' *Men and Masculinities* 12 (October 1998): 138–172.

Snitow, Ann, ed. *Powers of Desire: The Politics of Sexuality*. New York: Monthly Review Press, 1983.

Snyder, Katherine V. *Bachelors, Manhood, and the Novel, 1850–1925*. Cambridge: Cambridge University Press, 1999.

Sparke, Penny. *As Long as It's Pink: The Sexual Politics of Taste*. London: Pandora, 1995.

Stacey, J. 'The Families of Man: Gay Male Intimacy and Kinship in a Global Metropolis.' *Signs: Journal of Women in Culture and Society* 30, no. 3 (2005): 1911–1935.

Stallybrass, Peter, and Allon White. *The Politics and Poetics of Transgression*. London: Methuen, 1986.

Stanley, Liz. *Sex Surveyed, 1949–1994: From Mass-Observation's 'Little Kinsey' to the National Survey and the Hite Reports*. London: Taylor & Francis, 1995.

Stedman-Jones, Gareth. *Outcast London: A Study in the Relationship between Classes in Victorian Society*. Oxford: Clarendon Press, 1972.

———. 'Rethinking Chartism.' In *Languages of Class*. Cambridge: Cambridge University Press, 1983.
Steedman, Carolyn. *Landscape for a Good Woman: A Story of Two Lives*. London: Virago, 1986.
Stein, Marc. *City of Sisterly and Brotherly Loves: Lesbian and Gay Philadelphia, 1945–1972*. Philadelphia: Temple University Press, 2004.
Summerfield, Penny. 'Women in Britain since 1945: Companionate Marriage and the Double Burden.' In *Understanding Post-War British Society*, edited by James Obelkevich and Peter Catterall. London: Routledge, 1994.
Symonds, John Addington. *The Memoirs of John Addington Symonds*. London: Hutchinson, 1984.
Thane, Pat, ed. *Unequal Britain: Equalities in Britain since 1945*. London: Continuum, 2010.
'The Nude in Photography.' *The Studio: An Illustrated Magazine of Fine and Applied Arts* 1, no. 2 (June 1893): 104–107.
Thomas, N. 'Will the Real 1950s Please Stand Up? View of a Contradictory Decade.' *Cultural and Social History* 5, no. 2 (2008): 227–236.
Thrift, N.J., and Peter Williams. *Class and Space: The Making of Urban Society*. London: Routledge, 1987.
Thwaite, Ann. *Edmund Gosse: A Literary Landscape 1849–1928*. London: Secker & Warburg, 1984.
Tickner, Lisa, and David Peters Corbett, eds. *British Art in the Cultural Field, 1939–69*. Wiley-Blackwell, Chichester 2012.
Tosh, J. *A Man's Place: Masculinity and the Middle-Class Home in Victorian England*. New Haven: Yale University Press, 1999.
———. 'Imperial Masculinity and the Flight from Domesticity in Britain 1880–1914.' In *Gender and Colonialism*, edited by Timothy P. Foley. Galway: Galway University Press, 1995, 72–85.
Valocchi, Stephen. 'The Class-Inflected Nature of Gay Identity.' *Social Problems* 46 (1999): 207.
Van Leer, D. 'Saint Joe: Orton as Homosexual Rebel.' *Joe Orton: A Casebook* 32 (2002): 109.
Vicinus, Martha. *Intimate Friends: Women Who Loved Women, 1778–1928*. Chicago: University of Chicago Press, 2004.
———. 'Male Impersonation and Lesbian Desire.' In *Borderlines: Genders and Identities in War and Peace, 1870–1930*, edited by Billie Melman. London: Routledge, 1998.
Vickers, Emma. 'The Good Fellow: Negotiation, Remembrance and Recollection – Homosexuality in the British Armed Forces, 1939–1945.' In *Brutality and Desire: War and Sexuality in Europe's Twentieth Century*, edited by Dagmar Herzog. Basingstoke: Palgrave, 2009.
Vickery, Amanda. *Behind Closed Doors: At Home in Georgian England*. New Haven: Yale University Press, 2009.
Voeller, Bruce, and James Walters. 'Gay Fathers.' *The Family Coordinator* 27, no. 2 (1978): 149–157.
Von Krafft-Ebing, Richard. *Psychopathia Sexualis*. London: Rebman, 1893.
Walkley, Giles. *Artists' Houses in London 1764–1914*. Aldershot: Scolar Press, 1994.
Walkowitz, Judith. *City of Dreadful Delight: Narratives of Sexual Danger in Late-Victorian London*. Chicago: University of Chicago Press, 1992.

Walter, Aubrey, ed. *Come Together: The Years of Gay Liberation (1970–73)*. London: Gay Men's Press, 1980.

Ward, Elijah. 'Homophobia, Hypermasculinity and the US Black Church.' *Culture, Health & Sexuality* 7, no. 5 (2005): 493–504.

Warner, Michael. *The Trouble with Normal: Sex, Politics and the Ethics of Queer Life*. New York: Free Press, 1999.

Waters, Chris. 'Havelock Ellis, Sigmund Freud and the State: Discourses of Homosexual Identity in Interwar Britain.' In *Sexology in Culture: Labelling Bodies and Desires*, edited by Lucy Bland and Laura L. Doan. Cambridge: Polity, 1998.

Waters, Chris, and Matt Houlbrook. 'The Heart in Exile: Detachment and Desire in 1950s London.' *History Workshop Journal* 62 (Autumn 2006): 142–163.

Watney, Simon. *Policing Desire: Pornography, AIDS and the Media*. London: Comedia, 1986.

Weeks, Jeffrey. *Coming Out: Homosexual Politics in Britain from the Nineteenth Century to the Present*. London: Quartet Books, 1977.

———. *The World We Have Won: The Remaking of Erotic and Intimate Life*. London: Routledge, 2007.

Weeks, Jeffrey, Brian Heaphy, and Catherine Donovan. *Same Sex Intimacies: Families of Choice and Other Life Experiments*. London: Routledge, 2001.

Weissman, David, and Bill Weber. *The Cockettes*, 2002.

Weston, Kath. *Families We Choose: Lesbians, Gays, Kinship*. New York: Columbia University Press, 1991.

———. *Render Me, Gender Me: Lesbians Talk Sex, Class, Color, Nation, Studmuffins*. New York: Columbia University Press, 1996.

White, Jerry. *London in the Twentieth Century: A City and Its People*. London: Vintage, 2008.

Whitman, Carl. 'A Gay Manifesto.' In *We are Everywhere*, edited by Mark Blasius and Shane Phelan. London: Routledge, 1997.

Wilcox, Michael, ed. *Gay Plays*. London: Methuen, 1984.

Williams, Fiona. *Rethinking Families*. London: Calouste Gulbenkian Foundation, 2004.

Wilson, Elizabeth. *Bohemians: The Glamorous Outcasts*. London: I.B. Tauris, 2000.

———. *Only Halfway to Paradise: Women in Postwar Britain 1945–1968*. London: Tavistock, 1980.

Wintle, Claire. 'Career Development: Domestic Display as Imperial, Anthropological, and Social Trophy.' *Victorian Studies* 50, no. 2 (Winter 2008): 279–288.

Wohl, Anthony. 'Sex and the Single Room: Incest among the Victorian Working Classes.' In *The Victorian Family: Structures and Stresses*, edited by Anthony Wohl. London: Croom-Helm, 1977.

Wollen, Roger, ed. *Derek Jarman: A Portrait*. London: Thames & Hudson, 1996.

Wymer, Rowland. *Derek Jarman*. Manchester: Manchester University Press, 2006.

Wynne-Tyson, J. *Accommodation Wanted: A Short Guide to the 'Bed-Sitter'*. London: Britannicvs Liber, 1951.

Yates, Chris. *Building for Immunity: Housing People with HIV Disease and AIDS*. London: National Federation of Housing Associations, 1991.

Zukin, Sharon. *Loft Living: Culture and Capital in Urban Change*. Baltimore: Johns Hopkins University Press, 1982.

Index

Nb. Areas of London are listed under 'London'

Ackerley, J.R, 9, 7, 12, 15, 17, 62, 89, 92, 111–32, 141, 143, 152, 155, 157, 161, 169, 171, 177, 251
  My Father and Myself, 117–21
  My Sister and Myself, 113, 123–4
  Prisoner of War, 113, 121
  We Think the World of You, 15, 113, 125–6
Ackerley, Roger, 112–13, 116–21
Adoption, 1, 68, 89, 92, 100, 103, 109, 131–8, 140, 189, 194, 225
  See also: Parents and Parenting
Aestheticism, 31, 33, 34, 36–8, 40, 43, 46, 59–60, 69
AIDS and HIV, 1, 4, 17–18, 54, 78–9, 125, 135–7, 141, 170, 191, 193–4, 216–17, 223–4, 225, 228, 234, 240
  Housing and AIDS, 196–8
  Cultures of care and AIDS, 242–6
AIDS quilt, 248–9
The Afro-Caribbean and Afro-Caribbeans, 123, 148–9, 161–2, 193, 200, 209, 211–13, 221–2
  See also: Black queer experience; Immigration; Race and ethnicity; Racism
Aging and old age, 81, 51–3, 169–73
Ajamu X, 4, 12, 17, 192, 198, 212, 218–25, 241
Alma-Tadema, Sir Lawrence, 33
The 'Amusing' style, 55, 64–70, 76, 185
Albany, Piccadilly, 98–9, 102, 229
Albany Trust, 99
Antiques, 3, 34, 37, 73, 133, 157, 165, 189
  See also: Collecting

Ancient Greece, *see: Hellenism and Classicism*
Apartments and apartment blocks, 68, 73, 77, 79, 157.
  See also: Tower Blocks
The Army, 154, 163, 171, 236. *See also: Guardsmen; RAF*
Art and design schools, 77
  Bournemouth Art School, 72
  City and Guilds Technical Art School, Kennington, 31
  New York Art School, Paris, 64
  Slade Art School, 227
  See also: Guild of Handicrafts
Art Deco, 65, 67
Artificial insemination, 106, 134, 279
  See also: Parents and parenting
Arts and Crafts, 35, 56–63, 83
Artist and Journal of Home Culture, 42–3
Asceticism, 41–2
Ashbee, C.R., 55–65, 70, 76–7, 100, 102, 104, 138–9, 165, 233
  See also: Arts and Crafts; Guild of Handicraft
Ashbee, Henry Spencer, 56
Ashbee, Janet (formerly Janet Forbes), 56, 104, 108
Australia and Australians, 106, 202, 205, 210, 211
  See also: Immigration

Bachelors, 41–2, 64, 73–4, 83, 114, 116–17, 120, 123, 138, 147, 150–1
  Bachelor chambers, 98–9, 102, 104, 129
  See also: Singleness
Ballet Russes, 44
  See also: Nijinsky; Diaghilev
Barracks, 61, 74–5, 77, 118

Bars, pubs, and clubs, 3, 83, 144, 169, 175
   A&B, 175
   Bang, 232
   Candy Lounge, 175
   Colherne Pub, 165
   Comptons, 232
   Heaven, 232
   Le Duce, 175
   Porchester Hall Drag Queen Balls, 170
   Shebeens, 161–2, 212
   Subway, 232
   Tattersalls, 74
   The Fridge, 219
   Substation South, 219
Bartlett, Neil, 4, 54, 81–5, 229, 233, 247
Batten, Rex, 143, 145, 151–3, 154–73
BBC, *see: Television and radio*
Beckford, William, 42
Bedsits, 12, 17, 25, 54, 70, 84, 144, 149–52, 154–73
   See also: Rented rooms and flats
Bell, Vanessa, 61, 62
Bermondsey (1972, BBC drama), 276 n86
Bohemians and Bohemianism, 7, 22, 33, 42, 49, 59, 62, 65, 70, 99, 100, 105, 201, 209
Booth, Charles, 32–3
Bournemouth, 72
Black queer experience, 161–2, 212–13, 218–22
   See also: Race and ethnicity; Racism; Immigration; and The Afro-Caribbean and Afro-Caribbeans
Blackmail, 122, 148
Bloomsbury group of artists, 61–3, 67–8, 83, 185
   See also: Vanessa Bell; Duncan Grant; Harold Nicholson; Virginia Woolf
Bloch, Iwan, 90–1, 136
   See also: Sexology
Bradley, Katherine, *see: 'Michael Field'*
Brighton, 56, 80–1, 181
British Society for the Study of Sex Psychology, 106–7, 110
   See also: Sexology

Cabbage Town, Toronto, 216
Cambridge, 40, 133, 189, 236
   University of, 56, 98, 107, 112, 114, 119
   See also: Fitzwilliam Museum
Camp (and kitsch), 4, 18, 42, 50, 65, 76, 84, 153, 160–1, 171, 177, 180, 195, 203
   See also: Effeminacy; Drag
Campaign for Homosexual Equality (CHE), 107
Campaign for Nuclear Disarmament (CND), 175
Capital Gay, 194
Carpenter, Edward, 26, 56–7, 61, 63–4, 90–2, 100, 103, 105, 107, 112, 114, 192, 233
The Census, 26, 100, 146, 192
Chaeronia, Order of, 61, 96, 99, 107–9, 110
   See also: George Ives
Children and childhood, 4–5, 10, 15, 17, 31, 36, 43, 57, 61, 70, 81–2, 87, 97, 100, 102, 121, 124, 161, 163, 189, 205, 226–7, 234, 236
   See also: Parents and Parenthood
Children Act (1989), 134
Chilham Castle, Kent, 23, 29, 44, 53
   See also: Charles Shannon; Charles Ricketts
Civil Partnership, 1, 18–19, 135, 137, 225
   See also: Marriage
Civil Rights, 175
Class, 8–9, 200, 208
   Cross-class connections, 56, 70, 75–6, 103 113, 124, 126, 127–8, 157, 239
   Middle class, 10–11, 23, 25–7, 30, 45–6, 56, 92, 99, 102, 123, 145, 147–9, 151, 156, 177, 180–1, 189, 208, 215, 226
   Upper class, 65, 76, 105, 107, 119, 157
   Working class, 21–6, 75, 96, 105, 110, 112, 119, 128, 131, 141, 148–9, 151, 153, 161, 167, 176–7, 180–2, 108, 209
   See also: Royalty

Classicism, 32, 37, 42, 54
    See also: Hellenism
Clause 28 of Local Government Act (1988), 3, 141, 193, 134, 135, 194, 197, 240
The Cockettes, 201
Come Together, 192, 201
Collage, 176, 179, 182, 184, 186, 189
    See also: Murals
Collecting, 4, 34, 35, 38–43, 47–72, 83, 229
    See also: Antiques; Eclecticism; Furniture
Collin, Keith (HB), 234–5, 237–49
'Coming out', 113, 131, 136, 170, 184, 193, 195, 207, 213, 229, 240, 245
Communes, 103, 105, 192, 201, 205, 212
Consenting Adults: The Men (1967, ITV), 125
Conservative Party (and Government), 133–4, 197, 214
    See also: Margaret Thatcher and Thatcherism
Cooper, Edith, *see: 'Michael Field'*
Councils
    Greater London Council, 196, 202, 215, 219
    London County Council, 26, 68
    Local London, 1, 11, 25, 133, 191, 196–7, 201, 207, 215
    See also: specific councils listed under 'London'
Country Life (magazine), 29, 237
Court cases, 23, 24, 35, 37, 74–6, 79, 108, 132–4, 166, 229
Coward, Noel, 62, 184
Cleveland Street scandal, 165
Craik, Dinah, *John Halifax, Gentleman*, 92
Crisp, Quentin, 87–8, 110, 116, 152

Department stores, 10, 30
Diaghilev, Sergei, 50
    See also: Ballet Russes; Nijinsky; Diaghilev
Domesticity, meanings of, 8–9
Domestic service, *see: Servants*

Dorset, 154–8, 168, 173
Dover, Kent, 115
Drag, 83–4, 170, 183, 193, 204
    See also: Camp; Effeminacy
Drugs, 175, 204, 210, 213–14, 246

Eclecticism, 4, 18, 30, 40, 67, 84, 229, 249
Edinburgh, 134, 157
Eighteenth Century style, 42, 66, 73, 76, 237
    See also: Queen Anne
Effeminacy, 64, 161, 171
    See also: Camp; Drag; Mysogeny
Ellis, Henry Havelock, 24, 43, 90, 117, 251
    See also: Sexology
Empire, 22, 30
Engels, Frederick, 90
Englishness, 3, 9, 25, 246

Family, meanings of, 8, 87–93
    See also: Children and Childhood; Parents and Parenting; Siblings
The Family Way (1966, film, dir. Roy Boulting), 276 n84
Féré, Charles, 90
    See also: Sexology
Film, 70, 276 n84, 281 n45
    See also: The Family Way; Adrian Goycoolea; Hollow Reed; Home movies; Derek Jarman; Isaac Julien; Ron Peck; Victim; Oscar Wilde; Wizard of Oz
Fitzroy, A.T, *Despised and Rejected*, 108
Fitzwilliam Museum, 40, 42, 48, 53, 76, 247
Flower and floristry, 17, 30, 33, 37, 38, 40, 44, 236, 240
Fleming, Ronald, 55, 64–8, 70, 72–3, 76, 80, 144
    See also: Amusing style
Forbes, Vivian, 46, 50, 233
Ford, Oliver, 55, 64, 71–7, 180, 184, 227, 229, 231, 237, 248
Forel, Charles, 90
    See also: Sexology
Forster, E.M., 33, 109, 113, 124

Feeman Gillian, *The Leather Boys*, 148
  See also: Youth Culture
Freud, Sigmund, 48, 90, 113, 117, 244
Friendship, 29, 31, 34–5, 50, 55, 61, 93, 108, 140, 152, 240, 246
Fry, Roger, 35, 38, 50, 59, 60–1, 64–5, 77
Furniture, 57, 65, 69, 133, 157
  Makers, 224, 232
  Second hand, 167, 238
  See also: Interior design and designers

Gale, Patrick, *The Facts of Life*, 245
Gardens and gardening, 1, 11, 30, 53, 60, 72–3, 83–4, 122, 138, 203, 217, 227, 234–8, 240–1, 246
  See also: Flowers and floristry
Garland, Rodney, *The Heart in Exile*, 70, 138, 159
Garrett, Agnes and Rhoda, 63
Gay, meanings of, 203, 206–8, 210, 212, 213–14, 234
Gay Liberation Front (GLF), 192–3, 201–5, 207–8, 212, 215, 225, 231–3, 242
  South London GLF, 203
Gay Left, 192, 203
Gay News, 192, 194–5, 203
Gay Pride, 194, 208
Gentrification, 11, 79, 170, 181, 189, 215, 216, 225, 229
Gilbert and George, 54
Glasgow, 131, 138
Gosse, Edmund, 117–18
Goycoolea, Adrian (dir.), *Uncle Denis*, 87–8
Grant, Duncan, 35, 61, 84, 99
Gray, Thomas, 42
Greater London Council,
  see Councils
Greenwood, James, 24, 32
Grey, Anthony, 25
Guardsmen, 55, 60–1, 74–6, 112, 115, 118, 119, 128, 157
  See also: Army; RAF
Gielgud, John, 73, 115
Guild of Handicraft, 23, 56–7, 59, 61–2
  See also: Art and design schools

Haeg, Fritz, 1
Hall, Radclyffe, and *The Well of Lonliness*, 62, 108
Halliwell, Kenneth, 7, 54, 84, 132, 176, 178–89
Harwood, Anthony, 229, 230
Haweis, Mary Eliza, 63
HB, *see Keith Collins*
Hellenism, 35, 42, 50, 58, 68, 108
  See also: Classicism
Heritage, 248
Heterosexuality, 90–2, 98, 102, 112, 125, 137, 140–1, 146–7, 156, 178, 205, 211, 217, 237
Heteronormativity, 136–7
Hockney, David, 231
Hollow Reed (film, dir. Angela Pope, 1996), 134
Home–meanings of, 8–9
Home movies, 87, 166
Homes and Gardens (magazine), 167
Homelessness, 5, 7, 21–5, 27, 115, 134, 163, 195, 197–8, 208, 239
  Homeless Persons Housing Act, (1985), 196
  Vagrancy Law Amendment Act, (1898), 24
'Home beautiful', 35–8, 182
  See also: Aestheticism
Homophobia, 17, 136, 165–7, 192, 246
The homosexual and homosexual 'type', 5, 7, 8, 11, 25, 27, 41, 43, 6, 48, 76, 90–1, 111, 125, 145–8, 151, 168, 180, 183, 189, 207, 229
  See also: Gay; Queer; Invert
Homosexual Law Reform Society, 99, 107
Hospitals, 161, 243, 244
Hotels, 3, 9, 24, 26, 72, 104, 110, 113, 127
Hotel workers, 3, 9, 26, 110, 150
Housing policy, 191–8
  Housing Acts (1980), (1985), (1996), 197
Housing shortage, 145
Housing Trusts and Co-ops, 191, 195–7
  Brixton Housing Co-op, 199–200, 215–18, 224

Housing, council, 26, 196, 197, 198, 214, 217
Housman, Laurence, 110
Huysman, J.-K, *A Rebours,* 38
Hyndman, Tony, 128

Immigration and immigrants, 123, 148, 150, 152, 161, 193, 202
  See also: Afro-Caribbean and Afro-Caribbeans; Australia and Australians; Ireland and Irish
Interior design and designers, 55–76, 88, 138–9, 181, 230
  On styles see also: Aestheticism; The 'Amusing' style; Art Deco; Asceticism; Camp (and Kitsch); Eclecticism; Eighteenth century; Japan and Japanisme; Modernism; North African; Victorian
  On interior designers see also: C.R.Ashbee; Ronald Fleming; Agnes and Rhoda Garrett; Mary Eliza Haweis; Philip Johnson; Oliver Ford; Ralph Lamprell; Peter McGraith; Jane Ellen Panton; Justin Ryan and Colin McAllister; Alan Tag; Elsie de Wolfe
Interwar period, 25–6, 53, 55, 62, 65–7, 103, 115, 144–5, 174, 236
The invert and inverted 'type', 2, 4, 7, 11, 27, 33, 43–4, 46, 64, 90, 104, 105, 117, 130
  See also: Gay; Homosexual; Queer
Ireland and Irish, 138, 164, 199, 202, 210, 213
  See also: Immigration
Isokon flats, Hampstead, 67–8
  See also: Modernism
Ives, George, 4, 7, 11, 51, 61, 89, 95–112, 116, 122, 127–8, 130, 155, 157, 229, 243

Jackson, Charles Kain, 42, 84, 50
Japan and Japanisme, 30, 36, 133
Jarman, Derek, 4, 7, 15, 17, 54, 71, 84, 107, 122, 175–6, 193, 198, 212, 226–50
  Bankside warehouses, 229–32, 238

Films, 233
The Garden (film, 1990), 236
Modern Nature, 228, 235, 237
Phoenix House, Charing Cross Road, 231, 232, 234, 239, 243
Prospect Cottage, Dungeness, Kent, 271, 231–48
Smiling in Slow Motion, 242
Jews and Jewishness, 21, 24, 25
Johnson, Philip, 230
Julien, Isaac, 212

Kent, county of, 15, 44, 54, 62, 115, 155, 227, 237–8
  See also: Chilham Castle; Derek Jarman
King, Francis, 111, 113, 124
Krafft Ebing, Richard von, 43, 45, 90
  See also: Sexology

Labour Party, 194, 196, 202
Lamprell, Ralph, 237
Lanchester, Elsa, 68, 265
Landlords and Landladies, 7, 12, 26, 115, 118, 146, 151, 159, 160, 162–3, 166–7
  See also: Bedsits; Rented rooms and flats
Laughton, Charles, 68
Leeds, 148, 218
Lesbians and lesbianism, 4, 6, 18, 108, 133, 134, 193, 210, 216
  See also 'Michael Field'
Letting agents, 78–80
Livingstone, Ken, 17, 219
Legitimacy Act (1959), 134
Legitimacy and Illegitimacy, 97–8, 112, 134
Leighton, Lord Frederick, 37, 41, 259 n69
Lesbian and Gay Switchboard, 195
Lewis, Cecil, 39, 40–1, 49–50, 52
Loft and warehouse apartments, 2, 79, 229, 230
  See also: Derek Jarman
London, 11–12, 22, 25–6, 30, 68, 71, 196–7. *See also: Councils*
  Belgravia, 205
  Bermondsey (market), 228–9

London – *continued*
  Bethnal Green, 201, 231
  Bexley Council, 133
  Bloomsbury, 56, 68, 228. *See also: Bloomsbury group*
  Bounds Green, 201, 212
  Brixton, 4, 199–226, 230–1
  Camden, 69, 153, 155, 160, 201
  Carnaby Street, 175
  Chelsea, 21, 32, 36, 49, 57, 61, 65, 70, 149, 152, 163, 175, 210
    Cheyne Walk, 21, 57, 59, 61, 63, 165
    Kings Road, 175, 229
  Clapham, 224
  Clerkenwell, 21, 79
  Covent Garden, 21, 232
  Croydon, 97
  Crystal Palace, 79
  Dulwich, 153, 155, 167–8, 175, 206
  Earls Court, 165, 207
  Hackney, 153, 162, 169, 170
    Hackney Council, 196
  Haringey Council, 196
  Highbury, 163, 165, 173, 179
  Holloway, 138, 176
  Holland Park, 41
  Hampstead, 68, 159, 176
    Hampstead Heath, 167, 232, 248
    West Hampstead, 176, 178, 179
  Hammersmith, 115–16, 118
    Hammersmith and Fulham Council, 196
  Hoxton, 79
  Hyde Park, 23, 163
  Islington, 17, 54, 79–80, 149, 176, 181, 201
    Islington Council, 196
  Kennington, 31–2, 37, 170
  Kensington, 29, 79, 84
  Knightsbridge, 74, 118
  Lambeth, 201
    Lambeth Council, 196–7, 215, 219
    Lambeth workhouse, 24, 32
  Leicester Sq., 159, 163
  Little Venice, 112, 115, 149
  Maida Vale, 115, 149
  Mayfair, 33, 68, 70, 73, 77, 79, 157, 163, 267 n17
  Muswell Hill, 212
  Notting Hill, 12, 149–50, 153, 161–3, 169–70, 172, 175, 201, 205
  Oxford Street, 21
  Paddington, 149, 161
  Penge, 212
  Piccadilly, 98, 210, 229, *292* n24
  Portobello (market), 228
  Putney, 115, 123, 152
  Queensway, 170
  Regent's Park, 29, 31, 98, 138
  Richmond, 31, 119, 121, 122
  Russell Sq, 155, 160
  St. James, 68, 79, 98
  St. Pancras, 72, 149
  Shoreditch, 79
  Soho, 18, 71, 110, 148, 175, 216, 242
  South Bank (Southwark), 1, 87, 229–32
  Stockwell, 166
  Sutton, 87
  The Strand, 36
  Swiss Cottage, 4, 95, 163
  Wandsworth Council, 133
Lord Montague, 15
Louis, Alan, 4, 16, 143, 149, 151, 153, 159–63, 169, 174, 176, 224, 229, 248

Macauley, Pauline, *The Creeper*, 189–90
Mapplethorpe, Robert, 79
Marigny, New Orleans, 216
Marriage, 17, 34, 45, 50, 62, 64, 144–6, 169, 187
  Marriage and queer men, 42, 46, 56, 61, 68, 83, 90–2, 101, 104–5, 117, 162, 177, 241
  See also: Civil Partnership
Marshall, Carl, 12, 14, 16, 143, 151, 153, 163–8, 170–3
Mass Observation, 54, 148, 156
Maupin, Armistead, *Tales in the City*, 162
Melly, George, 185

Memory and remembrance, 13, 16, 110, 122, 154, 169–73, 179, 222–5, 247–8
Merrill, George, 57, 103
McAllister, Colin and Ryan, Justin, 1, 80
McGraith, Peter, 4, 131, 137–41, 220
'Michael Field' aka Katherine Bradley and Edith Cooper, 44, 46, 48, 50–1
Millthorpe, Yorkshire, 56–7, 103
  See also: Edward Carpenter
Misogyny, 3, 44–5, 124, 183. *See also: Sexism*
Modern Family (US sitcom), 1
Modernism, 41, 50, 67–8, 185
Molly Houses, 91
Montaigne, Michel de, 29, 31
Moore, Oscar, 240, 243–5
  A Matter of Life and Sex, 245
  PWA, 244
Morris, William, 40, 44, 56, 59, 61, 232
Mortgages, 18, 78, 206
Murals, 59–62, 64, 184–6, 189
  See also: Collage
Murder, 31, 126, 132, 150, 176, 189

Nicholson, Harold, 62, 99
Nijinsky, Vaslav, 50
  See also Ballet Russes; Diaghilev
National Gallery, 22, 33
National Service, 126, 175
Neo-liberalism, 135–6
The 'new woman', 6
New York, 79, 152, 163
Newspapers, 3, 14, 35, 42, 58, 73, 75, 133–4, 145, 150, 157, 240
  For queer newspapers see: Artist and Journal of Home Culture, Come Together, Gay Times, Capital Gay
North Africa and north African decoration, 36–7, 74, 181–2
Novels and novelists. *See: J.R.Ackerley; Neil Bartlett; Rex Batten; Dinah Craik; Patrick Gale; Rodney Garland; Ronald Firbank; A.T.Fitzroy; E.M.Forster; Gillian Freeman; Radclyffe Hall; Francis King; Armistead Maupin; Oscar Moore; Mary Renault; Sins of the Cities of the Plain; Andrew Salkey; Teleny; Edmund White*

Orton, Joe, 4, 7, 17, 54, 71, 74, 84, 132, 152, 174–91, 207, 228, 237
  Entertaining Mr Sloane, 176–7, 187–8
  Loot, 176, 183, 189
  The Ruffian on the Stair, 176, 187–8
Orwell, George, 7, 24–5
Osborne, John, 3, 132
'Outrage', 135

Panton, Jane Ellen, 63–4
Parents and parenting
  Queer parents/parenting, 1, 18–19, 68–9, 90, 101, 104–7, 109, 131–42, 198, 240
  Parents of queer men, 17, 56, 88, 91, 112, 117–22, 125, 146, 155–6, 160, 168–71, 195, 205, 208, 212, 221, 226, 228, 234, 236, 244
  See also: Children and childhood
Parsons, Talcot, 125
Pater, Walter, 36, 45
Pets, 112–13, 116, 120, 123–6
Peck, Ron (dir.), *Nighthawks* and *Strip Jack Naked*, 212, 222–3
Philpot, Glyn, 46, 50, 83, 114, 233
Photos (family), 87, 247
Porchester Hall Drag Queen Balls, 170
Portsmouth, 115, 127, 128, 153, 160–2
Pornography, 122. *See also: Teleny; Sins of the Cities of the Plain*
Post-war period (1950s and 1960s), 70–1, 76–7, 107, 112, 123–4, 126, 135, 143–91, 196, 226
Prostitution, 26, 37, 74 118, 143, 162–3, 174, 193, 233
Psychoanalysis, 10, 65, 90

Queen Anne style, 66–7, 73, 84, 265, 267
'Queer', definition of, 7–8
  Queer theory, 8, 136–7
  See also: Gay; Homosexual; Invert
Queer as Folk (UK TV series), 1, 2

Race, 123, 148, 151, 161–2, 193, 199, 200, 208–9, 211–13, 218–22

Racism, 151, 162, 182, 211–12, 220
RADA (Royal Academy of Dramatic Art), 153, 176, 178
Royal Air Force (RAF), 72
Ramsay, Peggy, 179, 182–8
Renaissance art and style, 54, 184
Renault, Mary, *The Charioteer*, 70, 159
Rent Act, 1957, 151
Rent boys and renters, *see prostitution*
Rented rooms and flats, 12, 25–6, 98 115, 118, 120 128, 146, 151, 159–60, 162–3, 166, 179, 182, 191, 195, 201, 231
  See also: Bedsits; Apartments and Apartment Blocks; Tower Blocks
Respectability, 23, 25, 41, 63, 129, 133, 160, 171, 221, 230
Rickard, Norman, 150
Ricketts, Charles, 1, 7, 10–12, 15, 17, 22–3, 29–55, 57, 59, 61–3, 73, 76–7, 84, 90, 99, 114–15, 138, 185, 227, 229, 233, 237–8, 244, 247–8
  Townshend House, 29, 33 39, 40, 41, 52
  Lansdowne House, 39, 47
  See also: The Vale; Chilham Castle, Kent
Romantic Socialism, 55, 56, 107
  See also: Arts and Crafts; C.R.Ashbee; Edward Carpenter
Ross, Robert, 22, 34, 50, 53, 84, 100
The Royal Academy, 33
Royalty, 72
  Princess Margaret, 72
  Queer Elizabeth, the Queen Mother, 55, 72, 76
  Duke and Duchess of Windsor, 72, 75
  Royal homes, 75–6
Rukus! Black LGBT archive, 220
Ruskin, John, 56, 59
Ryan, Justin and Colin McAllister, 1, 80

Sackville West, Vita, 38
San Francisco, 162, 201
Schofield, Michael (*pseud*. Gordon Westwood) 146, 148, 159, 166, 169–70, 174, 179, 187

Section 28, Local Government Act (1988), *see: Clause 28*
Servants, 26–7, 33, 48, 96, 98–9, 102, 115, 123, 173
  See also: Hotel workers
Sex, 61–3, 104
  Male-male, 9–11, 26–7, 34–5, 52, 57, 75, 78, 92, 99, 101, 104, 112, 114, 120, 126, 138, 147–8, 152, 154–6, 161, 163, 179–80, 193, 195, 203, 219, 220, 230–32, 234, 246
  Public, 22–5, 126, 145, 172, 176, 178, 181, 190, 213, 236
  Male-female, 47, 64, 90, 105, 118, 126, 134, 135, 144
  and crime, 6, 26, 75, 112, 169, 175, 194. *See also: Sexual Offences Act*
  and identity, *see: Homosexual; Heterosexual; Invert; Gay; Queer*
  See also: Prostitution; Pornography; Sexual Liberation
Sexism, 192, 211. *See also: Misogyny*
Sexology, 1, 3, 6–7, 10–11, 24, 27, 35, 43, 64, 90–2, 104, 108, 110, 117, 125, 131, 136
  See also: Henry Havelock Ellis; Richard von Krafft-Ebing, Richard von; Iwan Bloch; Charles Forel; Charles Féré
Sexual Liberation, 233. *See also Gay Liberation; Women's Liberation*
Sexual Offences Act (1967), 75, 112, 168, 177, 190
Shannon, Charles, 3–4, 10–12, 22–3, 29–55, 57, 59, 61–3, 73, 75, 77, 84, 90, 99, 115, 138, 185, 229, 233, 236, 238, 244, 247, 248, 256
Sharpe, Mordant, *The Green Bay Tree*, 68–70, 77, 189
Shebeens, *see: Bars and clubs*
Siblings, 4, 18, 57, 60, 63, 88, 97–8, 100–2, 108–9, 111, 113, 115, 119, 123–5, 188, 195, 112, 176, 220, 222, 236, 244

Sins of the Cities of the Plain, anon, 118
Singleness, 64, 68, 75, 93, 96, 105, 110, 133–4, 150, 152, 169, 189, 195–6, 202, 208, 215. Men, 75, 93, 105, 133, 169, 189; Women, 50, 174, 194
See also: Bachelors
Sitwell, Osbert and Sacheverell, 64–5, 67, 69, 76–7, 84
Squats and squatting, 2, 4, 12, 17, 191, 199–226, 228, 230–2, 236, 238, 240–2, 248
Slater, Nigel, 122
Solomon, Simeon, 21–3, 37, 81, 83, 143
Somerset, Lord Henry, 105
South London Gay Centre, 200, 202–3, 207, 211, 213
Spender, Stephen, 128
Swinburne, Algernon, 21, 25
Switzerland, 133
Symonds, John Addington, 33–4, 43, 50, 104, 117–18, 251, 255, 260
Suburbs and suburbia, 10–11, 45, 53, 68, 70, 79, 95, 100, 118, 138, 144, 149, 151–2, 181, 201, 226, 228–9, 232, 244–5
Suffrage, 32, 64
Salkey, Andrew, *Escape to an Autumn Pavement*, 159
Surrealism, 65
Surrogacy, 131, 134
Sussex, 41, 42, 62, 81, 110, 122

Tagg, Alan, 64, 72
Taylor, Charles, 26, 37, 41
Teleny, or the Reverse of the Medal, anon, 37
Television and radio, 39, 80 115, 125, 176, 232, 276, 286
See also: Bermondsey; Justin Ryan and Colin McAllister; Modern Family; Queer as Folk; The Family Way; Consenting Adults, Will and Grace
Terraced housing, 11, 79, 149, 175, 201, 205

Thatcher, Margaret, and Thatcherism, 72, 135, 193, 214–15, 226, 231, 233
Theatre, 42, 44, 52, 64, 72, 99, 113, 126, 176, 184, 186–7
See also: John Gielgud; Charles Laughton; Elsa Lanchester; Pauline Macauley; Joe Orton; Peggy Ramsay; Mordant Sharpe; Kenneth Williams; Tennessee Williams
Theatricality, 35, 43–5, 150, 156, 165, 239
Theban Bands, 107, 110, 233
Thornicroft, Bill, 200
Toms, Carl, 64, 72, 181, 242
Toynbee Hall, Whitechapel, 56, 102
Tower blocks, 11, 175
Townson, Ian, 200
Tudorbethan style, 53, 238
Tuke, Henry Scott, 114

Universities, 107, 209
See also: Cambridge

The Vale, Chelsea 33, 37, 49, 52, 62, *The Vale Press*, 34
Venice, 104, 236
Victim (1961 film, dir. Basil Dearden), 70, 148, 276 n86
Victoria and Albert Museum, 33, 72
Victoriana and Victorian style, 30, 36, 40, 57, 65, 167, 215
Vietnam war and anti war movement, 175, 202
Vigar, Alan, 150
Vogue, 65, 230

Wagner, Richard, 44, 51, 260, 303
Walpole, Horace, 42
Warhol, Andy, 79, 230
Warren, Edward Perry, 21, 41–2, 46–7, 50–1, 122
Walker Brown, Ted, 211, 219
Watney, Simon, 84, 244
Whistler, James McNeil, 31, 61–2
White, Edmund, 242
Whitman, Walt, 107

Wilde, Oscar, 15, 22, 24, 26, 31, 33–4, 36–8, 41–6, 49–51, 57–9, 63, 69–70, 77, 83–4, 90, 98–9, 104, 129, 165, 184, 186
   The Picture of Dorian Gray, 36, 38, 98, 261 n130
   'The Decay of Lying', 44
   The Importance of Being Earnest, 98
   The Portrait of Mr WH, 37, 46
   Oscar Wilde (1960 film), 70
   The Trials of Oscar Wilde (1960 film), 70
Wildeblood, Peter, 15
Will and Grace (US sitcom), 1
Williams, Kenneth, 72, 73, 180
Williams, Tennessee, 182
The Wizard of Oz, 15, 235
De Wolfe, Elsie, 63–4
Wolfenden Committee and report, 53, 145, 168, 174, 190
Women's Liberation, 135, 192, 10
Woolf, Virginia, 62, 113, 115
Workhouses, 21, 22–4, 32, 37
World War I, 53, 96, 113, 121
World War II, 72, 109, 115, 125, 153, 160, 175

Youth Culture, 71, 148, 152, 162, 189, 193, 201, 203

Printed in Great Britain
by Amazon